YALE AGRARIAN STUDIES SERIES
JAMES C. SCOTT, SERIES EDITOR

The Agrarian Studies Series at Yale University Press seeks to publish outstanding and original interdisciplinary work on agriculture and rural society—for any period, in any location. Works of daring that question existing paradigms and fill abstract categories with the lived experience of rural people are especially encouraged.
—James C. Scott, *Series Editor*

James C. Scott, *Seeing Like a State: How Certain Schemes to Improve the Human Condition Have Failed*

Steve Striffler, *Chicken: The Dangerous Transformation of America's Favorite Food*

James C. Scott, *The Art of Not Being Governed: An Anarchist History of Upland Southeast Asia*

Michael R. Dove, *The Banana Tree at the Gate: A History of Marginal Peoples and Global Markets in Borneo*

Edwin C. Hagenstein, Sara M. Gregg, and Brian Donahue, eds., *American Georgics: Writings on Farming, Culture, and the Land*

Timothy Pachirat, *Every Twelve Seconds: Industrialized Slaughter and the Politics of Sight*

Alon Tal, *All the Trees of the Forest: Israel's Woodlands from the Bible to the Present*

Felix Wemheuer, *Famine Politics in Maoist China and the Soviet Union*

Jenny Leigh Smith, *Works in Progress: Plans and Realities on Soviet Farms, 1930–1963*

Graeme Auld, *Constructing Private Governance: The Rise and Evolution of Forest, Coffee, and Fisheries Certification*

Jess Gilbert, *Planning Democracy: Agrarian Intellectuals and the Intended New Deal*

Jessica Barnes and Michael R. Dove, eds., *Climate Cultures: Anthropological Perspectives on Climate Change*

Shafqat Hussain, *Remoteness and Modernity: Transformation and Continuity in Northern Pakistan*

Edward Dallam Melillo, *Strangers on Familiar Soil: Rediscovering the Chile-California Connection*

Devra I. Jarvis, Toby Hodgkin, Anthony H. D. Brown, John Tuxill, Isabel López Noriega, Melinda Smale, and Bhuwon Sthapit, *Crop Genetic Diversity in the Field and on the Farm: Principles and Applications in Research Practices*

Nancy J. Jacobs, *Birders of Africa: History of a Network*

Catherine A. Corson, *Corridors of Power: The Politics of U.S. Environmental Aid to Madagascar*

Kathryn M. de Luna, *Collecting Food, Cultivating People: Subsistence and Society in Central Africa through the Seventeenth Century*

Carl Death, *The Green State in Africa*

James C. Scott, *Against the Grain: A Deep History of the First Civilizations*

Loka Ashwood, *For-Profit Democracy: Why the Government Is Losing the Trust of Rural America*

Jonah Steinberg, *A Garland of Bones: Child Runaways in India*

Hannah Holleman, *Dust Bowls of Empire: Imperialism, Environmental Politics, and the Injustice of "Green" Capitalism*

Johnhenry Gonzalez, *Maroon Nation: A History of Revolutionary Haiti*

Christian C. Lentz, *Contested Territory: Điện Biên Phủ and the Making of Northwest Vietnam*

For a complete list of titles in the Yale Agrarian Studies Series, visit yalebooks.com/agrarian.

CHRISTIAN C. LENTZ

Contested Territory

ĐIỆN BIÊN PHỦ AND THE MAKING OF NORTHWEST VIETNAM

Yale UNIVERSITY PRESS NEW HAVEN AND LONDON

Published with assistance from the Association for Asian Studies and from the Mary Cady Tew Memorial Fund.

Set in Scala and Scala Sans type by Newgen North America, Austin, Texas. Printed in the United States of America.

Library of Congress Control Number: 2018953984
ISBN 978-0-300-23395-7 (hardcover : alk. paper)

A catalogue record for this book is available from the British Library.

This paper meets the requirements of ANSI/NISO Z39.48-1992 (Permanence of Paper).

10 9 8 7 6 5 4 3 2 1

To my mother, Patricia McLaughlin-Lentz, whose stories about Bangkok in their own way took me to Southeast Asia and beyond

CONTENTS

ACKNOWLEDGMENTS

In many ways, this book traces how historical actors produced powerful knowledge about the Black River borderlands at a pivotal moment in the area's longer history, that is, when the region became known and governed as Northwest Vietnam. It is also a repository of what I've learned about the region, Vietnam, and Southeast Asia more broadly over years of study and research. I've accrued many debts along the way.

This project began long ago as a dissertation. I thank my PhD committee—Shelley Feldman, Phil McMichael, Max Pfeffer, and Eric Tagliacozzo—for patient support, sharp insights, and steady guidance. As my advisor, Shelley taught me to think about state making and helped me balance the demands of academia and family. Phil provided a model of mentoring that combined humor, wisdom, and deep—some would say world-historical—knowledge. From my early days on campus, Max's door was always open: he reminded me to value good writing and showed me how to bring theory and practice together. Eric deserves special thanks for his mentoring and friendship. An outstanding scholar, he has given unflagging support to my graduate studies and my intellectual development since then. My cohort in the Department of Development Sociology, including Alex and Dia da Costa, Emelie Peine, Kelly Dietz, Sergio Chavez, Upikwira Djalins, and Jason Cons, helped disparate ideas come together. In both graduate and undergraduate studies,

Cornell University's Southeast Asia Program was a deep reservoir of intellectual resources, camaraderie, and lasting friendships. Thak Chaloemtiarana, Benedict Anderson, and John Wolff were excellent teachers, and I am grateful for how they shaped my encounter with an endlessly fascinating region. Keith Taylor introduced me to Vietnam's history and has remained an invaluable resource ever since. Quang Phu Van, Tạ Thị Phương Quyên, Nguyễn Phương Chung, and Thúy Tranviet taught me Vietnamese, imparting words and opening worlds. At Yale University, the Agrarian Studies Program as well as students and faculty of the Council on Southeast Asian Studies offered an intellectual home. James Scott and Michael Dove taught me to think broadly about agrarian change and in depth about highland Southeast Asia.

My research in Vietnam has benefited immeasurably from the support of many kind teachers, colleagues, friends, and interlocutors. Without the hard work, devoted interest, and sponsorship of Dr. Trần Đức Viên, the staff of the Center for Agricultural Research and Ecological Studies (CARES), and other colleagues at the Hanoi National University of Agriculture, my research would never have been possible. In 2006–7, the university's beautiful campus in Gia Lâm became a second home to me, and I am grateful to the many talented scholars and teachers there, including Neil Jamieson, who took me in as one of their own. Likewise, the staff of the National Archives of Vietnam Center 3 steered me through their impressive collections and offered insightful readings of their own. Among the many kind people in its reading room, Nguyễn Tiến Đỉnh in particular helped me navigate the records of Vietnam's complex past, pointing out landmarks and shoals along the way. Archive directors Trần Việt Hoa, Vũ Thị Minh Hương, and Phạm Thị Bích Hải distinguished themselves as model leaders and collaborators. Philippe Le Failler and Andrew Hardy at the École Française d'Extrême-Orient in Hanoi not only shared documents and experiences but also provided early encouragement and lasting collegiality. Jason Morris-Jung, Đinh Hưu Hoàng, Phan Thị Kháng Hoa, Nguyễn Anh Tuấn, and their lovely families became good friends, neighbors, and lifelong colleagues.

The University of North Carolina at Chapel Hill and its Department of Geography provide an enriching intellectual home and a great place to hang my hat. Gaby Valdivia, Elizabeth Havice, Scott Kirsch, Banu Gokariksel, John Pickles, Betsy Olson, and Steve Birdsall understood this book project and its place within geography from the get-go. They are also fun colleagues, and I cherish our hallway chats and lunches in the shade. Thanks to other friends in the Triangle for conversation, camaraderie, and solidarity on and off campus, especially Brett Whalen, Kat Charron, Townsend Middleton, Morgan Pitelka, Emily Burrill, Wayne Lee, Laurent Dubois, Charlie Kurzman, and Dirk Bonker. As I have traveled hither and yon to complete this book, they and other friends have been the village my family relies on. Additional thanks in this regard to Perri Morgan, Malissa McLeod, the McRae family, and the Dailey clan.

I am grateful to the funding agencies, centers of learning, and other sources of financial, intellectual, and logistical support for this research. My study in and of Vietnam was funded by a Fulbright Foreign Scholarship Award, Foreign Language and Area Studies (FLAS) Fellowships, the Andrew W. Mellon Foundation, and Cornell's Southeast Asia Program and Einaudi Center for International Studies. In 2004, the Vietnamese Advanced Summer Institute (VASI) brought me to Vietnam for the first time and immersed me in language and cultural study. Duke University helped me land on my feet in North Carolina, and Phil Morgan opened the doors to its Department of Sociology and let me crash his office. At the University of North Carolina, the Carolina Asia Center, Department of Geography, Center on Global Initiatives, and an IBM-Reynolds faculty development award enabled me to travel abroad, collect more data in Vietnam and France, analyze results, and present findings at scholarly venues. A publication grant from UNC's University Research Council and a First Book Subvention from the Association of Asian Studies generously supported this book's publication.

I am also grateful to the institutions and the individuals I encountered during fellowships at crucial moments in this book's composition. In fall 2016, the Institute for Arts and Humanities at UNC enabled me to complete a full manuscript free from customary academic duties. Further, weekly meetings at Hyde Hall created invaluable space for scholarly and practical discussions, encouraging all of us to push onward in difficult times and to find joy in small things. A sojourn in spring 2017 at the Institute for Advanced Study (IAS) was nothing short of an academic paradise. My appointment to the School of Historical Studies introduced me to a remarkable intellectual community, facilitated new thinking about old problems, and fed me the best cafeteria food on the planet.

I am particularly grateful to Nicola Di Cosmo, Patrick Geary, Jonathan Haslam, and Karina Urbach for their enlightening conversation, model scholarship, and outstanding collegiality. I enjoyed numerous conversations over lunch, dinner, and after hours with Antoine Borrut, Andrew Chittick, Thomas Dodman, Elizabeth Kaske, Yu-chih Lai, Klaus Larres, Fabien Montcher, Giuliano Mori, Ohad Nachtomy, Klaus Oschema, Columba Stewart, Mark Tauger, Roberto Totolli, Matt Waters, and Xin Yu. Meanwhile, Céline Bessière, Teng Biao, Nick Cheesman, Lee Ann Fuji, Vanja Hamzic, Pascal Marichalar, Reuben Miller, Juan Obarrio, and Didier Fassin welcomed my trespassing into the School of Social Sciences. Fadi Bardawil and Peter Redfield have carried this spirit and our conversations back to North Carolina. Living and working in Princeton also embedded me in a community of scholars at the university next door, including Janet Chen, Andrew Johnson, Daena Funahashi, He Bian, and Michael Laffan. My work is better for it.

Professional workshops, conference presentations, and timely retreats gave me opportunity to develop the ideas and arguments contained in this book. I gained invaluable perspective and disciplinary knowledge at annual meetings of the American Association of Geographers. The Association of Asian Studies has consistently enriched my work, and the scholars in its Vietnam Studies Group are a cherished resource. Hue-Tam Ho Tai and participants in the 2010 Space in Vietnam workshop at Harvard University jump-started my conceptualization of Vietnamese territory. Conversations with Hue-Tam, Bradley Davis, Erik Harms, John Whitmore, Ken MacLean, David Biggs, and Christina Schwenkel remain vivid to this day. My conversations with Bradley there are part of our lasting intellectual friendship. Also in Cambridge, Vince Brown and Ajantha Subramanian led inspiring discussions about region formation and offered excellent feedback on the spaces of revolution. Presentations at the University of Michigan, Copenhagen University, Irmgard-Coninx Foundation in Berlin, Duke's Nicholas School, UNC's Cultural and Political Sociology Workshop, University of Wisconsin–Madison, Max Planck Institute in Göttingen, Vietnam Academy of Social Sciences, and the IAS helped hone my ideas and advance chapter drafts. Thanks to Ian Baird for arranging conversations in Madison. Last and certainly not least, my participation in the indomitable Skagen School breathed fresh air into this work and filled my scholarly sails for years to come. I'd like nothing more than to spend more time in the redwoods of Santa Cruz, on a beach by the North Sea, or in a stuffy conference room in Boston talking shop with Zach Anderson, Erin Collins, Jason Cons, Mike Dwyer, Michael Eilenberg, Reece Jones, Christian Lund, Duncan McDuie-Ra, Jonathan Padwe, Nancy Peluso, and Emily Yeh.

My participation in the conferences and venues mentioned above has introduced me to outstanding scholars and engaged me in lively and ongoing intellectual exchange. In addition to their inspirational written work, timely collegial support from Pierre Asselin, Tâm Ngô, Pam McElwee, Jamie Anderson, Oscar Salemink, Tuong Vu, Philip Taylor, Lien-Hang Nguyen, Nga Dao, Chris Goscha, Mitch Aso, Jamie Gillen, Kimloan Hill, Merav Shohet, and Ben Kerkvliet helped each in its own way to bring this project to fruition. Vietnam studies is a more fruitful field because of these individuals' committed efforts.

My ethnographic work in Hanoi and Điện Biên Phủ owes too much to too many people to name here. My neighbors in an alley off of Phố Lò Đúc tolerated my sometimes clumsy presence and taught me more than I can say about life in Vietnam and the histories they experienced. My interlocutors on Điện Biên's plain and the surrounding mountains did the same and still more. I could not have imagined my way through archival records without their presence, guidance, and interpretations. Whether by welcoming me into their homes, treating me to meals, walking me through their fields, hosting my stays, raising a glass, offering advice, or answering difficult questions, they opened new vistas into Vietnam's past, present, and future.

Transforming a manuscript into a book is a long process, and a handful of talented people provided much needed assistance toward that end. Cartographers Amanda Henley, Philip McDaniel, and Hannah Reckhow designed original maps using GIS software. Alexis May scanned photographs from Vietnam's archives, and Trần Thị Hoàn secured permission to print them. Hà Việt Quân answered pressing questions about historical actors and genealogy. Artist Đức Hoà generously allowed his painting to grace the book's cover, and the Vietnam National Museum of History provided a photograph of it from their collections. Oliver Tappe and Deirdre de la Cruz commented insightfully on chapter 6. Ben Kiernan and two anonymous reviewers offered constructive criticism on the manuscript that has no doubt improved its content. Ben's close attention to the full text distinguished him as an exceptional reviewer, and I am eternally grateful for his writerly advice, insightful comparisons, and historical insights. My editors at Yale University Press, Jean Thomson Black and Michael Deneen, have expertly shepherded this manuscript through its publication and encouraged me to persevere at all the right moments. Robin DuBlanc did heroic work copyediting the manuscript.

Finally, my family nurtured me through this long process in ways thoughtful, kind, and caring. Erin Lentz and Jason Cons started graduate school with me and have since become formidable scholars in their own right. But they have always been first and foremost my dear sister and brother in arms. Likewise, in the time it took me to write this book, my brother Jon Lentz earned his own PhD and started a family. I cannot count the times he and I have talked about fatherhood and scholarship, trying always to walk both paths gracefully. I reserve my deepest thanks for my loving wife and closest colleague, Adriane D. Lentz-Smith. Gorgeous writer and fearsome editor, Adriane is my best reader ever. She helped this sociologist turned geographer to think like a historian and kept a steady hand on this ship's sometimes wavering rudder. On this journey, we welcomed Zora Holloway and Langston Thomas who, in addition to giving us daily joy, also managed to discipline my working hours and make them more fun.

Notwithstanding all this assistance, any mistakes are my own.

A NOTE ON VIETNAMESE LANGUAGE AND SOURCES

This book largely adheres to the Romanized system for transcribing Vietnamese known as *quốc ngữ*. The script renders the language's six tones and other distinctive vowel and consonant sounds through diacritical marks. For example, the term for "people's laborer" is written *dân công*. It begins with a soft *d* which, in the north, is pronounced like an English *z*, as in *zip;* by contrast, a hard *d*, written Đ/đ, sounds like the normal English *d*, as in *door.*

Several exceptions to Vietnamese orthography facilitate readability, use alternative spelling for Vietnamized words, and reflect historical sources. First, I prefer common names for places familiar to many readers, such as Hanoi (Hà Nội) and Vietnam (Việt Nam). Conversely, the toponym Điện Biên Phủ adheres to Vietnamese spelling to stress its original meaning as "border post prefecture." Second, ethnic Tai peoples are referred to as "Thái" in Vietnamese, but I have adhered to "Tai" in keeping with scholarly convention; the same goes for Hmong (rather than H'Mông) and other ethnonyms. Likewise, I use the standard phonetic transcription for *muang*, a Tai word for governed spatial unit, rather than its Vietnamese spelling (*mường*), except when invoked as a formal place-name, as in Mường Phăng. Third, my citations of Vietnamese archival documents from the 1940s and 1950s preserve the original spelling of author, title, and content. To write the mostly typed reports, authors relied on old French typewriters unequipped with most diacritical marks.

That these early Vietnamese government documents did not use diacritics points to a larger process of translation and interpretation. For many native Tai speakers and non-Kinh revolutionaries, an ability to write in standard Vietnamese developed over time with exposure to literacy campaigns, formal training, and everyday practice. Visible in the documents themselves, unconventional spellings, nonstandard grammar, and creative syntax all attest to the novelty of the Vietnamese language in the post–World War II Black River region. I have attempted to retain these idiosyncrasies with one exception: adjusting the capital letters originally used in report titles, names of government agencies, and the like from all uppercase to lowercase. Reading these reports seventy years later parallels the kind of work that people there had to do to make the region knowable to a larger audience.

Unless otherwise noted, all translations are my own.

CONTESTED TERRITORY

Introduction

A WORLD-HISTORICAL PLACE

THE BATTLE OF ĐIỆN BIÊN PHỦ changed the world. It began in November 1953 when French paratroopers landed in an isolated mountain valley, built a fortified airbase out of rice fields, and challenged the Vietnamese army to a set-piece battle. In turn, the Democratic Republic of Vietnam (DRV) deployed its army over rugged terrain, surrounded the colonial force, and mobilized a massive logistics operation—all largely on foot. Geopolitically, the confrontation figured in Asia's emerging Cold War, leading the United States to offer the French two atomic bombs. After grinding artillery duels and siege warfare, the battle ended on 7 May 1954 in a stunning victory for the DRV.[1] The outcome compelled negotiators in Geneva to conclude the First Indochina War (1946–54), earning independence for Vietnam, Laos, and Cambodia. As a liberatory symbol and fait accompli of armed decolonization, the battle was a fulcrum in a global transformation from European empire to national self-determination throughout Asia and Africa, inspiring anti-colonial activists from Accra and Algiers to Bandung, Beijing, and beyond.[2]

But Điện Biên Phủ's significance as pivot and symbol can overshadow the many other things it was and remains. Just as scholars must often remind readers that Vietnam is a country, not just a war, so too is Điện Biên Phủ a place, not just a battle.[3] Situated in a broad plain near the Black River, the town was home to ethnically diverse peoples who had turned the plain into a rice basket, covered the mountains in food and cash crops, and plied trade routes to China, Laos, and Thailand. They called their home Mường Thanh, or heavenly *muang*, using a Tai language term for governed space to signify the place's centrality, not isolation. In Vietnamese, by contrast, Điện Biên Phủ means "border post prefecture," a place-name that positions it on the inside edge of territory claimed by downstream Kinh/Việt peoples, now the country's national ethnic majority. That one place has two names indicates not only different ideas about space but, moreover, competing claims on it. Therefore, although the battle of Điện Biên Phủ has come to symbolize Vietnam's national liberation, it was never certain that the place would become Vietnamese—even after 1954.

Emplacing Điện Biên Phủ in the Black River borderlands during the long 1950s, from 1945 to 1960, frames a new story about Vietnamese territory, the battle central in its making, and the many associated contests that carried into the postcolony. When French troops dropped from the sky, the supposedly remote place's productive landscape and strategic terrain had been contested by global forces for over a decade. Just as Tai farmers had turned its plain into a regional rice basket, Hmong cultivators covered its hills with lucrative opium poppies. In addition to lively trade led by Chinese merchants, the plain's airfield and the mountain passage to Laos attracted powerful interests. In 1945, French forces held off the advancing Japanese army there before retreating with Tai partisans north to Yunnan. After two hard months during which locals lengthened the runway with unpaid labor, Chinese Nationalists (KMT) moved south to disarm the Japanese, then fleeced the countryside until the Franco-Tai force returned in spring 1946.[4]

Not simply a war of Vietnam versus France, the First Indochina War initiated lasting and unpredictable contests in the Black River region over its incorporation into Vietnam. The returning Franco-Tai forces set about suppressing the revolutionary activity, led by Việt Minh cadres and allied Tai elites, that had flourished in the confusion over who, exactly, was in charge. DRV guerilla organizing contested colonial reconquest in the late 1940s but, after winning Điện Biên Phủ in the autumn 1952 Northwest Campaign, the People's Army lost it a year later when the French paratroopers landed. Now, the People's Republic of China and the United States complicated questions of sovereignty even more by backing proxies in a heating Cold War conflict. In late 1953, therefore, which state controlled Điện Biên Phủ—whether DRV, France, or some other polity—was openly contested and deeply uncertain. So too was the underlying legitimacy of any one claim on its territory and resources.

This is a book about the construction of national territory and the many struggles underlying anti-colonial liberation. It is also a historical and political geography of Điện Biên Phủ and the Black River borderlands when the region became known as Northwest Vietnam. Drawing on Vietnamese and French archival records, I explore worlds transformed through revolution and the tense relations of rule that revolution produced. My historical narrative begins in the wake of World War II when Vietnamese revolutionaries and Tai elites imagined liberatory spaces, traces how they assembled a larger coalition through coercion and consent, and focuses on the everyday work of territorial construction during and after the First Indochina War.

Elite actors socialized their vision of national space, or the Vietnamese geobody, by enlisting the borderlands peoples in logistics work. The strategy yielded staggering quantities of labor and food to support the People's Army and build the infrastructure necessary to defeat colonial forces. Mass mobilization also fashioned diverse inhabitants into citizens of Vietnam and subjected them to nation-state power. Yet the DRV's heavy claims on the region's agrarian economy bent its political trajectory in unexpected ways. During and after the war, hungry residents sought not just food but meaningful political change. After 1954, as the DRV sought more—not less—of their scarce resources, they turned to cultural traditions rooted in place, animating an alternate geobody and driving a movement for autonomy shaped to their mountain homeland. The narrative ends in 1960, when the DRV crushed the movement and initiated another round of territorial construction, this time in the south, where another Vietnam had emerged to rival its sovereign claim.[5]

SPACES OF STRUGGLE

A contested and indeterminate process, making Vietnamese territory in the Black River region offers insight into the concept of territory. This book's theoretical premise is that territory is never given—even when treated as such by historical actors or scholars. Rather, territory is an ongoing social process, a ruling strategy, and a contingent outcome.

Defining territory in this way encapsulates my analytical argument about power and space. By incorporating the unintended outcomes of territorial production, *Contested Territory* complements prevailing geographic theories of territory as a political technology and a space always in formation. Exploring the production of Vietnamese territory in a fiercely contested place serves as a concrete case in point and a primary goal in itself.

Challenging notions of territory as a given object, critical geographers conceptualize territory as a product of powerful processes. The processual approach critiques the notion of territory as merely a fixed unit of sovereign space or a spatial container. This ahistorical treatment remains common both in military and diplomatic histories based on French sources—territory as a thing just fought over—and in nationalist Vietnamese accounts—territory as an expanse always already there.[6] Instead, territory is an expression of the powerful processes through which relations of rule are spatialized, what geographers call territorialization. These varied processes operate at multiple scales—from macro to micro, globe to body—and give shape to hegemonic relations of state and society. Always in the making, territorial relations are continually generated through material and symbolic contests, landscape transformations, and spatial practices. Borders, here, represent the edges of a sovereign claim on space, not its final extent as though full, forever, and insurmountable.[7] These territorial claims often work through memory, as Điện Biên Phủ illustrates. In Vietnam, the site is remembered for national triumph and named after a border post. But this dominant meaning has involved forgetting, silences, and erasures that speak to contests lingering in the postcolony.

Supplementing the processual approach is a more recent theorization of territory, led by geographer Stuart Elden, as a ruling strategy and political technology. As a governmental project seeking to control space, territory is a technology of social and spatial organization based on techniques of knowledge production, like cartography or cadastres, for measuring land and securing terrain. More succinctly, according to Elden, territory is a calculative political technology that encompasses relations of terrain (its military-strategic value) and land (political-economic value, or property). Consistent with this view, maps represent a spatial argument, not a neutral description, as well as a powerful way of knowing

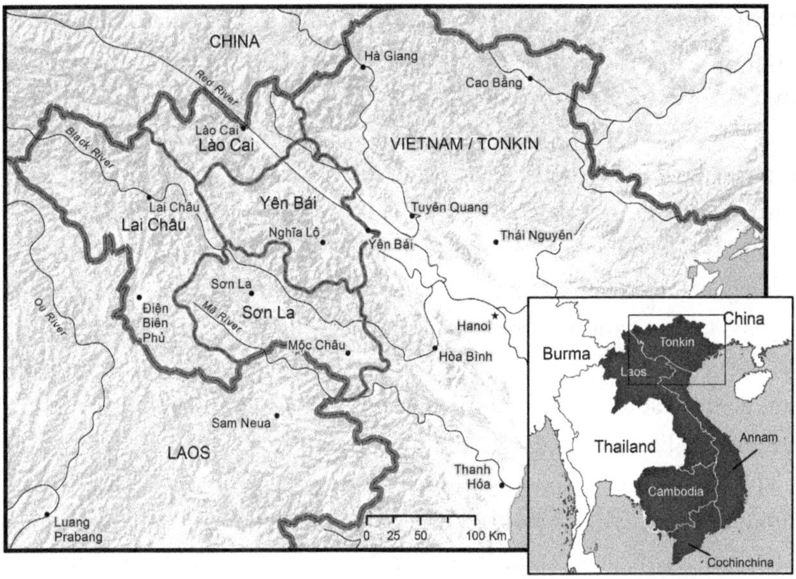

FIG. 1. Map of the Black River region claimed by Vietnam and France (1946–54). The inset shows the five territories of French Indochina (in bold); Tonkin, Annam, and Cochinchina are now known as Vietnam. (Map by Amanda Henley, Hannah Reckhow, and Philip McDaniel.)

society.[8] The historic maps, land appraisals, distance measurements, and other official data presented later ought to be read this way, as technical statements regarding space and its control. In light of the hazards involved in portraying just one biased perspective, figure 1 portrays two competing arguments about spatial sovereignty made in the period covered in this book, the First Indochina War. The map situates the Black River region in a bordered area contested by Vietnam and France. The region roughly spans the four historic provinces of Lào Cai, Sơn La, Yen Bái, and Lai Châu.

Contested Territory argues that understanding territory in terms of contest, context, and contingency enriches the geographic theories outlined above. Rethinking territory in the space of a multiply contested Vietnam contributes to a geographic dialogue about an idea conceptualized largely on the basis of the European and North American experience.[9] Defining territory as strategy and process leaves questions open about why space is imagined in particular ways and how to explain unintended outcomes. Why did Vietnam take the spatial form it did in the 1950s? How did unpredictable contests shape this form? And how did this form, in turn, shape ongoing contests?

The territorial imaginary, what scholar Thongchai Winichakul memorably called a "geobody," can take many forms and acquire meaning through any number of arguments. But in the modern era, territory has come to be associated with the nation-state, a political form that rests heavily on nationalist arguments for state legitimacy and spatial sovereignty. Like a national community, its coeval space must be imagined; neither can ever be known except as abstractions. Just as maps simplify the world, national maps represent that world in particular, often emotive, ways. Especially fraught and embattled, Asia's postcolonial spaces display what one scholar aptly calls "cartographic anxiety," an effect of producing national sovereignty and inscribing identities in binary terms of self and other, citizen or foreigner.[10] Operating in hand with this anxious awareness in Vietnam was and remains another process that classifies varieties of national self by way of ethnicity.

Vietnam's geobody now has an "S" shape that traces its territorial form along the eastern littoral of mainland Southeast Asia. Often projected anachronistically into the distant past, this nationalist vision of Vietnamese space recently aligned with actual state control over an equivalent territory. The territorial formation rests on long and violent histories of Vietnam's expansion, including the 1471 conquest of Champa in the south, and between its kings and neighboring kingdoms, notably the millennium-old relationship with China to the north. Following centuries of separation and brutal civil wars, only in 1802 did a Vietnamese king come to rule a domain stretching along the coast from the mountains north of Hanoi all the way south to Saigon and the Mekong Delta. French colonial rule in the nineteenth and twentieth centuries divided Vietnam again but, ironically, introduced the linear terrestrial borders that still lend shape to the dominant cartographic imaginary of the Vietnamese nation. Even since the DRV's Declaration of Independence from France in 1945, this S-shaped geobody has remained but one of many ideas of the nation and its rightful space. Although this book does not treat in detail the breakaway southern Republic of Vietnam (1955–75), it explores how Black River peoples imagined and enacted a space alternative to (northern) nation-state territory.[11]

The geobody has large discursive potential in relation to nationalist ideas of space, but scholars of Vietnam have not fully explained how elite visions of the geobody garnered mass appeal, gained traction on the ground, and drove territorial processes. In order to bridge this gap between a spatial idea and its realization as territory, my analysis examines everyday politics over agrarian resources during and after anti-colonial warfare. Understanding politics in rural Southeast Asia, as in other contexts where subaltern voices often go unheard or rarely recorded, means expanding an idea of the political to capture meanings produced relationally and in specific historical-geographic contexts. As peasants struggle in quotidian ways over labor, land, and food, their thoughts and actions acquire meaning both culturally within communities and politically in relation to larger economic forces, social movements, and state claims.[12]

Combined with an understanding of bodies as agents in territorial production, the agrarian approach grounds an analysis of territory in everyday resource struggles. In a very concrete way, the tens of thousands of civilian laborers who fed and moved the People's Army, like the soldiers themselves, enlivened the Vietnamese geobody even as many contested the work it required of them. Telling their story also offers insight into the lived experience of revolution, the consequences of warfare, and the embodied struggles underlying both. As much in postcolonial Vietnam as in colonial Indochina, then, peasant protests over taxation and labor service strike at the core of state legitimacy, or the rightfulness of sovereign claims on scarce agrarian resources.[13]

Questions over the sovereign control of resources were at the center of decolonization struggles and national territoriality. But armed struggle, like militarization more generally, was a tense and contradictory process. In Vietnam, revolutionary leaders like General Võ Nguyên Giáp advanced a strategy of politico-military struggle, *đấu tranh*—or People's War—to mobilize the countryside against colonial domination.[14] Giáp understood that an army did not simply win territory; rather, newly liberated territory resembled a stage on which the People's Army enacted exemplary civil-military relations. Thus, DRV cadres engaged rural audiences with a powerful appeal: if you support the army now, we can relegate colonial exploitation to the past and develop together in the future. During the military campaigns that went into making Northwest Vietnam, the local audience greeted the official performance with enthusiasm and anxiety, affective responses that registered the contradictory effects of territorial construction.

Governing logistics in the First Indochina War configured lasting relations of territorial rule—but not always as intended. In contrast to scholarly claims that logistics and territory constitute distinct spaces, this analysis demonstrates how militarization compressed them into one.[15] The everyday work of logistics constructed tense relations of territorial domination. Educating peasants in the rights and duties of citizenship, DRV cadres mobilized their labor power to build roads and move an army. Stressing fairness and equality of democratic participation, they also taxed their rice to feed soldiers. The logistics strategy yielded great sums of resources and generated calculative knowledge of population and territory, consistent with Elden's concept. But strategic practice unintentionally compromised agrarian production and household reproduction. Among other contradictory outcomes, the hunger that rode in the wake of every campaign deferred visions of a better future, provoking debates about the morality and fairness of DRV rule in postcolonial territory.

More than a contested process and not just a ruling strategy, territory is also a contingent outcome of grounded struggles. In support of this argument, *Contested Territory* emphasizes relations between the national state and citizen-subjects and traces the battle forward into an unpredictable moment in the longer production of Vietnamese territory. After war ended and the DRV secured independence from France in 1954, logistics labor flowed into infrastructure, taxation expanded, hunger increased, and political tensions reached new heights. Practiced in guerilla warfare and emboldened by ideas of self-rule, Black River peoples now turned logics of revolutionary state formation against the DRV. Drawing on millenarian traditions, they mobilized a countermovement, created spaces of autonomous social action, and called for deliverance by an alternate sovereign.[16] The movement's ideas and actions cap the analytical argument, demonstrating that an idea of territory must incorporate the contingencies, indeterminacies, and dead ends observed in the actual making of territory. By extension, understanding territory and its production must also incorporate the relevant spatio-temporal context—in this case, the Black River borderlands after World War II.

MUANG GEOGRAPHIES

The Black River's course through the borderlands of Vietnam, Laos, and China defines a region based on ecological and cultural similarities. Originating between the Mekong and the Red Rivers, the Black River flows a total of one thousand kilometers through steep valleys and drains high mountains—including Vietnam's highest peak, Mt. Fansipan (3,143 meters)—before joining the Red River, spreading into a delta around Hanoi and spilling into the Gulf of Tonkin. Under a tropical climate regime, monsoon rains normally arrive in the summer months and alternate with a long dry season punctuated by strong westerly winds, a pattern that varies by topography and elevation.[17] Climate and relief shape agricultural possibilities, enabling irrigation and wet rice in the valleys while suiting the region's forested hills, slopes, and mountains to swidden cultivation and rain-fed cash cropping. Since ancient times, waves of in-migration, social differentiation, and agricultural specialization have reshaped these landscapes, generating settlement patterns that resemble a patchwork quilt of about twenty ethno-linguistic groups. More powerful and numerous among the others, Tai peoples have achieved a measure of autonomy by negotiating with large polities, mediating long-distance trade, and brokering sometimes tense relations with smaller groups, notably Hmong, Dao, and Khmu peoples.

Challenging conventional analytic frames, scholars of upland Asia have recently offered ways to reframe the Black River region as part of a world unto itself—but not a world apart. Peering across national boundaries and querying given categories brings into focus an underlying and contiguous social formation in the borderlands of China, India, and mainland Southeast Asia. Roughly spanning the eastern Himalayan massif, this world encompasses peoples and terrain characterized by high altitude, rugged topography, low population density, cultural and linguistic diversity, and—until recently—political autonomy. Though they largely agree on these core features, scholars vigorously debate this world's name, precise dimensions, and political relations. James Scott's influential conceptualization of this world as "Zomia" offered a point of departure for rethinking the highland region as a space of escape inhabited by refugees from lowland state-making projects. Yet scholars critique a Zomian binary that posits lowland states versus highland non-states, arguing instead for more nuanced interpretations of local political agency. In this vein, historians James Anderson and John Whitmore conceptualize "the Dong World" to analyze the complex and varied relations between external powers, especially China, and the diverse highland communities organized around valley settlements, wet-rice agriculture, and local rule known in Tai/Chinese as *dong* and in Tai/Vietnamese as *muang*.[18]

Placing emphasis on local agency and geographic adaptability, this book treats the consolidation of nation-state territory as a conjunctural event, one that unfolded variously across Asia's highland world. Since ancient times into the modern era, local rulers have contended with powerful state forces, exchange relations, and civilizing projects rising from the lowlands. As these processes intensified and drew the highland world into competing domains, particularly in the nineteenth and twentieth centuries, local actors continued to negotiate, accommodate and, sometimes, resist relations of external domination. Coupled with these processes, modern communication and transportation technologies closed the distance that had enabled local autonomy, but they still offered opportunity to adapt to changing circumstances and shifting alliances.[19] In short, grounding the construction of Vietnamese territory in the Black River borderlands throws its political strategies, contested processes, and uncertain outcomes into sharp relief.

In the mid-twentieth century, the Black River region was home to diverse peoples poised at the precipice between an old history of adaptation and a new territorial alignment. Statistics describing the region from the early 1950s hint at the contests driving knowledge production. Official French and Vietnamese estimates of the region's population range from 260,000 to 320,000 residents. The sources enumerate subpopulations by ethnicity (listed by new/old ethnonyms): Tai/Thái peoples were the largest at 57 percent, followed by Hmong/Mèo at 19 percent, Khmu/Xá at 6 percent, Dao/Mán at 6 percent, Mường at 6 percent, Tày/Thổ at 3 percent, Kinh/Việt at 1 percent, and less than 1 percent each for Lao, Sing Moon/Xinh Mun/Puộc, Giấy/Nhắng, Lự, Chinese/Hoa, Akha/U Ni, and Lô Lô. Finally, a Vietnamese source from 1955 estimated the region's area at 55,000 square kilometers, and a French politician estimated its area in 1952 at 50,000 square kilometers.[20]

Far from a neutral endeavor, counting population by way of territory was a strategic form of knowledge production used by France and Vietnam alike. Competing against a colonial strategy of territorialization, the national political project conceptualized Black River space by using the same borders and quantitative measures on its population. As such, three statistics here deserve critical attention. First, Tai peoples were a demographic majority in the upland region (57 percent), far outnumbering Kinh peoples (1 percent) who had settled there from downstream. The latter group, also known as Việt, was a demographic majority in Vietnam's emerging, yet still contested, national territory (85 percent of 28 million). Second, the region's low population density relative to Vietnam's Red River heartland and its enormous area—over one-third of the DRV's total territory (158,000 square kilometers)—drove a frontier discourse dating to the late 1940s. In years to come, the Kinh population in the Black River region would swell with inflows of soldiers, officials, and migrants. Third, the range between upper and lower population estimates was likely due to wartime displacement and popular evasion, the latter an old tactic to avoid taxes, conscription, and labor service.[21] Deployed by competing state projects to control the same space, enumeration itself was a site of contest between each project and a footloose population.

These data provide a snapshot of a region in flux, but official figures on ethnicity point again to powerful ways of knowing but not necessarily understanding Asia's socially complex borderlands. In the early 1950s, Vietnamese officials were embarking on a classification project based on ethnicity or nationality (*minzu* in Chinese; *dân tộc* in Vietnamese) not altogether different from that of the French and much like an ambitious project then under way in China's Yunnan Province. Aiming to integrate different groups into a centralized and territorially stable state, both Vietnam's and China's classification projects exposed problems in the category of ethnicity. First, an official ethnic group often amalgamated socially meaningful distinctions: for example, the category for Tai peoples (Chinese *Zhuang*; Vietnamese *Thái*) glossed over the distinction between White and Black Tai; the same goes for internally diverse Hmong, Khmu, and Dao peoples. Amalgamation figured in a state strategy of categorization and classification that operated in relation to, but in different ways than, ongoing social processes of diversification and adaptation. This second problem, as anthropologist Edmund Leach had just observed in the mountains of neighboring Burma (Myanmar), meant that ethnic identities were and remain highly mutable, oscillating in response to social interaction and political circumstance. In line with these scholarly critiques, ethnicity here is defined as a situational identity and a form of social organization constructed in relation to self and other, environmental conditions, cultural influence, and political power.[22]

Understood as situational and adaptive, ethnicity helps explain the spatial distribution of social groups in the Black River region at a moment of incipient and lasting change. Broadly speaking, its human geography displayed a threefold elevational pattern—upland, midland, and highland—stratified by ethnic identity, residence time, and agricultural specialization. The pattern was contiguous with the middle Mekong basin, or present-day upper Laos, where, wrote anthropologist Karl Izikowitz, "the distribution of ethnic groups is layered." His findings, like those of Leach, offer an approach to highland Asia's complex social world that crosses the boundaries imposed by colonial and nation-state frames. Izikowitz, who coined the term *swidden* for shifting cultivation, did the fieldwork for his classic study in late 1930s Laos.[23] Yet his analysis describes mid-twentieth-century Black River conditions more accurately and comprehensively than comparable work from that time on Tonkin or Vietnam.

Social layering roughly corresponded to the type of swidden cultivation practiced by ethnic groups in the region's four main language families: Hmong-Mien and Sino-Tibetan groups at the highest elevations, Mon-Khmer in the midlands, and Tai-Kedai in the lowlands. Dominant Tai peoples, including the Lao, primarily inhabited the plains and river valleys, used irrigation to grow wet-rice, and organized themselves by muang, a spatial unit governing relations of land, labor, and ritual activity. For them, swidden cultivation, used to grow dry rice and cash crops, was secondary; it also offered poor peasants an escape from muang obligations or a temporary alternative in the event of displacement. Khmu groups mainly inhabited the midland slopes and foothills, relying primarily on rotational, dry-land swidden cultivation to grow rice. Although the region's original inhabitants, Khmu peoples became subordinate to the Tai within the muang order. By contrast, groups of Dao and

Hmong—the latter a relative newcomer, arriving en masse from China in the nineteenth century—settled the highlands and mountain ridgelines. Buffered from muang politics by forests and rugged terrain, they practiced pioneering swidden cultivation, opening forests to cultivate dry rice, tubers, maize, and opium and to raise livestock. If the opportunity arose, Hmong people could grow wet-rice but Khmu people largely did not, sometimes forbidden by muang custom.[24]

Spread unevenly across the rugged landscape, the Black River population was underlain by a muang geography: people clustered in the valleys, dispersed in the forested mountains, and connected by way of trade. Towns, administrative centers, and other sites of relatively dense settlement were all built on historic muang, and each Vietnamese placename still coexists alongside a Tai toponym. Prominent towns included Lai Châu (Muang Lai) to the north, Sơn La (Muang La) to the south, Điện Biên Phủ (Muang Thanh) to the west, and Nghĩa Lộ (Muang Lò) to the east. Serving the region's agrarian economy, markets in these lowland towns funneled agricultural produce and forest products from the surrounding highlands and functioned as nodes in a larger upstream-downstream network. Among other goods, including livestock, cotton, and cardamom, opium produced by Hmong and Dao swidden cultivators at heights above a thousand meters figured both locally in exchanges for rice grown by midland Khmu and lowland Tai peoples and extra-locally for salt, silver, and metal wares originating from the Red River Delta and brokered by Tai, Kinh, and Chinese merchants.[25] Upstream-downstream trade flowed principally along the Black River and met the Vietnamese lowlands at the historic Riverside Market (Chợ Bờ) in present-day Hoà Bình. By contrast, rugged terrain, river crossings, and monsoon flooding limited overland routes largely to mule trains and foot traffic, preventing most long-distance automobile traffic into the 1950s. Just prior to the Điện Biên Phủ Campaign in 1953, for example, a crucial eighty-kilometers-long segment of Road 41 linking the battleground to depots at Tuần Giáo and other towns east was, according to a military historian, "little more than 'a mule track.'"[26]

In addition to settlement, economy, and communication, the Black River's muang geography structured internal and external relations of political domination. According to a classic analysis by Georges Condominas, the muang exemplifies an intermediate social space that governs relations both within Tai communities and between them and larger polities. A flexible unit, the muang operates at multiple scales in what Condominas called *emboîtement,* translated literally as "emboxment" and rendered by others as "containerization" or "encapsulation."[27] In other words, the muang may simply include constituent settlements (*bản*) like villages, expand to encompass many muang ruled by a supreme leader, as in a country like Thailand (known as Muang Tai before 1941), or function in between the two, like a county, district, city, or community. Condominas's analysis of Tai political systems advanced an important agenda—namely, to study "their articulation with the state"—that has inspired scholars working across highland Asia, including this one. Just behind the front stage at Điện Biên Phủ another drama was playing out: a foundational moment in the longer integration of Tai political spaces with Vietnam's postcolonial state, society, and territory.[28]

Within the larger Dong world and its overlapping and shifting spheres of influence, the historic durability of muang relations distinguishes the Black River region from its neighbors. East of the Hoàng Liên Sơn Range and across the Red River is a region known as the Việt Bắc, where Tai peoples (including Tày, Nùng, and Giấy) have longer histories with Chinese and Vietnamese kingdoms. Vietnamese revolutionaries established an important base there in the First Indochina War, and their formative relations with Black River peoples are one subject of this book. West of the Nam Ou River and southwest of the Mekong's left bank, the muang organizes similar peoples and spaces in similar ways. But Tai and Lao groups there are more influenced by Theravada Buddhism and have longer histories with Lao and Siamese kingdoms. Situated between these regions, the Black River basin was the site of the Sip Song Chau Tai (Twelve Tai Principalities) in the centuries prior to French colonial rule. A confederation of muang leaders led by the Đèo clan of Lai Châu, the Sip Song Chau Tai earned autonomy by maintaining tributary relations with Chinese, Vietnamese, and Lao kingdoms.[29]

Well into the mid-twentieth century in the Black River region, the muang organized relations of land, labor, and rule under control of a hereditary Tai elite. Vested with ritual authority, male Tai aristocrats served as "protectors and organizers of the community," according to Condominas, and oversaw a hierarchical social order. "In return," he continues, "the lord [Tai: *tao,* or chief] enjoys considerable privileges," such as allocating wet-rice land to "free peasants" but keeping choice parcels for himself; commanding peasant manpower, owed as corvée, to work these parcels; collecting taxes in kind, usually rice; and exerting monopoly rights over the goods exported out of the muang, especially forest products and opium. Non-Tai peoples could be included within the muang's domain but usually on a subordinate basis, as was the case with the midland Khmu, whose archaic ethnonym (*Xá/Tsa*) also indicated status as slaves or servants (Tai: *kha*). Consequently, Khmu dress, language, diet, architecture, and other cultural forms exhibited the influence of Tai-ization, a way of elevating their lowly status. But the muang elite's considerable power over lowland sites faded with elevation and diminished in the highlands and forests, landscapes that Tai peoples considered "wild" or undomesticated. By inhabiting these spaces, Hmong and Dao peoples, among other Tai and non-Tai swidden cultivators, strove to live outside the muang's reach. Even as they maintained cultural distinctions, they still engaged with muang communities in sometimes tense exchange relations and political negotiations. A Tai-language term but used by more than just Tai peoples, the muang also functioned—as it still does—as an idiom and a model of political organization for diverse peoples at a regional scale.[30]

The Black River's muang geography shaped the construction of French and Vietnamese territory there, incorporating social cleavages that widened with the First Indochina War. After World War II, French administrators reinvigorated a special relationship with the powerful Dèo clan of Lai Châu. They recognized the Tai Federation in 1948 as a semi-autonomous unit within Indochina, its capital at Lai Châu, and Đèo Văn Long its president. Modeled on the historic Sip Song Chau Tai, the federation occupied strategic territory along Tonkin's porous borders with China and Laos—demarcated in the late nineteenth century with the assistance of Long's father. Among other so-called Highlander Countries, the Tai Federation in northwest Tonkin earned autonomy over its budget, administration, and education in exchange for cooperating militarily and politically with the French against the DRV. French policy aimed to exploit regional fault lines, fragment nationalist sentiment, and divide territory claimed by the DRV, the result amounting to a civil war.[31] Divisive as it was, the strategy did not always work as intended, especially among increasingly restive Black River peoples.

Tensions growing out of the Tai Federation split in favor of Vietnam's surging anti-colonial movement, tying the upstream region to a national state and society rising from downstream. Favoritism toward the Đèo clan amplified rivalries between muang elites, and disaffected Tai leaders gravitated to the Việt Minh. In the revolutionary situation, personal feuds often blurred into disputes over office, and political relations colored economic exchange and cultural difference. Hmong opium growers chafed at the federation's taxes and trade monopoly, and they backed guerilla units operating in the highlands.[32] Radical DRV cadres taught poor Tai and Khmu peasants about alternatives to muang domination, and they rallied behind socialism and land reform. Bolstered by a push from downstream, these political, economic, and cultural relations would pull Vietnamese territory upstream into new highland worlds. Opposed to France's colonial division of territory, Vietnam pushed forcefully to unify nationally, incorporating the muang into local government and socializing the geobody through logistics work. Like French Indochina's strategy, however, the DRV's did not always work as intended, especially as warfare appropriated ever more local resources and Tai elites secured privilege in a new regime. Like the DRV state itself, the territory this state co-produced was never monolithic but patchy, permeable, and contested.[33]

Challenging conventional spatial frames benefits from challenging temporal ones as well. As such, this study adopts a novel periodization to account for local changes and continuities during an era of rapid decolonization, nation-state formation, and territorial production. Called the long 1950s, this period traces the processes—flowing from revolution in 1945, driving anti-colonial warfare, and suppressing a local countermovement by 1960—that produced Vietnam's national territory in a highly contested and culturally different place. My approach engages three tendencies in the scholarly literature. The drama of Điện Biên Phủ has been told many times over, but conventional histories tend, first, to focus on combat at the expense of local noncombatants and, second, to begin or end narratives in 1954. By contrast, this study elevates local actors in order to analyze how their everyday participation helped win a war and transformed the very ground under their feet. Furthermore, working across the conjuncture of 1954—often used to signify rupture between colony and nation—both follows continuities in rule and analyzes the changes, like national citizenship, that resulted.[34] Third, studies of present-day Northwest Vietnam have surged with scholarly interest in highland Asia, but many reproduce binaries of Cold War or Zomian varieties, such as communist and anti-communist, highland or lowland, state and non-state, majority and minority, and so on. In contrast, this study analyzes how the Black River's threefold social formation interacted with downstream forces, generating alliances and exposing fissures that shifted rapidly over time and stretched unevenly across space.

In sum, the wartime struggles that culminated in the Điện Biên Phủ Campaign involved enlisting local peoples and militarizing spaces, and they realized a national territorial project that transformed the Black River region into a frontier of Vietnam. In the late nineteenth century, French cartographers and local elites mapped the region within the Tonkin Protectorate, establishing external borders with China and internal borders with the Lao Protectorate, also part of French Indochina. Not until after World War II, however, did Vietnamese anti-colonial revolutionaries imagine the space as integral to the Vietnamese geobody by externalizing its borders with Laos and administering its territory as the DRV's Northwest Zone. Yet the vanguard faced two significant obstacles. First, imperial France, ruling indirectly through its Tai Federation proxy, challenged the DRV's nation-state claim. Second, local support for the DRV did not extend far beyond local elites, reaching the Tai muang chiefs but not necessarily their subjects or the upland ethnic groups. Subsequently, as war escalated from 1952 to 1954, DRV elites socialized their vision of national territory through mass participation in everyday logistics work. In so doing, they endowed an old colonial border with new meaning on the ground, gradually aligning military fronts with a national frontier and turning the rear into sovereign territory. They also destabilized a preexisting social formation, an outcome no one had predicted but that nonetheless grew out of the grounded struggles constitutive of Vietnamese territory.

ARCHIVAL APPROACHES, FIELDWORK, AND NARRATIVE ORGANIZATION

Research for this book tacked between the archives and the field. Consulting archival sources required thinking carefully about their content and the conditions under which they were produced, stored, and accessed.

My reading of archival documents, therefore, engages the connections between epistemic claims and state power; explores tensions between textuality, orality, and polylinguality; analyzes categorical construction in moments of cultural encounter; and strives to identify voices silenced in the production of history. Neither repositories of truth nor transparent records of thought and action, archives instead house what historian Ann Stoler characterizes as "records of uncertainty and doubt in how people imagined they could and might make the rubrics of rule correspond to a changing imperial world."[35] This book shows how reading along and against the grain applies not only to colonial archives, as Stoler observes, but to the national kind as well.

The book draws primarily on sources housed in Vietnam's National Archives, especially its enormous and still largely untapped trove of Vietnamese-language documents on early DRV state making. An archive built by and for the postcolonial state, Center 3 in Hanoi stores central, regional, and local reports dating from 1945 onward.[36] The collection captures the uncertain processes of territorial construction at each administrative scale. During the First Indochina War, for example, the DRV's "Center" (*Trung ương*) was something of a misnomer. It was located not in Hanoi—still held by France—but in the Việt Bắc base area. Only in 1955 did DRV leaders align the government's centralized institutions with the nation-state capital, building over what had been the capital of French Indochina.

The relationship between the DRV central government and Black River actors depended on a volatile military situation that, in turn, influenced source material in substantive ways. First, reports from the region date to the onset of guerilla warfare in the late 1940s, stop for two years following a French counterattack in 1950, and then resume in late 1952 with the first of two large military campaigns. The gap indicates a nonlinear process of state making, an empirical finding that contradicts a linear telos underlying nationalist narratives, including that of the archive itself. Second, reporting agencies change as well, ranging from—among others—the Sơn-Lai Administrative Committee from 1948 to 1950 to the Northwest Zone Party Chapter from 1952 to 1955 to the Thái-Mèo Autonomous Zone after 1955. The institutional and scalar variability indicates the diversity of perspectives affiliated with, and the evolving capacities of, DRV territorial administration. Far from monolithic, the nascent DRV state was a work in progress all over its claimed space of "Vietnam," and this was very much the case in the physically distant and culturally different region studied here.

Just as the DRV state was mutable, patchy, and permeable, so too are the voices in its archived reports variable, situational, and polyvocal. In spite of official exhortations to follow a unified line, ostensibly allied activists, soldiers, officers, cadres, and bureaucrats rarely if ever spoke as one.[37] As best as the sources allow, my narrative excavates the stories of these individuals and situates their actions within the relevant geographic and institutional context. Doing so reveals how local cadres mediated between center and locality and adapted, adjusted, and altered policy during its implementation. Not simply practitioners, local Tai cadres also formulated policy by guiding their nominal superiors on ways to incorporate the muang into territorial administration. Far from automatons, downstream Kinh cadres, too, recorded differences with superiors over policy, even splitting factionally over land reform, mass mobilization, and taxation. In short, official motivations were about as diverse as the conditions in which officials operated.

Officials aside, everyday folk enter the archive at key moments, not always for reasons of their choosing. If "the peasant's job," to quote Scott, "is to stay out of the archives," then flagging when and why they appear, and those instances when they do not, is the job of the scholar. In revolutionary Vietnam, peasants entered the archive not only as suspects and counterrevolutionaries but also as exemplary producers, heroic laborers, and model citizens. Even rebels might be cited as champions—provided they were on the right side. More frequently, as Scott observes, peasants appear as "statistical abstractions," recorded by the state in terms of their manpower, taxed grain, workdays, and so on. Yet, like other DRV state capacities, accounting practices developed unevenly over time in relation both to the military situation and a partially legible society. Notably, the Điện Biên Phủ Campaign heralded the achievement of a new statistical capacity, what scholar Timothy Mitchell calls "a character of calculability," that the DRV wielded to gather military supplies and coordinate logistics on a grand scale. Rather than accept the archived statistics as given facts, my analysis aims to render the numerical abstractions concrete again, thereby humanizing people counted as numbers.[38] Further, approaching these sources critically unpacks the social processes driving development of calculative technologies, thereby revealing the methods used and abused by the counters. In sum, reading Vietnam's National Archives against the grain uncovers the territorial traces of a state project left behind in places with distinct histories and, sometimes, orthogonal trajectories.

French-language archival sources consulted in Hanoi and in France document an earlier territorial project and how it shaped the more recent Vietnamese one. Hanoi's Center 1 stores documents from colonial offices and agencies, including detailed maps of northwest Tonkin produced by French colonial cartographers. Yet, as with maps stored at Center 3, reproducing cartographic documents was forbidden, an indication of how officials still treat national territory and its colonial antecedents as sensitive spaces.[39]

Working in France's archives offers easier access and quicker service than in Vietnam, but these same features risk enrolling an uncritical reader in the reproduction of epistemic violence and flawed analytical terms. The long entanglement of colonial categories, Cold War strategies, and academic research in Vietnam means that critical scholars must contextualize the ethnographic assumptions and representations embedded in archival documents. Thus, my analysis here treats seemingly neutral categories and information sources as themselves politically laden. Treading carefully at the Defense Historical Service in Paris, I read military intelligence reports that referred routinely to Vietnamese soldiers as "terrorists" and drew heavily on captured individuals and translated documents. But reading the transcripts of interrogations performed on the young captives—including intimate details of biography, home, and family—and wondering about their fate reminded me to interrogate the interrogators.[40] Further, translations offered their own biases. Official renderings of Vietnamese into French facilitate understanding in the target language but add another layer of powerful, sometimes biased mediation. Approximations at best and willful distortions at worst, the (mis)translation of revolutionary ideas fails to convey their full meaning but does other work instead. Laden with ideological intent, colonial documents aimed to legitimate a coercive territorial project and cast doubt on that of its rival, or "enemy." Although its ideological register differs, the DRV pursued a similar project.

My archival approach was complemented by a parallel investigation of actual conditions in the Black River region. Although the sources cited are historic documents, it would have been impossible to write about the peoples and places the sources represent without acquainting myself with conditions on the ground over a decade of fieldwork. Through ethnographic participation and site observation, oral histories and interviews, and studying up as much as down, I learned about Điện Biên Phủ as a hallowed site and commemorated event as well as a lived-in place, market hub, and administrative node. My understanding of state-society relations, boundary-making processes, and territorial administration in Vietnam comes as much from the accidents and processes involved in negotiating research clearance as from scholarly texts and standard research methods.[41] In an everyday way, veterans in Hanoi and farmers in Điện Biên helped me comprehend the physical distance and cultural difference separating these places in the 1950s as well as the tremendous amount of work they did to close the gaps. Traveling on the roads they built connected me with the landscapes they helped transform, even though my experiences were but a pale approximation of their longer struggles.

Just as the larger story here is one of historic conjuncture, my ability to tell it likewise emerges out of conjunctural experiences, relationships, and forces. My dissertation fieldwork in 2006–7 coincided with a longer rapprochement in U.S.-Vietnamese relations. As a Fulbright grantee, I participated in diplomatic and scholarly exchanges as well as the opening of state archives to foreign scholars. Living in Hanoi and Điện Biên Phủ for a year and a half positioned me in the same socio-spatial relationship I studied. Whether residing in a tight-knit urban community or visiting highland villages, my neighbors and interlocutors were as interested in me—a young, white American man—as I in them.[42]

The book's six chapters are organized by rough chronology and analytical scale. The first and last chapters take the reader into and out of the long 1950s through the biography of Lò Văn Mười, a Tai man who rose from colonial jailer to regional judge and national hero. Opening with the August Revolution of 1945, the narrative ends with the DRV's forceful consolidation of territory in 1960. The middle four chapters are grouped in pairs to analyze the social transformations accompanying two large military campaigns: the 1952 Northwest Campaign and the 1953–54 Điện Biên Phủ Campaign. Each pair analyzes an overlapping time period: first from the top down and second from the bottom up. Like adjusting a camera's zoom lens, toggling the level of analysis highlights the production of territory at multiple scales as well as a quantitative and qualitative shift in the latter campaign. Logistics capacity advanced in step with calculative knowledge of society and resources, enabling a state project to climb the hills, enlist swidden cultivators, and generate Vietnamese territory above and between muang spaces.

In all, *Contested Territory* uncovers hidden histories about a place often invoked but poorly understood. Điện Biên Phủ was and remains powerfully significant in Vietnam, especially as a symbol of hard-fought Vietnamese independence, state legitimacy, and national territory. The epilogue examines the construction of this dominant meaning through a brief survey of archival production, military campaigns, and official commemorations. Such narrative recounting, I argue, depends both on prior acts of counting and accounting as well as on continually discounting other memories and stories. As a result, scholars know little about the events discussed in this book. While *Contested Territory* in the main offers up a forgotten history of Điện Biên Phủ, it closes with a discussion of the place in relation to the battle's anniversaries, commemorated every decade since 1964. Local peoples there now inhabit a valley floor carpeted with memorials and cemeteries, the meanings of which they still produce in relation to their everyday struggles.

CHAPTER ONE

"Vast Area, Sparse People"

NEAR THE END OF WORLD WAR II, a humble man took a radical turn. On 9 March 1945, the Japanese forces occupying French Indochina staged a sudden well-prepared coup against their increasingly uneasy allies, the Vichy French administration. Almost everywhere else in Vietnam, Cambodia, and Laos, Japanese troops rounded up French military and civilian personnel and their families, forcibly detaining them in camps. In the Black River region, they escaped to China alongside local officials, adding to a temporary power vacuum created by the colonial regime's disruption. Seizing the initiative, no fewer than two hundred communist prisoners escaped the Sơn La Penitentiary, where a local Tai prison guard, Lò Văn Mười, had joined their movement. He went on to help lead Vietnam's August Revolution in Sơn La Province.[1]

Joining Sơn La's revolution not only required navigating a complex international situation, including colonial reconquest, it also helped initiate a longer and highly contested process of Vietnamese state making in the Black River borderlands. Beginning on 22 August 1945, revolutionaries captured weapons from Japanese soldiers, raided grain warehouses, seized government offices, and hoisted Vietnam's new red flag with a yellow star. As a local Việt Minh Front leader, Mười openly challenged French control over Sơn La's muang—places of concentrated Tai residence, agriculture, and power. Yet the uprising was short-lived. On

31 August, Nationalist Chinese forces charged with demobilizing the Japanese army also disarmed Việt Minh activists and assisted a rival nationalist organization (VNQDĐ). Mười and his peers scattered. Worse, French forces returned in February 1946 and set about installing their own regional leader, Đèo Văn Long. When the Chinese left that spring, the Franco-Tai alliance began restoring the colonial order to Sơn La's muang, a task largely accomplished by 1947.[2] Picking up the story in 1948, this chapter examines a two-year period when Mười pursued Vietnam's anti-colonial revolution and helped transform it into DRV state administration. He, and other local Tai cadres like him, were crucial in Vietnam's 1954 victory over France at Điện Biên Phủ and in the ruling relations that enabled and flowed from it.

Making Vietnam in the Black River region meant encountering socially diverse peoples and confronting the colonial barriers erected between them. Although Mười's actions in the August Revolution and ensuing First Indochina War (1946–54) earned him a Presidential Independence Award in 1998, he recalled that being an "ethnic minority" had made his path to the Communist Party "very awkward." He hailed from Thuận Châu (aka Muang Muổi), settled in the twelfth century and rivaling Điện Biên Phủ (Muang Thanh) as a center of regional Tai authority. Coming from a "high-class" Tai family spared him the "humiliations felt by most of my ethnic compatriots" and provided "privilege and profit from the local regime," including an education in French schools, enough to eat, and a civil service post. Expecting "power and benefit," he joined the colonial native guard in 1931 and rose to warrant officer in the Sơn La Penitentiary. His high-status Tai background fit a colonial jailer's ideal profile, matching what anthropologist Oscar Salemink calls a "divide-and-rule-policy on the basis of ethnographic knowledge." French officials sequestered Kinh political prisoners from Hanoi and the Red River Delta far up and away in Sơn La's prison where they believed interethnic hostility would prevent illicit discourse.[3] Mười came of age poised to uphold a colonial order that privileged Tai elites, pitted them against downstream Kinh, and reproduced an old muang hierarchy.

But serving in the notorious penitentiary changed Mười in ways the French did not anticipate. Jailed members of the Indochinese Communist Party (ICP) and its vibrant party cell educated him and, he recalled, "awakened my consciousness." He felt sympathy for poor, oppressed people and "heartfelt exposure" over his own privilege. Indeed, the same qualities that endeared Mười to colonial officials made him a catch for communist organizers. The Việt Minh, founded in 1941 and led secretly by the ICP, proclaimed a regionally specific message of "Tai-Kinh unity" through national salvation organizations and bilingual newspapers, especially the Tai Youth League and its organ, *Lắc Mường*. The message resonated among an upper strata of Tai society, including wealthy peasants burdened by taxes, students educated in French schools and modern ideas, and hereditary elites alienated by French colonial rule. Together, writes scholar Cầm Trọng, they organized to "resist the lords (*phìa tạo*) holding power."[4] In years to come, Mười would play a pivotal role in expanding the message's appeal to include common Tai folk in muang spaces and the many non-Tai peoples outside of them.

Mười figured prominently in an emerging political alliance between upstream Tai elites and downstream Kinh radicals. After the two hundred prisoners, all of whom were party members, escaped in March 1945, Mười served on Sơn La's Việt Minh Council alongside former inmates and better-known Tai revolutionaries, including Xa Văn Minh and Cầm Văn Dung. Hailing from the Xa clan of Mộc Châu (Muang Xang), Minh had served in the colonial administration in the 1930s but achieved lasting prominence by incorporating traditional Tai administration into DRV territory through the 1950s. Dung, accused of poisoning a French ex-Resident in 1933, had been imprisoned in Hanoi's Central Prison at Hỏa Lò, another site of communist strength and sanctuary for political activists. Like Mười, Dung joined the prison's thriving ICP cell, allied with Vietnamese radicals there, and—after his escape on 11 March 1945—returned home to help open the new Black River front. Scion of the powerful Cầm clan of Mai Sơn (Muang Mụa), Dung leveraged his local "prestige" to lead Sơn La's provisional government and put Tai-Kinh unity into practice. But after his arrest for allegedly assisting the Chinese takeover in 1945, Dung grew disillusioned with the Việt Minh, feared for his life, and thereafter adopted a low profile. Meanwhile, another Tai elite and rising star, Lò Văn Hặc (no family relation to Mười), had served the colonial administration during World War II in his home of Điện Biên Phủ. But by 1946, he supported the Việt Minh and, with his family, was persecuted by the Đèo clan. Hặc fled, and he would not return to the region until 1953.[5]

It was left to prominent Tai men like Minh and Mười to territorialize the revolution, a story little known to scholars and the subject of this chapter. In 1948, they began constructing the Democratic Republic of Vietnam's regional resistance government in opposition to, and in territory claimed by, France's regional proxy, the Tai Federation. Hired to enforce colonial boundaries, Mười instead unlocked doors separating Vietnamese revolutionaries from muang places to carry revolution into its next phase.

"Vast Area, Sparse People" explores this early phase of postcolonial Vietnamese state making in the historically Tai-dominated Black River region. It focuses on relations and tensions within DRV territory forming in opposition to French colonial rule from 1948 to 1950. Though the state project temporarily failed, the relationships, ideas, and personnel formed in this two-year period would structure larger interventions still to come. The chapter tells how Kinh radicals and local Tai cadres worked to incorporate Sơn La's muang into DRV regional government and appealed to highland peoples between the valleys. To varying degrees, all of them engaged cultural, political, and economic processes fraught with conflict and uncertain outcomes. The chapter ends when a Franco-Tai assault drove out cadres and guerillas, punished supporters left behind, and severed local archival production.

BIRTH OF A FRONTIER DISCOURSE

Operating a resistance administration in the Black River region contested territory subject to indirect French colonial rule. As declared by Hồ Chí Minh in 1945, the DRV claimed three of Indochina's five territories for an independent Vietnam—Tonkin, Annam, and Cochinchina. In 1948, the French sponsored a rival government to rule the same spaces, known as the Associated State of Vietnam, but maintained a separate hold on its strategic highland areas. In northwest Tonkin, the Tai Federation offered Tai-language education, ran a civil service, commanded several Tai battalions, and collected taxes to support its budget. But the French maintained military and administrative oversight. Indeed, separate territorial administration of this Northern Highlander Country (Pays Montagnard du Nord), like that of the Southern Highlander Country, was a neocolonial strategy wielded by France in a war against Vietnamese independence. Led by Đèo Văn Long and backed by the French, the breakaway polity aimed to split upland Tai from lowland Vietnamese—just as the Việt Minh and DRV aimed to bring them together.[6] Their war generated processes that contested Vietnamese territory in other ways as well. Replacing colonial rule constructed alternate relations of domination, endowed landscapes with new meanings, and entangled resource rights in powerful but unstable alliances.

The everyday work of the Sơn La–Lai Châu Administrative and Resistance Committee aimed to transform guerilla resistance and revolutionary fervor into legitimate institutional power. Beginning in spring 1948, armed propaganda teams deployed to the Black River region along Indochina's Lao-Tonkin border. Known as "advance to the west" (*Tây tiến*) units, they followed ICP strategy by waging war not just in Vietnam and its northern salient (Tonkin or Bắc bộ) but in Laos and Cambodia as well. Their efforts enabled early DRV administration under the Sơn-Lai Interzone. In this embattled space, the Sơn-Lai Committee administered territory along Sơn La Province's southern tier and constructed local government of and for its population. At its peak in late 1949, the Sơn-Lai Interzone stretched south from the Hoàng Liên Sơn Mountains across the Black River to the Lao frontier, and east from Sơn La Town along upland river and road routes above Hoà Bình and the Red River Delta. Its estimated population of twenty-five thousand people comprised about 10 percent of the Black River region's total, the rest of which remained under Tai Federation control.[7] It fell on Mười and Minh, among other Sơn-Lai administrators, to establish district- and commune-level Administrative and Resistance Committees (UBHCKC) in line with DRV central government decrees.

Crafting DRV state power in the Black River region required maneuvering in a mountain landscape and adapting to its social terrain. Vietnam's new government institutions incorporated old Tai muang elites who appealed to popular legitimacy by presenting a recognizable alternative to the increasingly unpopular Tai Federation. More than just unilaterally implementing orders from above, Tai cadres Mười of Thuận Châu and Minh of Mộc Châu engaged in a process of interpretation and negotiation with the central government. As Sơn-Lai Committee members, they led discussions about the size, shape, and personnel of local government units. Their correspondence with superiors raised crucial concerns about state power.[8] In the process, Mười articulated an influential idiom, "vast land, sparse people," that did much more than merely describe his home region. Conjuring a particular vision of Black River places and peoples, he opened a discursive space through which he and other Tai cadres engaged an uncertain process, one that would help shape the region's relationship to Vietnam over the next decade and beyond.

Drawing on his knowledge of political customs specific to the Tai muang, Mười identified a cultural dimension of legitimacy, what he called "prestige" (*uy tín*), and argued in favor of local representation. In October 1949, he directed "special attention" to inspection tours conducted by fellow committee members Trần Quyết and Xa Văn Minh in newly created districts of Mường La, Mai Sơn, and Mộc Châu. He explained that military advance and revolutionary agitation were not enough to win political support from Tai villagers unfamiliar with outsiders, such as Kinh people like Quyết, who was the party secretary of Sơn La Province.[9] For the "simple, rustic" people of Sơn La, "each time a resistance committee member comes inspecting they are happy and realize they have a local government." Without those visits, they "know only the sibling cadres of the Việt Minh Front and army, thereby reducing the local government's prestige." In other words, before Tai folk could believe in DRV institutions, they had to see their own leaders act as leaders. More than just a means for superiors to check on subordinates, then, inspections offered a stage for homegrown political leaders to perform their prestige and earn popular recognition.

Based on this savvy analysis of how to secure local consent for DRV rule, Mười appealed for more resources and coined a powerful idiom. In particular, he asked superiors in the Việt Bắc Interzone—ICP headquarters and center of the DRV's resistance government—to organize transport and secure travel funding in order to conduct more inspection tours in the new districts and communes. More than the request itself, the language he used was and remained significant. "The geographic scale of one commune in Sơn La Province [where] land is vast [and] sparsely peopled (*đất rộng, dân thưa*)," he explained, is such that "one commune is as spacious as one or two districts below downstream." His geographic description accurately conveyed the larger region's gross demographic features: its population of approximately 260,000 was spread out over an enormous space and rugged terrain, averaging a density of just 15–20 people per square kilometer.[10] Much more than a neutral description, however, the idiom functioned also as a prescription for a lasting frontier relationship.

Mười's idiom of "vast land, sparse people" articulated a powerful representation of a region during a historic conjuncture when external relations of exchange and domination were in play. More than just asking for a car or an armed escort, he claimed to know the region and to represent it. He wrote in a language, Vietnamese, that most Black River peoples did not (yet) speak and referred to Vietnamese administrative units very much in the making. The Tai cadre indexed his knowledge of mountain conditions by offering a strategic comparison with the Kinh heartland where, a saying goes, "land is tight, densely settled." More than merely comparing relative scarcity and abundance, his terms of upstream (*ngược*) and downstream (*xuôi*) invoked older relations of exchange linking the Black River tributary to the main stem Red River, its delta, and the sea.[11] As such, he gestured to Tai-Kinh unity and confirmed its state representation on the Sơn-Lai Committee. He also coined a discourse that represented rugged places and unfamiliar peoples as a land-rich frontier ready with unclaimed resources. In short, he advanced a discourse of regional difference within a larger space of equivalence and solidarity.

Taken as a whole, the idiom of "vast area, sparse people" conceived a singular region and allied it to a revolutionary territorial project emerging within an area first delimited by French cartographers. By hitching the space to a rising DRV, Mười bounded it *within* larger relations of spatialized domination. The situation was not unlike the late nineteenth century when Tai power broker Đèo Văn Tri worked with French explorers to map the disputed space and secure its domination.[12] At this juncture, however, Mười accepted these colonial borders but represented the area's population as unified under, and loyal to, DRV rule. He wrote: "Among all strata of Mountain compatriots like Thái [Tai], Mường, Mán [Dao], Mèo [Hmong], Puộc [Sing Moon], Xá [Khmu] beats one heart loyal to the government proving unity between them. We pay closest attention to Mán and Mèo compatriots, who during the French period did not have to corvée or provision like the Thái or Mường; now they have to provision and labor not as though the [DRV] regime forced them but, rather, because they remain pleased to follow orders from above." Far from exhaustive, this list of peoples hints at a complex social landscape caught in a moment of jarring political transition. Yet to call them suddenly loyal and unified under the DRV fit policy prescription closer than empirical description. His report's language echoed an August 1948 ICP policy promulgating a "united national front" between ethnicities and inclusive of "all strata" within each.[13] As such, cloaking a desired political outcome in the guise of observation concealed manifold tensions.

Read closely, in fact, the statement suggests good cause to suspect conditions of actual disunity. In keeping with divide-and-rule strategy, French policy levied labor and military supply duties on the basis of ethnicity, exempting hill peoples from what was required of their valley neighbors.[14] Now, by universalizing these duties, the Sơn-Lai Committee reversed a half-century-old norm and required Dao and Hmong peoples to labor and provision on its behalf. While relatively few actually did so in 1949, DRV expansion of mandatory labor service in the early 1950s would generate broad and lasting grievance. Further, in spite of their supposed "pleasure" (*vui lòng*) to follow orders, the regional committee nonetheless monitored Hmong and Dao compliance. If they were truly happy to obey, why suspect them of disobedience?

Moreover, at this historical juncture, any "unity" among and between Black River peoples was patently false, for the following reasons. French forces fought revolutionary partisans with the assistance of local Tai battalions. The Tai Federation controlled Lai Châu and contested Sơn La ferociously. DRV officials, Tai cadres, and Việt Minh organizers violently opposed the federation, particularly in Sơn La and Yên Bái Provinces. All over, poor peasants did the hard work that officially recognized muang leaders commanded of them. Perched at the interstices between muang spaces, Dao and Hmong peoples appeared wary of Tai power—whatever its form.

Finally, colonial tactics were not the only source of division, as Mười himself demonstrated by offering to capitalize on rivalries within the Tai Federation. Popular struggles had eroded confidence in Sơn La's "puppet officials," he wrote, prompting French administrators to approach Lai Châu Province's officials with a deal: should they suppress the struggles, then the French military would grant the disputed Mường La District to "Lai Châu to rule." As a result, Sơn La's colonial officials held little love for their colonial masters, prompting the Tai cadre to approach his superiors with a plan "to split the puppet ranks." By issuing passes to turncoat officials, a tactic already in place for deserting soldiers, the Sơn-Lai Committee would win over muang elites, secure Mường La, and further isolate the colonial regime in Lai Châu.[15]

This anecdote calls into question what revolutionary activists and officials attributed *only* to colonialism: a strategy of divide and rule. Evidently, an emergent coalition of elite Tai partisans, party cadres, and Việt Minh agents countered colonial strategy not only by "unifying the nation" but also by using divide and rule against itself. In his own words, Mười described how two competing "regimes" pursued strikingly similar goals: to gain the loyalty of Tai "lords"; to "win over" their muang spaces, populations, and resources; to enlist them as local officials in a state "apparatus." It went without saying that securing these elites could shore up a strategic edge of sovereign territory.

Conceived as such, the newly emerging frontier reproduced many old frontiers and social cleavages. What Sơn-Lai officials told their superiors about the resident population, namely, that "all people [here] are mountain people," denied the locally meaningful distinctions between lowland, midland, and highland social groups. Once again, Tai elites were jostling one another for external recognition. But they were one among many peoples in the Black River region—some of whom had long chafed at the powers accruing to lowland Tai. Hmong communities, for example, had led a series of revolts before World War II against Tai domination and French rule.[16] In years to come, as DRV territory incorporated the muang and expanded its reach, midland Khmu peoples and highland Dao and Hmong would fall under renewed Tai power. When they began seeking an alternative to external rule through Tai elites in 1955, their discontent kindled a broader countermovement from within but against Vietnam's territory.

At its inception, therefore, the idiom of "vast area, sparse people" framed complex and emerging relationships in binary terms of periphery and center. The bifurcation worked through a register of mountain and lowland, upstream and downstream, Tai and Kinh. Just as the discourse advanced ideological claims to ethnic unity and state loyalty, it also disguised multiple forms of social difference and denied the many political contests within and between diverse peoples. At a moment of fierce territorial contest, the language of "vast area" telegraphed an idea—of a unitary region steered by knowledgeable and loyal local leaders—to a distant revolutionary vanguard eagerly in search of local support. As much as it privileged Mười and other radical Tai elites, the representation obscured other peoples inhabiting their own places, all of whom were traveling along an indeterminate and ultimately fractious historical trajectory.

In years ahead, "vast area, sparse people" became a dominant regional representation and the Vietnamese language a means for expressing it. Yet when Mười first used it in 1949 to position the region in a communal space of revolutionary solidarity, that space's final form was still far from certain. Whether this imagined communal space, or geobody, would take the form of Indochina or Vietnam was still undecided—and would remain so for several more years. Even as the idiom's meaning shifted with these and other changing conditions, its power has endured right up to the present. Over its long life in Vietnamese reports, everyday speech, and nationalist histories, "vast area, sparse people" has evinced malleable meaning yet retained ideological significance.[17] In ways he could not foresee, Mười coined a lasting frontier discourse that, depending on its usage, might locate the region inside a territorial edge of state power, privilege Tai-Kinh political relations, broadcast resource scarcity or availability, and define its peoples as equivalent to but also somehow different from dominant social norms.

ADMINISTRATIVE ADJUSTMENTS

It was no accident that this prescriptive description of local conditions appeared in DRV correspondence when it did. In response to centrally issued administrative decrees, Sơn-Lai cadres were negotiating with bureaucratic superiors on the one hand and diverse constituencies on the other regarding the size, shape, and personnel of local government units. Their negotiations threw into sharp relief powerful norms shaping territory and bureaucracy as well as the contests that would determine their final forms.

Evidence of maneuvers by local Tai cadres on the Sơn-Lai Committee challenges conventional interpretations of DRV state structure. Based on readings of central orders but not their local implementation, Cold War scholars accepted that the DRV's principle of democratic centralism meant "uninterrupted routine subordination" by what was called "local organs" to the central government.[18] This image of totalitarian rule fails to account for practices that counterbalanced centralization and enhanced strategic flexibility during war, features that a military historian attributes to the DRV's "inherent regionalism." Indeed, local cadres played a crucial role in state formation by constituting its regional bureaucracy, shaping territorial administration, and constructing the ideological effect of an emerging state. Such local agency complicates teleological narratives of a steady Vietnamese advance from the lowlands into the mountains. Further, analyzing how Tai cadres built the muang into DRV state structure suggests how the state did not just climb hills but was pulled upward as well. This finding complicates James Scott's argument about modern state sovereignty among Southeast Asia's highland peoples, some of whom sought to achieve "degrees of potential sovereignty and cultural influence" not just against the state but also within it.[19]

Guerilla warfare opened spaces for savvy local leaders to negotiate the terms of DRV territorial sovereignty. Because armed struggle for Sơn La's southern tier had created "wide and growing space" for DRV government in 1948, Xa Văn Minh requested an influx of cadres trained in "resistance administration" in January 1949. Cadres from the Việt Bắc came bearing orders freighted with historical import and cultural baggage. Signed by President Hồ Chí Minh in November 1948, Decrees 254 and 255 specified the composition, function, and organization of administrative committees and popular assemblies.[20] These local government units followed the Vietnamese administrative model of province (*tỉnh*), district (*huyện*), and commune (*xã*) first promulgated by Emperor Minh Mạng in 1831. Yet these lowland units required major adjustments in the muang-based world of the Black River region. In April 1949, Lò Văn Mười reported that communes in the districts of Mai Sơn and Mộc Châu had yet to implement the decrees, in part blaming a lack of paper for election ballots. Three months later, reporting on inspection tours in those two districts plus Mường La, Mười deployed a curious kind of double-speak. His report both confirmed that each commune had organized assemblies and committees "completely" yet stipulated that "not even one" conformed to the new laws.[21] What was happening on the ground?

The regional committee's awkward attempt to implement central decrees generated problems and stimulated debates regarding the appropriate units, shapes, and personnel of territorial administration. What was, and what should be, the fundamental unit for local government? On the one hand, Sơn-Lai's leaders now had orders "to organize a people's local government . . . only as far as the commune," that is, not recognizing leaders at the village level.[22] On the other hand, Tai people in these "upstream" areas were accustomed to a muang where villages (bản) were the basic unit of organization. Further, each "commune" organized on the *bản muang* model featured not just the village but additional units connecting villages to larger subdistricts (*lộng*) and smaller neighborhoods (*xóm*).[23] Settlements also displayed high geographic diversity: villages ranged from several households to over seventy; households might be packed densely together or spread hither and yon across the landscape. As a result, the new communes reproduced large size ranges (from twenty to two hundred villages) and expansive distances within them (up to thirty kilometers from the nearest office), both of which compromised the ability of local government to function as intended.

The revolutionary leaders inherited a system in which French administrators had addressed distance and diversity by recognizing the village unit, and village chiefs (*tạo bản*), as the fundamental form of local government within the muang. Just as the subdistrict extended administrative services to far-flung villages, the neighborhood connected households distant from one another. As such, colonial rule in the Black River region, much like in Laos, recognized the underlying Tai model of administration in which smaller muang could be absorbed by a larger muang or political center. In premodern Siam (now Thailand), for example, the largest muang was the royal realm which, in turn, encompassed many smaller muang, the lords of which negotiated with overlords and governed the corresponding population. By adopting this preexisting order to rule northwest Tonkin in the late nineteenth century, the French positioned themselves as the ultimate overlords of the Tai domain, retained the subsidiary muang, and recognized traditional leaders as bureaucrats. Then they reproduced the system in July 1948 by recognizing the Tai Federation and its president, Đèo Văn Long, who handed down positions to loyal muang leaders, such as Bạc Cầm Qúy of Sơn La and Đèo Văn Ân of Phòng Thổ.[24] The historic legacy and ongoing practice of Tai rule, therefore, presented the Sơn-Lai leadership with a difficult choice. "If we dismiss the person responsible for the village," rued Mười, "then we either follow the decree and work will not happen; or we do not dismiss them and violate the government's decree."

"Even more difficult" than the village issue, Mười continued, were problems administering Hmong and Dao peoples who settled the slopes, ridgelines, and mountaintops between and amid Tai settlements. Working with the Tai Federation, French administrators had applied a principle of proximity by drawing spatially contiguous polygons and including upland peoples with adjacent communities.[25] In so doing, colonial administration reproduced the muang and its political, cultural, and demographic domination by valley Tai and Mường peoples. Now, fighting against colonial rule and organizing a resistance government offered highland peoples an opportunity to vent discontent with Tai domination and express "aspirations" for an alternative. In one district, Hmong and Dao peoples "proclaimed" their own ethnically distinct communes by creating patchy units to connect their own villages over a hundred kilometers apart. Their unorthodox solution—a spatially *non*contiguous unit—allowed for people separated across space but linked by culture and custom (trade, language, kinship, and so on) to achieve democratic representation. For the Sơn-Lai Committee, such spontaneous communes pointed again to the problem of fundamental administrative units. "To dismiss the [offending] village head," lamented Mười, "makes work very hard."

The Sơn-Lai Committee thus faced a dilemma: either adhere to central government regulations abolishing village government or risk censure by incorporating the functional system. To follow orders jeopardized official work, "especially among the Mountain people," or Hmong and Dao groups, explained Mười, "because geographical conditions are such that people in these villages only know the person in charge of their village." In other words, the committee could ill afford to alienate trusted local leadership in spite of the colonial taint. Although the sources do not specify whether or not village leadership remained as before, it is clear that the parties reached a compromise. Officially, the Sơn-Lai Committee recognized no "village government." Yet it allowed Commune Administrative Committees to employ local "assistants" responsible for everyday correspondence between village and commune.

According to the Sơn-Lai Committee's assessments, these early attempts at creating an "administrative apparatus" or "local government" all failed because they did not conform with central decrees.[26] Yet what may have appeared a failure was in fact the result of negotiations between multiple constituencies regarding the terms of administration and democratic participation. These negotiations called into question underlying assumptions guiding the construction of spatially delineated local government. For peoples accustomed to, yet chafing under, historic Tai domination, regime change offered an opportunity to question old forms of spatial rule and advance new terms of political participation. For the Dao and Hmong, the normative construction of territorial units as spatially uniform and contiguous made little sense and worse, risked diluting their representative power. They proposed a solution, one based on partial sovereignty within the DRV, that linked villages at altitude like islands in the sky.

These debates on the administration of vast space raised another question regarding the allocation of office. With such a sparse population, who was qualified to staff and steer DRV government posts? Sơn-Lai leaders blamed a local shortage on two causes, one of skills fixable through education and another of irremediable otherness. On the one hand, they interpreted incomplete implementation of Decree 254 to mean "Representatives at districts and communes are all short of capacities; among them are commune representatives who cannot read *quốc ngữ*," or Romanized Vietnamese. The language of "capacities" indicates an assessment of skills that could be learned. Indeed, the capacity to read and write in Vietnamese was a crucial bureaucratic skill but in scarce supply among local candidates. To this end, the Việt Minh Front dispatched literacy teams to teach Vietnamese, the language of revolutionary solidarity and emerging bureaucracy. On the other hand, Mười reserved harsh evaluations for "Mountain people" who were, supposedly, "culturally insufficient" and "hygienically backward." This second assessment, a veiled reference to Hmong and Dao peoples, invoked a culturalist language of civility and savagery specific to Tai ideas of muang-based, wet-rice settlement and its opposite, a realm of swidden cultivators inhabiting a wild untamed forest.[27]

Pejorative descriptions of swidden cultivation speak to patterns common in Southeast Asia and, in keeping with this larger pattern, invoked a specific policy prescription that, in this instance, bolstered the Tai-Kinh alliance. Criticisms of shifting agriculture and its practitioners—whether technologically primitive, environmentally destructive, culturally backward, or politically suspect—often stand for larger civilizational projects pursued by lowland elites of Southeast Asia. What bears emphasis here, in 1949, was a convergence between Tai and Kinh ideas of their own civility counterposed against a savage Other out in the forest and up on the mountains. The DRV's regional leadership, Tai and Kinh alike, decided that the local population was either not yet qualified (for reasons of education) or fully unqualified (for reasons of culture) to lead itself. As a result, when Minh requested more Việt Minh cadres, he also rated commune leadership "lacking." Later, Mười echoed his colleague by asking for one cadre from "downstream," that is, someone of Kinh descent, to sit on each province and district committee.[28] In short, the Tai-Kinh alliance emerged as much out of political solidarity as from convergent cultural assumptions about their role as civilizing agents.

Cadres led everyday state formation and embodied these cultural assumptions. Trained individuals directly employed by party or state in an official capacity, cadres (*cán bộ*) were not everywhere the same, in spite of Cold War portrayals of them as Marxist-Leninist automatons. Vietnamese communist nationalism did carve important spaces for various non-Kinh peoples but did not eliminate feelings of Kinh cultural superiority toward them. Even as the party actively sought qualified local cadres (*cán bộ địa phương*), reports routinely deprecated their capacities or culture and, in contrast, exalted downstream cadres for their knowledge, skills, and "high degree of culture." Two seats on the Son-Lai Committee were explicitly reserved for "ethnic Kinh," one of whom was Trần Quyết, whose "capabilities" were rated higher than the "so so" marks assigned to an undifferentiated "Mountain people," or Minh and Mười. Local Tai cadres, in short, were second to Kinh cadres, valued both for administrative skills and for allegedly superior cultural attributes. Yet Tai cadres, too, rated themselves above a more nuanced but still blinkered version of "Mountain people," namely, the highland Hmong and Dao who kept the muang at arm's length. Mười had the latter in mind when he invited "lowland" cadres to improve personal hygiene and rectify work ethic.[29]

Though in high demand, Kinh cadres remained in short supply because of broad reluctance to make the arduous journey upstream. This was an old problem, not unique to anti-colonial organizing and DRV state making. From at least the Nguyễn Dynasty through French rule, Kinh officials considered the mountains to be a punishment post and an "unhealthy" place, owing in part to prevalent malaria.[30] In the late 1940s,

Kinh cadres routinely tried to avoid the Sơn-Lai post by citing distance from families, unfamiliar weather, and health problems. Of those who did make the journey, many either quit or fell ill with fevers, most likely malarial. Kinh cadres, in short, often feared and fled the same conditions they were supposed to improve.

In sum, a powerful idea of the Black River region—where land was vast, its people few by comparison with lowland Vietnam—emerged alongside administrative transformations, marking a new era of up/downstream relations. In a context of revolutionary state formation, the "vast area" discourse reveals relationships between Tai and Kinh leaders positioning themselves as leaders of region and center, respectively. It also conceals how power, knowledge, and difference intersected at lowland, midland, and highland scales *within* the Black River region. As a result, the rapid construction of local government along Sơn La's southern tier reproduced old patterns of rule. Debates about administrative units—whether commune and district or muang and village—opened onto enduring issues of spatial regulation, bureaucratic recruitment, and culture-bound logics. Local Tai cadres challenged central leaders to modify a system better suited to a Kinh socio-spatial context in and around the Red River Delta. Yet just as new districts and communes incorporated Tai muang in the valleys, the highlands above and between them mostly remained spaces apart—for now.

THE REVOLUTIONARY EXCHANGE; OR, SALT AND POWER

Alleviating popular hunger became closely linked to Việt Minh organizing at the end of World War II and to institutionalizing and legitimating DRV power for long afterward. During the Great Famine of 1945, mass starvation led to the death of an estimated 1 million people in the Red River Delta and adjoining provinces of Thanh Hóa and Nghệ An. Approximately 10 percent of northern Vietnam's population perished in five short months. "No disaster of this magnitude," writes historian David Marr, "had afflicted Vietnamese society in living memory." In stark contrast to weak or inept French administrators and the rapacious Japanese army, the Việt Minh Front mobilized peasants to raid government granaries, seize stocks from landlords, and redistribute rice to hungry people. However instrumental its aims or limited its impact, the Việt Minh was the only organization to alleviate famine conditions or even to understand their political implications. On 2 September 1945, in his Declaration of Independence of the DRV, Hồ Chí Minh cited the famine as evidence of how "our people" had suffered under the "double yoke" of French colonialism and Japanese fascism. Turning paternalist colonial rhetoric on its head, he observed wryly that the famine demonstrated France's incapacity to "'protect' us."[31]

Việt Minh and DRV cadres delivered food to upstream Black River peasants beginning in 1948. Learning from the Great Famine, they engaged peasants in state-making processes of reciprocal exchange, organizational development, and political recognition. In what I call the revolutionary exchange, agents not only improved conditions of scarcity materially but also worked both symbolically to legitimize their power as nurturing caretakers and organizationally to transform fluid relationships into durable institutions. By accepting these gifts, peasants entered into a debt relationship in which their material support was expected in return at a later date not of their choosing.[32] Over time, an evolving DRV state and military called on its peasant exchange partners to submit their resources, particularly labor and food, in the name of taxes or contributions. In so doing, and to varying degrees of success, cadres and soldiers legitimized state power, built institutions, and created political subjects. Always reciprocal, the relations made and unmade through this exchange were uneven, contingent, and ultimately bitterly contested.

Coming on the heels of world war, ongoing colonial warfare contributed to broader economic degradation in the Black River region. The Sơn-Lai Committee's first archived report from July 1948 provides a snapshot of difficult conditions and a footloose population. In areas controlled by the Tai Federation, farmwork had come to a "standstill" because of severe labor shortages. Men were forced to work off-farm to supply the military, work as corvée, or serve as soldiers. French and Tai soldiers shot water buffalo, wasting meat and draft labor. Imported goods like salt, knives, tobacco, and medicine sold at grossly inflated prices. As a result, the people in "enemy occupied areas" were "hungry and miserable." In "free areas" where the Sơn-Lai Committee claimed control, conditions were only marginally better. Only about one-third of the population had enough corn and rice to eat. Even these fortunate few supplemented their diet with forest tubers, an age-old food of last resort in Southeast Asia. Yet these latter conditions appealed to people "fed up" with the heavy federation labor requirements, enticing some to cross into Sơn-Lai zones where people were "happier and more comfortable." In the midst of combat, others chose not to choose sides: people "everywhere" either hid out in forest hollows and lived hand to mouth or left home and livestock behind to start all over again in Laos.[33]

This report, like any document produced by and for the state, deserves a critical reading. Descriptions of conditions in either "enemy occupied territory" or "free zones," as these value-laden terms indicate, may be self-serving. In fact, the Tai Federation's corvée requirements, military service, and bonded labor did reduce the supply of agricultural workers just as high prices on salt were, in part, due to Indochina's colonial monopoly. Yet the so-called enemy alone was not responsible for economic difficulties among the broader population. Rather, food shortages and high commodity prices stemmed as well from ongoing guerilla actions intended to "sabotage the economy," or disrupt trade, obstruct transport, and torch colonial granaries.[34] In short, both sides bore responsibility for disturbing agricultural production and reducing the supply of staple goods.

Given shared responsibility for conditions of scarcity, what accounted for socially recognized differences between two zones claimed by armed opponents? Except for those who fled to Laos or went into hiding, why did most peasants move from federation to Sơn-Lai territory and not the other way around? Why, in spite of ongoing labor and food shortages, did peasants go on to provide labor and provisions willingly to Sơn-Lai agencies and military?

The same mid-1948 report noting the recognition of "happier" conditions in DRV territory hints also at an explanation—salt and its political-economic value. In comparison with areas controlled by the "enemy," cadre Trần Quyết describes how "people in free zones are relatively happier and more comfortable. Especially since [we] have been able to provide salt, the people already feel that their lives are guaranteed, that the government cares for them with all its heart."[35] Of all the material goods DRV-allied agents and institutions brought into the Black River's disputed territory, salt was the most important. Known as "white gold" for its high exchange value, salt was a coveted commodity in a broader trade linking Asia's mountain highlands to downstream points of production. The French were aware of salt's economic value and, increasingly, its political implications.[36] By comparison with the DRV, however, they could not deliver. With no local sources and transport now disrupted, salt was so scarce in 1948 that "people say they have not seen a single scoop for three or four months," observed Quyết. In addition to contributing to everyday nutritional requirements and its use as a condiment, salt preserved meat and made medicine. Among all the goods that cadres and revolutionary agitators could pack upstream, salt's high value-to-volume ratio made it the most desired and transportable commodity.

Salt figured significantly in a revolutionary program that aimed to reconstruct political relations based on capturing and reconfiguring upstream-downstream exchange. Not simply sabotage, displacing lines of communication and transport indicates early attempts to replace political *and* economic flows. By ambushing boat traffic and blockading roads, armed propaganda teams wrested control over the principal river (Black) and road (Road 41) routes linking the region to downstream markets in Hòa Bình (Chợ Bờ) and Hanoi. As a result, the Tai Federation relied increasingly on French aircraft for transport and resupply which, not coincidentally, inflated commodity prices. Much like French officials in the Central Highlands—who wielded Indochina's salt monopoly "to maximum advantage" against the Việt Minh by importing from Thailand—those in Tonkin's Northern Highlands scrambled to lower salt prices, identify new sources, and secure the commodity's transportation. But flying salt by plane into Lai Châu did not solve the larger problem of the good's uneven distribution over rugged terrain. Meanwhile, the DRV and its military met growing transportation needs by capturing overland routes and blazing new ones. Heavy traffic on the east-west route through Yên Bái to and from the Việt-Bắc base area led the Sơn-Lai Committee to request construction of a north-south road through Interzone 4 to Thanh Hóa.[37] Little did anyone know that both routes would help supply the epic 1953–54 Điện Biên Phủ Campaign.

The delivery of salt facilitated organizing predicated on a dialectical process of recognition regarding the (il)legitimacy of power. Note how Trần Quyết presents "government" in the quotation above as a singular paternal figure, one that "cares" for its people in a manner akin to a parent rearing his or her own children. Rather than reject familial invocations of state as somehow aberrant from modern norms of rationality, attending to the idiom of kinship offers insight into Confucian ideals and Vietnamese forms of power. The 1948 report describes state recognition in terms of a caretaker affectively attached to a population and committed to caring for it materially. The population, in turn, rewards a parentalized state with something akin to filial attachment. In contrast, the "enemy" appears neglectful, either unable or unwilling to perform its normative duties: this logic delegitimized French colonialism as a form of "exploitation" (*bóc lột*) responsible for mass impoverishment, even famine. As President Hồ had declared in 1945, a state's intent and organizational ability to "protect" (*bảo hộ*) its population indicated its legitimacy. Contrary to Hannah Arendt, who considered mass poverty a revolutionary dead end, associating poverty alleviation with state responsibility endowed the "social question" with real political significance.[38] Salt brought these abstract ideas down to earth. By hitching salt to a political project, cadres provided concrete means and ends to differentiate one regime from another.

Salt indicates how some of the first revolutionary cadres working in the Black River's contested territory observed popular discontent and devised a means to capitalize on it. Through close observation of local labor and trade relations, cadres identified what goods were in shortest supply and, in turn, what they could deliver to solicit and confirm popular support. In terms of "our economic activities," Xa Văn Minh reported in autumn 1948, the Sơn-Lai government was "unable to do anything else besides bring salt, rice, and farm tools up to the people." The word "up" indicates the exchange's directionality—from seashore sites of production to mountain sites of consumption—and the political forces driving it. In a January 1949 report, salt features in two sections under the heading of "Politics" (*Chính trị*): Minh observed that the "masses" were suffering the short supply of salt, knives, and tobacco; and reported that the committee had dispatched its Economic Service to distribute those goods. By "helping" the people obtain "things they need most," the chairman observed an intended effect: "The people feel the care and encouragement of the Government truly and clearly."[39]

Just as cadres constructed an alternative system of exchange, they built also the institutions of an alternative local government. The timing was no coincidence: by joining economic activity to political transformation, the revolutionary exchange expanded participation and intensified commitment among a broader population. It also initiated a process through which cadres gained access to local resources. Beginning in late 1948, the movement of goods coincided with constructing mass organizations, such as women's and youth unions, and Sơn-Lai's district and commune committees. In addition to salt distribution, the Economic Service opened official markets; purchased opium and fiber crops from local producers; sold salt, tobacco, foodstuffs, and tools at subsidized prices; and issued DRV currency (đồng) to replace the Indochinese piaster.[40] Significantly, the Economic Service worked closely with commune committees to round up local resources. Indeed, much of the Sơn-Lai leadership's concern about the efficacy of commune committees was due to the latter's responsibility for extracting transport labor and provisions from constituent populations.

That salt became the Sơn-Lai Committee's favored currency in the local resource trade was the outcome of a longer contingent process of experimentation. At least initially, the yield of material and labor resources appeared spontaneous, even welcomed by the population. Following the establishment of the resistance government in late 1948 and early 1949, residents endowed its institutions with more than just abstract legitimacy. In April 1949, the committee reported: "Because of their enthusiasm, the masses have sacrificed all their rice, corn, [and] cassava in order to supply the military and each office in such large quantities that, in many places, the masses must eat forest tubers; and, on days they cannot find [tubers], they must beg."[41] While caution is required before accepting communist claims, the last statement is a revelation. Just as they drew from their own food stores to feed soldiers and cadres, the "masses" also left home and farm to participate directly in the labors of revolution. In spite of their "desperate straits," they remained "enthusiastically willing to participate in resistance activities" such as joining guerilla raids, transporting supplies, and guiding combatants. In so doing, they demonstrated solidarity with the anti-colonial, revolutionary project, recognized in approving terms of "sacrifice" (*hy sinh*). Importantly, soldiers and cadres shared in the conditions of shortage and, like their local supporters, went begging.[42]

That these exchanges unfolded in a context of warfare is significant. Giving up one's own food and labor for a broader cause brought danger, and potential death, to all participants, thus equalizing soldier, cadre, and peasant in an existential situation. Exchanging socially necessary goods and labor formed a relationship as partisans bound to one another through common danger: the very act of sharing began to constitute a community. In spite of deliberate attempts to steer popular support, such enthusiastic demonstrations of solidarity—and willingness to die—point to a sense of belonging and membership. Theoretically, the immanent prospect of shared death helped unify a community, one whose boundaries the state constructed yet whose unity was never guaranteed.[43] In other words, this emergent communal form was also subject to, and part of, a state-making project. What may have been a euphoric moment of recognition became, in short order, a relationship predicated on hierarchical terms of "government" and "masses," idioms for state and society.

Although enduring difficulty together indicated forms of solidarity and community, officials and soldiers did not live on popular legitimacy alone. As state consumption increased over time, so too did the demands placed on local resources. After all, cadres and soldiers needed food to subsist and labor to resist. After a recorded year in 1948 of providing the local population with the "things they need most," cadres and soldiers expected things in return. What may have started as sharing between equals evolved into a process of claim making between ruler and subject.

Even amid voluntarism in April 1949, official labor usage blurs descriptive supply with prescriptive demand. In spite of their "enthusiasm," for example, the committee stated that "the masses *must* go laboring." Did they volunteer? Or were they forced to work? Maintaining the distinction was crucial because the legitimacy of DRV resource claims hinged on explicit comparisons with colonial claims delegitimized as exploitative and impoverishing. In January, Xa Văn Minh had credited popular discontent with the Tai Federation to corvée and military duties and to "heavy" food contributions, both of which left people "hungry and dying." Yet his comparison of the "two apparatus," or political regimes, betrayed a distinction of degree, not of kind.[44] Indeed, by April, colonial and revolutionary regimes alike drew on people's labor and food stores. And the Sơn-Lai Committee, too, began to observe unintended effects.

In spring 1949, popular hunger emerged among the same people whom the Sơn-Lai Committee and Việt Minh organizers had promised to feed. How did this happen? First, available food supplies had plummeted. With no hint of irony, the April report chided peasants for "too zealously" supplying provisions, depleting already limited household stores. Evidently, many supporters had been operating on the assumption that such outlays would end quickly. But ongoing conflict meant that, as weeks turned into months, the additional consumption stretched everyone thin. Second, agricultural production fell. The use of adult labor off-farm left only the elderly and children on-farm, depressing overall output. Third, even the food of last resort was running out: forest foods were increasingly scarce.[45]

So, given structural similarities with colonial resource claims, how did the Sơn-Lai Committee solve the two pressing problems of labor supply and popular legitimacy? Regarding supply, the committee attempted a number of strategies—from markets and coercion to exchange and imported labor—few of which worked as planned, if at all. As discussed below, salt and its signal role in exchange emerged as a partial solution yet one that could not overcome the region's characteristic labor scarcity. As Mười stressed, people were relatively few and far between in the Black River region. Regarding legitimacy, salt's symbolic value could only partially compensate for the socially necessary things required in return. As the next section discusses, development arose at this time as a promise of a better future, one that might compensate more fully for the difficulties revolution was creating in the present.

To support military advances in 1948–49, officials initially created markets for labor and provisions. The Economic Service tried to entice "manpower" (*nhân công*) and hire "laborers" (*lao công*) at lucrative lump sums of 100 đồng and wages of 5 đồng a day. Yet wartime inflation had rendered even this high daily wage insufficient to purchase subsistence grain rations. Moreover, farmers expressed concern about the cost of such opportunity—working off-farm was not worth foregoing "care for home and hearth." Officials thus complained they "could not hire people at all." Similarly, the service tried to use proceeds from sales of salt, tobacco, and rice to purchase perishable produce, especially vegetables and meat. But the revenue stream amounted to a trickle when peasants refused to part with the sources of their own sustenance.[46]

The failure of markets to generate sufficient resources led the committee to draw on and exercise its growing institutional power. Just as cadres did not live on legitimacy, they did not make institutions for their own sake. It was the job of commune representatives to "help the military and offices, hands together with locality, to mobilize and collect labor, to collect provisions." Although their mandate was clear, the exercise of bureaucratic power appears alternately coercive and beseeching. Faced with peasants unwilling to use markets, for example, commune representatives invoked "the name of local government" to "take" (*lấy*) provisions and "request" (*nhờ*) farmers sell to the Economic Service. By July 1949, during the annual hunger season, food was so scarce that coercion resulted in perverse consequences: in order to meet required grain "contributions," some peasants sold water buffalo—their productive capital—to buy rice and corn from the Economic Service and then turned the grain over to military units and civil offices. Likewise, the committee used the "power of paper" (*sức giấy*)—issued written orders—to "request" commune officials to mobilize transport labor. With most men already pressed into Tai Federation service, they turned to women living on roadsides.[47] This gendering of civilian labor would grow in years to come as the First Indochina War escalated in the Black River region.

Although institutional coercion failed to yield sufficient resources, it strengthened the hand of local brokers. Significantly, Mười cited the region's "vast area, sparse population" as a reason the Sơn-Lai Committee had violated Decree 254's personnel guidelines by keeping old officials in place. To collect labor and provisions among hungry people, he explained, commune representatives had to trudge from village to village, "as though each step was climbing a mountain." In spite of poor clerical skills, widespread illiteracy, and colonial taint, in other words, every official was necessary.[48] Even then, the early DRV state still lacked the bureaucratic capacity to square its territorial ambitions with the population's spatial distribution.

Faced with these conditions of widespread hunger, market failure, and institutional incapacity, the Sơn-Lai Committee opted to increase the import of goods, especially salt, in pursuit of local resources. In late 1948, the committee began using salt and tobacco as payment for farmers who cached corn and cassava for guerillas and planted improved varieties of cotton.[49] Hiding grains from the Tai Federation and increasing the yield of cash crops fed back into resource availability; salt completed the loop. Moreover, and not unlike Tai Federation practices, salt increasingly became a reward for DRV loyalty. Whereas the federation gave it to individual snitches, the Sơn-Lai Committee distributed salt widely in support of armed resistance. In areas of "struggle," wrote Mười, the people "give all their energy to follow us but are short of salt and have no money to buy it." As a result, in July 1949 he requested two metric tons of salt every month "in order to do political work."

A strategic commodity, salt helped construct DRV territory in the Black River region. "If Sơn La has any land and any people now," declared Mười in the closing line of his July 1949 report, "one reason is because there is salt to conduct political work."[50] In this contested region, the distribution of salt enabled the DRV state to configure itself territorially and to appeal popularly. "Political work" (*công tác chính trị*) meant the activity of legitimation. Salt stood for a larger pattern of exchange in which the rising DRV state achieved popular legitimacy by remediating everyday shortages and rewarding popular support. In so doing, the DRV expanded its territory but not necessarily its military's capacity to secure it and protect the population.

In an ironic twist, importing more salt jeopardized its political value because doing so required more pedestrian labor to move it. Aware of the paradox, Mười once again deployed his powerful discourse to justify an unorthodox solution. "The wide lands of the Interzone, its very vast and really sparse people," he stressed to superiors in July 1949, led the Sơn-Lai Committee to issue an order limiting collection of local labor. The porters who transported the ever larger flows of salt, weapons, and rice, he explained, now came from Phú Thọ Province—outside the Sơn-Lai Interzone. These Kinh porters stopped at a depot on the Black River's banks where local residents picked up the "heavy burden" and headed uphill to complete the transit. "Only by limiting the labor of Sơn La's people to the domain of Sơn La Province," concluded Mười, "do they obtain enough time to raise [agricultural] production."[51]

By appealing to an ethic of paternal state responsibility, Mười protected the Tai peoples in his domain from a long-standing Vietnamese practice of compulsory labor service.[52] By adapting the center's agenda to his assessment of regional conditions, he brought salt to Tai peasants in Sơn La and bought them time to grow more food. It was a sensible and, no doubt, popular move. But doing so acknowledged Vietnamese power in an area outside its customary domain. Indeed, boosting agricultural production was not simply a means to feed hungry people but also a way to increase future resource availability. Mười, then, ushered in a DRV strategy aiming to provide more resources for rising state consumption. New ideas and practices of rural development were emerging in the context of armed struggle and in its pursuit.

THE EARLY REVOLUTIONARY PROGRAM AND ITS LIMITS

The legacy and practice of colonial rule alternately hindered and favored oppositional organizing. On the one hand, some difficulties associated with cadre recruitment point to social conditions growing out of French colonial rule in the Black River region. Endemic malaria and waterborne diseases often went medically untreated. Widespread hunger, displacement, and forced resettlement all increased vulnerability to disease. Low access to formal education contributed to high illiteracy rates, estimated at 80–99 percent of the population.[53] As a result, many upstream leaders could not perform clerical work and qualified downstream cadres often fell ill.

On the other hand, cadres capitalized ideologically on these widespread social problems by blaming the colonial regime and advancing a revolutionary program in its place. The Sơn-Lai Committee chair, Xa Văn Minh, accused France and its Tai Federation proxy of withholding health and education resources in pursuit of a "policy to dumb down the people." Further, the Tai cadre charged colonialism with debauchery by creating "degenerate customs" such as gambling, extramarital affairs, opium addiction, and alcohol abuse. In sum, he diagnosed a policy of deliberate neglect and hinted at its revolutionary antidote: "The enemy does not pay attention to improving the countryside."

An idiom of modern rural development, "improving the countryside" emerged as a means to construct state power militarily opposed to colonial rule. In a dialectical twist addressing alleged colonial negligence, the chair advanced statist solutions to social problems: "We attend exhaustively and particularly to the problems of culture and society," citing eradication of vices as evidence that "the work of improving the countryside has been thoroughly implemented."[54] Following this social purification yet still limited in scope, the Sơn-Lai Committee's development agenda in 1949 emphasized mass political education and the revolutionary exchange to build support for armed struggle. But such support hinged as much on coercion as consent. Underlying development was a political ambition: to march toward a future down a path cleared by the army, guided by Việt Minh mass organizations, and overseen by DRV institutions. In short, the Sơn-Lai Committee advanced an idea of rural progress rooted in—and enabling—a postcolonial state with teeth.

In actual practice, any path to a better future was far from straightforward. The revolutionary program ran up against three limits—of language and literacy, consent and coercion, logic and reason—stemming from the Black River region's complex social geography. The region's rugged landscape offered spaces for clandestine activity but only at great distances from the main Việt Bắc base area. The region's social and physical features meant that early DRV state making there initiated contingent social processes further constrained by larger movements in the First Indochina War.

As elsewhere in the contested spaces of Indochina and an emerging Vietnam, the Việt Minh led literacy campaigns to educate youth and adults in the Vietnamese language and its Romanized script. Such public education was called "propaganda" (*tuyên truyền*) which, in revolutionary Vietnamese, means to broadcast and spread knowledge; unlike in English, the term does not carry a negative connotation. Still, the political content was central: propaganda in the late 1940s Black River region taught not only reading and writing but also how to distinguish between a just "democratic" government and unjust French "exploitation." After a year of work, cadres in the Popular Education Service reported results from two districts where the movement was most active. By April 1949, some 1,512 (13 percent) of Mộc Châu's 11,637 people aged eight and up could read and write quốc ngữ; out of 467 people in Phù Yên, 57 (12 percent) could do so.[55] Meanwhile, much of Sơn La's population and all of Lai Châu had no access to literacy training.

The literacy campaign's modest results explain neither the novelty of the Vietnamese language itself nor its political significance in the Black River region. Unlike other areas where campaigns were active, most residents here did not even speak Vietnamese, much less read or write it; they used local vernaculars instead. Like much of highland Southeast Asia, the Black River region was and remains home to an astonishing array of languages in no fewer than four linguistic families (Mon-Khmer, Tai-Kadai, Hmong-Mien, and Sino-Tibetan). Each family comprises a number of distinct languages, and each language features dialectical variations. Tai languages, like Black Tai (Tai Dam in Tai, or Thái Đen in Vietnamese) in much of Sơn La and southern Lai Châu, functioned as a regional lingua franca among a remarkably multilingual population. French was available in schools to sons and daughters of elite Tai families. As such, Vietnamese was likely the third or fourth language learned through literacy campaigns. Furthermore, the Tai Federation sought to obstruct just such education by outlawing local discourse in what locals called then, and still do now, the "Kinh language" (that is, Vietnamese). According to one scholar, this late colonial linguistic prohibition was a deliberate "barrier to assimilation" erected under French colonial rule to separate lowland from highland and perpetuate divide-and-rule policies.[56] For many reasons, then, learning Vietnamese was not easy for Black River peoples.

By mid-1949, regional promoters of literacy campaigns stopped reporting statistics and acknowledged broader limits instead. Adult learners had difficulty learning how to pronounce Vietnamese vowels and their six tonal variants. Written teaching materials did not feature local scripts, such as Tai orthography based on Pallava. The proposed solution, to provide more written materials translated into local languages, ignored the problem of illiteracy in *any* language yet underlines the vibrancy of the region's many spoken languages. For early learners, building schools "had no results" because "people don't want to go far from their home to study" and, among those living near schools, "the numbers are very small."[57] In other words, the long distances and montane topography separating village-based populations from commune-based services, including schools, increased the opportunity costs of formal education.

The problems of language and literacy carried immediate and lasting consequences for Vietnamese state making and cultural power in the Black River region. Among urban residents and downstream Kinh peoples, the Vietnamese language had already assumed what Benedict Anderson calls "politico-cultural eminence" and, as a result, was the primary medium for "print capitalism" and national awakening.[58] By contrast, in these mountains among mostly illiterate but multilingual peoples, political educators had to work hard just to spread Vietnamese as a bureaucratic medium and a common language. From the late 1940s into the 1950s, then, the language problem had two regional effects.

First, downstream cadres relied not on print but on oral communication to engage audiences, a strategy that required local interpreters. Second, limited local oral and written proficiency in Vietnamese privileged downstream cadres for whom it was their native tongue, empowering them to report and record state affairs. Since then, the work of cadres, bureaucrats, and teachers has equated Vietnamese with state correspondence and national communicability, adding a socio-linguistic dimension to emerging relations of political domination.

These linguistic problems aside, how did cadres establish relations with everyday people? How did the former inculcate in the latter a desire for education? In official parlance, how did cadres working in free zones or behind enemy lines "generate a political influence among the masses"? Early organizing efforts had to overcome two additional difficulties: a peasantry preoccupied with subsistence and a rival political program. Initially, peasants expressed a "desire" only to "make a living in peace." Evidently, "liberation" meant pursuing a livelihood untroubled by warfare—an aspiration diverging from cadres' expressed interest in armed struggle and social transformation. Meanwhile, Sơn-Lai officials observed how the Tai Federation supported a rival nationalist party (VNQDĐ), used propaganda to "split Tai from Kinh," built a military, and organized local government.[59] Given these similarities between the federation approach and its revolutionary antithesis, then, what did the Việt Minh do that the colonial regime did not?

In contrast to the federation, the Việt Minh Front developed a program that, by incorporating everyday conditions into education and propaganda, explained these conditions and promised a better alternative. Hunger and food shortages among peasants and cadres alike provided an immediate point of entry. The following quotation on "politics" from Xa Văn Minh's January 1949 report suggests how cadres first appealed to hungry people by linking the (bad) economy with (unjust) politics and then provided them with a revolutionary solution.[60] "We cope by opening eyes to the wallet of Đèo Văn Long and Bạc Cầm Quý, peeling away the skin so the people know that when the Tai Federation comes, all their draft animals are lost; all rice, chickens, ducks are lost; they die of starvation, die on corvée, die in military service." For cadres and allied educators, observing local conditions was part and parcel of using them to recruit popular support for the revolutionary cause. Peasants were taught to associate their suffering with the federation and, therefore, to find its form of rule unjust. Note the simple language accessible to an audience long denied formal education: colonial officials are named and recognizable; "wallet" stands for their wealth; "peeling the skin," as one does by opening eyes (or peeling a fruit), means exposing a purported truth lying just below the surface of lived experience. Like blaming the 1945 famine on foreign occupation, the logic aims to reveal colonial exploitation that, in this case, referred to Tai Federation claims on food and labor resources. By extension, cadres associated postcolonial legitimacy with restoring popular rights to these same resources.

Next, cadres attempted to cast pupil peasants within a broader community, one defined by violent opposition to alleged exploitation. The lesson continued: "[The people's] death can be replaced with the death of the enemy; to explain the story with pamphlets and National Salvation newspapers in all areas of enemy control; to announce the news from our front; to praise the masses who support the struggles rising to the surface in Mường Mân, Hát Lót, Mường Sai, Mai Sơn; to teach the people to plant a garden, not one planted by or for each house." During World War II, National Salvation (*Cứu Quốc*) newspapers and organizations had called on Sơn La's Tai elites to rally on the basis of "Tai-Kinh" unity.[61] Now, should elites *and* peasants heed the call, any and all upset with colonial rule were not alone: cadres cast them as part of a broader community, one constituted through struggle and shared danger. Coordinated by the Việt Minh Front, mass organizations gave form and leadership to this emergent community, one "rising" in neighboring muang populations too. In this regard, planting a garden for public use, rather than private household subsistence, worked in a double register: metaphorically, to think collectively and cultivate shared benefits; literally, to provide sustenance for visiting cadres and soldiers.

Once revolutionary consciousness and community were kindled in the local population, the lesson provided concrete steps to support the cause: "Assist cadres to go deep, to get to their target in all rear areas in order to organize and create secret base areas. Persuade puppet authorities and mobilize puppet soldiers. Organize the provision of salt, tobacco, knives, etc. in order to create a political influence among the masses." That cadres required guides indicates how they needed local knowledge to navigate unfamiliar terrain among people they did not know. As discussed below, "persuasion" of colonial officials did not preclude violence. Moreover, and consistent with the revolutionary exchange's broader significance, the distribution of goods was but a material moment in a longer reciprocal process driving mass political participation. "Creating a political influence," therefore, encompassed a number of ideological lessons, the successful completion of which initiated material exchange.

As this quote demonstrates, revolutionary pedagogy involved making several cognitive leaps. Cadres instructed local people to imagine beyond the confines of regionally specific rule and to associate themselves with a broader movement, that is, "*our* front" or "*National* Salvation." They invited peasants to join a community uniting in opposition to colonial rule. Membership in this community portended benefits, such as salt, as well as responsibilities, such as feeding and guiding cadres. Who, or what, decided the terms of membership and exchange? Significantly, the above passage ends with an answer to this very question: "Create immediately a local people's government in the areas where struggles explode in order to call upon the masses to unify in killing the French enemy." In sum, convincing peasants to support the revolution meant first providing them with an explanation for their suffering and then offering a durable alternative to improve their lot. Once guerilla actions destabilized federation government and secured mass support, cadres built rival institutions empowering them to lead violent opposition. By containing in its start an antithetical end, the extended lesson in legitimation unfolded in a dialectical telos: a critique of local government initiated by, and ending with, an oppositional local government. Such self-conscious state making aimed beyond constructing an idea of the state as popularly representative and a set of institutions endowed with coercive capacity.[62] The program also strove to create a society, or "masses," willing to construct its edifices, feed its personnel, and heft its ammunition.

Among whom and on what terms cadres and soldiers gained access to the Black River's agrarian resources was, and would remain, a crucial point of contest both within the DRV and against the Tai Federation. Concluding his report with an assessment of the program described above, Xa Văn Minh acknowledged this very issue. Among "strengths," he included increasing popular support, instilling hatred for colonial leaders, and construction of secret base areas. Program "weaknesses" included insufficient funds for "political work" (that is, salt), the overuse of local labor, and heavy consumption of rice by cadres. By accusing the Tai Federation of unjust colonial rule based on its exploitation of agrarian resources, the revolutionary program made a lasting association between state resource claims and popular legitimacy. Yet the DRV, too, required agrarian resources to wage war and build its state, risking the terms of its own dialectically generated legitimacy. In this regard, Minh's report was prescient of the revolutionary exchange's haphazard unfolding in 1949–50: cadres and officials had to be very careful to avoid blame for worsening the social conditions they promised to improve.

Even at this early stage in postcolonial Vietnamese state making, relations between a newly conceived state and society were starting to assume socio-spatial patterns. In June 1949, six months after Minh outlined the program, his colleague Lò Văn Mười described its uneven impact. "In the Sơn-Lai Interzone," he reported, "there is *only* the Việt Minh Front operating and developing fast among the Hmong, Dao, and Mường ethnicities." Because the organization enjoyed strong "prestige among the masses," he continued, the front had six thousand members in its affiliated National Salvation organizations. His statement indicates that highland peoples supported anti-colonial activities but remained out of touch with DRV state institutions. To drive home his point, he warned that Việt Minh organizing and guerilla activity had expanded "free zones" beyond the local government's capacity to administer them. Important base areas, such as one in Mộc Châu close to the Lao border, were located in the same forests and mountains that Hmong and other highlanders called home.[63] But unlike lowland muang communities, DRV institutions and state relations did not form in highland communities until the massive Điện Biên Phủ Campaign of 1953–54. How these relationships and spatial patterns evolved, and how claims organized by and for the new state grew with respect to an emerging society, would construct DRV territory in unexpected ways.

Whereas the revolutionary program's use of force exposed a limit to consent in the transformation of muang spaces, non-Tai peoples outside the muang questioned the program's underlying logic. "Beginning in early 1949," Mười reported of the former, "the army has arrived up here in large numbers" and, through its armed challenge, had made people "gain confidence." In apparent fulfillment of the program, he described how committees and line agencies, cadres and mass organizations had all quickly "grasped the opportunity" by explaining the situation, seizing popular "optimism," and harnessing it to a long-term resistance struggle. "In order to handle the movement," he described how the Sơn-Lai Committee constructed local government, trained its leadership, and oriented state activities toward supplying the military, remediating local shortages, and boosting agricultural production.[64]

Whatever happened later, he seems to say, the armed challenge came first. Although the sequence may have varied, it is clear that nascent state institutions relied fundamentally on military force. Regular and guerilla units destabilized the Tai Federation, demonstrated its vulnerability, and secured territory for DRV administration. When wielded tactically against civilians, revolutionary violence appeared more orderly and selective than its colonial antithesis. In deliberate contrast to French and federation soldiers, who might kill one's family, torch a village, or gang rape a man's wife, Vietnamese partisans assassinated or intimidated individuals more selectively.[65] As the intended audience in the DRV's violent performance, peasants and colonial Tai officials played complementary roles: peasants marched into revolutionary service as porters and food providers; to avoid execution, officials switched allegiances and used their power to mobilize the peasants in said service.

Loyalties of the Tai muang elite became the focus of sustained, often violent, contest. The hereditary nobility (*châu muang*) serving the French found themselves, their families, and their staff targeted for assassination by guerilla agents and armed propaganda teams. Similar to their tactics in Hanoi, Việt Minh agents took advantage of chaotic conditions after World War II to murder political rivals in the Black River region. In October 1946, during negotiations organizing the Tai Federation, the French political attaché explained why Bạc Cầm Qúy had been promoted so quickly to the post of Sơn La's provincial mandarin: in addition to his support for the French cause, "all the other hereditary chiefs in Sơn La have been executed by the Việt Minh." In fact, not all of them were killed. Some chose to switch sides, often with Lò Văn Mười's encouragement. Nonetheless, the murder of "important traitors," including Xa Van Nuc and Xa Kim Tien on 12 August 1948, persisted on the Sơn-Lai Committee's watch, serving as a violent tool to enforce allegiance among lords of hotly disputed muang.[66]

Caught between federation collaborators and Vietnamese revolutionaries, many muang chiefs remained equivocal during and after guerilla advances in 1949. Even the powerful Qúy expressed ambivalence in April: "I want to come out very badly, but am suspicious of the Việt Minh [which] have killed two of my younger siblings, suspicious of what might result." His caution turned out to be well founded: a few months later, a guerilla offensive in Sơn La wounded him and his wife.[67] In another case, Mười revealed how a group of chiefs declared revolutionary support when faced with force but still whispered among themselves, "When the Việt Minh come, just let them be, attend to them, and don't tell the French anymore." Many elites played both sides of a moving fence, apparently supporting French soldiers by day and Vietnamese agitators by night.

Other officials changed sides more openly for reasons departing from revolutionary fervor. The vice chairman of Mường La issued an order calling on "all his colleagues" still loyal to the French to "turn"; his title indicates that by "turning," he retained his position in DRV local government. Yên Châu's chief, who "worried about his fate" after his father's assassination, chose not to turn but announced to subordinates: "Should you see the Việt Minh coming, don't say anything and give them food and drink secretly." Personal relations often proved influential. Lò Văn Puôn, for example, had served the Vichy administration under Japanese occupation and, following the latter's coup d'état in March 1945, fled with French officials to China. On their return, he served the postwar colonial administration in Mường Chanh. Expressing a desire to turn in 1949, he appealed directly to Lò Văn Mười by deprecating himself and praising the Sơn-Lai official for abandoning his family and resisting the French. "Mười and I have no issues and, further, Mười is a good person," he declared. "As such," he continued, "I'll come out in favor of the Việt Minh as long as Mười can protect me and I don't wind up killed by the Việt Minh."[68]

Inquiring why these elites supported the revolution exposes one limit to consent and underlines the significance of incorporating muang spaces and social relations into the emerging postcolonial state. Coercion divided the loyalties of Tai officials, sometimes even within one person, and forced them to make a difficult choice. As a result, some joined the movement not because they bought the program. Rather, as these examples indicate, some pledged allegiance to preserve their status and position or, simply, to save their own skin. Moreover, any new allegiance to the DRV preserved their traditional power over muang domains and subject populations. Citing the Mường La and Yên Châu cases as exemplary, Mười explained to his superiors that, rather than murder lords and risk losing their popular support, it was better to retain their "influence." For the moment, in other words, he cared less about revolutionary consciousness than importing muang domains and leaders into DRV territory and administration.

In the mountains above muang spaces and on the fringes of Tai dominion, the revolutionary program reached another limit among non-Tai peoples, who acted less according to the program's logic and more in line with their own form of reason. To seek legitimacy based on rejecting exploitation and embracing freedom rested on a foundation of rationality—that is, convincing an audience to weigh the costs of unjust rule against the benefits of a just alternative. Education and propaganda used a logic of persuasion to peel the skin away from perceived reality, thereby exposing the underlying injustice of the French colonial project and its local instantiation, the Tai Federation. The program presented an alternative, one that could be achieved only through politico-military struggle (đấu tranh) and by uniting as a national community transcendent of local differences and inequalities. Once the locals identified with this struggle, accepted its burdens, and unified as a nation along the way, then a new state would appear to represent their interests justly. True progress could then begin—or so the program went. Diverse Black River peoples did not always act in concert with this determined logic.

To take social difference seriously means accepting that the revolutionary program's underlying rationality was not the only reason motivating diverse peoples—even if the outcome was the same. Even as he boasted of increasing Việt Minh membership among Hmong and Dao peoples, Mười indicated his failure to comprehend why, in fact, they had joined. A story he recorded in July 1949 illustrates the depth of difference in a moment of encounter:

> At a French post in Mộc Ly one day, a lightning bolt struck the French flagpole, smashing it to pieces and hanging the flag in tatters; one time a wild rooster came to the post to flirt with a

> domestic chicken and it was captured and eaten; another time a deer came to the French post and was also captured and eaten; the masses in the occupied area who were reactionary or still of superstitious mind read [these events] as inauspicious omens meaning the French would lose to the Việt Minh; and they looked for a way to cross over to our free zone.
>
> Result: as many as 20 people close to our position in Mộc joined us.[69]

What are we, as scholars, to make of this story? Whether or not these instances happened exactly as recorded is beside the point: the text presents these events alone as enough to convince a group of people to join the revolutionary cause. Some signifying events appear self-evident, such as the lightning bolt striking the French flag. Others, such as the appearance of the wild rooster and deer, were incomprehensible to the report's writer yet fully comprehensible—as "inauspicious omens"—to the historical actors. The story is a conversion narrative, yet the reason underlying why this group converted was—and still is—unclear for everyone except them. Even though the report claimed achievement of its stated goal (support for "us"), the actors' collective decision appears unrelated to the program's professed rationality. In short, why exactly these twenty people decided to take a deadly risk remains unknown.

I argue that such inexplicability carries important implications for a study of state making in an area of profound and multiple forms of social difference. The report's author, a local Tai cadre, was a trusted source on local custom but did not understand the motivations of these people. It is safe to assume, therefore, that the report's contemporaneous readers shared his lack of understanding. To call the historical actors "reactionary" does not begin to explain why these twenty people suddenly abandoned their homes and crossed military lines at great personal risk. To call them "of superstitious mind" was a pejorative dismissal of irrational thinking. Yet the dismissal itself betrays the limits of a self-revealing logic oriented always toward building a national community with its own form of rule. It also points to unwillingness among Tai and Kinh cadres to think beyond a shared culture-bound logic by comprehending a series of events as the historical actors themselves did. The actors were highland swidden cultivators, the same "Mountain people" whom the emerging Tai-Kinh political coalition treated as inextricably Other, yet whose participation they nonetheless sought.

Although the story was and remains ambiguous on its own terms, its location in a Vietnamese state archive tells us something about a region in the making.[70] The story's archival trace reveals the limits of a teleological, culture-bound logic informing cadres in a strange environment among unfamiliar peoples. Embedded within ostensibly undifferentiated "masses," in other words, were diverse communities and social cleavages that belied the unity of this revolutionary category. The Black River region presented radical cadres with social differences beyond class and status and rooted instead in traditions of language and culture, identity and agriculture. The report recorded this encounter in a language and idiom its official audience understood: written in Vietnamese and indexing a discourse of reasonable self and unreasonable Other. Archived in state documents, traces of the region's many and fluid social forms reappear in muted guise: cast as irrational actors on the fringes of governed space and national community; simplified as a regional difference between frontier and center; and already attached to Vietnam as a "vast area, sparse people."

Persuasion did not always win over the population on the merits of education, reason, and rationality. However the twenty people arrived at their decision, their sudden pledge of support was historically contingent. Like the Tai elites who changed allegiances to save themselves or preserve their position, the many peoples populating the Black River region sometimes acted according to their own interests and for their own reasons. Even among revolutionary converts, social difference did not melt away; joining a movement might mean sublimating differences, not transcending them fully and forever.

The story inaugurated lasting relationships but also foreshadows an oppositional social movement that would rattle postcolonial state formation. In years to come, Mộc Châu became an important base area where Hmong partisans sheltered and assisted soldiers as they waged guerilla warfare against French colonial rule. Once this struggle ended in 1954, however, other struggles rose to the surface in 1955. Calling to a supernatural sovereign for deliverance, highland peoples not only belied the ascribed unity of a nation-state frontier, they also animated an alternative form of community transcending its social and spatial boundaries.

If armed struggle did ultimately produce a local coalition to topple the colonial regime, then any unity achieved was, at best, temporary. In this region particularly, as in a decolonizing Vietnam more generally, disunity and unity were locked in a dialectical tension that generated indeterminate outcomes.

The Sơn-Lai Committee's last locally produced report is dated 20 November 1950. From then, the National Archives of Vietnam contain virtually no documentation from the Black River region until December 1952.[71] What happened during this period? How do Vietnamese-language secondary sources handle the two-year gap? What do the last available primary sources tell us? The short answer to all these questions suggests a final limit in the DRV's early revolutionary program: its local outcome was contingent on politico-military strategy decided elsewhere.

The victory of the People's Republic of China (PRC) in October 1949 altered the political and strategic calculus in Indochina generally and along Vietnam's northern border particularly. The Indochinese Communist Party seized the opportunity to open communication with an international ally and receive its material, ideological, and strategic support. In January 1950, the PRC and the Soviet Union formally recognized the DRV. Adapting Mao Tse Tung's stages of revolutionary military development, Party Secretary Trường Chinh and General Võ Nguyên Giáp shifted military strategy in early 1950 from guerilla to mobile warfare. Becoming the People's Army of Vietnam as of mid-1950, DRV forces would advance to the final, fixed position stage four years later at Điện Biên Phủ. Meanwhile, mobile warfare spread French forces thin and concentrated attacks on weak points. In its autumn Borderland Campaign, the army launched a running offensive on French posts guarding the northeastern Sino-Viet frontier. Its victory expanded the Việt Bắc base area, secured an overland route to China, and emboldened ICP leadership. Yet Mao himself warned, "Fighting in this stage will be ruthless and the country will face devastation."[72] Indeed, concentrating the People's Army in Vietnam's northeast had left its northwest flank exposed and vulnerable—an opening the French now exploited.

French forces counterattacked in the Black River region to great effect: recovering contested territory, allocating it to the Tai Federation, and severing upstream-downstream links. The formation in 1949 of a third

Tai battalion under federation command, writes colonial official Jean Jerusalemy, "permitted the recovery and pacification of all Black Tai country in Sơn La." Through 1950, he continues, "the entire country between the Red and Mã Rivers, between the Chinese and Lao frontiers was calm and pacified." The Tai Federation regained territory, in other words, at the expense of the DRV's Sơn-Lai Interzone—an outcome confirmed by Vietnamese sources. Beginning in June 1951, Jerusalemy explains, French forces built a series of blockhouses "to reinforce all the Tai country's front, facing East." Guarding a line extending 150 kilometers from Việt Trí, where the Black and Red Rivers join, south to Phủ Lý, French soldiers interdicted the upstream movement of peoples and goods from the Red River Delta. Completion of the so-called De Lattre Line in late 1951 followed a series of French victories over the People's Army in the same lowland areas.[73] As a result, the revolutionary exchange in the Black River region largely dried up.

The ICP's strategic decision to de-emphasize territorial control in the Black River region bore grave consequences for an emerging postcolonial state and society. Military and party histories mention in passing how French-led raids and military sweeps destroyed "revolutionary infrastructure" from Điện Biên Phủ east along Road 41 through Sơn La's southern tier and north into Yên Bái. Cadres either went into hiding or fled to the Việt Bắc and Laos.[74] The colonial counterattack crushed nascent forms of DRV administration in all the places—especially the Sơn-Lai Interzone—where they had only recently appeared. Yet these official accounts focus on political-military institutions to the exclusion of the local people who supported them. Further, they skim over this period of loss in favor of a narrative emphasis on a steady advance to victory at Điện Biên Phủ, as though the war's end in 1954 exerts a teleological pull on all that came before it.

What happened to the people left behind? Rather than fill this silence, let this chapter end instead with two archival documents from 1950 that, admittedly, only hint at what was to come. In June, the Sơn-Lai Committee reported on conditions in old and new language: "Land is spacious, people few, forest and mountains many; its few valleys have many bandits and are in enemy hands. Nonetheless, over the past few years, laborers have continually supplied transportation and provisions to the military, guerillas, and offices; [we] *don't know how they can love* [us] *any longer.*"[75] Here, the discourse of "vast area, sparse people" celebrates people who navigated rugged terrain, endured hardships, and braved death to feed and move the resistance forces. That valley floors were now held by French and federation forces indicated the outcome of increasingly violent contests over muang spaces. In Yên Châu, for example, the report explains how people in areas reoccupied by the French still struggled to evade capture and relocation in "concentrated settlements" (*ở tập trung*), wishing instead "to return to their old villages and make a living." Forced to live in confined spaces under harsh military command, residents of these settlements faced strict restrictions on mobility that limited their access to swidden plots, forest tracts, and fishing spots. Euphemistically called "large villages" (*gros villages*) in French, the internment camps were of a piece with Cold War counterinsurgency practices used at the time by the British in Malaya ("New Villages") and later by the United States in southern Vietnam ("Strategic Hamlets").[76] Local people who had pledged revolutionary support now suffered terribly from hunger, displacement, and collective punishment. Nonetheless, many *still* worked to transport military supplies, join guerilla teams, and provide soldiers and officials with food.

The quotation above offers a rare glimpse into the genuine emotions imbuing a relationship between soldiers, cadres, and their peasant supporters. In spite of worsening conditions, the fact that peasants continued to work and supply provisions astonished the report's author, leading him to wonder how or why they still "love us." His description of popular affection for soldiers and cadres demonstrates an affective depth infusing relationships formed over the previous years of shared hardship. The report's author, no longer a Tai cadre, has a Kinh-Việt name, pointing ahead to a broader shift in regional DRV leadership. Evidently, he did not expect to find such devotion among the same people he labeled "culturally backward." As such, he inserted a marker of difference between state and society in spite of an otherwise politically and affectively meaningful relationship. This relationship entailed many difficulties for those who labored on its behalf and, not long after, stayed behind and bore even heavier consequences.

The last archived report of the Sơn-Lai Committee dates to November 1950 and provides a rejoinder to the above description. Under the heading "political conditions in areas of armed struggle," the report describes the consequences of participation in revolutionary activities: "Initially, the masses were healthy and eager to struggle. After a time, they were cruelly repressed, fled to the forest, and wound up hungry, cold, sick, and in miserable straits (eating tubers instead of rice year-round means the tubers are also gone). There are places where two to three dozen people die of starvation."[77] While cadres and soldiers escaped counterattacks by fleeing to base areas in Laos or the Việt Bắc, the people they left behind suffered alone for all their previous activities together.[78] Three years of relying on forest tubers meant that even foods of last resort were now depleted. Starvation added to the severe consequences the local population already faced for allying itself with Việt Minh and DRV.

The chilling depiction concludes this early period of political organizing. Subsequently, the Sơn-Lai Committee ceased reporting from within the Black River region, indicating the degree to which the colonial counterattack had damaged the DRV's local infrastructure. The next archived report from this area comes two years later when the People's Army returned in force. The gap speaks loudly of indeterminacy in postcolonial state making. The absence speaks mutely of loss.

CHAPTER TWO

Vietnam on the March

IT WAS A DARK, moonless night when the People's Army of Vietnam began crossing the Red River at Yên Bái. Using hundreds of boats, the soldiers forded waters swollen with rain and pink with silt. It took from 7 to 10 October 1952, four successive nights, to shuttle over thirty thousand combatants and laborers to the western shore. They landed at the foot of looming mountains, peaks shrouded in mist. Marching single file, they climbed over forested passes and converged on the wide, rice-rich valley of Nghĩa Lộ for their first battle in the Northwest Military Campaign. The French fort collapsed quickly. After breaching the colonial barrier, the army moved west and staked a territorial claim by the Democratic Republic of Vietnam stretching across rugged landscape all the way to Laos.[1]

Vietnam was on the march around the Black River region. No longer willing to relinquish the region to French colonial forces, as they had two years earlier, DRV leaders aimed to secure territory deemed "strategic and important, now and in the future." Military tactics shifted with territorial emphasis from guerilla warfare to regular combat and overwhelming force. The People's Army rolled back the neocolonial Tai Federation to Lai Châu and surrounded French troops at Nà Sản. By December 1952, the DRV commanded the provinces of Sơn La, Yên Bài, and Lào Cai and gateways to northern Laos. Its rivals largely vanquished and on the run, the DRV commenced intensive state-making and nation-building activities in its new Northwest Zone—established by decree just four months earlier as a "vast land [and] sparse people, almost all of whom are ethnic minorities."[2] The "Northwest Zone" was but the latest in a long line of place-names projected onto the Black River region—Tai Federation, Zone Autonome Nord-Ouest, Sơn-Lai Interzone, IVème Territoire Militaire—each of which indexed different ruling projects, albeit with similar spatial and social assumptions.

Illustrating more broadly the contests and tensions embedded in territorial strategies of rule, this chapter examines how DRV state making entangled Vietnamese territory in local interests and agendas. The Northwest Zone was not simply a spatial container captured by an army; it was territory established by decree and produced through spatial practices, social processes, and military force. If scholars conceptualize territory as a governmental project operating at multiple spatial scales, then we should consider, too, how the same project worked on population as well—in this case, constructing diverse borderlands peoples as "ethnic minorities" in relation to community imagined nationally. In other words, Vietnam was "on the march" in multiple ways. The phrase speaks to an embattled practice of Vietnamization, one contending not only with the French Expeditionary Corps (CEFEO) but also indigenous forms of social and political organization. Relatedly, this chapter's title refers to contingent processes and indeterminate outcomes springing from DRV incorporation of Tai chiefdoms (muang) on the "march," or bordered frontier, of its claimed sovereign territory. Vietnamizing the Black River region worked with, and sometimes against, a preexisting practice and process of Tai-ization among non-Tai peoples, including Hmong, Dao, and Khmu groups.[3]

This chapter explores a key moment in the longer making of Vietnamese territory and population in the Black River borderlands. Its focus on the construction and layering of authority relations begins in 1951 when radical Vietnamese articulated a national geobody, or a territorial definition of nation. An imagined spatial expanse, the geobody exerts classificatory effects on places, peoples, and relations; its primary technology is the map.[4] The moment ends in 1953, when DRV cadres configured Northwest Zone territorial administration through muang spaces and elites. The chapter opens at a conjuncture in the First Indochina

War (1946–54) when the communist vanguard envisioned Vietnam's national space and community on the model of colonial French Indochina. Communist decisions projected the borders of Vietnamese territory outward and classified the diverse, non-Kinh peoples within those borders as "ethnic minorities." The second section discusses plans to enforce the geobody in the Black River region by conquering and governing it as the Northwest Zone. The final section shifts from abstract ideas and spatial planning to concrete implementation in Tai places newly won but not fully secured. Indeed, the DRV's incorporation of muang spaces and power relations built lasting tensions in Vietnamese territory, especially among poor Tai peasants and non-Tai peoples. Though strains among the former were already evident by late 1953, they were less so among the latter. Most highland swidden cultivators began to experience the full weight of DRV power only with the massive Điện Biên Phủ Campaign, a topic discussed in chapters 4 and 5.

By examining the articulation of a national geobody and the subsequent construction of national territory in a complex social landscape, in this chapter I analyze how powerful tensions became embedded in regional authority relations. Organized in rough chronological sequence, the sections zoom in spatially from largest to smallest scales, from imagined national space to regional policy down to administered places. Covering the same moment, the next chapter continues to zoom in—down to the scale of farms and bodies—in order to show how territorial ruling relations shaped, and were shaped by, contests over agrarian resources. In so doing, I demonstrate how Vietnamese territory became increasingly contested *within* the DRV prior to its decisive confrontation with France at Điện Biên Phủ.

IMAGINING VIETNAM IN INDOCHINA

Vietnam's spatial imaginary, its geobody, emerged at a conjuncture when Cold War international developments shaped the possibilities of anticolonial liberation. In January 1950, the People's Republic of China and the Soviet Union formally recognized the DRV led by Hồ Chí Minh. A month later, the United States recognized the French-backed Associated State of Vietnam led by former emperor Bảo Đại. Just as diplomatic relations with world powers increased material and strategic support to opposing forces, the outbreak of war in Korea in June 1950 intensified ideological commitments on each side.[5] Enmeshing the colonial conflict in a Cold War confrontation internationalized the war and prompted radical Vietnamese leaders to come to terms with the national dimensions of state, territory, and population.

A pivotal moment in this long conjuncture came in February 1951 when the Indochinese Communist Party convened its Second Congress and decided in favor of national over international solidarity. Founded as the Vietnamese Communist Party in February 1930 by Hồ Chí Minh, its name had changed to the ICP that October after receiving a Comintern directive. If Hồ had indicated his preference for Vietnam, then the reaction suggests a larger uncertainty among his fellow travelers over whether to pursue a nationalist or internationalist agenda. For the next twenty years, the ICP continued to reflect the spatial organization of its avowed enemy: allying radical anti-colonial activists from all five of French Indochina's colonial territories of Laos, Cambodia, Tonkin, Annam, and Cochinchina (figure 2). Now, party delegates from each voted to dissolve the ICP and divide into three national branches. As such, they recognized a Vietnam formed out of Tonkin, Annam, and Cochinchina and created a corresponding Vietnam Workers' Party (Đảng Lao động Việt Nam). In turn, the VWP announced leadership of the DRV state and set a revolutionary agenda for national liberation and socialist transformation.[6]

Signaling much more than simply a name change, delegates at the Second Congress settled a long-standing question regarding the spatial dimensions of Indochina's communist movement. How did the revolutionary vanguard imagine postcolonial territory? Would it look like Indochina or Vietnam? Like the preference he expressed in 1930, Hồ Chí Minh had declared in September 1945 the independence of a Democratic Republic of *Vietnam,* not Indochina. He had also recognized an independent government of Cambodia led by Son Ngoc Thanh, underlining a distinctly national view of Vietnam and its neighbor. By contrast, the ICP had retained its Indochinese orientation through the August Revolution and September declaration. Then the party publicly dissolved itself in November 1945 while in reality continuing its activities in secret and through the Việt Minh Front. Within the party, according to scholar Huỳnh Kim Khánh, a Vietnamese faction was rising at the expense of its Indochinese rival. Thus, following the self-dissolution of the

FIG. 2. Map of French Indochina in Southeast Asia, 1928. (Detail from Service Géographique de l'Indochine, "Asie politique," in *Atlas de l'Indochine*.)

Indochinese party in 1945, the (re)appearance of a Vietnamese party in 1951 marked the triumph of a strategy that prized national independence and unity over internationalist solidarity.[7]

In his 1951 keynote speech, Party Secretary Trường Chinh stepped forward decisively to define Vietnam's space nationally and assert the party's right to govern it. He distinguished a Vietnamese "nation" (*quốc gia*) from Laos and Cambodia, calling the latter two's affairs "international" (*quốc tế*). His use of the Sino-Vietnamese term *quốc gia* was significant: unlike another word for nation (dân tộc), meaning a people or ethnicity, *quốc gia* also connotes state, or a form of rule attached to sovereign territory.[8] His terms reflected a savvy appraisal of a post–World War II global order—based on the nation-state—emerging from the wreckage of European overseas empires. Departing from the ICP's long commitment to internationalist struggle, he set the coordinates for three new nation-states. Vietnam's space now constituted the territorial objective of a *national* liberation struggle led by a renewed communist vanguard in command of the DRV state founded in 1945.

If deciding in favor of Vietnam over Indochina gave birth to a modern Vietnamese geobody, then the decision raised three fundamental ambiguities regarding its temporal, spatial, and social dimensions. First, articulating a Vietnamese geobody in early 1951 far outpaced the sovereign control of Vietnamese territory. The temporal lag influences both how history would be written in Vietnam and how historical actors conceived of contested space at the time. Viewed in hindsight and from the VWP's perspective, the 1954 Geneva Agreement ended war against France but divided Vietnam in two at the 17th parallel with American support. The partition of Vietnam lasted until 1975, when People's Army tanks rolled into Saigon to unify the northern and southern republics. Privileging the intact geobody in historical accounts lends inevitability and coherency to what was, in fact, an indeterminate outcome of decolonization, Cold War interventions, and civil war.

At the time, the VWP's 1951 resolution conceived of Indochina's regions of Tonkin, Annam, and Cochinchina as Vietnam, aligning the party with the DRV's 1945 declaration. Yet five years into a bitter and protracted war, political elites at the Second Congress actually commanded precious little of the geobody they aimed to realize as DRV territory. Because their area of control was limited to the Việt Bắc base area, they expressed an aspiration, not an achievement, in relation to France's colonial dominion. Emerging dialectically as a deferred yet desired space, the national geobody was an elite imaginary oriented toward the future. The geobody's temporal quality—its future orientation—imbued territory with teleology, or a state space predetermined by its final shape. The territorial telos appears in maps and reports that refer routinely to colonial space in terms of a "zone still temporarily occupied by the enemy."

Categorizing space as "temporarily occupied" implies it already belongs in the geobody yet remains to be "liberated" as territory. Once conquered and consolidated, the space is classified as "our zone," invoking a national "we" to signal the geobody's full realization in territory.[9]

Second, the force required to close the gap between geobody and territory raised questions about Vietnam's strategic space during the First Indochina War. Where was the terrain of anti-colonial liberation struggle? How would party-state elites treat territorial borders established during the colonial era? Trường Chinh called these spatial issues the "Lao question" and offered a response at the Second Congress. "Vietnamese communists," he stated, "do not take lightly their own international duties, especially the duty to help the Cambodian and Laotian revolutions." In other words, Vietnam's political organizing continued as before in Indochina, even as it now crossed what were seen as international borders with Laos and Cambodia. Over the course of the war, the number of cadres sent from Vietnam to strengthen Khmer Issarak and Pathet Lao party organizations grew steadily. Just as Vietnamese radicals were wary of being overwhelmed by Chinese advisors, so too did Cambodian and Lao radicals chafe at relying on Vietnamese "brothers." What brought them together, according to Trường Chinh, was "a common enemy in French colonialism and American interventionism."[10]

In order to fight the foreign enemy, the operational sphere of Vietnam's political and military strategy expanded beyond its geobody. Indochina remained constitutive of Vietnam's territory by virtue of its terrain, a space defined by politico-strategic relations. Indeed, the Second Congress advanced General Giáp's idea of geostrategic space: to match French forces by conducting war on "the single battlefield" of Indochina. In April 1953, shortly after the Northwest Campaign, the People's Army launched a secretive campaign against French forces in Laos. "Our attitude regarding the Lao question," Trường Chinh instructed VWP members in May, "is to do much and speak little, or just do it but don't speak."[11] Secrecy cloaked the violation of territorial sovereignty. So, what was the Lao terrain's value to Vietnam? Officially, the People's Army set out to "assist" their allies, the Pathet Lao, by clearing a base area to stage guerilla warfare. Not coincidentally, expanding the battlefield dispersed French forces over a wide area and weakened their strength in Vietnam. The timing also overlapped with the opium harvest in the Lao highlands, suggesting its land value was also at play. Most of all, the "liberated" Lao area—an enormous swath stretching from Phongsaly through Sam Neua to Xiang Khoang—bordered territory in what was, by then, claimed as Vietnam's own "northwest." In military practice if not diplomatic rhetoric, then, the Black River region remained a borderland, its frontier crisscrossed by Lao and Vietnamese revolutionaries. "By helping the people of an allied country," wrote Hồ Chí Minh in a letter to the People's Army in Laos, "it means we are helping ourselves."[12] Ultimately, even if the three countries of Indochina formed one strategic unit, Vietnam's national revolution was for and of itself.

Third, the elite articulation of a Vietnamese geobody structured understandings of the peoples within and outside its borders. Stated differently, delineating Vietnam's spatial limits also marked its external and internal social boundaries. International borders distinguished peoples Vietnamese from non-Vietnamese, establishing the outer bounds of national community. Not included in, but friendly to, Vietnam's national community were Lao, Cambodian, and Chinese radicals. Violently excluded from, and hostile to, the Vietnamese nation were foreign enemies identified as French and American. The latter two served what historian Thongchai Winichakul calls the "enemy function," a form of negative identification that works to consolidate the geobody's "we-self."[13] Within this national we-self party leaders defined inner boundaries of ethnicity or nationality (dân tộc). In so doing, they identified a cultural trait as a means to classify the national population. This classificatory operation was the basis for DRV Ethnic Policy, and it would bear lasting and profound implications for the Black River region's socially diverse peoples. As discussed below, to become Vietnamese meant fixing fluid ethnolinguistic identities and demoting their status.

Imagining national space encouraged political leaders to reconstruct multiple peoples into a singular people indexed by ethnicity. As in Siam, so too in Vietnam: writes Thongchai, "the geo-body had set the direction and established the foundation for a new classification of people." The classificatory exercise operated on the basis of dân tộc identification. Scholars and political actors alike have long debated this term's meaning—as nation, ethnicity, or nationality—and its relation to Vietnamese-ness. The compound word combines two Sino-Vietnamese roots: *dân*, or social person, member of a community; and *tộc*, or type, ethnos, relation. The term *dân tộc* exemplifies what anthropologist Katherine Verdery calls "kinds of people," or a typology according to which nationalist ideologies "sort the world" in relation to an "actual or potential political entity." Although nation and ethnicity both signify community and bear a shared kinship idiom, they display distinct genealogies. Whereas the construct "nation" is defined at the level of state, "ethnicity" occupies a lower order, Verdery writes, "to be managed during the process of state consolidation."[14]

Not simply implicit in the geobody, classifying Vietnam's population by way of territory and ethnicity was on its way to becoming an explicit state project. Defining dân tộc as "ethnicity" and ranking it below national identity enabled Vietnamese political elites to organize forms of social difference within (claimed) sovereign national territory. In years to come, this particular meaning of dân tộc hardened in the context of an ethnic classification project in the Black River borderlands and northern Vietnam more broadly. Meanwhile, a PRC project next door in Yunnan catalogued China's ethnic groups (*minzu*).[15] Running almost simultaneously and to similar ends, these two projects used territory to distinguish borderlands peoples long linked through ties of trade, kin, culture, and landscape.

At the time, Trường Chinh used his platform at the Second Congress in February 1951 to ascribe social boundaries, rank ethnicity below nation, create minorities and a majority, and imbue them with cultural norms. In a crucial passage called "resolving the ethnicity question," the party secretary ventured a solution: "Vietnam includes many *dân tộc*." The seemingly simple statement bore profound implications: at a stroke, he ranked communal forms and assigned them relations to state power. If Vietnam, defined as quốc gia, delineated the outer bounds of nationhood, then dân tộc, defined as ethnicity, demarcated a subsidiary form of difference within. In this light, quốc gia's slippage between nation and state simultaneously concealed and revealed an emergent form of postcolonial rule: the nation-state. Trường Chinh simultaneously pointed to nation as the highest form of communal identity and enlisted it as a device to legitimate the emerging state. On behalf of the enmeshed DRV and VWP, Trường Chinh had performed a powerful discursive act: he drew community boundaries and ordered them in relation to state power.

Ranking ethnicity below nation established the former as a regulatory category under nation-state purview. With this in mind, the secretary described the Vietnamese geobody in terms of its ethnic composition, population counts, and cultural attributes: "Next to the Việt people, there are some ethnic minorities. There are some races of small population scattered about haphazardly like Mèo [Hmong], Trại [Sán Dìu], and Lô Lô compatriots, etc. There are some ethnicities living in relatively dense clusters . . . like Mường compatriots living in the Northern Salient's southwest and in the Central Salient's north; the Thái [Tai] living in the Northern Salient's northwest; the Ra Đê [Rhade] living in the Central Salient's northwest plateau."[16] Note the recitation of regions: Northern and Central Salients recall as well a Southern one. Also known as Tonkin, Annam, and Cochinchina, the regions bespeak a Vietnamese geobody laden with colonial past and present. Though imaginary, it still frames the classification of social difference in terms of ethnic typology. His vague "Việt people" (*người Việt*) hints at Vietnamese nationals but, more likely, refers to numerically dominant ethnic Kinh folk who usually settled lowland areas and spoke Vietnamese as their first language. Next to this Kinh majority, his "ethnic minorities" refers to numerically smaller populations living in highland areas and distinguished by varying degrees of linguistic, cultural, and ecological otherness. Tai and Mường peoples cultivated wet rice, a land-intensive form of agriculture that enabled them to live in "dense clusters" similar to Kinh norms. Hmong (Mèo) peoples, by contrast, earned a marker of racial difference (*chủng tộc*) in part because their land-extensive swidden cultivation techniques generated "scattered" and "haphazard" settlement patterns different from Kinh norms. In short, he conflated cultural attributes with ethnicity and valued some forms of settlement and agriculture over others.

The Vietnamese geobody's underlying equation between nation and territory raised another question regarding the relation between ethnicity and its rightful space, one the secretary answered in terms of limited autonomy. Unlike the colonial practice, he argued, autonomy does not amount to having one's own "country" (*nước*). He accused the French of "division and trickery" by creating the Tai Federation, one of several Montagnard Countries in Tonkin and Annam that deliberately excluded Kinh peoples. In contrast, the secretary modified long ICP policy by proposing to unify Vietnam's ethnicities on the basis of equality, self-determination, and interdependence and by holding out the possibility of autonomy (*tự trị*) according to ethnic type. "We decide," he declared, "to recognize a right to local autonomy for those ethnic minorities living in relatively dense clusters in certain established regions." Referring to the above typology, he recognized a right to self-rule among Mường, Tai, and Rhade peoples but not their "scattered" Hmong, Sán Dìu, and Lô Lô neighbors. He added two important caveats. First, a densely clustering ethnicity may be entitled to "all forms" of autonomy ("political") or only its "administrative" variant. Second, for fear of these areas falling prey to "imperialist invaders," he insisted on delaying any immediate implementation.[17]

Not only did the speech articulate a category of "ethnic minorities," it also contributed to the making of a nationally determined, ethnically defined majority. "It is easy to forget," writes political scientist Benedict Anderson, "that minorities came into existence in tandem with majorities—and, in Southeast Asia, very recently."[18] Dialectically reconstituted as a singularity, the Kinh population outnumbered all other ethnically identified, nationally enumerated populations. In addition to numerical dominance, Trường Chinh endowed this one ethnic group with cultural and economic superiority and ordered it to wield that superiority among a panoply of inferior others. He obliged the majority "to help ethnic minorities build their economies and cultures in order to catch up with the ethnic majority."[19] The language echoes France's civilizing mission: one "ethnicity" now became standard-bearer for *national* norms, privileging one bundle of cultural attributes with the same normative status earlier accorded to French civilization.

The creation of a national ethnic majority out of a historically fissiparous population contributed to a powerful naturalization of Kinh cultural norms, including language. Prior to French conquest in the nineteenth century, Kinh or "Việt" peoples had long fought among themselves in pursuit of hegemonic rule over eastern mainland Southeast Asia.[20] Trường Chinh himself hailed from the province of Nam Định, located in the Red River Delta heartland. During his speech before the party delegates, he spoke in the first-person plural inclusive "we" (*chúng ta*).[21] Given the presence of Lao and Khmer representatives, the use of "we" hints at more than just the we-self constitutive of nationalism. He also gestures to a Kinh majority, Indochinese radicals, and/or VWP members. What the "we" seems to signify, then, is an anti-colonial alliance whose composition might shift depending on circumstance as much as calculation. His medium was also the message: now that French was on the ropes, the Vietnamese language wielded increasing political, cultural, and economic clout, privileging those for whom it was a native tongue.

Subsequent versions of what Trường Chinh first articulated in 1951 as Vietnam's ethnic policy (*chính sách dân tộc*) adhered to egalitarian principles yet glossed tensions between nationalized majority and ethnicized minorities. Promulgated as VWP Ethnic Minority Policy in August 1952 and later as DRV Ethnic Policy in June 1953, both embraced ideals of equality, interdependence, and self-determination among all ethnicities. Yet Kinh peoples, estimated in 1952 at 90 percent of the national population, greatly outnumbered all other groups combined, threatening to overwhelm interethnic equality with sheer numerical dominance.[22] Furthermore, this one group bore cultural traits and linguistic skills equated with national norms, reproducing a sense of lowland superiority in relation to highland peoples.

Amid these larger continuities, territorial expansion in the Black River region drove debates among revolutionary leaders over when and in what terms to recognize self-determination. The successful Northwest Campaign emboldened President Hồ Chí Minh at the VWP's Fourth Plenum in January 1953 to broach the topic in his opening address, declaring it now time to resolve the "ethnic question." In contrast to "false autonomy" under the French Empire and the Associated State of Vietnam, Hồ offered "true autonomy" within the DRV in order to "unify all ethnicities."[23] The party nominally accepted his proposal yet stipulated military security before establishing what it called "zones of ethnic minority autonomy," underlining a subordinate position within the nation.[24] Five months later, Vice President Phạm Văn Đồng signed the DRV's Ethnic Policy, which advanced autonomy as a goal but as one "to be defined later."[25] Ambiguity on autonomy would last through the First Indochina War. Not until May 1955, one year to the day after the victory at Điện Biên Phủ, did the DRV unveil the Thái-Mèo [Tai-Hmong] Autonomous Zone—its latest place-name for the Black River region. Yet its powers adhered to Trường Chinh's 1951 definition of administrative, not political, autonomy. As discussed in chapter 6, what these terms meant in practice raised new questions about community and its rightful space, stoking contests over equality and self-rule.

Underlying all these wartime questions and policies was a powerful vision of a Vietnamese geobody, of national space and community imagined together. By deciding in favor of Vietnam over Indochina, Trường Chinh's speech aligned the communist movement with the same space declared independent by Hồ Chí Minh in 1945. This consolidation of a Vietnamese geobody generated classificatory effects on people by including Vietnamese nationals and friends but excluding foreigners and enemies. The DRV's 1953 Ethnic Policy exemplifies how the geobody frames national space and people normatively. Its preamble reads, "All ethnic majority and minorities long living together in Vietnam's homeland have come together to build the nation of Vietnam." This fusion of territory with community in "Vietnam" gestures at a nationalist trope mixing ancestral lands with a rightful claim. It also suggests the geobody's influence on the construction and forceful expansion of DRV sovereignty, what the policy called "nation-state-making" (*kiến quốc*). Advancing in step with the People's Army, a reinvigorated Vietnamese political project was on the march.

MARCHING ORDERS

Identifying the Black River region as Vietnam's "Northwest Zone" was an act of imagination and aggression. Decreeing it an integral part of Vietnam's geobody, effacing its colonial past and present, constituted the first of several marching orders issued in summer 1952 and executed that autumn. When the VWP established the Northwest Zone (Khu Tây Bắc) on 17 July, it staked a claim on territory and population actually under French Indochina's control, administered as the Tai Federation. Built from the same Black River bedrock, national and colonial spaces were virtually identical, sharing strategic value, external borders, internal provinces, and cartographic orientation to the city of Hanoi. Yet the principle of exclusive territorial sovereignty meant that only one could reign supreme over the same subject population. Projecting Vietnam's geobody in place of French Indochina, therefore, foreshadowed a military confrontation followed by sustained territorial administration and resource extraction.

This section explores the underlying processes and emerging tensions through which central decision makers regionalized the geobody.

In particular, it analyzes three VWP policies on space, people, and force that guided soldiers and cadres in the construction of Northwest Vietnam, including its cartographic representation. Conceived at the center before delivery at the margins, the marching orders bore the geobody's hallmarks of bounded space, classified people, and military enforcement. They also functioned as plans that, as the next section demonstrates, could be implemented only by negotiating with local actors and accommodating unforeseen conditions. The policies mediated the smooth geobody and its realization in uneven territory. They also opened a new phase in longer, and still unfolding, processes of Vietnamizing the Black River region.

Creating the Northwest Zone projected a future Vietnam onto colonial space co-produced through French domination and local Tai rule. The 17 July orders stated simply that the zone's space included four provinces—Sơn La, Lai Châu, Yên Bái, and Lào Cai—previously under the putative administration of the Việt Bắc Interzone. Much like imagining Vietnam on the basis of Indochinese space, however, VWP leaders shaped the zone in mirror-like opposition to the actually existing Tai Federation. Its four provinces had been formed during the previous half century of indirect colonial rule. Moreover, the zone's external borders with China and Laos followed those surveyed in the late nineteenth century by cartographer and explorer Auguste Pavie, whose "mapping projects," writes Thongchai, "spearheaded French colonial power." By working closely with regional power broker Đèo Van Trì, Pavie had established the basis for France's sovereign territorial claim, one Vietnam now contested. Not coincidentally, the Tai Federation's president in mid-1952 was none other than Trì's son, Đèo Văn Long, who embodied a tradition of regional Tai rule under French protection (figure 3). Finally, the zone's status as a politico-military unit reflected the French Expeditionary Corps' operational area, ZANO (Zone Autonome Nord-Ouest), designed to defend the federation and guard its strategic gateways to Laos.[26] Like the French unit, Vietnam's cartographic referent was Hanoi, to which both zones lay west by northwest. Naming the place by cardinal direction signaled where VWP leaders imagined their future political center to lie—squarely in the place of French Indochina's capital.

The toponymic orientation to the imagined Vietnamese capital of Hanoi suggests how the VWP aimed to reorient and centralize regional

FIG. 3. Đèo Văn Long with a map of the Tai Federation, June 1952. (© Jean Péraud/ Établissement et Centre d'Archives Production Audiovisuelle de la Défense [hereafter ECPAD/Defense].)

decision making. The Northwest Zone Party Committee (Khu ủy Tây Bắc) led the region's military, government, and party cells. While its long-term goal was to lead "resistance and nation-state-making," its immediate goal was to "prepare the battlefield." Prioritizing the war effort signaled a broader tactical shift from guerilla warfare waged against a superior enemy to mobile warfare designed to put it on the defensive, stretch its forces thin, and attack weak points. An increase in force size from small bands to infantry brigades implied a more hierarchical command exerted over broader territory and longer duration. Consequently, the socio-spatial dimension of political organizing in Black River terrain would also shift: cadres no longer hid out and moved among far-flung, mountaintop swidden cultivators, as they had since 1951, but spilled into the valleys to secure muang spaces of dense settlement, wet-rice cultivation, and local administration.[27] Not until late 1953, when the People's Army adopted fixed-position warfare in the Điện Biên Phủ Campaign, would cadres climb back uphill to construct DRV local government among highland peoples.

The tactical shift and territorial emphasis inflected regional leadership and reporting. Bùi Quang Tạo (1919–76) became the region's political commissar (*Chính ủy*), indicating the rise of Kinh cadres into positions chosen by, and in communication with, the "Center." Born in the lowland province of Thái Bình, Tạo was appointed by the Politburo and received his nom de guerre, Nguyễn Kháng, personally from President Hồ. When the president signed over the Party Committee's powers to a DRV Administrative and Resistance Committee in January 1953, Commissar Kháng remained the region's highest official.[28] Meanwhile, local Tai cadres like Xa Văn Minh and Lò Văn Mười, who had organized muang districts from 1948 to 1950 and reported on their activities, no longer authored reports held in the national archives. Instead, these locally born leaders assumed positions in Sơn La's provincial administration, where they represented the party-state as recognizable, even familiar figures.

In keeping with Vietnam's emerging nation-state form, centralizing and expanding the bureaucracy closely tracked powerful processes of national incorporation. The July 1952 establishment order described a "mountainous region where land is vast [and] people sparse, almost all of whom are ethnic minorities."[29] The language of "vast land, sparse people" indicates how far an idiom coined in 1949 by Mười had traveled, resonating among central decision makers interested in expanding the DRV's territorial claim. As before, the discourse (mis)represented the embattled Black River region as a singular upstream frontier, one already unified and hitched to Vietnam where, according to downstream idiom, land was scarce and packed with people. Now that the geobody exerted classificatory effects on the Black River population, however, the terms of community membership had changed from one of revolutionary solidarity to national belonging. Ascribing "ethnic minority" status to its diverse peoples counted them as Vietnamese yet marked them as different from Kinh cultural norms and small in number relative to a rising national ethnic majority.

A second marching order elaborated the terms of national incorporation and applied them to state formation in the Northwest Zone. In August 1952, the party issued instructions for Ethnic Minority Policy in the "complex and backward" area based on nationalist social classifications. Using the "weapon of propaganda," cadres would educate the population in, and select leaders based on, categories of enemy and friend. The alleged enemy referred to foreign French and "great traitors" ensconced in colonial administration, both of whom deserved hatred and violent resistance. Prescribed friends aimed to unite the Kinh national ethnic majority with the many minorities who mistakenly blamed one another for problems stemming from divisive colonial rule. The instructions reserved leadership positions in local government for Kinh cadres, ordering them to "help" local cadres and the masses follow the party line. Among minorities themselves, members of the upper class were to be "won over" because they "still have much influence among mountain people." The instructions preserved the positions of chiefs (*thổ ty*) and hereditary Tai nobility (phìa, châu) in local government until the people could select their own "good persons," that is, landless, poor, and middle peasants. Departing from the socialist revolution it promoted elsewhere in Vietnam, the party ordered the *regional* construction of state and society on the basis of national unity, not equality of class and status.[30]

For the time being, the party's ethnic policies maintained social hierarchies in order to take advantage of elite influence and harness it to the national cart of anti-colonial struggle. In so doing, party leaders aimed to consolidate territory won in the Northwest Campaign. As such, ostensibly new territorial administrative committees actually entrenched an old elite in positions of local rule dating back hundreds of years. Since the thirteenth century or so, Chinese and Vietnamese courts alike had recognized local chiefs (thổ ty in Vietnamese; *tusi* in Chinese) as officials in the far reaches of their sometimes overlapping frontiers.[31] Recognizing them again in a context of radical social transformation must have appeared jarring to cadres committed to overturning the social order. Precisely because building alliances with this allegedly "feudal strata" was so strange, the August 1952 instructions were crystal clear: "Regarding those Tai elites (*thổ ty, châu, phìa*) who have prestige among the people, we need them to participate in local government, though we must help re-educate them."[32] The party ordered downstream cadres, in other words, to incorporate upstream elites and use their elevated status (*uy tín*) to legitimize institutions of local government. In deference to this functional territorial administration, it placed any radical agrarian reform on indefinite hold. In 1950, cadre Mười had stressed that the Sơn-Lai Committee had *not* implemented DRV programs to reduce rent and interest or redistribute land. Now, even allegedly "feudal exploitation," such as the *cuông* practice of bonded labor, was exempt from any immediate "limitation." Cadres interested in "eradicating" any such practices had to submit formal requests to the Northwest Party Committee which, in turn, forwarded its findings to the "Center" which, finally, would issue a ruling.[33]

Planned as temporary but with no expiration date, prioritizing national unity and territorial stability over social transformation would bear far-reaching and unintended consequences in Northwest Vietnam. Binary categories of friend and enemy could not account for the shifting alliances—colonial bureaucrats recognized as DRV officials, for example—generated by years of bitter warfare and territorial contest. As the next section shows, the ranks of local government swelled with Kinh cadres and Tai elites, embedding new forms of territorial administration in old social hierarchies and muang spatial practices. As we will see in the next chapter, allowing unequal relations of land access to continue much as before angered poor peasants and radical cadres, resulting in splits within and between state institutions. As chapters 5 and 6 demonstrate, the arrangement would alienate other peoples long chafing at Tai domination, such as Hmong and Khmu, reproducing social cleavages in a national community increasingly dominated by a Kinh majority. In short, extending Vietnam's geobody to include the Black River region emplaced its peoples in heavily disputed relations of territorial administration, ethnic classification, and agrarian resource control.

In late September 1952, the VWP issued a third marching order directly to the People's Army: prepare for a military assault on the newly declared Northwest Zone. Two weeks later, the army commenced the Northwest Military Campaign and conquered much of the Tai Federation's territory. The results are illustrated in figures 4 and 5, and their representation suggests a bout of cartographic anxiety symptomatic of a society suspended in the space between former colony and "not-yet nation."[34]

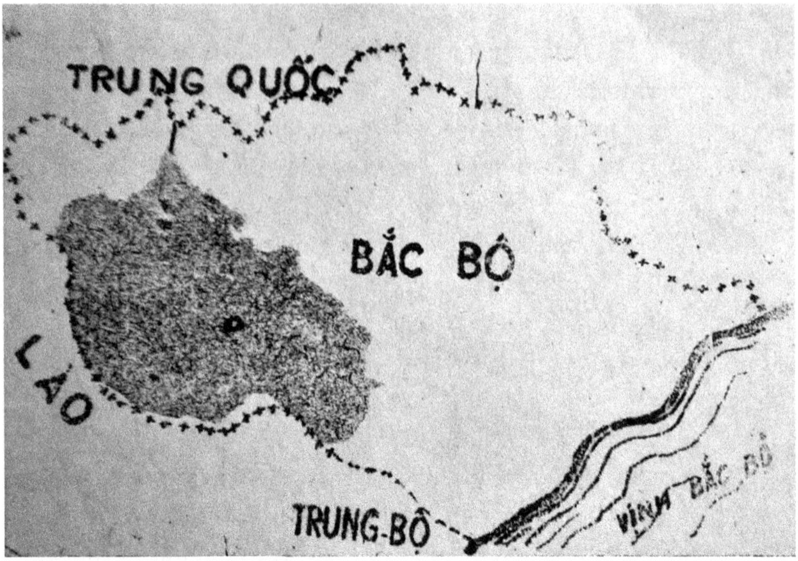

FIG. 4. Detail from map of the Northwest Campaign, October 1952. The shaded black area indicates territory won by the People's Army of Vietnam inside the borders of Tonkin (Bắc Bộ). (1306/Phủ thủ tướng [hereafter PTTg] [1945–54]/National Archives of Vietnam Center 3 [hereafter NAVC3].)

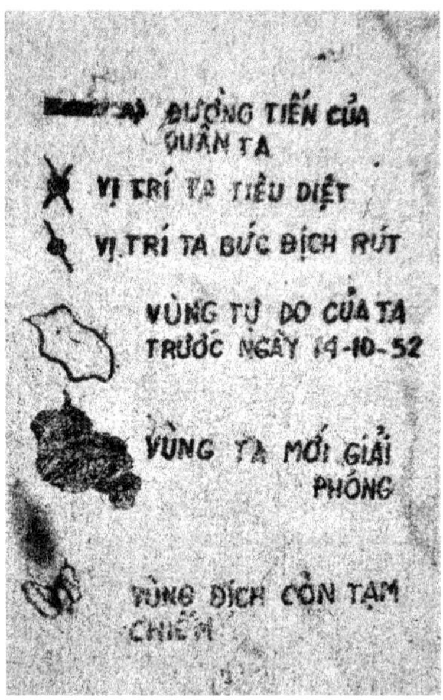

FIG. 5. Legend from map of the Northwest Campaign featuring tripartite zonation. (1306/PTTg [1945–54]/NAVC 3.)

Although the archived campaign map itself is too large to reproduce here, its inset (figure 4) and legend (figure 5) display the Vietnamese geobody's effect on space, time, and community. Effacing colonial traces, the geobody simplifies each dimension as national. The inset shows the military's territorial advance within the space of Bắc Bộ, the Vietnamese name for French Tonkin, lying just to the north of Trung Bộ, or Annam. The underlying but obscured equation positions the two protectorates plus the colony of Cochinchina (Nam Bộ) as equal to the national geobody. International borders with Laos (Lào) and China (Trung Quốc)—originally surveyed by Auguste Pavie and Đèo Văn Long in the late nineteenth century—now indicate a sovereign claim not (yet) realized. This desired outcome structured the cartographic representation of past, present, and future space. As the legend shows, space inside these borders features a tripartite zonation: "our free zone as of 14 October 1952" (blank), "our recently liberated zone" (dark), and "zone still temporarily occupied by the enemy" (cross-hatched). Implying full liberation soon to come, the temporal distinction indicates the telos driving Vietnam's geobody. Its future orientation neatly inverts a past orientation displayed by contemporaneous French maps: in place of territory newly liberated, a French-language map of the same region, called the "Tai Country," described the space held by the Việt Minh as "no longer liberated." Finally, community appears only in binary terms of friend and foe: either as "enemy" (as in "temporarily occupied by") or a statist we-self (as in "our" free zone).[35]

The map captures a moment in the longer imagination and production of Vietnamese territory in the Black River region. Declared in 1945 but not consolidated until 1951, the national geobody began a lasting transformation into territory through the use of force there in 1952. But that is the end neither of territory nor of this story. In addition to national imagination and regional military conquest, Vietnamese territory was made and contested at smaller scales as well. The military victory initiated spatial practices of government administration and resource appropriation, each of which generated contingent social processes.

ADMINISTERING THE NORTHWEST

Only days after the People's Army swept through Sơn La, a public bulletin announced the arrival of DRV rule. Dated 16 October 1952 and headed by the slogan "Independence, Freedom, and Prosperity," the "NOTICE re cancellation of cruel prohibitions levied by western enemies" stated that President Hồ and the Government had sent the military to liberate residents from French enemies and Vietnamese traitors.[36] The province's Administrative and Resistance Committee hereby annulled colonial restrictions and granted "rights" and "freedoms" in the following areas: settlement choice; rice ownership; payments to military posts; nighttime fishing and farming; movement, assembly, and worship. Residents who had questions or difficulties were encouraged to consult their village head or commune committee. Finally, the bulletin exhorted its audience to fight the French in order to become "forever free and happy." It was signed by Sơn La Province committee chairman and native son Xa Văn Minh.

Notable for its discursive flourish as much as its conspicuous timing, the bulletin simultaneously explains, legitimates, and demarcates emerging relations of territorial domination. Indexing units of the DRV state—from government to province, commune, and village—explains a system of administration classified from largest to smallest scale. Naming Hồ Chí Minh in the company of Sơn La's own Xa Văn Minh connects national to local leadership and flags revolutionary solidarity between Kinh and Tai peoples. Celebrating the Vietnamese state and military as guarantors of freedom opposed to foreign cruelty appeals to nationalist sources of legitimacy, a gesture made concrete by lifting onerous grievances. Finally, granting popular rights over resources, settlement, military duties, and public gatherings indicates a field of governance that the DRV was organizing on a territorial basis.

Contrary to the bulletin's statement of given powers, the system of territorial administration was not created overnight, nor did the field it governed go uncontested. Rather, DRV administration of Northwest Vietnam built on indigenous muang spatial units and incorporated a Tai hereditary elite. In so doing, the new local government entangled its capacity to administer rights in old norms and practices. The following discussion unravels the territorial knots produced when the nationally imagined space of a Vietnamese geobody met the locally lived and socially diverse places of the Black River region. Snarls over the class backgrounds of local Tai officials, for example, indicate tensions woven into the fabric of Vietnamese national territory. Springing from these tensions, subsequent contests over resource extraction suggest what scholars rightly call the "instability of the territorial strategies of the modern state."[37]

Whereas public bulletins heralded newly delivered freedoms, early post-campaign reports signal a shift in leadership and agenda corresponding to DRV territorial command. No longer do local Tai cadres like Xa Văn Minh or Lò Văn Mười boast of sabotaging roadways or burning granaries, as during guerilla warfare from 1948 to 1950. Following the Northwest Campaign's conclusion in late 1952, senior Kinh cadres authored reports in a tone of managerial responsibility, describing how engineers now built bridges and soldiers assisted farmers harvesting rice. Ministerial delegate Phan Mỹ and zone party commissar Nguyễn Kháng acted as representatives in territory secured with overwhelming People's Army force. Like Kháng, Mỹ drew on close ties to DRV leaders: born in Hà Tĩnh Province and the younger brother of Phan Anh, who served as the DRV's first minister of defense, Mỹ was known as a valuable troubleshooter.[38] The two Kinh cadres reported directly to the "Center" (Trung ương) and managed regional party, state, and military institutions on its behalf. Meanwhile, the Tai cadres Minh and Mười served on Sơn La's Province Committee, represented the DRV publicly, and sought popular legitimacy. This emerging pattern—where local government came to be dominated by Tai elites and party ranks by Kinh cadres—was the latest configuration of Tai-Kinh unity first promulgated by Việt Minh organizations during World War II.

As central government delegates, it was Kháng and Mỹ's job to make Northwest Zone territory and population legible, to render them known and governable from afar. Their December 1952 reports inform central leaders about the latest addition to DRV territory, opening with calculative descriptions of area and people. Their quantitative assessment matched the underlying logic of their colonial rivals even as they parted ways on evaluating its strategic and economic significance: whereas the French minister of defense downplayed the loss, the Vietnamese victors trumpeted the spoils.[39] The victors estimated that the "newly liberated area" covered three-quarters of the zone, or 28,500 square kilometers, and most of its population, some 250,000 of the 300,000 total. A majority of Tai lived in dense valley settlements growing wet rice. Dao and Hmong peoples practiced swidden agriculture, the former along high mountain streams and the latter "even higher up" on peaks and ridges. The largest of four rice baskets was the great plain at Điện Biên Phủ, measuring 20 by 9 kilometers. Trade in "local forest products" such as opium, cinnamon, and deer antlers floated down the Black River in seven hundred boats to Hòa Bình's market. Overall area was reported in straight lines, "as a bird flies," from Mộc Châu to Ba Nậm (270 kilometers) on the Chinese border and from Bao Ha, across Road 41, to Điện Biên Phủ (250 kilometers) on the Lao border.

Such calculative descriptions suggest that scholars would do well to conceptualize territory not just as governing technology but also as an outcome of practices dependent on context. Take, for example, the cartographic distances tracing the Northwest Zone and routes within it. Read from a scaled map, the straight lines measured points from internal crossroads to external border crossings, serving to demarcate sovereign territory and delineate road and river routes with strategic allies. Certainly, the measures reveal territory's strategic and economic dimensions, what geographer Stuart Elden calls its terrain and land values.[40] The measures also confirm how modern mapping informs a territorial definition of nation, what Thongchai calls the geobody. But reading distances from a map neglects landscape features—high mountains, fast rivers, thick forests—that made any straight line the business of birds, not earthly people.

For the Northwest Zone to become an on-the-ground reality, territory had to be put into places in the Black River region. In late 1952, practice constrained technology in two important ways. First, state knowledge was far from complete, evinced by Mỹ's frequent apologies for data "not yet enumerated" (*chưa thống kê*), literally, made into statistics. Such knowledge would be generated through practices like labor service and agricultural taxation, as the next two chapters discuss. Second, implementation was the responsibility of a local government very much under construction. As discussed below, it would be a mistake to assume that local officials shared the same ruling logics as their nominal superiors.

The ministerial delegate's report did not simply describe internal state space as such, but rather prescribed and participated in its administrative transformation. In order to decolonize local government, guidelines allowed temporary retention of village chiefs (tạo bản) until establishment of a "new local government." Gradually, cadres consulted with residents to select village heads (*trưởng bản*) and replace chiefs. Once village leadership was secure, the work of building a commune committee (*Ủy ban xã*) began; cadres from the area in question had priority as representatives. In the interim before commune leadership was fully vetted, province- and district-level cadres supervised administrative affairs. "In general," summarized Mỹ, "these are the procedures but the work of implementation is up to the locality."[41] As with decrees implemented two years earlier, centrally issued bureaucratic guidelines required local negotiation. Now, the pressing need to administer territory gained through the Northwest Campaign accelerated the Tai muang's incorporation into, and unexpected influence on, the Vietnamese administrative system.

Although the delegate recognized negotiation processes, his representation of territory and population only partially acknowledged the effects these processes had already exerted on his spatial categories. As illustrated in table 1, Mỹ presented Northwest Zone area and people according to four provinces (tỉnh), twelve districts (huyện), and estimated population. Not included are areas around Lai Châu Town still under Tai Federation control. Population data marked "unclear" corresponds with districts farthest from the DRV center, illustrating geographic limits to state knowledge. Nominally, province and district units follow a Vietnamese administrative model dating back to early nineteenth-century Nguyễn Dynasty reforms.[42] Yet underlying each Vietnamese district was the Tai muang's administrative bedrock.

Now recognized as Northwest Zone districts, the underlying muang spatial unit had long formed the basis of local administration, settlement, and agrarian relations in the Black River region. All twelve districts above also have a Tai name, such as Muang Thanh for Điện Biên Phủ, and carried with them noble families, clustered villages, and norms of resource control. As Jim Scott notes of the Southeast Asia–China borderlands more generally, the Tai muang often functions as a bureaucratic segment in larger socio-political assemblages, including this region's precolonial Sip Song Chau Tai. The unit had already undergone an initial transformation when French colonial rule recognized the muang as administrative spaces and their hereditary chiefs as ranked officials. During the Sơn-Lai Interzone's brief existence, described in the previous chapter, local Tai cadres painstakingly adjusted Vietnamese district and commune (xã) to accommodate the muang. Now, it offered a durable

Table 1
Northwest Zone administrative divisions and estimated population, December 1952

PROVINCE (*TỈNH*)	DISTRICT (*HUYỆN*)	POPULATION
Yên Bái	Văn Chấn (Nghĩa Lộ)	30,000
	Than Uyên	20,000
Sơn La	Phù Yên	30,000
	Mộc Châu	12,000
	Yên Châu	12,000
	Mai Sơn	20,000
	Mường La	20,000
	Thuận Châu	30,000
Lai Châu	Quỳnh Nhai	"unclear"
	Tuần Giáo	"unclear"
	Điện Biên Phủ	"unclear"
Lào Cai	Phong Thổ	"unclear"
Total estimated population		300,000

Source: Phan-My, "Bao Cao So Luoc vê tinh hinh cong viec chinh quyên trong hai thang 10 va 11 nam 1952 tai vung moi duoc giai phong o Tây-Bac," 22 December 1952, 1306/PTTg (1945–54)/ NAVC 3.

basis on which to configure DRV local government. If this strategy enabled the DRV to "aggregate political power without having to organize completely new structures at the local level," as scholar John McAlister asserts, then doing so also created powerful entanglements that snarled Vietnamese territory in local contests and interests.[43]

Whereas projecting district onto muang attracted little notice, subdividing districts into communes, reported Mỹ, led to "unsolvable" problems. In Phù Yên District, local implementation produced a gigantic Quang Huy Commune including ten thousand people in thirty-six villages and spanning ten kilometers in length by one to four kilometers in width. "The commune committee," complained the delegate, "cannot grasp [its jurisdiction] at all, especially villages on mountain tops." In Văn Chấn District near the town of Nghĩa Lộ, one Hmong commune included mountaintop villages interspersed by separate Dao and Tai communes, producing a spotty administrative unit.[44] Both examples demonstrate how altitude intersected with ethnic difference to advance local interests but vex DRV administrators. In the former, valley officials had the desire but not the capacity to "grasp" highlanders who, based on their high-elevation villages, preferred to stay out of arm's reach. In the latter, Hmong peoples connected settlements into a noncontiguous unit, the shape of which enabled a measure of autonomy but confounded an administrative preference for neat polygons and contiguous boundaries.

More generally, these two examples illustrate how DRV territorial administration initiated the muang form's latest transformation. Historically, the muang had fuzzy boundaries, variable scale, and might change shape over time. Their malleability was consistent with ruling strategies focused on people and manpower, not territory and borders.[45] The spaces betwixt and between offered refuge for swidden cultivators who sought to avoid labor claims and open forest land. Now, more than just layering Vietnamese names onto Tai administrative space, the DRV introduced a cartographic conception of spatial borders, what Thongchai calls "a new exercise of administrative power on a territorial basis."[46] Each district fit together like a jigsaw puzzle and, theoretically, left no gaps or overlaps between constituent communes. In the case above, Hmong and Dao swidden cultivators, as with other peoples historically outside of Tai muang power, now faced Vietnamese and Tai officials intent on mapping them inside districts. Fixing non-Tai peoples within administrative units enabled powerful claims on their land, labor, and opium resources. This process accelerated a year later with the Điện Biên Phủ Campaign, and the next chapters discuss the contests and consequences that resulted.

As of late 1952, very few non-Tai spaces and peoples fell under immediate muang/district administration, usually communities with strong revolutionary credentials and sizable populations. In December, for example, Commissar Kháng located the code named Hmong Zone 99 (Khu Mèo 99) in Sơn La Province either in Phù Yên District or lying alongside it. Unlike in other districts, where "governments are being established," he stated that Zone 99 "still allowed the old regime principle" of leaving local leaders in place with distinct titles. In fact, these titles—*thong ly, thong quan, Xa phai*—may have originated with fifth-century Chinese courts, long before the community migrated south to escape imperial expansion.[47] Earning their stripes during guerilla war against French forces, leaders of the "old base area" evidently earned an additional reprieve from DRV administrative reforms. "Although the upper class is rightist deviationist," reads a VWP report from March 1953, "they still have prestige among the people and we have held onto old leaders." Their acceptance as and by DRV officials indicates the persistence of culturally specific ruling relations amid larger transformations in territorial administration. In 1955 the DRV would recognize Hmong Zone 99 as one of three Hmong Autonomous Counties (Châu Mèo tự trị), along with Mù Cang Chải and Tủa Chùa, within the Thái-Mèo Autonomous Zone.[48]

Old officials in Tai and non-Tai areas alike thus carried into the new Northwest Zone administration. As mobile warfare rapidly expanded DRV territory, demand for local bureaucrats rose just as rapidly to govern it. As a result, a bureaucracy overseen by Kinh cadres swelled with local elites, many of whom were former colonial functionaries. Pardoned under the leniency policy but often still derided as "puppets," they possessed authoritative knowledge of local custom and protocol invaluable to newcomers from downstream and unavailable among the common peasantry. Furthermore, as Kháng noted above, they also possessed "prestige" (*uy tín*), what prevailing Ethnic Minority Policy held up as a key criterion for selecting representatives of DRV local government. Not simply top-down, the policy echoed Tai cadre Lò Văn Mười, who in 1949 had stressed local forms of legitimacy and their significant role in securing DRV rule. One case shows how, even when ignored, high status remained operative: zealous cadres appointed a commune committee sui generis, but because the new representatives lacked "sufficient prestige among the people," Phan Mỹ recorded their appointment as an "error."[49]

Constructing a regional bureaucracy of local elites and Kinh cadres offered a pragmatic response to rapid territorial expansion but entangled administration in contradictory agendas and authority relations. Kinh cadres possessed bureaucratic requirements: Vietnamese-language literacy and fluency, clerical skills, and commitment to anti-colonial revolution. If such technical knowledge is a hallmark of what sociologist Max Weber termed "legal authority," then what Mỹ, Kháng, and the Ethnic Policy recognized as prestige points to "traditional authority," or a claim to legitimacy based on "age-old rule and powers." Although tradition must be socially reinvented, reinvested with power, and often appears in hybrid forms, Weber explains how power must be recognized as legitimate before becoming socially accepted as authority.[50] As such, considering the sources of legitimacy also points out the sources of instability in DRV regional administration. Kinh cadres committed to decolonization and radical equality hitched their wagon to prestigious Tai lords and other elites vested with cultural influence and control of agrarian resources. Further, the latter's knowledge of bureaucratic procedure came through serving a colonial administration that had buttressed their allegedly "feudal" social positions.

Retaining old officials and local elites complied with central policy but generated increasing concern among regional leaders. "Organizing the local government," observed Kháng in December 1952, "has brought along all sort[s] of reactionary traitors, leading the people to resent and dislike the local government." Further, he observed that Tai "lords" (phìa) held positions as commune chairmen or on distribution committees, enabling them to divert "national" labor and food aid to their own households, shirk labor service, avoid taxation, and control common land. Evidently, the traditional authority of powerful Tai men, like Tai Federation officials from Quỳnh Nhai (figure 6), outmatched any bureaucratic authority held by their Kinh superiors. Overall, Kháng worried that these "comrades" failed to grasp the importance of "building a government and using the government to execute each Party policy and, by contrast, still do whatever—sickening and loosening the trust between people and local government."[51]

Enabling old elites to represent "the Government" to "the people" in everyday affairs compromised institutions and risked state legitimacy. In contrast to an ideal of radiant light, Commissar Kháng called DRV institutions "dim" because local personnel effectively blocked implementation of central policy. Mixing colonial with anti-colonial regimes even blurred fundamental ideological distinctions in an area that had been a revolutionary stronghold. In July 1953, nine months after the People's Army secured most of Sơn La Province, people in its "valley communes," where cadres had organized muang populations between 1948 and 1950, "do not yet know who is the enemy, who is the friend."[52]

However much regional officials complained about their local counterparts, importing more Kinh cadres created still more problems. Their

FIG. 6. Tai notables and muang leaders in Quỳnh Nhai, 1952. (© Jean Péraud/ECPAD/Defense.)

prized technical knowledge did not prepare them for socially complex and ecologically varied conditions, making them all the more reliant on local partners. Unfamiliar with local languages, downstream cadres could communicate only through interpreters, many of whom were former "puppet authorities" (*ngụy quyền*) who rendered "the voice of the Government unable to reach the people." Accustomed to flat lowland landscapes and urban settings, Kinh cadres "did not yet understand the rural situation" in the mountains where ideas of wealth and poverty varied widely from place to place. During the military campaign, for example, cadres in Nghĩa Lộ calculated household rice taxes based on per capita village production. Averaging across a highly unequal community, however, taxed poor people beyond their means and lost their support.

In spite of limited familiarity with local customs, Kinh cadres nonetheless "acted like poohbahs," contributing to the "utter confusion" of committee work. It did not inspire confidence when, like the late 1940s and earlier, Kinh cadres often complained of their post and requested one "closer to their families."[53]

As a result of policy and functional necessity, Kinh party cadres became entangled with a Tai bureaucracy carried over from the old colonial regime. Out of 443 of the zone's total 513 VWP cadres in February 1953, 425 were "ethnic Kinh" and only 18 "ethnic minority." Such a small party contingent could not possibly oversee all local officials, never mind a resident population estimated at three hundred thousand individuals spread over thirty-eight thousand square kilometers. Moreover, the regional dimensions inverted national majority and minority ethnic relations, placing Kinh cadres in a structural position analogous to the displaced French administrators. Like their colonial forebears, Kinh cadres were a distinct regional minority and had little choice but to work with Tai muang elites in command of a regional ethnic majority. In six surveyed districts of Sơn La and Lai Châu, between 60 and 95 percent of commune representatives and village heads were "old puppet authorities" and hailed from Tai hereditary nobility. Nonetheless, except for a few cases requiring dismissal, the regional committee acknowledged that their technical qualifications and specializations made them "comrades" suitable for DRV local government.[54]

When the revolutionary agenda shifted in early 1953 to embrace radical agrarian reform, it amplified tensions within the DRV state itself regarding how to govern northwest territory—whether for territorial consolidation, social transformation, or another purpose altogether. On the one hand, as the People's Army roamed west into Laos in April and fought French forces at Nà Sản through August, maintaining stability on the home front demanded pragmatism. For this reason, delegate Mỹ argued for flexible implementation, a principle that built coalitions out of preexisting social formations, especially the muang, yet compromised a reformist agenda. On the other hand, a growing emphasis on class purity offered ideological ammunition to radical cadres, like Commissar Kháng, who now proposed to staff local government with poor peasants trained through mass organizations. But he admitted that a majority of these front organizations, as with local government, were dominated by "landlords and kulaks who obstruct implementation of Party and Government policy."[55] Indeed, the old elite worked as much with as against central policy by using their status and office in unpredictable ways. In one egregious case, a vice-lord ensconced as commune representative fed French bombardiers the coordinates of a field hospital, subsequently destroyed.[56] More routinely, the old elite leveraged their new positions to access government largesse and maintain control over agrarian resources.

In addition to policy impediments, legitimacy problems, and contested resource control, Northwest Zone territorial administration suffered from deep ambiguity over the extent of agrarian social transformation. In May 1953 Vice Prime Minister Phạm Văn Đồng ordered commune rectification (*chỉnh đốn*) by selecting officials with "clean" class backgrounds, that is, poor and landless peasants, consistent with radical agrarian reform. "The commune is the fundamental unit of organization," he decreed, because in addition to administration, the unit functioned as a "resting place for the peasantry's struggle."[57] Yet the order contradicted the Ethnic Policy's emphasis on a united front among "ethnic minority" peoples (that is, inviting elite participation in government) *and* the leniency policy's forgiving treatment of low-level colonial officials. Northwest Zone cadres were left wondering which policy took precedence. In October, Phạm Văn Đồng renewed the rectification order but stipulated an important caveat: in "areas of many ethnicities," commune committees must reflect "that ethnic situation," hence waiving class and gender considerations.[58] A month later, when the Điện Biên Phủ Campaign commenced, mass mobilization shifted emphasis back onto class background but, as discussed in the next chapter, exempted the Northwest Zone from land reform.

While other parts of Vietnam and other nations of Southeast Asia also carried an old bureaucracy into the postcolonial state, doing so in the Northwest Zone destabilized its territorial attachment to Vietnam.[59] If we conceptualize territory as a strategy of rule, then we must also consider how disputes within a ruling coalition influence the state of territory. However clear the geobody looked from afar, expanding territorial control on the ground embedded the new DRV in old social formations, particularly indigenous muang spaces and administrators. As such, incorporating traditional authority reproduced elite control over agrarian resources, especially land and labor. The pragmatic administrative choice thus exposed the DRV regime to a damning contradiction: radical leaders collaborated with the same "traitors" and "feudalists" they identified as enemies of the people's revolution.

When Party Secretary Trường Chinh spoke out in favor of Vietnam over Indochina in early 1951, he resolved a long-standing ambiguity among political elites about the imagined space of postcolonial territory. Departing from an internationalist line, he realigned communists, led by the new VWP, with the nationalist vision of Hồ Chí Minh, aired at the Declaration of Independence in 1945. Yet consolidating the Vietnamese geobody raised other ambiguities that bore directly on the early transformation of the Black River borderlands into Northwest Vietnam—an entity that did not exist until July 1952, and then only on paper. Initiated with force during the Northwest Campaign, the process of making Vietnamese territory in historically non-Vietnamese places raised lasting questions about the space of anti-colonial struggle, the status of ethnic identification, and the distribution of powers between center, region, and locality.

Never fully resolved, these questions became sources of political tension built deep into the regional foundations of Vietnamese territory. Socializing the geobody through logistics work enlisted Tai peasants (and later non-Tai peasants) in the people's war. At these smaller, everyday scales, the tensions registered affectively as anxiety and enthusiasm. Stemming from the lived experience of territorial construction, such ambivalence led participants to question DRV authority entangled with customary forms. Far from stable, Northwest Zone territory in years to come would shake with struggles against French counterattack and from contests within.

CHAPTER THREE

Anxious Economies

WHEN THE PEOPLE'S ARMY STORMED the Black River region and revolutionary officials began reassembling its local government in autumn 1952, residents greeted soldiers and cadres with expressions oscillating between enthusiasm and anxiety. On the one hand, military defeat of the French-backed Tai Federation inspired popular enthusiasm and excitement (*hăng hái*) accompanied by help carrying supplies and gifts of fresh vegetables and rice. On the other hand, local peoples expressed anxiety and worry (*thắc mắc*) over declining food stores and increasing claims on their labor. Over the next year, while regional officials incorporated the muang and party elites weighed social transformation against national solidarity, folks on the ground expressed their sentiments in this distinctly double register.

Archival records chronicling local conditions in the year after the Northwest Campaign thus present a puzzle. Focused instead on the military situation, French documents say precious little about the so-called Tai Country (Pays Thai) itself—except for passing comments in late 1952 on "annoyance about [Vietnam's] taxes" and in late 1953 on "preoccupation with the coming harvest."[1] By contrast, Vietnamese records say a lot about local livelihoods and popular conditions rooted in an agrarian economy: virtually all do so in binary terms of worry and excitement. So, how does the analyst reconcile such contradictory social responses?

Did initial enthusiasm give way to anxiety as obligation began to weigh on those who bore its load? Or did worry lurk behind excitement, only to surface when and where the possibilities of liberation yielded to the realities of domination by Vietnam's Democratic Republic?

Both sequential in time and simultaneous across space, anxiety and enthusiasm are affective responses that indicate deep ambivalence over an emerging state of territory. Affect here is an indicator of power relations, their legitimacy in particular, constituted through contests over land, bodies, and food.[2] Only one among many contests, military conquest did not secure the agrarian resources necessary to feed and move an army. Empowering local government to do so constructed institutions but stopped short of actually transforming rice into provisions and farmers into porters. Rather, resources resulted from everyday negotiations between cadres, soldiers, elites, and peasants over the rightful ownership, movement, and placement of people and things. Micro-scale contests over labor service and agricultural taxation imbued resources—and the territorial relations structuring their distribution—with meaning and affect, power and its social effect.[3] Not just sources of subsistence, more than simply factors of production, and never things as such, agrarian resources were inextricable from relations of territorial rule.

Covering a period of one year beginning in late 1952, "Anxious Economies" examines a politics of resource production, consumption, and exchange in the making of Vietnamese territory in historically Tai places. Whereas the previous chapter analyzed the construction of DRV authority relations in Black River muang during and after the Northwest Campaign, this one investigates how these relations realized a wartime economy and generated resources necessary to secure Vietnam's Northwest Zone. What officials called "making the Northwest's human and material resources into a reserve force" underlines powerful processes of state appropriation yet glosses the state's entanglement in complex relations of resource access and control.[4] Land reform looms over this story, but "land to the tiller" never happened. Tai elites maintained control over land by resisting rent reduction and despite popular calls for land redistribution. Ensconced as new DRV officials, they also transformed muang spatial units into district and commune which, not by accident, opened state access to the labor and food resources traditionally in their domain.

Continuing an analytical approach that tacks between national, regional, and local scales, this chapter zooms in on households and bodies, fields and roads. "Anxious Economies" peers behind ideological edifices like "the state" and "the people" to investigate actual relations of domination and subordination as well as their recognition or rejection as legitimate. In so doing, it uncovers conflicts over strategies of resource allocation, uncertainty about relations of property and exchange, splits within the DRV state, and the deadly unintended consequences of hunger.

WITHHOLDING LAND REFORM

Peasants in the Black River region had good reasons to hope and worry in autumn 1952. Just as their wet-rice crop reached maturity in October into November, so too began the work of liberating them from French colonial rule. Released from internment camps far from home, people returned to villages close to rice fields and ancestral tombs. The People's Army seized granaries, returned rice to residents, and lent a hand in the field. The DRV government pardoned former Tai battalion soldiers and annulled colonial taxes, payments to military posts, and corvée labor duties. For the first time in years, farmers brought much of the harvest back home to eat, contributing to a recognition of revolutionary possibility, what an official called "a clear vision that they can be liberated, can be free." Yet people also expressed "worry and alarm" over French warplanes and the destruction combat wrought on a productive landscape. Further, popular "anxieties" included serving the army as porters, loaning rice to feed soldiers, and the hunger caused by outflows of scarce household labor and nourishment.[5]

Virtually all these popular expressions of worry and enthusiasm sprung from powerful contests over agrarian resources. Expressions of anxiety in 1950s Vietnam point to feelings of deep unease regarding rapidly changing power relations.[6] Enthusiasm, on the other hand, signals awareness of revolutionary possibility and willingness to participate in radical political activity. Anxious and excited, then, Black River peasants in autumn 1952 did not know what would happen to their land, labor, and food under the new regime. They faced Vietnamese officers and cadres who needed access to rural resources but had yet to determine how to obtain it. Their negotiations unfolded in sharply differentiated communities, during larger debates over land reform, and amid ambiguity over the extent of state-led social transformation. At the blurry interface between state and society, where DRV government merged with a Tai hierarchy, agrarian resources figured at the core of rapidly evolving relations of territorial rule.

As the harvest season gave way to a new year in Vietnam's Northwest Zone, land and its unequal distribution once again became a focal point of popular ambivalence and official concern. Early efforts by the Sơn-Lai Committee to regulate agrarian reform had already sown confusion. In May 1950, a Kinh cadre reported that the temporary distribution of wet-rice land had not "yet" taken place. In December, Tai cadre Lò Văn Mười overruled his colleague, declaring that such redistribution had not, and would not, take place. Now, two years later, as regional officials constructed a local government based on the Tai muang, they sought the loyalty of Tai nobility (phìa tạo)—and the peasants bonded to them—by, in some cases, fending off radical cadres intent on redistributing land resources. In November 1952, Phù Yên's newly formed People's Committee stripped nobles of their "official" land and then redistributed it to poor peasants to cultivate. Contrary to expected class solidarity, "some people responded with anxiety," presumably peasants loyal to nobles, and regional commissar Nguyễn Kháng rebuked "comrades" on the committee for their "error." Evidently, the radical actions threatened the holdings of a prominent Tai clan (the Cầm) whose powers were deeply embedded in the DRV. Reflecting on this event, Phan Mỹ explained, "The Northwest generally and Tai majority areas especially have many complex social problems, many feudal relationships." Continuing, the prime minister's delegate warned, "If cadres do not investigate thoroughly, do not adhere to guidelines closely, then the reactionary feudalists can easily spread counter propaganda."[7] Radical social transformation, in other words, threatened the same local hierarchies that DRV leaders sought to formalize in local government and territorial administration.

Long before the Vietnamese arrived, Tai control over choice land in the Black River region had grounded resource allocation and spatial domination in places. Located in far-flung valleys and basins in the tropical mountain area, land suitable for wet-rice cultivation was, like the labor needed to work it, in short supply. Tai nobility controlled access to irrigable fields and commanded manpower, all of which were situated in the muang. Not privately owned but held in common, land was allotted annually by hereditary male elites, largely to themselves and their families as "official land," and in smaller parcels proportional to social rank down to nominally "free" peasants. Compelled to submit labor service (*cuông*) and grain taxes (*nguột*) in exchange, Tai peasants ranked just above bonded house servants, often people of Khmu origin. If relations of domination grew too onerous, peasants and servants might escape to the forest, open swidden plots, or flee to another muang. Whereas people could move and bring their labor along, land and its productive value always stayed put. Land's materiality grounded power in muang places. Territorial control over muang land, then, offered means both to rule subordinate populations and gain access to their labor, food, and livestock.[8]

At the moment of large-scale Vietnamese arrival in late 1952, Tai muang hierarchies continued to shape profoundly uneven access to agrarian resources, land and labor particularly. Despite earlier French efforts to privatize land resources, most wet-rice land was still held in common and benefited elites above others. DRV agricultural investigations document both how Tai Federation rule had affirmed such muang-based inequality and how warfare added to burdens borne by poor Tai peasants. In Sơn La's Yên Châu District, elites commanded the lion's share of wet-rice fields as official land. Further, a lord (phìa) was entitled not just to four *mẫu* (about seven hectares) of wet-rice land but also twenty field laborers (cuông) and two household servants; a vice-lord (*phó phìa*) to two mẫu of land, twelve laborers, and one servant; a village chief (*tạo*) to one mẫu and two laborers. Free peasants owed taxes in rice and livestock, including five pigs per household, to these same official elites as well as regular outlays to military posts and traveling officials. Upstream/downstream trade in forest products had largely ceased due to blockades, and forced resettlement reduced agricultural production overall. As a result, an average peasant household kept only one-third of its rice harvest, producing a hungry majority who dug tubers in the forest. In neighboring Mộc Châu District, another investigator described how "old forms of feudal exploitation" combined with wartime provisioning, corvée, and internment to immiserate the Tai peasantry. As a result, out of the district's original population of seventeen thousand prior to French reconquest in 1951, over six thousand residents fled across the border to Laos or to neighboring districts. Although the exodus made more land available, the remaining Tai peasants chose instead to avoid burdensome claims on self and stock by abandoning wet-rice fields in favor of swiddens on the hills, in some cases even living hand to mouth on forest tubers.[9] In sum, while Tai elites lived like lords over the muang domain, Tai peasants had only partial control over their labor, even less over land, and often went hungry.

Agrarian conditions in the Black River region may have been ripe for reform, but reform neither unfolded there as elsewhere in Vietnam nor did it take place as most scholars have recounted. Whereas a rich literature analyzes land reform and its consequences in downstream Vietnam, the Northwest Zone illustrates how withholding land reform upstream was itself a choice, one that unfolded contingently and carried distinct consequences. In contrast with renewed scholarly focus on violence and errors committed against lowland landowners between 1953 and 1957, my account emphasizes how blocking the program in these highlands contributed to costs and consequences borne disproportionately by poor peasants. Though some scholars note the decision to exempt the zone from land reform, they devote little attention to how the decision was made, the prolonged debate and ambiguity surrounding it, and the territorial effects flowing from it. Indeed, to many historical actors from late 1952 through 1953, including the authors of the reports cited above, conditions of agrarian inequality and exploitation seemed opportune for socialist transformation consistent with long-held, core revolutionary aims.[10] But agrarian reform threatened a territorial ruling strategy grounded in the muang and dependent on its relations of domination and subordination. Ultimately, the decision to withhold land reform from the Northwest Zone brought the muang into local government and formalized traditional access to its resources—both of which helped achieve victory in the First Indochina War. Hitching the socialist DRV to an allegedly "feudal" system, however, compromised the revolutionary agenda, split the state against itself, and amplified divisions within the peasantry.

At the Fourth Plenum of the Vietnam Workers Party's Central Committee in January 1953, senior DRV leaders shifted revolutionary strategy away from united front policy in favor of class struggle. Inspired by land reform's "great success" in China, President Hồ Chí Minh declared it time to commence its first stages in Vietnam through a process of mass mobilization. The struggle against foreign imperialism, explained VWP Secretary Trường Chinh, could succeed only by striking feudalism at home, making land reform the "crux" of the national democratic revolution. The January 1953 decisions urged the peasant masses to push back against landlords, first with rent and interest reduction and then with seizure and occupation of land held by "traitors" and in common. Only later and when conditions permitted, the secretary added, would the program evolve into full-scale land confiscation and equitable redistribution, or "land to the tiller." Recognizing that the radical and potentially divisive program required a broad mandate, he called for a vigorous discussion "at all levels."[11] In short, the leaders renewed national debate about agrarian inequality and proposed an agenda to fix it.

In fact, not only was agrarian reform already under way but its curious course in the Black River region would bear directly on Vietnam's war for independence and its postcolonial territory. First, state-led transformation of agrarian relations of production had started in 1951 with a progressive agricultural tax paid in kind. This tax on farm produce, discussed below, was in many ways more regionally transformative than land reform proper. Second, what party leaders did in early 1953 was to dispatch special teams of cadres throughout the north to mobilize peasants and demand lower rent and interest payments from landlords. After the National Assembly passed a Land Reform Law in December, land redistribution commenced in spring 1954 on an experimental basis in the Việt Bắc and then expanded over the next two years to cover much of lowland northern Vietnam. The process was so fraught with tension, replete with false accusations, and beset by violence that party leaders changed course in autumn 1956 and announced a rectification of errors campaign lasting into 1957.[12] But the state project unfolded very differently in the new Northwest Zone, especially in Tai muang communities where land access was deeply connected to authority relations. Telling this story uncovers heightened uncertainty at an early stage in socialist reforms and exposes sharp tensions within the DRV state. It also explains how a little-known decision not to implement land reform there both secured the logistical resources necessary for military victory at Điện Biên Phủ in 1954 and set the course for political instability in its wake.

Heeding the party secretary's January call to put land reform at the top of their agenda, party cadres in the Northwest Zone convened in February 1953 and agitated on behalf of poor peasants. Led by Commissar Kháng, the region's Executive Committee reported that the people were "very enthusiastic" about agricultural production and worked diligently from dawn to dusk. "Any place where anyone has no land," the report continued, "they all request that the government divide the land of traitors and officials among them. Their aspiration is to redistribute common land fairly and appropriately." As such, the report amplified an appeal filed one month earlier that had described how people "responded warmly" to a production campaign, leading them "in each and every place" to request that the government redistribute official and common land fairly.[13] At face value, poor peasants appealed to the central government to implement radical land reform. At second glance, it is unclear who really was enthusiastic—whether the peasants themselves or the cadres who claimed to represent them. Either way, regional VWP leaders clearly advocated in favor of land reform, targeting both land held in common by the Tai nobility and land used to remunerate federation officials. Such consistent advocacy suggests a real or potential alliance between radical cadres and poor Tai peasants, one that challenged party-state superiors to clarify fundamental ambiguities regarding incorporation or dissolution of muang hierarchies.

Even as agrarian reform expanded everywhere else in DRV territory over 1953, however, the spaces of debate and implementation in the Northwest Zone shrank rapidly, effectively privileging ethnic unity over class solidarity. In March, DRV leaders approved regulations to determine rural class strata and initiated a strict rectification campaign aiming to expel "landlords" and "rich peasants" (*phú nông* or "kulak") from local ranks in favor of select "middle peasants" and "poor and landless peasants." But, as discussed in the previous chapter, subsequent orders waived class considerations in the zone owing to its particular "ethnic situation."[14] Likewise, Decree 149-SL of 12 April 1953 issued a formal mandate both to reduce rent and interest and to redistribute land commonly held and confiscated from traitors. Yet Trường Chinh then instructed cadres in "areas of entirely ethnic minorities, especially those still adhering to local chiefs (*thổ ty*)"—the Northwest Zone, in other words—to postpone mass mobilization toward such redistributive ends. To avoid "disagreement between ethnicities," he stressed that class struggle proceed only with central government approval.[15]

In compliance with the revised party line, the Northwest Zone's VWP leadership closed debate and shifted from advocating land reform on paper toward undoing it on the ground. Rules issued in March 1953 ordered that the region's official land be "reassigned" to peasants temporarily but, echoing the secretary, warned against "redistribution" of official or common land without the Center's formal approval. In practice, however, the fine verbal distinction between forms of land reallocation was lost on, or ignored by, radical activists. Much like Phù Yên District in fall 1952 but now on a larger scale, widespread actions in Sơn La Province to "solve the land problem" exceeded their mandate. In March and April, district officials in Mường La, Tuần Giáo, and Quỳnh Nhai "decreed the limited distribution of official and common land." In addition to providing land to poor peasants, local officials sought to fulfill another regional priority: to increase production by bringing fallow land back into rice rotation. Commissar Kháng reacted by rolling back the local initiative, what he called "hasty implementation without decisive preparation." He dutifully reported the "errors" to superiors and ordered subordinates to "repair" them.[16] The reprimand notwithstanding, these local actions demonstrate how poor peasants and radical cadres coordinated efforts to challenge muang power. As such, they also indicate emerging splits within the DRV state's territorial configuration and internal contests over its revolutionary agenda.

Meanwhile, Tai elites fended off early agrarian reform, including rent and interest reduction, and reasserted control over land and other productive resources. The practice of allocating common property based on political office, not market price, rendered rent and interest control mostly moot. In select areas where rent was relevant, landlord reactions through 1953 fit a regional pattern of elite resistance that subverted any actions in favor of poor peasants. In Yên Bái and Lào Cai, where cadres had seized and redistributed thirteen fields in 1950–51, poor farmers had by early 1953 returned the plots to their former proprietors. Landholders there continued to charge "excessive" rents either in secret or through payment in labor. Elites also seized the same agrarian capital, such as seed stock and draft animals, that cadres had just distributed to the poor.

Further, allocating land on area alone overlooked distance from home and productive quality, leaving poor farmers—once again—working faraway fields of low fertility. More broadly, even though membership in Farmers Councils had soared, these were no match for entrenched elite power, and as a result popular "enthusiasm" waned. "Landlords and hereditary rich peasants," wrote Commissar Kháng in mid-April 1953, undermined rent reduction and interest control "by drawing on many tricks to exploit poor peasants." By July 1953, the commissar reported how a recent last-ditch push to "reassign land temporarily" in time to plant spring rice "did not work as intended." Instead, he explained, "wet-rice fields were divided according to old custom," wherein the Tai elite still captured the best and most land as well as the workers to plant it.[17] Even if unintended, the outcome was unsurprising. Vested with the bureaucratic administration of territory, muang elites outmaneuvered reformist cadres and poor peasants to renew traditional control over land, labor, and agrarian capital.

More than capital or resources per se, Tai elites took advantage of government positions granted by senior state actors to renew dominion over local muang spaces and peoples. They received the blessing of central and regional party-state leaders who sought their customary power, grounded in land, to secure the Black River region's contested territory and ethnicized population. By September, Tai elites and senior DRV officials had closed ranks to prohibit full agrarian reform in the Northwest Zone in favor of a "unified ethnic front." They did so by jointly recognizing a key land law article (37/CT/TW): "Areas of ethnic minorities with regimes of local chiefs and Tai aristocracy (*chế độ thổ ty, phìa tạo*) do not mobilize the masses by implementing land policy."[18] In fact, then, exempting "ethnic minority areas" from land reform took effect in the Northwest Zone months ahead of the exemption's official proclamation in December 1953 pursuant to the National Assembly's Land Reform Law. In line with a territorial ruling strategy and prevailing DRV Ethnic Policy, the September provision encouraged cadres to "win over" the Tai aristocracy in order to build an ethnically representative local government administering commune, district, province, and zone.

At a regional crossroads in the Vietnamese revolution, securing territory and population trumped reforming class and status. Yet fulfilling regional priorities had stacked the socialist state with avowed class enemies, as the September provision admitted. More than just odd bedfellows, the provisions enabled exploitative Tai practices and disabled a source of revolutionary legitimacy. First, even though the allegedly "old feudal system" had allied with French "imperialism" to make "serfs" of peasants, the rules nonetheless forbade attack on the system itself. In some cases, provided "lords" were not traitorous, the rules explicitly allowed customary forms of bonded labor and tax in kind, even spelling them out by name in Vietnamized Tai (cuông nguột).[19] Second, as might be expected, the privilege afforded to Tai elites came at the expense of poor peasants. For these peasants and the cadres who advocated on their behalf, the promise of revolutionary socialism began to fade from the Northwest Zone.

In a region where colonial divide-and-rule tactics had and still did produce enmity and rivalry between peoples defined ethnically, the decision to unify nationally across ethnic groups does seem warranted. Yet the decision carried consequences as well, as indicated in a corresponding affective shift from popular enthusiasm for reform into anxiety and anger over its compromise. As resource struggles would increasingly lay bare, withholding land reform generated bitter contests within differentiated Tai communities that quickly scaled up from land, labor, and muang to territory, nation, and state. Later that year, beginning with mass mobilization in the Điện Biên Phủ Campaign, such multi-scalar resentment emerged among midland and highland peoples as well, many of whom resented Tai control over muang land and the privileged place it earned in DRV territory.

NATIONALIZING LABOR

Whereas withholding land reform reinscribed power relations in the muang, mobilizing labor returned to Vietnam's territorial imaginary, its geobody. As with other revolutionary initiatives, serving the DRV as a "people's laborer" (*dân công*) elicited responses ranging from enthusiasm and participation to anxiety and avoidance. While packing supplies for the People's Army in the Northwest Campaign, downstream women from Phú Thọ Province inspired upstream women to break with custom and venture far from home, leading many to take part "enthusiastically." An elderly blind woman in Phù Yên joined lines of porters while a Hmong child took rice from home all the way to the storehouse just to see the soldiers. But others harbored deep "anxieties" about dân công service, noting how poor people picked up more than their fair share and likening the obligation unfavorably to colonial corvée. Some hid their rice and scattered: in Nghĩa Lộ, three hundred out of a thousand would-be laborers fled the first recruiting wave while another six hundred out of a thousand did so in Phù Yên.[20]

In the months after the campaign, such ambivalent affect and behavior traced the expansion and intensification of dân công service. At a construction site in Sơn La, a worker declared his "elation" for the DRV government, likened its social effect to life after death, and joined similarly "excited" compatriots building roads and bridges, transporting provisions, and standing sentry. Behind the same scenes, however, officials vented about policy failure while roadworkers broached "many anxieties" over personal safety, site sanitation, and missing out on farmwork back home.[21]

The diverse attitudes and actions regarding dân công labor index the powerful expansion of Vietnam's geobody in the Black River region. Like the geobody itself, serving it bodily was, in the words of Thongchai, a "source of pride, loyalty, love, passion, bias, hatred, reason, and unreason." In a very concrete sense, mandatory labor service connected the elite imaginary of national territory to the embodied practices of everyday folk. Cutting foundational policies from the same cloth, party-state elites issued dân công regulations on 14 July 1952, decreed the Northwest Zone days later, decided Ethnic Policy in August, and ordered military enforcement of said labor, territory, and population measures in September. In addition to generating much-needed manpower, the Temporary Regulations on Mobilization and Use of *Dân công* (183-TTg) sought to apportion duties through "fair and rational" assessments to maintain economic production and uphold revolutionary principles. In October, after leaving home behind and rice fields in the care of work teams, actual dân công fell in line behind soldiers, carried heavy loads, and studied propaganda for upward of two months. In December, DRV officials rewarded model farmers-turned-porters who had embodied principles of contribution, sacrifice, and enthusiasm. In line with old Vietnamese traditions of social learning known as emulation or mirroring, the desired effect was to perform exemplary national service and encourage others to do the same.[22]

While labor practice linked scales from geobody to body, the idea of dân công operated morally to bind individual citizens to national society. A new Vietnamese-language concept in the early 1950s, dân cộng and its meanings required explanation and, inasmuch as they evoked comparison to corvée labor, were not evenly accepted. Nonetheless, rendering dân công in English as "conscripted laborer" or in French as "coolie" both posit a one-way exercise of power and overlook dân công's normative dimension, namely, a moral imperative linking society to individual. "Each and every person," explained a typical bulletin, "must understand their obligation to *dân công* as a duty to the resistance." The definition draws on a Confucian precept of duty, of moral responsibility to society, and obliges individuals to serve an incipient nation emerging through anti-colonial warfare. "Citizens (*công dân*)," declared the Temporary Regulations' first article, "have a moral obligation to do *dân công*."[23] Here, a bond normally linking parent to child operates in relation to a rights-bearing subject, one obliged to work for state and army but entitled to equal, fair, and rational treatment. The implied relationship builds on a clever etymological twist: reversing the particles in "citizen," from *công dân* to *dân công*, generated an idea of "people's laborers" morally obligated to struggle for national liberation. The rights and responsibilities of citizenship were, literally, two sides of the same compound word.

The embodied practice and moral meaning of dân công raise important questions about power, resources, and their representation in the Black River region. Vietnamese was and remains a language of power in a polyglot region. Associated not only with bureaucratic position, national community, and revolutionary possibility, the Vietnamese language also conveyed cultural meanings that did, and still do, dominate others. As such, gaining access to manpower was a powerful economic process and a cultural negotiation. Like withholding land reform, nationalizing labor built on preexisting notions and relations of resource use and access. Through what practices did officials make farmers into state laborers? How did people express agreement or discontent? What relations did Vietnamese officials efface or incorporate? In sum, who worried about work and why?

Introduced with the Northwest Campaign and expanding in its wake, the dân công system transformed relations and representations of labor, though not always as intended. Archival documents no longer refer to "manual laborers" (lao công) or "manpower" (nhân công), as they did in the late 1940s. From autumn 1952, all workers serving DRV and People's Army were called dân công. Whereas underlying conditions of labor scarcity had not changed, official personages, attitudes, and practices most definitely had. As local Tai cadres moved out to administer the provinces, Kinh officials from downstream assumed command of the new Northwest Zone. Although initially constrained by the limits the Ethnic Policy placed on local labor recruitment, they applied a calculative logic to the population consistent with the governing technology of territory. "The military victory is making human and material resources in the Northwest into a reserve force," declared Commissar Kháng, "a reserve that must be trained into becoming a resistance force."[24] Aiming to turn Black River peoples into dân công and their food into provisions, DRV regional leaders initiated contingent and contested processes that would intensify and expand again in the 1953–54 Điện Biên Phủ Campaign.

Calculative descriptions of the population under colonial rule assessed its labor power yet underestimated the consequences of appropriating it for anti-colonial warfare. Delegate Phan Mỹ described how the Tai Federation had forced all men either to do corvée an average of twenty days per month or, alternatively, to join the Tai battalions. Faced with the frequent beatings by Tai chiefs and the occasional unceremonious death that accompanied corvée, some 446 of 2,451 men in Yên Châu aged eighteen to sixty years, or 20 percent of the district's male population, opted to go soldiering. As a result, farm households lost their adult male labor, leaving people increasingly hungry.[25]

Mỹ's descriptions were more than neutral observations; the delegate referenced a significant policy tension and gestured toward an untapped labor source. To differentiate dân công from colonial corvée and maintain agricultural output, the DRV sought to mitigate negative production effects stemming from the use of agricultural labor in dân công work. Early regulations from 1951 limited service duration to ten to fifteen days and recruitment to slack periods in the agricultural calendar, except in an emergency. Yet as warfare escalated and expanded to distant fronts, the military required constant rotations and extended service. As a result, both the 1952 Temporary Regulations on Mobilization and Use of *Dân công* (183-TTg) and the final version decreed on 10 September 1953

(308-TTg) acknowledged the tension but glossed any service limitations, instead splitting the difference by integrating labor mobilization with a movement to boost production. Second, the short supply of male labor gestured toward a supposedly ample supply of female workers. Whereas Kinh women were already part of the dân công force, Black River women rarely worked far from home. In battles to come, recruiting local women opened new opportunities outside the household. But their participation further decreased the already scarce supply of farm labor which, as noted by French intelligence agents, again depressed agricultural production and increased popular hunger in 1953–54.[26]

Nationalizing labor put local government to work by bringing calculative logics of population and territory down to the scale of households and bodies. To make new subjects into citizen laborers, the central government instructed Administrative and Resistance Committees (UBHCKC) at each administrative unit—from military interzone to civilian province and district—to formulate plans based on their own requests and on those gathered from subordinates. Significantly, tasks of collecting data on eligible workers and ensuring their compliance fell on the commune (xã), the branch of government in daily contact with the village-based population. Commune committees had already begun working with Farmers Councils (Nông hội) to tax agricultural produce through household assessments, generating both grain for soldiers and data on society's productive capacity. Now, the Temporary Regulations charged commune and council with expanding data collection to include potentials for off-farm labor, including women. In partial recognition of production trade-offs, the regulations also ordered them to organize work teams to assist farming households depleted by a member's dân công service. Among Tai communities, recruiting labor and organizing work teams would transform gendered divisions of labor: women who moved off-farm experienced new mobility while those staying home learned tasks, such as plowing, normally reserved for men.[27]

Just as withholding land reform grounded DRV territory in old muang places, nationalizing local labor helped secure Northwest Zone terrain by increasing force mobility. Understood as resources, land and labor differ in materiality and, as such, play different roles in the construction of territory. Whereas land is fixed in places and cannot move, labor can and does move between places. This material quality of labor, and its ongoing mobilization, enabled the DRV to secure its territorial claims in two ways during and after the First Indochina War. First, the People's Army was still a pedestrian force largely dependent on foot traffic to supply its soldiers. Maneuvers in and around the Black River region made the army increasingly reliant on local dân công. After the Northwest Campaign ended in December 1952, one column of the People's Army roamed into Laos in April–May 1953 while another column laid siege to the French troops and Tai battalions dug in at Nà Sản until August. Other units engaged the Tai Federation, squeezed onto remaining territory in Lai Châu, finally routing it in December. All the while, and even more so in the 1953–54 Điện Biên Phủ Campaign, dân công labor fed, armed, and moved the troops who enforced DRV spatial claims.

Second, local dân công laborers began work in spring 1953 on large transportation projects, especially roads, designed to facilitate overland transport linking western frontier reaches to secure base areas back east in the Việt Bắc. Roadworkers built a new segment on Road 13 (present National Road 37) that linked Yên Bài to Sơn La by way of a Black River crossing at Tạ Khoa. The ninety-two-kilometer segment ran up, over, and around mountain ranges to connect two older spurs, both of which were upgraded along the way, and merge at the Cò Nòi intersection with Road 41 (National Road 6), the principal artery running along the southern tier. Overseen by two hundred Chinese advisors and untold Kinh cadres, upwards of fourteen thousand workers served ten to fifteen day stints felling trees, hauling dirt, and enduring bouts of illness. In this regard—and again, even more so in the Điện Biên Phủ Campaign—the region's own material qualities seemed to push back on human labor. Just as rushing rivers, steep slopes, and thick forests challenged military engineers and exhausted roadworkers, endemic malaria and scarce food weakened them both. Such rugged landscape features compound any straightforward measures of distance, long as they were already, with what scholars call the friction of terrain.[28] Meanwhile, aerial bombardment and strafing by French warplanes further endangered foot traffic and roadwork, underscoring their strategic value. Indeed, these transportation arteries not only expedited force mobility in time of war but connected the upstream Black River region to the downstream Vietnamese heartland.

As state labor recruitment expanded and intensified over 1953, so too did the problems that accompanied its regulation and use. After household recruitment, commune leaders often failed to oversee the movement of laborers from village to site, presenting ample opportunity to flee. Moreover, in spite of official emphasis on fairness and equity, the application of dân công duty was uneven socially and spatially. As with elite resistance to land reform, muang elites shirked their duties and exempted family members, leaving poor families to bear a disproportionate burden. Worse, wartime roadwork in unsanitary conditions not only risked one's health and well-being but also jeopardized household food security back home. These injury and opportunity costs followed status and gender inequities and, further, traced the spatial expansion of DRV authority relations west to the Lao frontier. Whereas Yên Bái had clinics to treat and inoculate laborers, for example, the western reaches lacked comparable health facilities and personnel. Such institutional unevenness mapped onto the differential normalization of citizenship duties. In places where service was more routinized, like Yên Bái and Lào Cai, farmers requested time limits to "put their minds to rest and make a living" but did the work nonetheless. By contrast, the provinces of Lai Châu and Sơn La lacked institutional capacity at the local level to furnish even basic data on worker origin, service duration, and labor supply. Still largely unfamiliar with dân công, residents remained "anxious," complained vociferously, and often fled when asked to work on road crews or to transport salt and farm tools. Worst of all, parts of Lai Châu and Sơn La reported increasing hunger and scattered starvation.[29]

The region's officials and residents shared the same worries. Commissar Kháng fretted about poor dân công recruitment and fragmented management as well as consequent transportation blockages and increasing hunger. He attributed these problems to the DRV's regional inability to meet the population's material needs and generate the ideological support necessary to sustain state labor claims. Salt and farm tools, he explained, remained scarce, especially in Sơn La and Lai Châu. The shortage of spades limited farmers' ability to reopen fallow land and increase production. When provided with these tools, residents responded "enthusiastically" and said, "the Government's provision of one spade is equal to one basket of rice." From an ideological standpoint, he noted, material shortages and resentment toward dân công tracked one another: after the initial "enthusiasm" of liberation wore off, peasants still bereft of salt and farm tools in western reaches became "anxious" and "insufficiently believed in the Government and cadres."[30] In other words, the same transportation difficulties that limited the provision of locally scarce goods also explained the spatially uneven legitimacy of state claims.

However partial, the commissar's explanation nonetheless points to a breakdown in the revolutionary exchange and a growing emphasis on new forms of DRV power. Unlike colonial corvée and except for beatings in 1952 Lào Cai, reports of corporeal violence inflicted on dân công are remarkably rare. When the exchange worked as intended, as in Sơn La in the late 1940s, the terms of trade legitimated the terms of rule, leading people to provide labor consensually. Yet the victorious Northwest Campaign, by increasing the dimensions of territory and population exponentially, outstripped the DRV's limited transportation and exchange capacities. Kháng's warning in spring 1953, then, decried a major shift in state claim-making practices, from reciprocal exchange to intensive mobilization. If the former was more voluntarist and predicated on legitimating power as authority, the latter was less voluntarist and predicated more on wielding institutional and disciplinary power. Though still reciprocal, mobilization required greater institutional powers, especially surveillance but also coercion. A July 1953 police report indicates the growth of such capacities. Patrols along the Red River found hideouts where "gangs of *dân công* hide from their duties to the resistance."[31] Correct about their intent, the chief of police was wrong about these people in an important way: they neither considered themselves nor wanted to be known as dân công. But he, like other powerful DRV officials, was increasingly able to treat them as such, with or without their consent.

By overlooking social inequities and complex interethnic relations, moreover, the commissar's analysis effaced underlying problems rooted in the entanglement of muang in DRV territory and the entrenchment of elite Tai control over agrarian resources. Recall that most DRV officials in the northwest were former colonial officials accustomed to conscripting corvée (*bắt phu*), particularly for roadwork. Further, their new district and commune bailiwicks incorporated hierarchies of resource control that, thanks to withholding land reform, survived largely intact. As such, officialized Tai chiefs were accustomed to still older—and, in some nominally DRV districts, ongoing—relations of labor control, whether servants bonded to households or peasants beholden to labor payments in exchange for land access. At the massive Road 13 construction site in October 1953, for example, many "anxious" local laborers still considered dân công akin to corvée and a few even thought the work fit for "slaves (*tôi*), captured by the government."[32]

Kinh cadres could do little to overcome such (mis)interpretations. Very few had the local language skills necessary to elucidate "people's labor" as a citizenship requirement distinct from colonial corvée or customary bondage. Although linguistic barriers certainly inhibited legitimation work, any justification in any language was sometimes superfluous. Among other "errors" and "worries" at the Road 13 site, a contingent of Kinh cadres was "scared" of Tai elites, "feared" reporting back to superiors, and refrained from "criticizing" local practices.[33] If rulers and ruled in Tai communities remained much the same, then how the former put the latter to work must have remained much the same also.

More was at play than simple historical continuity, though—the muang itself was undergoing a spatial transformation in line with its use in DRV territorial administration. Stretching the Tai bailiwick to fit district and commune was reaching up to incorporate places, peoples, and resources historically out of reach. Notably, colonial policy had exempted Hmong and Dao peoples from corvée duties, illustrating a divisive French strategy of "racial politics" (*politique des races*) but recognizing a measure of autonomy that the highland peoples had in relation to lowland Tai.[34] Even though the majority of laborers at the Road 13 site identified as Tai and Mường, the presence of some Hmong, Dao, and Khmu workers foreshadowed how DRV labor claims—funneled through the muang—would, over the course of 1954, come to weigh heavily on them as well. Applying citizenship duties equally and fairly to all peoples within DRV territory not only eroded the labor autonomy of swidden cultivators but also threatened them with Tai domination.

Not simply commandeering people and forcing them to work, nationalizing labor was a transformative social process that linked bodies to geobody, expanded membership in a larger community, and exposed households to new risks and rewards. For the region's diverse peoples, serving as a dân công laborer embodied one's national citizenship and constructed territory in everyday ways. Always arduous and sometimes deadly, participating in the work of armed resistance enabled civilian noncombatants to learn about, and make claims on, the same Vietnamese nation-state-making claims on their labor power. The women and poor men who picked up a large share of the burden built roads beyond the muang that led, for better and worse, to more egalitarian possibilities. Expressing as much anxiety as excitement, they faced conditions not always of their choosing but nonetheless a product of their labors.

TAXING FOOD

Much as they did about labor, peasants and officials shared worries about their principal food: rice. As stalks ripened and bent with seed in late October 1952, Black River peasants grew "alarmed that airplanes might destroy [the plants], concerned about leaving for *dân công* duties, and, overall, very worried about the harvest." People's Army maneuvers invited French warplanes to bomb and strafe rice fields doubling as battlefields. With so many men drafted into the Tai battalions, households were already short-handed when cadres called on women and remaining men to carry supplies and work on roads. As a result, their collective anxieties tempered the excitement that normally accompanied the run-up to harvest season. Meanwhile, senior DRV officials and People's Army officers understood that long supply lines required them to secure a local food supply to provision soldiers. In anticipation of the harvest, therefore, the Northwest Party Committee convened a Cadre Conference to stress the "crux" of government activities: "calm the people's hearts and safeguard the rice crop."[35]

Redeployed to rice fields, cadres and soldiers in November 1952 worked with local producers to protect the crop, and in so doing began to transform agricultural work. In Yên Bài Province, now behind front lines, soldiers helped bring in the harvest. Around its market town of Nghĩa Lộ, cadres sold badly needed sickles to reap rice. Along the southwesterly road to Sơn La, where French planes frightened farmers from fields, cadres instructed the people to avoid white shirts and wear camouflage, to harvest in sections before seeking cover in the forest, and to disperse into small groups so as not to draw fire. More broadly and lastingly, cadres taught efficient techniques like cutting in bunches rather than individual stalks. They imparted a sense of time discipline by encouraging farmers to work longer daylight hours, extend the work week, and do fieldwork by night. In order to expand the pool of active labor, they organized mixed-gender youth groups to reap and thresh rice, aiming to discredit local customs structuring such tasks as appropriate for women only or for men of the "correct age." A year later, agricultural agents reported "solving the labor shortage" in two ways: first, women who had never ploughed fields before now did; second, work teams had expanded as far west as Lai Châu, increased membership all over, and exchanged not just labor but also seed, livestock, and tools.[36]

In addition to transforming worlds of agrarian work, the DRV agenda sought to transform ownership of its products, especially rice but also opium, in pursuit of territory. Once the fall 1952 harvest came in, cadres levied a tax on rice, paid in kind, and borrowed more grain against future tax payments. Beginning with Decree 13/SL of May 1951, the central government had simplified and centralized the agricultural tax (*thuế nông nghiệp*) along a progressive scale based on household assessments. Taxed rice belonged to the central government which, in turn, distributed most of it to feed the growing People's Army, leaving a smaller portion in local granaries to balance regional budgets. In explicit contrast with a heavy, multifarious, and hated colonial tax burden, DRV public education now emphasized equitable, appropriate, and voluntary contributions to the national resistance.[37] Comparable to what dân công service did for transportation labor, then, the agricultural tax not only secured a strategic military resource, in this case provisions, but also legitimized its appropriation. In ways similarly real and imagined, taxing food connected bodies to geobody by enlisting a source of sustenance in a national territorial project.

Food value aside, one of the main aims and outcomes of agricultural taxation was calculative knowledge of an agrarian society. In December's evaluation of the Northwest Campaign, Commissar Kháng cited statistics on locally collected labor and rice and credited cadres with "mobilizing human and material resources" for the military. Yet he criticized "shortcomings and errors in their work," particularly failures to investigate production capacities by area, determine targets for each, and fine-tune the latter. He heaped criticism on cadres "hesitant" to register variations in household assets who simply collected a per capita levy instead, blaming them for lingering popular "anxiety" regarding the new DRV tax.[38] His emphasis on quantitative data and the mistakes made in collecting them reveals an abiding interest in counting people and things in space, of knowing population and resources by territory.

Subsequent rounds of taxation, including iterative corrections and reassessments, fulfilled this official drive to know the population and render it legible. In April 1953, the commissar cited the eastern province of Yên Bái and its 100 percent achievement of targets, based on 5,363 tons of rice revenue, to exemplify how, just four months after campaign's end, the province command had "already figured out how to concentrate forces and capacities through the work of taxation." Lào Cai came in second, achieving 88 percent of targets based on revenue of 1,941 tons. Conversely, he reported "no results" from the western province of Sơn La and did not even mention liberated parts of Lai Châu, like Điện Biên Phủ.[39] Significantly, state knowledge in these latter places not only lagged behind territorial conquest and resource appropriation but was also obscured by these same contested practices.

Not only did taxation share a calculative logic with territory: it also shared practices fraught with contest and destabilizing outcomes few predicted. Theoretically, to focus narrowly on the logic of taxation—and by extension territory—would be to overlook the broader conditions and consequences of its actual implementation. Empirically, it was the latter that threatened to unravel the DRV's fragile territorial configuration in the Northwest Zone. The revolutionary and postcolonial Vietnamese experience demonstrates that, more than a ruling logic, territory is also a grounded practice and negotiated process that must be understood historically—including all the contingencies, compromises, and unplanned outcomes that history entails.[40] In short, taxation was a territorial strategy that itself destabilized the territorial outcome.

In the case above, to take the commissar at his word on official failures traces a calculative logic running through statecraft but follows his attention away from real local anxieties and tense power struggles. From the perspective of statecraft, not until the Điện Biên Phủ Campaign would the DRV achieve a centralized capacity to calculate and regulate agrarian resources in the Northwest Zone. Developing and wielding this capacity would cause its own problems, as discussed in chapters 4–5. From a local angle, years of warfare and colonial exploitation had left Black River peasants hungry and rice scarce, giving them good reason to worry. In Sơn La and Lai Châu especially, taxing food generated contests over its distribution and increased popular hunger, both undermining the legitimacy of state resource claims and skewing data collected on agrarian production and population. That muang chiefs intimidated DRV tax assessors yet still retained their ruling positions indicates the complex negotiations involved in making Vietnamese territory. These hidden histories also suggest the unstable accommodations built into its spatial form.

Multiple contests over taxation both against the French colony and within the emerging nation contributed to Vietnam's territorial project as well as its inherent fragility. Emphasizing what he called "the economic fight," the commander of French forces in North Vietnam ordered officers in mid-1952 to refocus on "another form of combat" by deploying "all available means" to disrupt enemy resupply and provisions. In keeping with such objectives, French military intelligence kept a close eye on what its analysts called the "heavy and unpopular" agricultural tax, highlighting its "essential" significance to DRV finances (as the single largest source of state revenue) and describing its role in broader economic "difficulties" (the progressive scale depressed overall production by discouraging peasants from growing more than necessary to meet minimum household needs). "The agriculture tax has run up against serious difficulties," reads a French diplomatic report that attributed a "missing spirit of sacrifice among the population" in northern Vietnam to a government "error" allowing powerful rich and middle peasants to oversee local tax processes. The diplomats predicted correctly that senior DRV officials would rectify the situation by "cracking down" on wealthy peasants in downstream areas.[41] Little did the French officials know that such punitive measures, meted out during land reform beginning in 1953, were suspended in the upstream Northwest Zone to maintain the support of local elites.

Far from neutral observations, knowledge of population gleaned through taxation underwrote a form of territorial warfare waged less with guns and coercion than with propaganda and persuasion. DRV and French Indochinese officials fought over the Red River Delta rice basket, aiming to funnel or block, respectively, the flow of provisions to the People's Army as it maneuvered in the surrounding highlands. Their weapons were cartoons and propaganda. A flyer published by a local DRV Information Bureau features a series of captioned illustrations and asks rhetorically, "How can compatriots in temporarily occupied areas emulate patriotism?" Near other blockprints of a worker sabotaging machinery and a teenager knifing a Frenchman, a peasant rakes his paddy next to a water buffalo (figure 7). The caption reads, "Peasant Emulation: increase production to assist the activities of soldiers and cadres."[42]

Whereas the DRV legitimated taxation as a contribution to national resistance, the French-backed Associated State of Vietnam counterattacked with media representations that stressed the consequences of losing food. "Because of the agricultural tax," reads one bulletin, "compatriots in Việt-Minh areas work hard all year, but still go hungry." Another cartoon (figure 8) illustrates how paying the agricultural tax led stepwise to self-destruction: circular arrows point from rice to DRV flag and then weapons, combat, and finally villages aflame; at the center is a satirical play on President Hồ Chí Minh's famous statement ("There is nothing more precious than independence and freedom"): "Nothing is strange here at all, because you have killed yourself!"[43] Although it is unclear whether these media reached a Black River audience, they nonetheless

FIG. 7. Pro-DRV agrarian propaganda stored in France's archives. (2369/10H/Service Historique de la Défense [hereafter SHD].)

FIG. 8. Pro-French agrarian propaganda stored in Vietnam's archives. (1394/PTTg [1945–54]/NAVC 3.)

indicate how contests over food and its rightful distribution were embedded in larger struggles over the legitimacy of state claims on territory.

While French forces waged a frontal attack on the legitimacy of DRV taxes, local contests between Black River peasants and Northwest Zone cadres threatened to undermine the tax agenda from below. Initiated after the late 1952 Northwest Campaign, taxes in newly liberated Sơn La and Lai Châu focused on autumn's main wet-rice crop, granting a holiday to spring's secondary crop and, significantly, all swidden produce. Confirming the commissar's criticisms and French findings alike, early agricultural taxation collected grain and discontent in equal measure, prompting investigations and extensive reassessments during 1953. "High contributions have drained the peasants' energy," warned the region's party executive in March, "so we have not fulfilled the Center's policy of bringing them benefits and increasing their enthusiasm for the resistance." Signaling much more than declining calories, the change in popular affect indicated how DRV taxation had confused a radical, anti-colonial project with a detested colonial practice. Cases of intimidation in Yên Châu, where a district representative threatened jail time, and in Mộc Châu, where an official backed by commandos brandished leg fetters, aimed to spur peasants to declare their stores.[44] While such coercion had been common under colonial rule, the threats now jeopardized a spirit of voluntarism based on legitimating tax payments, like labor service, as contributions to nation and resistance.

Investigators found the inaugural tax process riddled with false declarations, inaccurate assessments, and inflexible procedures, all of which worked against DRV efforts to centralize authority, collect grain and data, and reform society. A report on regional finances urged harsh penalties for those cadres and VWP members whose "suicidal self-interest had mistaken policy, violated people's rights, and destroyed Party policy." Such dire problems, the report continued, risked support for the anti-colonial resistance: after French counterpropaganda left people "puzzled" about DRV taxes, cadres did not explain how taxed rice would "nurture the army, smash the enemy, protect country and home," leaving people still confused but now also worried and reluctant to participate. Cadres had succeeded in collecting grain, in other words, but they had failed to legitimate its appropriation in line with self-professed care for the population. Further, muang-based inequalities remained largely intact, as evinced by Tai elites who sought to reduce rice payments by underreporting land area and yield, dispersing their fields, and even disguising themselves as poor folk. In Tuần Giáo and Thuận Châu, truly poor peasants deferred to the elite's "kind yet contriving" ways and took them in, even hiding them as their own. In Mường La and Mai Sơn, where peasants boldly accused elites of false declarations, the latter dodged the charges, and evaded the punishment of reeducation, by using "prestige" to influence commune committees in their favor. In all these cases, the fact that the "upper class" dominated the ranks of local cadres—ninety-two out of one hundred in Tuần Giáo, for example—helped buttress the old order and fend off DRV efforts to centralize authority and reform society.[45]

Taxation in 1953 revealed and exacerbated the spatial unevenness affecting both regional state capacity and local inequality. Elite resistance to taxation not only confounded state efforts to determine production capacities but also, like dân công labor service, left poor peasants to pick up a disproportionate share. If the province of Yên Bái had exemplified coordination between taxation and data collection in April, then subsequent experience on the region's far frontiers shows how the two programs still had yet to work in harmony. As late as October 1953, agricultural agents detailed exact figures for Yên Bái regarding land area restored to production but reported "no data" from Sơn La and Lai Châu.[46]

Uneven state knowledge of society tracked a larger spatial pattern characterizing DRV capacity in the Northwest Zone. The further west by southwest toward Điện Biên Phủ and Laos, the less state actors knew of the population and the weaker the official flows of transportation and communication. Tax collection also amplified the same social inequalities its architects aimed to level. Actual grain payments strayed far from the policy's egalitarian ideal, generating "unfair contributions" that, in places, "bore an impact on the lives of ethnic minority compatriots, especially laboring peasants." Now hungry and no longer enthusiastic, disaffected peasants strayed from the revolutionary fold, in extreme cases gravitating to colonial forces wielding slogans like "Lift the cangue of agricultural taxation" and "Liberate the *dân công*."[47] No wonder people were confused: such counterrevolutionary wordplay savvily appropriated revolutionary rhetoric but referred to a form of punishment—a cangue is a wooden block hung from the neck—often used in the colonial era.

Through late 1953, Northwest Zone officials worried as much about the unintended consequences of taxation as did the peasants they taxed, if for different reasons. Withholding land reform not only preserved a social order but enabled elites to shirk their duties and shift the weight of DRV resource claims onto poor peasants. Consequently, officials fretted over splits in the national coalition along lines of class and status; unlike elsewhere in northern Vietnam, they risked alienating poor and landless peasants, not landlords and wealthy peasants. Officials were also anxious about ethnic cleavages growing out of colonial rule and spreading with neocolonial agitation. Accusations that "Kinh cadres are evil" were not easily dismissed as mere counterpropaganda given that so many downstream cadres did in fact supervise assessments and oversee grain storehouses. Moreover, the tax holiday granted to swidden crops largely benefited highland Hmong peoples, inspiring lowland, tax-paying, wet-rice-growing Tai and Mường folk to charge the government with unfairness. Meanwhile, Hmong peoples figured at the center of violent contests over the valuable opium crop—what they called "black rice" for its food exchange value—as DRV buyers and guerillas maneuvered against Tai Federation tax collectors and soldiers.[48]

Altogether, then, the popular mood shifted with growing state claims on increasingly scarce agrarian resources. No longer excited but more and more worried about dwindling food supplies and farm labor, many peasants became angry and emboldened, demanding that cadres redo their work. Others fled for the hills or escaped over the montane frontier, prompting one Lao official representing Sam Neua and Phong Saly to worry about feeding and clothing refugees from Sơn La.[49] Still others suffered hunger silently, as discussed below.

In addition to generating provisions and knowledge, taxation illustrates how resource claims linked state legitimacy to population and territory in concrete and sometimes unexpected ways. Calling taxed rice "contributions" enrolled peasants in a national territorial project, sometimes against their will. Claiming their scarce food resources risked their health and bodies, enlisting them in an existential struggle alongside soldiers and cadres who, according to the party line, protected and cared for them in return. Yet such efforts to legitimize the DRV through taxation could just as easily backfire, particularly when undermined by counterpropaganda, sloppy implementation, and heavy-handed enforcement. Like nationalizing labor, then, taxing food generated contingent social processes that exposed the tense ties between bodies and geobody and between resource control and territorial domination. The epic Điện Biên Phủ Campaign would expand and intensify these same processes, as discussed in the next two chapters. Beginning in late 1953, the agricultural tax would climb up the hills and eventually include swidden crops too, notably opium, further expanding fields of contest along with the growing reach of Vietnam's territorial state.

A POLITICS OF HUNGER

Two waves of acute hunger swept the Black River region in 1953. In spring, while the secondary wet-rice crop matured, hunger affected some five thousand people, mostly Tai, in Sơn La Province alone. Five people starved to death in Quang Huy Commune and another nine died in Mộc Châu and Phù Yên districts. More perished in Yên Bái Province. Highland Hmong and Dao peoples as well as midland Khmu survived mainly on starchy tubers, such as cassava and yams, while waiting for corn to mature. A second hunger wave arose in summer, affecting swidden cultivators in particular, after spring rice yielded only one-third of normal levels, multiple corn plantings failed, and forest foods became depleted. Severe food shortages lasted into autumn, abating only when the main wet- and dry-rice crops and the second corn crop all came in, one year after the Northwest Military Campaign had formally ended.[50]

While seasonal hunger was and remains a fact of life during intercrop periods (*giáp hạt*) in the region's agricultural calendar, hunger and starvation in 1953 did not just "appear" or "happen," as officials described it, as though these conditions were independent of shifting territorial rule.[51] Even if generated contingently, food shortages were caused, at least partially if not substantially, by DRV state claims on agrarian resources. Resource appropriation had three interrelated effects on consumption, production, and distribution. First, the worst affected districts were conspicuously close to sites of increased military consumption, whether at the Nà Sản siege (Mường La, Mộc Châu), a staging area for the Lào offensive (Mộc Châu), the Tai Federation front (Quỳnh Nhai, Tuần Giáo), or crossroads with the Việt Bắc base area (Phù Yên, Than Uyên, Văn Chấn). Simply put, more soldiers meant more mouths to feed. Second, pressing peasants into dân công service left farm households short of labor, depressing agricultural production. Such was the case in Sơn La, where off-farm labor led to a decline in total cultivated area, contributing in turn to the disappointing spring rice harvest.[52] Over and above the direct loss of household food supplies to taxes, dân công laborers and their families paid an opportunity cost bodily, experienced as hunger and expressed as anxiety.

Third, and in addition to increased consumption and decreased production, agricultural taxation disrupted the routine redistribution of post-harvest rice in and around the muang. Functioning as important redistributive mechanisms, vibrant local markets had long linked groups that varied not simply by ethnic identity but, moreover, by settlement elevation, climatic exposure, and agricultural specialization. Trade helped balance the relative shortage and abundance of food caused by environmental factors exerting differential effects across rugged terrain. But taxing food reduced an already diminished supply of the rice sought by swidden cultivators, for example, in exchange for their livestock, opium, and other cash crops. As cadres collected more and more tax payments in kind, the official price of rice in DRV currency (đồng) grew exponentially. In Yên Bái, for example, rice's price quintupled from January to February 1953 (from 950 to 4,680 đồng per kilogram) while salt's rose only marginally (from 14,000 to 15,000 đồng per kilogram).[53] Preoccupied by what they saw as currency inflation, economic planners overlooked how the grain's rapid price increase owed more to diminishing supplies than undervalued paper money. In any case, swidden cultivators earned too little from cash crops to buy food at such high prices.

Across northern Vietnam more broadly, in 1953 shortfalls in agricultural production became a serious problem for local cultivators and DRV leaders alike. Following the Tết holiday, rice stores ran dry in the Red River Delta and hunger spread south. Before spring rice added to desperately low stocks, hunger in the northern midlands turned into starvation: some 168,500 people in Quảng Ngãi Province went hungry and 1,272 starved to death. As with any famine or hunger crisis, multiple natural and social causes limited food production and distribution, all of which contributed to human suffering.[54] As in the case of the Great Famine of 1945, who bore responsibility for this latest episode of hunger and starvation was a politically sensitive question, yet one that now threatened to reflect poorly on the upstart postcolonial regime.

Official assessments of hunger's causes deflected culpability from DRV activities, reflecting less an accurate analysis than a politics of blame. Agriculture officials harked back to August 1945 as the last worst hunger epidemic, recognizing how DRV legitimacy still rested in part on reducing hunger and maintaining food security. "*It is not the agricultural tax which causes hunger,*" they stressed, pointing instead to pest outbreaks, natural disasters, and warfare, including scorched-earth tactics by French forces. Adding to these stated causes, central party leaders cited the legacy of colonial exploitation and traditions of village "feudalism." The latter suggests how fingering landed elites helped justify land reform but still denied any causal role for the state appropriation of grain and labor. Commissar Kháng, too, blamed colonial exploitation and displacement for pauperizing the peasantry but withheld judgment on the Black River elites whom he had helped exempt from land reform. In the main, DRV officials dodged responsibility for reallocating scarce resources away from peasant producers to military consumers. Instead, they blamed capricious nature, careless swidden cultivators, and foreign occupiers.[55]

However common rural privation was during the First Indochina War, the 1953 experience distinguished the Northwest Zone from other parts of an emerging Vietnam in three important ways. First, conditions may have been worse in the northern midlands and Red River Delta but, because of French occupation there, they did not necessarily impugn the postcolonial state. In the "newly liberated" northwest, by contrast, where DRV territorial rule was now ascendant, hunger jeopardized regime legitimacy predicated on caring for a national community and associating misery with foreign others. Second, a given cadre's identification as Kinh did not signal solidarity with diverse, upstream locals but rather differentiated him. By and large, the newly arriving male cadres were not *of* Black River peoples: they had grown up far away, dressed in uniform shirts and trousers, spoke Vietnamese, ate water spinach, and called somewhere else home. As a result, their communal recognition was associated with an aspirational project—national liberation—that actually contributed in everyday ways to local suffering. Finally, hunger in 1953 was different again from the 1950 experience in the Sơn-Lai Interprovince. Earlier Kinh guerillas and cadres had earned a measure of solidarity by enduring hardship together with local partisans. Now, formal territorial rule meant that most Kinh in-migrants worked at a distance from locals either as regular soldiers on the front lines or as bureaucrats in district offices, the latter often complaining of local conditions and requesting posts closer to home. In sum, using hunger as a cause to unify a collective self against a grain-hording other was far more complicated and ultimately less successful. After all, storehouses were no longer in the hands of some foreign "enemy" (whether Japanese or French) but rather belonged to a state(d) "friend," that is, the grain-collecting, tax-assessing DRV.

Although officials realized how regime legitimacy hinged on alleviating hunger, their efforts to do so became entangled in the same bureaucratic knots, resource hierarchies, and flawed programs they had helped produce. Preventing and relieving hunger were already items on the Agriculture Ministry's regional agenda. Yet the program's "long-term goal," determining household production capacities and overall targets for state appropriation, articulated with taxation's calculative logics and unintended effects. Indeed, tax collection continued even as production dipped and conditions worsened. In May, after the first hunger wave and just before the second, central party-state leaders ordered Northwest Zone counterparts to work with district and commune to "prioritize hunger prevention above all else," because "hunger prevention and relief *are important political work*."[56] Just as ongoing hunger in DRV territory eroded state legitimacy, they figured, solving the problem would buttress popular consent.

Given circumscribed understandings of the problem, however, it is not surprising that official solutions largely adhered to business as usual. Aid efforts included loaning out relief rice borrowed from storehouses and wealthy farmers, offering food in payment for road and irrigation work, and exchanging cash crops and forest products for rice. In one measure of aid's bitterly ironic limitations, prescribing more off-farm labor only exacerbated the same on-farm shortages created by dân công recruitment. Further, food aid was insufficient and failed to reach the people who needed it most. An after-the-fact report cited "landlords [who] did not loan the proper amount," both displacing blame and indicating elite resistance to redistribution. Further, the report continued, people with "means" managed to borrow emergency provisions while "poor people" were unable to do so because they could not repay the loans. Meanwhile, aid efforts focused on Yên Bái and Lào Cai, hardly reaching Sơn La and Lai Châu.[57] Like so many other programs at the time, aid wound up buttressing social and spatial inequities.

Much more than a passing phase, hunger and the politics it generated were integral to relations of DRV territorial rule in the Northwest Zone. Officials acknowledged the links between political legitimacy and full stomachs. But the land, tax, labor, and aid programs they put into place jeopardized popular support by allocating scarce resources from farm to front and amplifying local inequality. Further, the 1953 hunger episode signaled how an old tension—whether to leave labor on-farm for production or move it off-farm for transportation and warfare—had returned under new circumstances and with deadly consequences. Despite policy efforts to defuse this and other tensions, conditions of hunger and scattered starvation indicate unresolved contradictions in the DRV's regional agenda.

GROUNDED CONTESTS

At a crucial moment in the First Indochina War, then, contests on the ground threatened to unravel the DRV's territorial arrangement in a place rapidly becoming its most strategic site. Circulated just two days after French paratroopers landed in Điện Biên Phủ, a fiery report analyzed the Northwest Zone's tense and tangled relations of rule and production. Written by a Chinese observer named Duong Hông Quang, the report was titled "Land Holding and Feudal Power in Ethnic Tai Areas of the Northwest" and reflected critically on a region ostensibly liberated a year earlier.[58] The reading below analyzes how agrarian power relations, in their polyvalent economic, political, and cultural forms, worked with and against the territorialization of DRV state power.

That the author was not Vietnamese and outside DRV channels perhaps enabled him to challenge—in writing—the Northwest Zone's highest official, unnamed but presumably Commissar Nguyễn Kháng, on the state of agrarian power relations. In September 1953 at a regional assembly, according to Duong, the commissar had maintained that because "the Tai aristocracy no longer has economic power"—having with the Northwest Campaign supposedly lost its official land, labor to work it (cuông), and rice payments (nguột)—its members were, instead, really just landlords and middle peasants "capable of taking things from peasants." The commissar's claim denies how region and center had actually approved, in the same month, the exact same labor obligation and rice payments under the Ethnic Policy discussed in chapter 2. Duong responded acidly, asking "on what basis" the commissar had reached his conclusions. Basing his rebuttal on regional data and a field study conducted in Sơn La's Phù Yên District, site of spontaneous land reform in autumn 1952 and acute hunger in 1953, he highlighted the Tai elite's ongoing, manifold powers.

The Cầm clan's capacity to retain office, dominate land access, and avoid state resource claims exemplifies the reproduction of muang power in DRV guise. Led by the "very powerful" Cầm Văn Khoa, prominent clan members held colonial office in the 1940s, turned out in support of the August 1945 Revolution, and then fled into exile during French reconquest. After the Northwest Campaign, these Tai elites returned to positions of prominence. Former county chief (*tri châu*) Cầm Văn Nô became district chairman of Phù Yên. Among his three sons, all of whom were VWP members, one became secretary of Quang Huy Commune's party cell, another held a seat on the district's standing committee, and a third served as an army political officer. Ensconced in these positions and backed by senior officials, the clan maintained a grip on "good land" while poor peasants continued to labor on "poor land." Like muang elites elsewhere, Cầm kin avoided DRV tax and labor duties and shifted the brunt onto poor families. Through such covert resistance and overt political participation, male Tai elites fused economic and political powers to press their own familial advantage.

Incorporating hereditary hierarchies into a socialist bureaucracy split supposedly unified entities, notably the DRV state itself, and exposed potentially violent factionalization within it. No longer enthusiastic and more than just anxious, poor peasants joined with radical cadres to vent anger and frustration. Noting an entrenched Tai elite who bent any attempt at agrarian reform to their advantage, Duong described the land situation as "very severe" and the people as "very discontent." Unable to "reform society" as elsewhere in the DRV, radical cadres spoke out against what they called "the Central Government's circumscribed policy of [so-called] 'mass mobilization.'" Their "zealous" counterproposal, quoted Duong, offered "to liquidate all unclean elements belonging to the upper class."[59] Radical cadres, in other words, clamored for a violent purge of class enemies in the DRV's own ranks. Their call to "liquidate" or "purge" people like the Cầm clan—recognized party members, military officers, and government officials—points to the tensions embedded in regional authority relations. Through 1953–54, the Center worked through the Northwest Party Committee to moderate the ambitions of such radical cadres, often backed by poor peasants, who were violently opposed to institutionally recognized traditional power. Such splits within "the state" reveal the formation of factions belying any neat state-society divide: poor peasants allied with radical cadres, local elites with regional cadres and central leaders.

Even as class-status cleavages proved a potent source of division, not all peasants responded according to rational interests. Like the story of the lightning bolt at Mộc Ly discussed in chapter 1, the persistence of popular traditions running counter to class-status position points to the limits of revolutionary logic. Power in Tai communities was diffuse and permeated everyday social life—at once outside of, yet still embedded within, positions of authority and relations of production.[60] "The veneration of the masses regarding the house of Cầm," observed Duong, "is very clear in everyday activities." In rituals accompanying harvest, prayers, feasts, funerals, and other holidays, Tai peasants continued to bestow elevated stature on the Cầm. Returning from exile to reclaim their hereditary positions in the muang, for example, members of the Cầm clan likened their homecoming to a welcoming flower:

> A lotus flower in a pond, for many years did not bloom,
> this year it blossoms.
> Because the Cầm clan was dispersed the flower did not bloom,
> now they have returned and the lotus flower blossoms.[61]

Many people believed the metaphor to be "true," endowing the clan with powers beyond land as property to encompass land's generative properties as well. Similarly, when a stream in Quang Huy changed course, "everyone" interpreted the event to announce the defeat of French military forces and, further, believed that subsequent French failure was caused by Cầm ritual efforts to alter the stream's course. Interpreting natural events as omens of social change points to an element of Cầm clan power that perplexed Kinh and Chinese cadres but swayed Tai peasants: elite domination extended beyond office and field to social meaning and cultural practice.

Elite cultural power fed into control over manpower and silenced dissenting voices. The capacity of members of the Cầm clan to call on peasant service exceeded even that which their office extended, a bureaucratic power that they also abused. When Cầm Văn Khoa, known as Lord Khoa, returned from exile, for example, he found his home destroyed by warfare. He said to peasants, "Now I am weak and poor, so [I] must request that you help me carefully." Many of them, though hungry and in need of their own labor power, nonetheless felt such love, respect, and fear that they built him a new home "voluntarily." Even radicalized peasants who expressed anger in private to cadres still fell silent in public. Splits among an old elite and a radicalized peasantry also had a generational dimension: while the elderly venerated the Cầm, the youth "hated" and spoke badly of them. Nonetheless, in meetings attended by Cầm clan members, the revolutionary youngsters "did not dare to speak." Despite their best efforts to forbid such deferential displays, reformist cadres could do little to stop them. Nor could they understand why a "liberated" peasantry continued to follow their former masters.

In spite of their ostensible liberation, peasants adhered to local hierarchies in part because of old traditions particular to the Tai muang or other cultural custom. Moreover, peasants continued to follow old masters because the DRV regime hitched the social hierarchies to territory and its administration. By prioritizing the category of ethnicity over class, status, and gender, the DRV granted local government office to male elites, Tai above others. The rising state offered ample opportunity to reproduce elite control over land, labor, and food—provided cadres and officers got the lion's share. As state resource claims expanded and intensified in 1953, most people grew hungrier and their affect shifted accordingly, from enthusiasm to anxiety, even anger. Amid growing popular dissatisfaction, the next military campaign, a still larger one, would begin. Hunger and anxiety would again follow, underlining how resource contests joined with military combat to constitute DRV territory.

Building on the late 1940s revolutionary exchange, official economic activities starting in late 1952 initiated longer processes of state and territory formation working to centralize control over resource flows—though these did not always play out as intended. Even as exchange remained reciprocal and generative of a state idea, tactics of resource extraction expanded and intensified in support of a rising territorial administration and its growing coercive apparatus—the People's Army of Vietnam. The DRV gained access to land and labor resources bound up in muang relations by withholding land reform, empowering a local elite to tax food, and constructing Vietnamese citizens in Tai communities. But these powerful processes generated other outcomes as well, notably producing hunger among the poor and reproducing privilege for the elite. These regional contingencies alienated many poor Tai peasants and radical cadres, undermining the regime's legitimacy and jeopardizing its territorial claim. This chapter's concluding portrait of anxious peasants allied with angry cadres ends in late November 1953—shortly before French forces landed at Điện Biên Phủ. Chapters 4 and 5 pick up when the Điện Biên Phủ Campaign propelled a much larger cadre corps to redouble its efforts in muang communities and expand into the midland and highland communities above and between these valley spaces.

CHAPTER 4

Điện Biên Phủ and the Logistics of Territory

"THE OUTSTANDING DIFFICULTY of such a long military campaign," stated General Võ Nguyên Giáp in his 1999 memoir, "was the problem of supplying food and ammunition." Although he referred to the 1952 Northwest Campaign, his statement on the centrality of logistics applies equally if not more so to the next year's Điện Biên Phủ Campaign. Only two roads reached the embattled Black River region from secure base areas in Thanh Hóa and Thái Nguyên, and each stretched hundreds of kilometers over rugged terrain. Transportation relied on thousands of civilian porters (dân công) who consumed much of the rice intended for soldiers. Meanwhile, local food and labor supplies were scarce. Aware of these formidable supply problems, French military planners in mid-1953 accurately foresaw how logistics would prove decisive in the coming campaign yet fatally underestimated their adversary's capacity. "Ironic, then, how this calculation," recounted the victorious general, "would contribute to the disaster of the French Expeditionary Corps at Điện Biên Phủ."[1]

Not simply moving and supplying armies, logistics did more still than help win the battle that won the First Indochina War. In early 1950s Vietnam, mobilizing logistical resources organized relations between state, economy, and society according to the calculative logic of territory.[2] Especially during the epic Điện Biên Phủ Campaign, an emergent logistics capacity equipped a central elite with spatial knowledge of things and people, enabling them to project military force and secure distant territory. Historically consequential, this link between territory and logistics is also contextually meaningful and theoretically significant. The Vietnamese word for logistics (*hậu cần*) shares meaning with the human body and abstract space, felicitously mapping onto a vernacular geobody and its realization as Vietnam's national territory.

Expanding iteratively, governing logistics applied military force to state knowledge of things and people in the Black River region. Its administration as the Northwest Zone began with the autumn 1952 Northwest Campaign, one year before the Điện Biên Phủ Campaign began to secure it fully. Figures from these two campaigns illustrate a quantum leap in DRV logistical capacity over that intervening year. The former lasted two and a half months, supplied 36,000 soldiers, and relied on 70,000 dân công, of whom 9,000 hailed from the zone. The latter lasted eight months, supplied 70,000 troops, and relied on 261,000 dân công, of whom 30,000 were local. Compared with its predecessor, then, the Điện Biên Phủ Campaign lasted three times longer, supported double the number of troops, and depended on four times as many laborers, including triple the number of locals. These statistics reflect a broader expansion and intensification of state power consistent with the tense and contradictory social process of militarization. Increasing mass participation drove, and was driven by, centralizing bureaucratic power and elite domination.[3]

Even though the estimates above indicate a leap in magnitude, to compare logistics by quantity alone would presuppose all the work necessary both to quantify things and people and, through that quantification, to empower a central elite with military force. Rendering resources legible was itself a powerful project that, logically and historically, preceded the development and routinization of bureaucratic accounting measures. Recounting supplies statistically, therefore, appears natural and straightforward only in retrospect. At the time, General Giáp did not actually know how many dân công laborers moved his army in the Northwest Campaign. In the months to follow, developing state capacity to count resources and account for their military use gave birth to new institutions and new forms of knowledge that, in turn, made the Điện Biên Phủ Campaign possible. These government agencies and the statistics they produced exemplify what Michel Foucault named "power-knowledge" (*pouvoir-savoir*). Indeed, the topic of this chapter—the governing of military logistics—speaks to the philosopher's interest in the "army as a matrix of organization and knowledge" and answers his call to study military campaigns geographically.[4]

Unlike much governmentality literature, which tends to decenter the state as a locus of power, however, the inquiry here refocuses analytical attention on the state itself, particularly how military and bureaucratic practice centralized state power and shaped knowledge of society. Counting people and things as quantities certainly implies discounting them in other, more human ways. But, as Max Weber stressed, bureaucracy works "according to *calculable rules* and 'without regard for persons.'" So the numbers remain analytically significant, not simply as given statistics but, even more, as artifacts of state learning practices. By tracing the production of statistics to bureaucratic decisions and military movements, this chapter also explains the logistical processes and militarist terms through which state came to know society, and exact claims on it, in pursuit of territory. Seemingly neutral and purely technical, logistics bears the epistemological stamp of what sociologist C. Wright Mills aptly labeled in 1956 "a military definition of reality."[5]

Logistical quantities indicate an underlying state capacity to generate resources and thus put people and things to work. In memory and archive, the two People's Army campaigns contrast in the "character of calculability," defined by scholar Timothy Mitchell as a calculative ability to realize an object of statistical enumeration and government policy. Unavailable during the Northwest Campaign, the enumerative capacity became part of the DRV arsenal through institutional construction in 1953–54. Ruing a "feature we did not expect," Giáp recalled in 1999 how porters in October 1952 had marched in a "seemingly endless file" six kilometers long. Notably, he did not count them, observing only that "*dân công* outnumbered soldiers." Archived reports are similarly uncertain, presenting labor figures that diverge widely and come to no agreement. When recounting the Điện Biên Phủ Campaign, by contrast, Giáp enumerated porters and supplies precisely, citing statistics originating in an authoritative account filed by the Central Front Supply Council in July 1954.[6] In short, only during the latter campaign did the DRV wield a new institutional capacity to calculate resources, mobilize society, and secure territory.

This chapter views the Điện Biên Phủ Campaign from the top down by analyzing the invention and operation of logistics in relation to the construction of Vietnamese territory. It traces how DRV leaders built institutions to mobilize the masses and applied calculative technologies to appropriate their food and labor. In a longer iterative process of state learning, officers and officials identified local barriers, standardized measures, compiled statistics, and established the Central Front Supply Council to coordinate all this work. By joining household counting with central accounting, they expanded the military's "rear," or area of procurement, across northern Vietnam, intensifying the transformation of Black River space into Vietnamese territory. Such counting and accounting tactics yielded the immense quantities of logistical resources required by the People's Army to defeat the French Expeditionary Corps. The tactics also generated new forms of knowledge: as Giáp's memoir suggests, the quantities still structure narrative recounting of past triumphs. Indeed, statistics on labor, food, and area animate the Vietnamese geobody by lending narrative fodder to nationalist-militarist reification of civilian "contributions" to the war effort. The calculations highlight the forms of abstract knowledge that enabled DRV rule of historically autonomous borderlands, especially the spatio-temporal boundaries that shaped the Northwest Zone and discounted local costs.

EARLY MISCALCULATIONS

General Giáp's inability to recount precisely the logistics required for the 1952 Northwest Campaign owed as much to local illegibility and colonial barriers as to limited bureaucratic capacity. During guerilla warfare in the late 1940s, a generation of local Tai cadres had begun to integrate the muang socio-political unit into Vietnamese administration. By translating the unit's governing customs and rules into Vietnamese, the local cadres initiated a state project to appropriate Black River resources, the significance of which only increased as war escalated. During mobile warfare in 1952, a second generation of Kinh cadres intensified processes of administrative incorporation and resource appropriation. When taking stock of local resources, however, they encountered diverse peoples who had developed ways and measures designed to thwart just such an extractive project.[7]

In the Black River region, downstream Kinh cadres confronted worlds where the unknown extended beyond quantities of agrarian resources to include the very metrics used to measure them. Units of land, weight, and labor all varied locally, often from muang to muang and between Tai and non-Tai communities. A unit of land area commonly used to measure wet-rice fields, known as the mẫu, serves as case in point. Etymologically related to the Chinese *mu* but larger in size, the Vietnamese mẫu unit varies between the north, where one *mẫu Bác Bộ* is equal to 3,600 square meters, and the center, where one *mẫu Trung Bộ* is equal to 4970.25 square meters. Yet both these equivalencies—between mẫu values and to the metric system—are themselves the outcome of longer efforts to standardize and centralize Vietnamese rule in the lowlands. Spared these processes until the 1950s, the Black River mẫu was, at the time, a highly variable measure. Each muang used its own mẫu unit sized three to seven times larger than one "downstream mẫu," presumably the northern one. In Mộc Châu District, an agricultural cadre found its unique mẫu measured not land area but weight in rice, "whereby each *mẫu* equals 150 *gánh,* and one *gánh* equals five *yến tạ,* or 30 kilograms."[8] Indeed, measures of weight, including the *gánh* (literally, shoulder load) and myriad others, varied as well. Likewise, relations of labor control were often illegible, much of it tangled in muang hierarchies specific to place. Finally, all these weights and measures were of mixed use outside the valley-bound wet-rice settlements, notably among swidden cultivators working dry rice, maize, and opium in the highlands, where measures changed all over again—if used at all.

The boundary between upstream and downstream itself became a fierce point of contest during the First Indochina War, underlining the political significance of transportation across it. Just as French colonial rule aimed to separate the Black River region from the Red River Delta, Vietnamese revolutionaries sought to cross these gaps and close the distance. Combining paternalism with divide-and-rule tactics, colonial policy in Indochina offered autonomy and protection to highland peoples, constructing physical and cultural boundaries between them and lowland Vietnamese. In exemplary fashion, France's attaché to the Tai Federation, Jean Jerusalemy, credited a string of blockhouse forts built in 1951 for "protecting the Tai country from the Red River and Việt Minh threat." Yet the colonial barrier, called the De Lattre Line to honor Indochina's high commissioner from 1950 to 1952, failed to withstand the late 1952 People's Army assault. Moving people and things upstream for military and strategic purposes, in turn, catalyzed longer processes of acculturation, exchange, and development still unfolding to this day.[9]

For the duration of the war, France held the sky while Vietnamese space expanded on rivers and over land into the upstream region. Warfare compounded old transportation problems. Slow and seasonal transport slowed still further with combat, particularly on the principal but treacherous Black River route. Before the war, ascending from the Chợ Bờ falls at Hoà Bình to the town of Lai Châu took three weeks, and the descent just six days. Navigable during the dry months from October to May, the river rose with rapids in the rainy season, burst its banks, and turned impassable. Facing delays in late 1952, DRV administrators assessed routes through the metric of salt, signaling its continued significance in exchange relations. Because aerial strafing forced boaters to travel at night and shelter by day, moving one ton of salt on a short segment from the Suối Rút depot (in Mai Châu) to forward positions at Quỳnh Nhai (below Lai Châu town) now took as long as the full route. Slower still, overland transport required enormous human resources: packing one ton of salt an even shorter distance required seventy people six days out and six back. "At problem's center is inadequate manpower," explained the prime minister's delegate Phan Mỹ, referring to transportation delays worsened by "imprecise planning and incomplete inspections."[10] Speeding material supply, he suggested, required more laborers as well as rational management and governmental discipline to make them work more efficiently.

Hitched to strategic and everyday transport, the problem of calculating labor supply became increasingly evident through Northwest Campaign logistical work. Moving thirty-six thousand People's Army soldiers into engagements with French and federation forces stretched a pair of supply lines some three hundred to five hundred kilometers from ready sources of labor, food, and supplies. One from the southern Red River Delta snaked from Thanh Hóa on Road 15 to join Road 41 (now National Road 6) at Suối Rút. Another from the northern Red River Delta wound through the Việt Bắc base and connected with Nghĩa Lộ along Road 13. Initially, the VWP's Ethnic Policy had instructed the military operating in "ethnic minority areas" to "limit collection of local *dân công*" so as to avoid "troubling the people" and damaging their livelihoods.[11] As General Giáp noted, however, relying on labor from afar formed a human freight train and multiplied provisioning requirements, generating logistical nightmares. Quantifying labor, therefore, was a matter of strategic interest and political sensitivity. So, how many dân công participated in the Northwest Campaign? How many were, in fact, local?

Answering these questions was and remains tellingly uncertain. Although planners estimated that 35,000 dân công would be necessary in the Northwest Campaign, they miscalculated the manpower actually required. By how many is still an open question. Official military histories state unequivocally that the campaign ultimately required a total of 194,000–200,000 dân công performing 7 million workdays. Yet these central secondary sources diverge sharply from primary sources, especially local ones—none of which reach agreement. In January 1953, the Ministry of Labor issued two reports on dân công that enumerated a campaign total of 54,449 dân công, including 1,000 locals from Nghĩa Lộ, and 490,041 workdays overall. Weeks earlier, in late December, delegate Mỹ gave no sum total but confirmed the Nghĩa Lộ figure, added another 3,000 from Sơn La, but "still did not know numbers" from Lai Châu. Meanwhile, Commissar Kháng and the Northwest Party Committee praised the campaign's 65,000 dân công and 5 million workdays, then added another 9,000 dân công from unspecified "newly liberated areas." In March 1953, the Party Committee reported a campaign total of 8,412 dân công from "free zones" in Yên Bái, Lào Cai, and Mộc Châu, then added another 16,421 "counted" as of January from similarly unspecified but possibly different "newly liberated areas." Finally, in October 1954, the Northwest Administrative Committee referred to 8,800 campaign laborers as a "target" and repeats the sum total of 16,421.[12] Which figures count the same people? Where were the zones of recruitment? When were the counting periods? Why do different agencies offer different amounts?

The point here is not to figure out fully and forever the most accurate or precise figures about a vital strategic resource, namely, transportation labor. Nor, for that matter, is the goal to resolve variable weights and measures once and for all. Rather, it is the range of and reasons for inaccuracy that are significant. Miscalculations matter too. Indeed, the institutional uncertainty and its underlying causes—visible in conflicting numeric data—demand analytical attention.[13] Across military, civilian, and party agencies, quantitative estimates of labor participation vary by a factor of four and of total duration by a factor of fourteen. Which counts are equivalent, additive, or subtractive remains unclear because, at the time, the DRV had no institutional consensus on fundamental accounting parameters.

Still yet to be delimited was a realm of accounting that governed the temporal and spatial boundaries of when and where people and things got counted. Different institutions generated independent counts, pointing to bureaucratically isolated accounting measures and suggesting what Mitchell aptly calls "political rivalry . . . affecting the growth of statistical knowledge."[14] Such bureaucratic rivalries indicate contests within the state itself, the outcome of which not only determined which agency's accounting would count above others but influenced what kind of knowledge would characterize Vietnam's population and territory.

Early miscalculations initiated a process of state learning. Not lost on DRV decision makers, awareness of the state's limited capacity to know society drove integrated processes of bureaucratization, centralization, and standardization. As the People's Army grew to some 250,000 regular soldiers in 1953, DRV elites developed a formidable logistical system to count and account for state claims on society, particularly military provisions and transportation labor. Members of the vanguard armed themselves with statistics and built institutions to process the data. In an iterative process, counting resources and accounting for their usage enabled them to plan and execute the next military campaign with increasing effectiveness which, in turn, expanded the people and space under their control. As the First Indochina War reached its peak phase at Điện Biên Phủ, these logistical measures equipped the army to secure even the most contested territory.

STATE LEARNING

"The logistics work we did for the Northwest Campaign bore useful experience," recounted General Giáp of planning in 1953 for what became the epic Điện Biên Phủ Campaign. He knew of what he spoke. Born in 1911, Võ Nguyên Giáp was a student and teacher of revolution before becoming one of its most accomplished practitioners. During French colonial rule in the 1930s, he studied European warfare and Vietnam's rural society with the pioneering geographer Pierre Gourou. Studying Napoleon Bonaparte, he must have learned the French general's famous dictum that "an army marches on its stomach." Studying conditions among the peasantry, he articulated a radical critique of colonial rule and how to mobilize the countryside against it. Then, as a history teacher in Hanoi, he delivered inspired lectures on the French Revolution.[15] He had already begun to turn the tables on his metropolitan masters: extending equality, fraternity, and liberty to colonial subjects would motivate an army and inspire a people. During World War II and through the Indochina Wars, Giáp applied himself to practical strategic problems, like logistics, but never stopped educating himself and others.

He continued learning in and from the Northwest Campaign, then shared the lessons with other DRV political and military leaders. His memory of planning in 1953 touches on a significant moment in state learning—a longer iterative process through which elites developed institutional capacity to wage war, mobilize resources, and secure territory on a grand scale. As military advances rolled back rival claimants to territory, administering this space opened access to new land and labor resources. Mobilizing agrarian resources, in turn, fed back into logistics, enhanced force mobility and, in the general's words, "bore useful experience." Generated in this way, knowledge of people, things, and how to enlist them informed military and civilian elites working to centralize state power and expand its reach through population and territory.

Prior campaign experiences in and around the Black River region taught Giáp and other Vietnamese officers how to balance formidable logistical equations, if not fully solve them. Foremost among others, the problem of military supply factored not only armaments and distance but also, and more vexingly, the consumption of provisions not just by soldiers but also by dân công porters. On a per-porter basis, longer distances meant carrying more food and fewer munitions, increasing again the number of porters necessary for supply. Schooled in "lessons" drawn from the winter 1951–52 Hòa Bình Campaign, cadres in the fall 1952 Northwest Campaign refined labor recruitment and organization but, as discussed above, still failed to provide reliable statistics. According to a quartermaster captured by the French, the spring 1953 Upper Lao Campaign required an aggregate ninety-five thousand porters to supply two People's Army divisions. The latter two experiences in particular furnished useful but worrisome data. Out of 5,000 tons of rice collected in the northern Red River Delta and Thanh Hóa, only 410 tons arrived at the Cò Nòi depot some four hundred kilometers on.[16] Of the rice meant for soldiers, porters ate an astonishing 92 percent. In short, the supply calculus pivoted on the distance between military front and sites of labor and food procurement.

By accumulating this numerical data and practical experience, DRV elites advanced the problem of logistics to a character of calculability. Having formulated a discrete statistical object, in other words, they aimed to solve it through government policy. Most important, their solution gave birth to a powerful new institution and reoriented supply strategies toward local resource collection. At its Fourth Plenum in January 1953, the VWP's Central Committee established the Front Supply Council (Hội đồng Cung cấp Mặt trận) in order to "guarantee supplies for the military," with a "special emphasis on transportation work." Appointing Vice Prime Minister and Politburo member Phạm Văn Đồng as the council's chairman prioritized military supply in civilian affairs and embedded the task among existing line agencies. Empowered to "work directly with all interzones, all provinces" by creating subcouncils in each military and civilian unit, the council's structure streamlined DRV territorial administration and strengthened the party's position overall.[17] Consolidating central control over territorial units enabled a shift in supply strategies away from distant but secure sources in the Việt Bắc and Thanh Hóa toward the near but still contested Northwest Zone.

The government's Front Supply Council worked closely with the army's General Supply Department to implement a policy, called "mobilizing logistics in place," that would distinguish the Điện Biên Phủ Campaign from its predecessors. General Giáp credits the policy to the department's director, Trần Đăng Ninh, who sought to reduce the staggering consumption rates observed in earlier Black River campaigns. Known for his sangfroid, analytical capacity, and sharp intelligence, Ninh, who was born near Hanoi in 1910, was held prisoner by the French at the Sơn La Penitentiary—where Lò Văn Mười was a guard—before breaking out in 1945 and assuming the directorship in 1950. In recognition for his role in the pivotal autumn 1950 Borderland Campaign, which opened the door of the Việt Bắc base area to Chinese aid, he earned membership on the VWP's Central Committee. In this capacity, he served alongside another former Sơn La prisoner and now party secretary Trường Chinh, with whom he established the General Department's civilian counterpart. In spring 1953, while campaigning in northern Laos just over the border from Sơn La and Lai Châu, Ninh began to gather provisions locally, both inspiring the policy shift and equipping him with experience in virtually identical ecological and social conditions.[18] Ninh's influence outlasted his own short life: after he fell ill in 1953, his deputy handled the Điện Biên Phủ Campaign's daily operations. Ninh died in 1955, the same year his agency was renamed the General Logistics Department.

If wars make states and states make war, as sociologist Charles Tilly famously argued, then governing military logistics played an outsized role in the Vietnamese case. Logistical organizing and bureaucratic learning centralized DRV state power and expanded its reach in relation to economy and society. Cross appointments in nominally "military" and "civilian" logistics agencies coordinated decision making among a small elite, glossed as "the Center" (Trung ương), and entrenched their power in relation to mass society. Operating over and through territorial administration, the elite's bureaucratic capacity spread to virtually all sectors of the rural economy. When the party secretary charged the council in July 1953 with guaranteeing food, transportation, and dân công for the military, the orders emphasized new accounting measures called "unified cost-benefit management." The measures sought to rationalize resource counts and collections already under way, especially the agricultural tax and labor recruitment. By managing resources rationally and increasing production overall, the secretary aimed for nothing less than "*to construct the material infrastructure of resistance and statemaking.*"[19]

The bureaucratic-military project advanced in waves of state learning, logistics operation, and resource appropriation. "The work of supplying the front will gradually become normal," the secretary advised party members coordinating northern Vietnam's "supply apparatus" in November 1953. He required them, after each operation, "to devote time to summarizing and learning from the experience."[20] Local institutions funneled statistical data to the DRV's central command which, in turn, used this knowledge to increase bureaucratic efficiency, scale, and discipline. As the knowledge loop tightened, the iterative process expanded spatially and intensified socially, ratcheting state resource claims steadily upward. As effective as it became in generating labor and provisions, however, the calculative way of knowing was always abstract, partial, and impersonal. By discounting local effects, officials were caught by surprise after May 1954 when Black River peoples went hungry and blamed the DRV.

Transportation was a key to territory. While French counterinsurgency strategy strove to inhibit upstream-downstream movement, Vietnamese revolutionary strategy aimed to improve road and river infrastructure and facilitate traffic into the mountains. In spring 1953, a team of high-ranking cadres traveled to the Northwest Zone to study its terrain, conduct topographical surveys, and learn how to realign its economy with defense priorities.[21] The cadres' findings demonstrate how friction of terrain, not distance alone, presented geographic obstacles requiring heavy manual labor and technical expertise to overcome. Trained as an engineer, the minister of transportation, for example, assessed the Black River route by locating dangerous falls and rapids, identifying them by name, counting traffic bottlenecks, detailing vessels by type, number, and tonnage, finding caves to shelter by day, and measuring distances by nights of travel. Such practical quantitative spatial knowledge facilitated ongoing logistics operations serving the Upper Lao Campaign and the Nà Sản front. It also informed preparation for the 1953–54 campaign, particularly the master transportation plan for northern Vietnam, written by none other than Trần Đăng Ninh. Aiming to secure territory by compressing time and space, his plan deployed dynamite and hard labor as what scholars call "distance-demolishing technologies."[22]

Carved into mountains and blasted out of riverbeds, new transport infrastructure bound the Black River region to downstream Vietnam and, in the process, surmounted or destroyed geographic obstacles that had long slowed traffic in goods, ideas, and people. Ninh's General Department flattened rivers, constructed roads, and established a system to move supplies along them. South of the Black River, sappers opened a new route on the Mã River by exploding waterfalls with dynamite, smoothing passage from its mouth in Thanh Hóa west into Laos, through Sam Neua, and back into Sơn La. Learning from the experience, army engineers then tamed the Nậm Na River to connect the Điện Biên Phủ front via Lai Châu with China's Yunnan Province, a route known in Vietnamese as the Glorious Line (figure 9).[23]

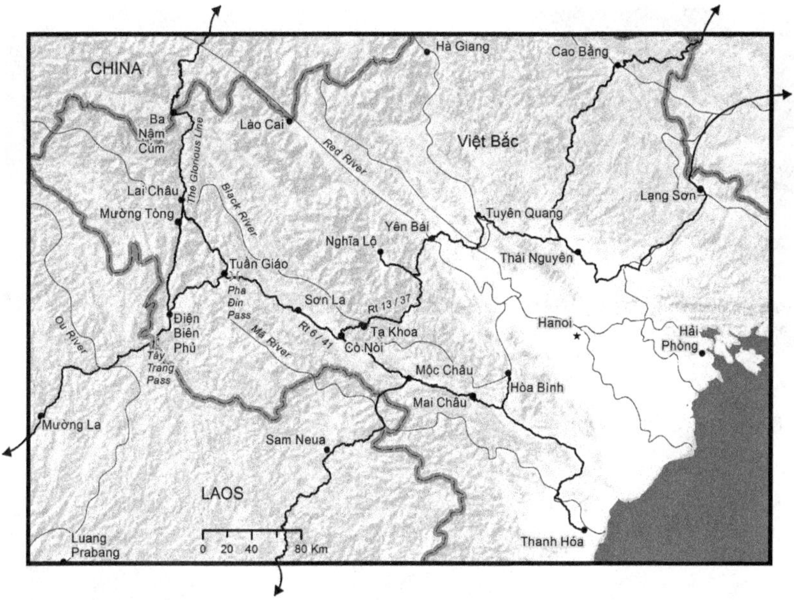

FIG. 9. Map of the main logistical routes to Điện Biên Phủ. (Map by Hannah Reckhow, Amanda Henley, and Philip McDaniel.)

Meanwhile, engineers and dân công workers built roads uphill from three directions (figure 10). From the north, they extended Road 13 across the Black River at Tạ Khoa, linking Yên Bái to Sơn La and intersecting with Road 41 at Cò Nòi. From the east, they lengthened and improved Road 41 from Hoà Bình up to Lai Châu town's doorstep. From the south, they extended Road 15 to link Interzones 3 (Red River Delta) and 4 (Nghệ An, Thanh Hóa) with Road 41 at Suối Rút. The northern road stretched six hundred kilometers from the Chinese border at Lạng Sơn, across Vietnam to Mộc Châu, and over the Lao border to Sam Neua. Adding a spur from Tuần Giáo to Điện Biên Phủ then linked the front by road to Thanh Hóa and Lạng Sơn, enabling supply over distances of six hundred kilometers and eight hundred kilometers, respectively. Along all these long river and road routes (figure 11), the General Supply Department established a system of wharves and depots where they divided transport responsibilities with the Central Front Supply Council and its local branches.[24]

Road and river routes reached beyond Vietnam to funnel aid from allied terrain in Laos and China. If Indochina was a single battlefield,

FIG. 10. Roadwork performed by downstream dân công. (3130/Bộ Ngoại Giao [hereafter BNG]/NAVC 3.)

FIG. 11. Heading upstream with supplies for the front. (3148/BNG/NAVC 3.)

as DRV leaders had already decided, then so too were food resources in Laos fair game for People's Army provisions. After all, Laos was next door to Điện Biên Phủ, its frontier visible from the plain and its landscape cut from the same cloth. Meanwhile, the People's Republic of China provided Vietnam with military aid, including weapons, provisions, advisors, and training—much as the United States did for its own Cold War ally France. The PRC even furnished Vietnam with American artillery captured during the Korean War (1950–53), later turned on the French to devastating effect.[25]

If transport was key to territory, then so too was transportation labor. The logistics of dân công mobilization involved not only institutional coordination but also ideological work and legal regulation, all of which centralized DRV power. In January 1951, the People's Army established a Department of Politics (Cục Chính trị) under its General Supply Department to conduct ideological training and political education among supply officers, cadres, and laborers. By late 1953, under the leadership of Trần Lương (aka Trần Nam Trung), the military subunit had developed an institutional network to propagate state priorities in village settings, educate folk in service obligations, and intensify collection of labor and food.[26] Working in this capacity was cadre Hoàng Công Phẩm, who recruited laborers, supervised their duties, and monitored their morale; his narrative opens the next chapter. Meanwhile, Phạm Văn Đồng exercised his bureaucratic authority as vice prime minister, Politburo member, and head of the Front Supply Council by codifying dân công use and recruitment. The latest labor regulations, signed by him in September 1953 (308-TTg) and amended by the Ministry of Labor a month later (12-LĐ/TTg), formally rationalized and enumerated service requirements.

Emblematic of an emerging character of calculability, the autumn 1953 dân công regulations enabled the statistical calculation of labor that had so far eluded logistics officers and government officials. At their core, the regulations instituted an accounting system to register individual performance according to the workday. "From before until now," explained the Ministry of Labor in its October circular, "there has been no organized way to record and count the labor of *dân công*." The Temporary Regulations of August 1952 (183-TTg), it continued, had no relevant mechanism, causing two problems: first, service durations ranged widely, from "vigilant" workers serving three to four months to "lazy" ones working five to ten days and even extending to problems of "hiding" and absenteeism; second, workers wished to know beforehand how long they were expected to work. As a result, overall labor productivity had stagnated. Now, building on over a year's worth of practical learning, September's regulation (308-TTg) standardized the workday labor unit (*công*) and accounted for the total performed by each person. The system was less simple than it sounds; the standard workday of a pedestrian porter, for example, was a function both of weight carried (twenty to thirty kilograms) and of the distance and terrain covered in one day (twenty to twenty-five kilometers on the flats; fifteen to twenty kilometers in mountains), where distance was deflated if work was by night (fifteen to twenty kilometers flat; twelve to eighteen kilometers in mountains). The transport workday varied again by alternate means of transportation, whether bicycle, automobile, or raft. And the standard varied still more by type of work, including also roadwork and construction.[27] Nonetheless, by counting and recording days worked, the accounting mechanism aimed to certify individual service and generate a paper trail for government inspections.

Far from alleviating a burdensome citizenship requirement, dân công regulations rationalized state labor appropriation in a double sense, both tuning it to territory's calculative logic and legitimating bodily claims nationally. The circular did acknowledge "legitimate aspirations of people" who wished to balance logistics duty with making a living. But the regulations still did not set an upper limit on service duration, working to the benefit of state management, not subject labor. More broadly, and in keeping with the contradictory and tense process of militarization, elites centralized their command of labor power even as they expanded and intensified mass participation. With each territorial advance through the early 1950s, logisticians enlisted more and more people in front supply, enrolling an ever-larger population in the name of nation. Recall that the word for people's laborer, *dân công*, contained its own source of legitimation, as a duty of national citizenship (*công dân*). Defining part of this word as a measurable and objective labor standard thickened its meaning: a polyvalent Sino-Việt particle, *công* means a public or community of equals, work itself, and/or the output of one's efforts.[28] Already embodied, nationalist, and contested, dân công service now incorporated a metric of individual performance, one measured and policed by a centralizing state.

Not just bureaucratic but social as well, the process of state learning gave rise to new everyday experiences and understandings of state power. Just as elites honed a character of calculability into an institutional instrument, so too did the enlisted masses experience the effects of accounting and surveillance tactics. In a letter to cadres and dân công building roads and bridges dated September 1953, President Hồ Chí Minh wrote: "I, along with the Party and Government, will always watch over each of your work." An idiom of surveillance and protection, "watching over" (*theo dõi* or *theo rõi*) captures the ambivalent way one feels when an authority figure, like a policeman or parent, follows one's movements closely, even from afar.[29] Registering citizen labor enabled bureaucrats to do just that. Built on a Confucian idea of state that personifies complex power relations in the form of a caring uncle or benevolent policeman, the idiom of watchfulness extends "his" reach, particularly when out of sight but not out of mind.

Generated by the bureaucratic use of calculative technologies, the intended effect of watchfulness disciplined individual behavior in performance of collective work. Party secretary Trường Chinh, for example, mandated that all provincial party officers "watch over on a daily basis, to lead bridge and roadwork based on plans and careful inspections."[30] Unified cost-benefit management and workday accounting, among other institutional tactics, enabled Vietnamese elites to keep one eye fixed on subordinates and subjects. As such, counting human and material resources and accounting for their use bureaucratically did more than boost labor productivity, increase logistics capacity, and expand transportation infrastructure. Counting and accounting also empowered supervisors to police cadres, soldiers, and peasants and to punish "lazy" or reward "vigilant" ones among them.

SPACES OF MILITARIZED DEVELOPMENT

Whereas building roads and transporting things enlisted labor, generating provisions enrolled land and food as well. Making and moving supplies to the front located resource contests in the military's rear, a space rapidly becoming national territory. Both tied to the social organization of violence, territory and logistics employ similarly calculative logics and forms of technical knowledge, especially mapping and accounting. Although geographers tend to distinguish and sequentialize spaces of territory from logistics—the first in terms of law, sovereignty, and borders; the second in terms of flows, infrastructure, and networks—their argument does not always work on the ground. Making Northwest Vietnam in a time of war not only drew on the same technical logics but compressed the two spaces together in line with the national geobody.[31] Working in tandem with military conquest, mobilizing logistics constituted Vietnamese territory in the Black River region.

Encoded in language and embodied in practice, the geobody permeates Vietnamese-language understandings of military logistics and national territory. In Vietnamese, as in English and French, rear (*hậu phương*) and front (*mặt trận*) are bodily distinctions projected onto space secured through force. Etymologically, the Sino-Việt root for rear (*hậu*) means "back of, after, behind," and is defined bodily in relation to the older Mon-Khmer root for front (*mặt*), meaning, simply, "face," that is, the front of one's head. In military usage, the front advances while the rear remains behind; the distinction maps onto forward, strategic decision making backed by civilian support in the rump or hind part. Significantly, the *hậu* particle also forms the root of logistics (*hậu cần*) or the work of military supply and transportation. This particle, then, constitutes words for a body part, a territorial place, and a circulatory system. Lest the rear be thought of as merely posterior, or an afterthought, to an anterior front, Asian revolutionaries advanced an alternate view. Mao Tse Tung, whose lessons and experiences in the Chinese Civil War inspired Vietnamese revolutionaries in the 1950s, emphasized the strategy of securing rural spaces by likening the rear to one's buttocks, as somewhere to sit down, rest, and regain strength.[32]

In spring 1953, development emerged in the Northwest Zone as a military provisioning strategy and a lasting regional agenda for the national economy. Far from an anti-politics machine, development in and of revolutionary Vietnam was explicitly political. The timing alone of development, originally articulated in support of military campaigning, suggests how state-organized violence enabled intervention in agrarian economies and constituted national politics through the resource struggles that ensued. In March, citing the VWP's Fourth Plenum that had founded the Central Supply Council two months earlier, the Northwest Zone Administrative and Resistance Committee pronounced a financial and economic policy "to integrate mass mobilization with boosting and rationalizing production."[33] Invoking the verb "to develop" (*phát triển*) for the first time, the committee members indexed a new idea of progress predicated on a transitive, subject-verb-object relationship, as in "State develops society." They also set the idea of development as such on its way to becoming a desirable thing.

A militarized idea of progress, development framed a pressing material and ideological project that targeted the rear. The regional administrators aimed "to develop productive infrastructure" broadly by "raising popular livelihoods" in the wake of colonial rule and, "particularly, by restoring agriculture and rebuilding livestock in order to provide people with enough to eat and wear and to contribute to the resistance." The materialist project worked in hand with an ideological message: ordered to "lead thought" (*lãnh đạo tư tưởng*) among the masses, cadres "must realize the significance of improving people's lives" while "guaranteeing military supply." The mechanism for obtaining provisions under the "integrated" military-economic-financial agenda was the agricultural tax, to be widely implemented in autumn.[34] In short, state-led development sought to increase farm output and legitimate taking a hefty bite.

More than simply an elite political project, however, development was and remained also a contested social process, one that articulated in unexpected ways with complex histories and other policies.[35] With no hint of irony, the March 1953 orders announcing new forms of development invoked the old discourse of "vast area, sparse people." Invoked by local Tai cadre Lò Văn Mười four years earlier to ease supply duties on local folk, the discourse now justified the expansion and intensification of state claims. In the late 1940s, Kinh-Việt guerilla fighters had established political-economic relations with local Tai peoples through the revolutionary exchange, trading salt for supplies and, in the process, fostering anti-colonial sentiment and training local cadres. But the informal exchange could not equip a regular army, ushering in new provisioning strategies, especially mobilization in place, coeval with the emergence of central planning, rational accounting, and economic development.

Part of a larger shift toward governing people and things through territory, strategic economic planning organized upstream-downstream relations by way of sovereign, homogenous, bordered space. Movement of goods and ideas continued much as before, both recapitulating older patterns of reciprocity built around trade in scarce material goods, especially salt for food, and rehearsing ideas of progress as a source of DRV legitimacy. Now, focused state learning enabled planners and supply officers to join the calculative logics of territory and logistics, generating a ratchet effect on local resources. Not only would claims intensify on peoples and places already enrolled, particularly Tai peoples in the valley muang, claims also expanded to include peoples and places hitherto spared, particularly Hmong and Dao swidden cultivators in the highlands, effectively filling in the cartographic gaps between the scattered muang and ensnaring their forest fallows and fields in lines of district and supply. All of these diverse peoples, positioned within Vietnamese space and territorial administration, were to be "watched over" and "carefully inspected" by cadres assigned to supervise their work.[36] As a result, the DRV state would climb the hills with force during the Điện Biên Phủ Campaign, enrolling new subjects in pursuit of supplies and territorial control. Enthusiasm and support as well as anxiety and hunger would all follow in equal measure.

As much a matter of practice as policy, local provisioning and economic development in the Black River region ran up against a landscape of places and things constructed to thwart just such claims. Overcoming landscape features required not only new roads and bridges, smoother rivers and flatter peaks but also, on a smaller scale, the standardization of things to render them countable and bureaucratically legible. "The problem of statistics is an important problem for the leadership of work," opens a July 1953 Ministry of Agriculture statement on a project to quantify production, "and particularly so regarding the work of *economics and finance*." Only by instituting statistical standards could the powers of accounting, and their centralizing effect, bring produce, livestock, and land to bear fruit. As a result, and in line with the aims of central planning and economic development, the DRV state led a march to calculability, opening a new front in what scholars call a powerful but ever incomplete "conquest of illegibility."[37]

Bemoaning diverse measures, tardy cadres, and allegedly "backward" peoples who may have wished simply to dodge state claims, the Ministry of Agriculture positioned itself as the vanguard agency in the central government's push to count rural things and account for their usage. Much as the Ministry of Labor standardized labor accounts through the workday measure, the Ministry of Agriculture instituted universal and standard metrics for all things made in or on Vietnamese soil, upstream and downstream alike. No longer would cadres record land and its products by such diverse units as "*mẫu* squared, stomach *mẫu*, quintal, barrel, estimate, stamp, etc.," but instead by the hectare and the ton, meter and kilogram. Any and all standing livestock would be measured by the head.[38] These same measures, not coincidentally, still structure narrative recounting of the role logistics played in the eventual Điện Biên Phủ victory.

Performing multiple roles and integrated tasks, cadres in the field endeavored to militarize Northwest Zone spaces and bend the region's economies to strategic advantage. They propagated not just seeds, stock, and techniques but also measures to facilitate agricultural development and mechanisms to appropriate a share for military consumption. Acting as extension agents and supply officers, cadres in spring-summer 1953 encouraged farmers to "produce enough meat to eat and supply the army," to plant vegetable gardens "in order to eat and sell a portion to the army" and, after the fall harvest, to "develop spring vegetables" and "develop a second, rapid-yield rice crop" in early 1954.[39] Acting as translators, cadres reported on outcomes in kilograms, a metric their superiors used to calculate local provisioning capacities.

Through all these activities, cadres embodied roles akin to stern teacher and kind policeman, acting as someone empowered explicitly to "watch over" production and reproduction, including family planning. Policing all manner of rural life, or at least aiming to do so, imparted a nationalist lesson. "From the moment of planting to harvest time," cadres prepared the ground for taxation in 1953 by teaching people "the idea of contributing one part to the resistance."[40] Whether people complied with these state claims, and to what effect, is the subject of following chapters. For the moment what matters is how such claims were officially counted, accounted, and recounted and the centripetal forces they generated.

PREPARATION AND CONTINGENCY

Vietnamese logistics planning adapted to manifold contingencies, not the least of which was France's forceful effort to regain colonial territory.

Renewing the imperial commitment to Indochina in May 1953, French military and civilian leaders promoted a new military commander, Henri Navarre, and supported his strategic assessment. Backed by the United States, the so-called Navarre Plan sought to recover the military initiative in order to negotiate a political settlement from a position of strength.[41] Backed by the People's Republic of China, DRV leaders accepted the military challenge, socialized logistics demands, and anticipated a quick victory. Neither side's plan worked as intended. Through it all, preparing to do battle could not predetermine the battle's outcome but bore lasting effects nonetheless, binding the Black River region ever more tensely to Vietnam.

Aiming to smash the Navarre Plan, the DRV Politburo met in September 1953 and ordered the People's Army, once again, to march into the Black River region. Chinese advisors had provided them a copy of the French plan, complete with maps. After reviewing it, the Vietnamese elite amended preparations for the winter/spring offensive. Chaired by President Hồ Chí Minh, the Politburo decided to avoid French strength in the Red River Delta and instead spread out and weaken French defenses by launching another operation in the Northwest Zone. Led by General Giáp and Chief of Staff Hoàng Văn Thái, the People's Army set its sights on Lai Châu, then lightly defended by two thousand French and federation troops. Aiming to topple the Tai Federation, army leaders sought to control all Vietnamese territory bordering China and join forces with Pathet Lao allies to the west.[42]

Marching back into the Northwest Zone meant that logistics preparation there particularly and across northern Vietnam more broadly reached a fever pitch in autumn 1953. Facing squarely the problem of supply at a distance, the People's Army relied on the integrated civilian and military supply agencies to "mobilize logistics in place," or recruit labor and gather provisions in proximity to the front. Securing food locally, according to policy architect Trần Đăng Ninh, trimmed dân công consumption rates and reduced the amount of labor necessary for transport. Nonetheless, central VWP orders issued on 9 November expanded the military's rear beyond the Northwest Zone—east to the Việt Bắc base area, down to the Red River Delta (Interzone 3), and through Thanh Hóa and Nghệ An (Interzone 4)—and charged people in this territorial arc with the duty of front supply. Warned the orders, "The duty is about to be very heavy."[43]

In terms of provisions, the Central Front Supply Council ordered each province and interzone to collect specific quantities and types of food while diffusing state ideas and lowland cultural practices. Rice and meat were a priority overall while, in the Northwest Zone, central planners placed special emphasis on rice milling, tax collection, and salt distribution. Sixty millers traveled upstream to teach the "ethnic people," according to the army's chief of staff, to husk and pound rice "like downstream people."[44] Cultural habits and social categories, in other words, marched in hand with development and military force. The agricultural tax remained a mechanism to learn about subjects, gauge rural production, and appropriate rice. Collected, milled, and stored at depots, rice became rations at storehouses, subsequently distributed by quartermasters (figure 12). Additional salt shipments buttressed legitimation work and turned standing livestock into preserved meat. Transforming farm capital and household food into portable provisions both provided the

FIG. 12. Rice storehouse for military rations. (3114/BNG/NAVC 3.)

army with logistical supplies and constructed the institutions and relations of territorial rule.

In terms of transport, the army's General Supply Department oversaw road and river work and, in line with state accounting measures, sought to increase manpower efficiency. What the civilian council did with provisions, the military department did with labor: working with provincial and interzone units to marshal resources and inculcate ideas of civic duty and rightful state management. "The work of *dân công* is political work," stressed the November orders, encouraging cadres to perform as leaders and paragons, "awakening the masses to follow." Adhering to Confucian principles of emulatory learning and parental responsibility, cadres were to act not just as foremen supervising labor but as teachers instructing labor and ethnicity laws and parents providing food, shelter, and medicine. Above all, continued the orders, "do not let the enemy cut off communications." Along supply lines, conducting regular inspections and holding labor in reserve aimed to repair damage from aerial attack and land mines, especially at chokepoints like mountain passes and river crossings. Finally, to "reduce human energy," the order drafted all manner of land and water vehicles. Singled out as the "best" form of transport, pack bicycles (*xe thồ*) offered higher load capacities (sixty to one hundred kilograms) and boosted productivity over pedestrian porters. Campaign photographs featured orderly processions, enshrining individual efficiency before a mass project directed by and for the state (figures 13 and 14).[45]

Calculating and collecting provisions commenced during 1953's autumn rice harvest. The General Department originally called for 7,730 tons of rice, of which 6,060 tons were to be collected mainly in Sơn La and Lai Châu. Working with the Northwest Party Committee to collect rice locally, supply officers hoped to reduce the amount consumed en route. In contrast to the Northwest Campaign, here both the site and means of collection shifted in line with intensifying state centralization, economic rationalization, and mass participation. Under Trần Lương's leadership, the army's Department of Politics promoted a guideline: "Vigilantly mobilizing rice in place is foremost." Unlike a year earlier, when soldiers and cadres had "helped" the peasantry to bring in the harvest, this time a specialized team visited each village to conduct assessments and appropriate resources. In so doing, the teams educated cultivators

FIG. 13. Dân công crossing a bridge in formation. These camouflaged porters came from French-occupied areas of northern Vietnam. Such pontoon bridges, built of bamboo, crossed streams and rivers at multiple points. (3142/BNG/NAVC 3.)

FIG. 14. Dân công with pack cycles in Thanh Hóa. Note the two steering poles: one horizontal in the back and a vertical one equipped with a brake. Pushing these modified cycles enabled dân công to carry much heavier loads than was possible on foot, increasing transport efficiency per person. (3181/BNG/NAVC 3.)

in the campaign's official meaning—"to liberate the Northwest's compatriots through all-out resistance"—and secured commitments to pay the agricultural tax, perform dân công duties, and increase production.[46]

The French military struck first at Điện Biên Phủ. On 20 November 1953, French paratroopers dropped from the sky and over the next two days reoccupied a town on the Lao border lost to the People's Army just a year earlier. They set fire to the Mường Thanh plain, dug into its earth, improved the airstrip, and turned hilltop pastures and valley fields into fortified garrisons. In addition to elite paratroop units, the Expeditionary Forces hailed from across France's global empire, from Algeria and Morocco as well as Vietnam, and harbored former Nazi soldiers in the Foreign Legion. On 23 November, they welcomed a Tai battalion from the Tai Federation's capital at Lai Châu commanded by President Đèo Văn Long's son-in-law. The battalion's withdrawal foreshadowed the final French abandonment of Lai Châu just two weeks later. On 8 December, the president himself, his family, and a troop of dancers left on a Boeing C-47 for Hanoi. Đèo Văn Long died in France several years later.[47]

A logical extension of the Navarre Plan and a strategic error of grand proportions, locating the air-land base at Điện Biên Phủ aimed to capture a gateway to Laos, concentrate strength, and lure the People's Army to its destruction. French military planners drew inspiration from the defense of Nà Sản, an airfield where their forces had regrouped in face of the Northwest Campaign, fended off repeated assaults, and airlifted safely back to Hanoi in August 1953. This time, they hoped to draw the People's Army to a fortified airbase, counterattack, and destroy its main force. Confident in their capacity to resupply the remote site by air, it was unthinkable to French planners that the People's Army could do the same over land.[48] But developing Vietnamese territory in the military's rear would make all the difference.

In addition to logistical miscalculation, French strategy mistakenly banked on local support from and for the Tai Federation. Ironically, locating a large military base in Điện Biên undermined the federation's remaining prestige in two ways. First, French planners overlooked historic rivalries between the Luang Prabang court and the Đèo family in Lai Châu. In fact, protecting Luang Prabang's flank came at the expense of Lai Châu, both subordinating the federation to French interests in Laos and exposing its capital to attack. Second, many Tai and Hmong residents of Điện Biên harbored hatred for the Đèo family, especially after a year or more of successful anti-colonial organizing by DRV cadres and guerilla soldiers.[49]

Dropped from the sky, French officers, soldiers, and logisticians would meet their Vietnamese counterparts on the ground. On December 6, the Politburo approved the General Command's Winter/Spring Plan.[50] Led by General Giáp, the main force once again crossed the Red River and marched upstream to the Black River region. The Điện Biên Phủ Campaign had begun. After toppling the Tai Federation and securing Lai Châu in December, soldiers in a branch of the People's Army launched a diversionary attack into Laos before regrouping on the heights above the Mường Thanh plain and surrounding their adversary. And then they, too, dug in.

Despite all the central planning and local preparation, DRV elites did not foresee a crucial contingency. Round-the-clock flights supplied the elite French Expeditionary Corps with American tanks and artillery as well as bulldozers and barbed wire to fortify their positions. By late January 1954, it became increasingly clear to General Giáp that his troops were still not ready to attack the bristling "porcupine" defenses nestled so firmly in the Mường Thanh plain. Worse, only days before the planned date of attack on 25 January, Giáp received notice that French intelligence had learned his plan's particulars, including its schedule, and knew that his forces still lacked enough rice for sustained combat. True to the Navarre Plan, the French planned a massive counterattack that promised to wipe out the People's Army's main force units. So, on the eve of attack, General Giáp changed his mind.[51]

After a sleepless night spent "waiting for the sky to hurry towards morning," General Giáp resolved to implement "the hardest decision of my entire life as a commanding officer." He decided to delay the battle's opening. In consultation with Chinese advisors and Hoàng Văn Thái of the Front Command, he shifted strategy from "fast attack, fast victory" to "steady attack, steady advance."[52] Changing tactics from rapid assault to protracted fixed-position warfare meant, also, that logistical demands skyrocketed.

During the period of extended preparation, General Giáp settled into a bunker at Mường Phăng, located high above the plain and dug into a forested mountain, where he solidified the international and local alliances providing his army with crucial tactical and logistical support. In early February, the Front Command celebrated the Lunar New Year (Tết) with two key allies. Wei Quoging of the Chinese Military Advisory Team shared documents from the People's Liberation Army on lessons learned in Korea regarding tactics for siege warfare. The Chinese also delivered 37-millimeter anti-aircraft guns and 105-millimeter howitzers, the latter just captured from the U.S. Army in Korea. Just as significant but often overlooked by scholars, local Tai power broker Lò Văn Hặc led a delegation of Tai, Hmong, and Dao compatriots who expressed their resolve to fight alongside the People's Army.[53] After the battle, Lò Văn Hặc would climb to the top of the DRV's regional administration.

The strategic delay enabled the People's Army to maximize the newest weapons in its arsenal. By digging artillery and anti-aircraft guns into the mountains ringing the Mường Thanh plain, the People's Army leveraged the local terrain to concentrate firepower on the valley below. Although the cannons ultimately tipped the balance of forces, deploying them added again to the military's civilian labor requirements. Some six hundred trucks, mostly Soviet Molotov and some American Dodge, towed the cannons to a depot near Mường Phăng where special teams literally picked them up and pulled them into position. Weighing in at about five tons, just one 105-millimeter howitzer required a team of five hundred soldiers and dân công using block, tackle, and chock to maneuver slopes as steep as sixty degrees. There were at least twenty-four cannons of this type alone. Deadly accidents were common. Furthermore, transporting artillery pieces from afar and moving them into position required even more infrastructure, both to widen switchbacks on Road 41 and to blaze another 160 kilometers of artillery roads through the forest.[54]

To achieve tactical advantage, then, the DRV had to mobilize still more labor and provisions. In early February 1954, the Politburo agreed with the Front Command's analysis and instructed Interzone and Regional Party Committees to extend the campaign into the summer and, moreover, to "prioritize above all the mobilization of manpower and materials to supply the front." Extending the campaign temporally multiplied initial provision targets, intensified local mobilization, and expanded the rear spatially if not territorially. The army called for 14,950 tons of rice, doubling its initial request. While still adhering to the guideline of mobilization in place, local production was no longer enough to fulfill overall logistics requirements. The Politburo, therefore, ordered intensified mobilization throughout all of northern Vietnam—the Việt Bắc and Interzones 3 and 4. Logistics collection reached beyond Vietnamese territory too, expanding abroad to China and Laos. By combat's end, the actual total of manpower and supplies had more than tripled the General Supply Department's initial estimates.[55]

On 13 March 1954, full-scale combat began with an artillery barrage that destroyed the French airstrip. At a stroke, the People's Army had severed its opponent's main supply line, rendering logistics a ground game only. The Expeditionary Forces had to rely on airdrops, many of which fell short and wound up feeding and arming the People's Army instead. Over the two-month siege, total French forces, including reinforcements, amounted to some fifteen thousand troops. Surrounding them were an estimated fifty thousand Vietnamese combatants, another twenty-three thousand troops protecting supply lines, and still another six thousand logistics officers, youth volunteers, and medical staff.[56] Some 261,000 dân công laborers, many of them local, hauled supplies, milled rice, and worked on roads. On 7 May 1954, the battle ended with the capture of the French command post, a stunning victory for the People's Army. The outcome catalyzed the peace talks at Geneva, ending the First Indochina War.

COUNTING AND RECOUNTING IN THE REALM OF ACCOUNTING

"The work of supply was one among several decisive factors in victory," declared General Giáp shortly after his army's triumph at Điện Biên Phủ. His French counterparts more than agreed, ruing the Expeditionary Forces' dependence on "*only* one means of transport, *the airplane*," and crediting the People's Army for "winning—on a magnitude it deserved—a real battle of the rear." Military historians concur, stressing the role of logistics—"traditionally defined" as the procurement and transport of military supplies—in determining the war's outcome.[57] But logistics did more than help win the battle that won the war for Vietnam.

A narrow military definition of logistics overlooks all the governmental work done in and on people in the so-called rear, or population in contested territory, who endured the work's lasting material and ideological effects. In the early 1950s Black River region, calculating and collecting military supplies configured relations of state, economy, and society according to the space and logic of territory. This section shows how producing logistics and territory together created a particular knowledge of places and peoples: statistical and spatial, partial but powerful, and predicated on all manner of counting practices. This calculative way of knowing, always abstract and often more precise than accurate, empowered central elites and traced the boundaries of Vietnam's geobody. In a two-way process, generating such knowledge facilitated bureaucratic centralization and efficiency gains which, in turn, enabled central elites to direct their regional counterparts more effectively. Metaphorically, counting and accounting filled the geobody's head with numbers and stimulated regional motion. After the fact, recounting the role of regions in logistics work animated the geobody's parts, displacing agency from people onto abstract space.

In a way befitting the elite's territorial imaginary of Vietnam, recounting logistics began soon after the battle's end, and its effects have lasted into the present. On 10 July 1954, the Central Front Supply Council delivered a conclusive account entitled "Report on the Work of Serving the Điện Biên Phủ Campaign" and promptly dissolved itself.[58] Wielding its institutional powers in the meantime, the council had collected, standardized, classified, and synthesized data from all relevant line agencies and territorial administrative units, both military and civilian. Its authoritative summary recounts, in exacting precision, all the provisions, labor, and means of transportation used in the campaign. Originally presented at a conference held to educate senior officials and officers in the campaign's "lessons" (*bài học*), the report provided curricular materials for another iteration of state learning. Vested with state power and truth value, the synoptic account has since outranked and overwritten virtually any other account. Though the report is stamped "secret" and remained classified as of 2014, its figures on logistics, reified as regional "contributions" (*sự đóng góp*) to nation and army, are recounted to this day as undisputed facts in Vietnamese-language memoirs, government documents, newspapers, commemorative volumes, and scholarly works.[59]

The council's final report begins by delineating the temporal and spatial boundaries that structure its statistical narrative, mapping a realm of accounting onto the geobody. "We began in October 1953," reads its opening lines, "by organizing the apparatus of supply and receiving the army's winter/spring supply duties. Counting until now finishes eight months of work." By counting only the Điện Biên Phủ Campaign proper, the temporal boundaries discount the earlier preparatory and infrastructural work done in situ, without which the outcome would not have been possible. Discounting also any and all supply duty that was, in fact, still ongoing in the Northwest Zone, the report's time frame ends when "the Northwest compatriots were completely liberated, our enemy suffered defeat," and "our nation's resistance stepped into a new era. That is our honor. That is our victory." Here the rhetorical flourish bespeaks more than pride in dealing a death blow to French colonial rule in May 1954. It also identifies an enemy and amplifies a "we-self," discursive features that geobody scholar Thongchai recognized as constitutive of nationalism's territorial imaginary and its attendant teleological history.[60] The spatial frame, in other words, cast a crucial part of national Vietnamese territory in the mold of colonial Tonkin and erased the latter's traces.

Based on these spatial and temporal parameters, the council presented knowledge on society and resources in a new and powerful way. Its report reflects a character of calculability built on years of state learning, institution building, and socializing territorial rule through logistics. When President Hồ Chí Minh stated in September 1953 that he, the party, and the government would "watch over" dân công roadworkers, he articulated an idea of paternalist surveillance and a project of bureaucratic oversight.[61] Ten months later, the idea and project had become embedded in relations and institutions of DRV rule; their effects were legible in the report's tabulated data. Effectively fulfilling the president's orders, the council discussed how the "state apparatus," by stationing supply cadres in "all localities, interzones, and provinces," had functioned to "watch over (*theo dõi*) normal, everyday work." Empowered and informed by years of state learning from logistical practice, the Central Council sat atop an organizational hierarchy constructed to centralize bureaucratic authority, rationalize its practice, and increase efficiency. Its command of local branches had expanded institutional capacity and intensified territorial administration, socializing both through everyday logistics work. The statistics in its report, then, as much record a moment in ongoing state learning processes as measure resources pried from a population mobilized in and for national territory.

Presented in tabular form and reproduced here, the report's most frequently cited data describe food and dân công labor. The council apportioned provisions along two metrics: the amount of supplies mobilized at point of origin and the amount turned over to the military's General Supply Department. By point of origin, the council referred to three zones and one province responsible for amassing the food and labor resources gleaned from resident populations. Reflecting the outcome of state-led standardization processes, units of measure follow the metric ton, head of standing livestock, or workday labor unit (công). Table 2 illustrates the amount of foodstuffs mobilized at the point of origin.

"The numbers . . . are truly great," declared the council. "Not only must a few enemies be horrified," its report continues, "but we must also be surprised. They speak to the great energy of our people." Compared with the army's original request of 7,730 tons, total rice collected had more than tripled to 24,086 tons. Whether this or other figures actually surprised the audience and convinced it of the "revolution's invincible strength" is unclear. It is also unclear why summing across the four regions yields an amount (23,055) less than that reported. Nevertheless, the statement contained a clear warning about Vietnam's military strength, discussed below.

Their magnitude notwithstanding, these figures undercount total actual provisions by adhering to spatial and bureaucratic boundaries. Mentioned elsewhere in the report, water buffalo from Lạng Sơn and Nghệ An are not included in figures from designated rear areas. Moreover, the figure for total rice excludes an estimated two thousand to four thousand tons originating in Laos and China. General Giáp recounted that seventeen hundred tons arrived from China on the Glorious Line alone, the

Table 2

Food supplies mobilized at point of origin for Điện Biên Phủ Campaign (in metric tons)

	NORTHWEST	VIỆT BẮC	ZONE 3	THANH HÓA	TOTAL
Rice	7,310	5,229	1,464	9,052	24,086
Meat	389	454	64	1,700 head	907
Dried foods	—	226	51	640	918
Sugar	—	42	2	18	62
Salt from Zone 3 and State Shops: 266					

Source: Hoi dong Cung cap Mat tran, "Bao Cao Cong tac phuc vu chien dich Dien Bien Phu," 10 July 1954, 1692/PTTg (1945–54)/NAVC 3.

story of which opens the next chapter. This tonnage may not have been included in the council's report because that particular line fell under the aegis of the military's General Supply Department.[62] Whatever the reason, any rice from outside the Vietnamese geobody goes uncounted in the report, serving to buttress the claim that Vietnam alone flexed the revolutionary strength necessary to throw off French colonialism.

Because gross provisions collected on site do not factor the amount consumed en route, a second set of statistics reports what the council delivered to depots managed by the army's Supply Department. The amalgamated statistics gloss a complex—and sometimes acrimonious—bureaucratic division of labor by representing all prior military and civilian efforts as harmoniously unified.[63] Nonetheless, the figures demonstrate the signal role played by local people in the Black River region, categorized as the Northwest. Table 3 illustrates the amount and origin of supplies delivered to the General Department's front depots.

These data inspired the council to single out each territorial unit for praise with respect to its particular "achievement." The Council commended the Việt Bắc for providing bicycles and dried foods, like cured meats, both quickly and beyond its acknowledged capacity. Interzone 3, or the western Red River Delta, earned praise for salt. Thanh Hóa Province provided enormous sums of rice at crucial moments, including another 367 tons delivered to road crews. Above all, the council celebrated the Northwest Zone for surpassing its target, providing almost one-half the military's request (revised upward to 14,950 tons in

Table 3

Supplies delivered to front depots by point of origin (in metric tons)

	NORTHWEST	VIỆT BẮC	ZONE 3	THANH HÓA	TOTAL[a]
Rice	7,143	4,660	1,485	3,994	17,282
Meat	389	394	33	18	834
Dried foods	—	177	51	320	548
Vegetables	700–800	—	—	—	700–800
Salt	—	—	126	16	142
Sugar	—	42	2	18	62

[a] Calculated by author.

Source: Hoi dong Cung cap Mat tran, "Bao Cao Cong tac phuc vu chien dich Dien Bien Phu."

January), and sharply reducing consumption rates among porters. This last point validates the policy of mobilization in place. Of the 9,052 tons of rice collected in Thanh Hóa, for example, only 3,994 tons remained on arrival. By contrast, of 7,310 tons collected in the Northwest Zone, 7,143 tons arrived at front depots. Its people and gardens were also the only source of fresh green vegetables.

In addition to provisions, logistics operation also required mobilizing people for transport and other everyday work. The third and final set of statistics enumerates dân công labor and pack bicycles employed in campaign transport, displayed by point of origin in table 4.

In all, the council counted a total of 261,451 people who worked as civilian dân công laborers in the Điện Biên Phủ Campaign, over five times the number of People's Army combatants. In the Northwest Zone, some 31,818 people performed "short-term duty" over 1,296,078 workdays. If so, then fully 10 percent of the Northwest Zone's population left home at some point over eight months to work on the campaign, averaging 42 days per person.

As planners had hoped and the statistics enabled, iterative state learning practices delivered significant efficiency gains and facilitated timely transport of goods over rugged terrain and despite aerial violence. As usual during the campaign, cadres led training sessions and emulation movements to discipline behavior and organize performance. In addition, when a given period of dân công service ended, cadres recruited the same workers, formed returnees into teams, and assigned them to units. Early results were encouraging: porters pushed pack bicycles with loads from 70–80 up to 300 kilograms; pedestrians bore loads from 15–20 up to 90 kilograms; and cargo crews unloaded trucks faster, from eight

Table 4

Laborers and means of transportation by point of origin

	NORTHWEST	VIỆT BẮC	ZONE 3	THANH HÓA	TOTAL[a]
Dân công	31,818	36,519	6,400	186,714	261,451
Bicycles	—	865	1,712	11,214[b]	13,791

[a] Calculated by the author.

[b] Includes 1,400 bicycles from Nghệ An Province.

Source: Hoi dong Cung cap Mat tran, "Bao Cao Cong tac phuc vu chien dich Dien Bien Phu."

to thirty minutes down to only four minutes per truck. Then, the cadres initiated another movement to increase load capacity per individual, averaging 25–63 kilograms per pedestrian and 100–140 kilograms per bicycle. Pointing to these achievements—what were, literally, staggering loads for each porter—the council underlined "several required lessons to emulate increased efficiency": organize drills, heap praise on and give timely awards to outstanding individuals, and socialize the experience. Lastly, pedestrians and cyclists as well as horses and other pack animals offered a crucial advantage over mechanized transport, namely, the Molotov and Dodge trucks plying the same embattled roads, hairpin turns, and steep slopes. Such admittedly "primitive" forms of transport, notes scholar Nguyễn An, not only maneuvered nimbly around broken bridges and cratered roads but also responded quickly to alarm and sheltered safely from French aerial strafing, bombardment, and napalm.[64]

In addition to desired efficiency gains, the state learning processes generated lasting relations of bureaucratic power based on precise if not always accurate statistical knowledge. In the example below, following the flow of logistical numbers traces the circuits of territorial administration from region to center and back again, revealing a power-knowledge feedback loop. The council's centralized bureaucratic authority empowered it also to stake claims on truth—however uncertain the figures were in fact. In turn, this truth claim reinforces the central government's claim to legitimate rule of regions.

Accuracy aside, the hierarchy of institutional authority determined whose numbers count and, to this day, still influences what knowledge is recounted. In June 1954, a month between the victory and the council's final report, the Northwest Zone's commissar complied with council orders to report the total labor and means of transport supplied by the region's residents in the Điện Biên Phủ Campaign. Commissar Kháng cautioned that the figures on hand were "not yet adequate." He reported, provisionally, that 31,818 dân công laborers had worked 1,296,078 days (*công*), led 872 packhorses, and floated on eighty-three watercraft. Ignoring his caveat, the council in July re-reported these same, precise figures as "summaries" in its final report, endowing the tentative estimates with truth-value and circulating them widely. Then, back in the Northwest, both the Party Committee in October and mass organizations in December *re*-re-reported these same, precise figures, implicitly recognizing the council's report as the final, authoritative source. At that point, it did not matter that local officials had collected other data and issued more accurate reports enumerating even higher amounts of what they, too, called "contributions."[65] What mattered was the central government's role as the final arbiter of "our people's great energy," as though the center alone could speak on behalf of the nation. To the single digits, the council's statistics live on in nationalist, militarist, and scholarly accounts of the military campaign—to the exclusion of more nuanced data collected locally.

Even more than the quantities themselves, the realm of accounting established by the council structures a way of knowing that discounts anything outside its temporal and spatial boundaries. Included in the realm's calculative space-time were four territorial units measured over eight months. Spatially, the realm excludes any other campaigns happening simultaneously, in the Central Highlands, for example, as well as any goods and labor from international sources. Temporally, the realm excludes earlier campaigns in the same place, such as the preceding year's Northwest, Roads and Bridges, and Lao Campaigns, all of which built the infrastructure that enabled the Điện Biên Phủ Campaign's outcome. Nor does the realm account for any goods and labor directed toward the region in mop-up operations ongoing through August 1954, such as Work to Eliminate Bandits and Kill Commandos.[66] Even the few Vietnamese scholars who draw on local sources and report figures diverging from the council's still adhere to the latter's accounting parameters and, by extension, official counting practices. As such, admits a People's Army logistics officer and military historian, the council's system did not count any food that passed directly from locals to soldiers, leading to what the author called "incomplete statistics."[67] Overlooking this informal exchange discounts a form of contribution more pure than the formal taxation used by administrators, registered with the council, and called such.

However necessary clearly defined parameters may have been for purposes of logistical calculation, the nationalization of accounting practices endowed territory with a particular meaning, one that animated the geobody. With sentences like "The Northwest fulfilled its duty" or "The Việt Bắc, for many years the largest campaign contributor, knew how to mobilize carefully," the report's prose endows territorial administrative units with person-like capacities. Enlivening territorial units effected a double abstraction and an inversion of agency: the animated geobody wields people and things known only by numbers, yet these statistics are shorn of all human qualities, like acting on one's own volition. Spatially, privileging Vietnamese regions as the sole supply sources—to the exclusion of Laos and China—threw the territorial borders of Vietnam into sharp relief. Within these borders, building a sophisticated transportation network connected far-flung regions, enabling logistical circulation between the geobody's parts. Knowledge generated along the way concentrated among an elite, headed by the central government, who then directed the geobody's motions. Temporally, treating the campaign as a discrete event, one ending with the enemy's final defeat, drew a liberatory rupture between colonialism and independence. This neat break valorizes a narrative of heroic national resistance against foreign invaders.[68] In so doing, the report's authors endowed "our nation" (*nước ta*) with an uncanny ability to think and stand on its own unaided, as though territorial sovereignty were isomorphic with national self-sufficiency.

Adding military force to the council's nationalist rhetoric armed the geobody with teeth. Behind the inclusive "we-self" lurked another collective invoking the first-person plural, namely a "state-we" that masqueraded as inclusive when, in fact, it signified an exclusive ruling elite in command of a battle-tested army.[69] Not only did the report unify the cadres and officers in attendance against foreign "enemies" (French and, increasingly, American), it also joined them in exacting claims on "our people" (*nhân dân ta*), as if these elites calling themselves the state could or did possess a population bounded nationally. In addition to pride, the elite claim to demonstrably vast quantities of logistics reinforced the People's Army with popular muscle. Referring to the statistics in table 2 and reflecting on General Giáp's statement regarding the decisive role of logistics, the report invoked the state-we to intimidate enemies abroad and spur mass action on the home front. "We realize ever more clearly," reads the report, "that the spirit and duty of supply work must, now and later, pervade collective consciousness." As much prescription as description, trumpeting past achievements while offering lessons for the future enlisted government officials in an ongoing project to militarize society. Anyone challenging this claim to sovereign territorial rule by breaking away and forming a separate republic—an item on the table at the Geneva negotiations—would face an elite willing and able to deploy a fearsome army backed by a formidable rear.

If nothing else, the council's aggregate statistics for labor in the Điện Biên Phủ Campaign reveal an astonishing but underappreciated fact: the number of participants was equal to if not greater than the population of the entire Northwest Zone. At the time, DRV administrators enumerated the zone's population between 300,000 to 320,000 residents. My conservative estimate of total active campaign participants, including soldiers and laborers alike, comes to a minimum of 314,000; the actual number was undoubtedly larger.[70] Even when soldiers and civilians formally demobilized after war's end, the effects of this mass mobilization would last long beyond 1954.

At the climax of the First Indochina War, the Điện Biên Phủ Campaign compressed spaces of logistics and territory through the attendant process of militarization. In addition to its cardinal role in military triumph, logistics work in the Black River region bound it to Vietnamese territory by constructing transportation infrastructure, knowledge of its population, and institutions to exact resource claims. Thus empowered, a central elite was able to marshal resources against a formidable foe, overcome unexpected delays, mobilize still more resources, and ultimately realize the Vietnamese geobody in territory. The victory aligned the military's front with national borders and its rear with sovereign national territory. Yet contingencies ceased neither with the battle nor with the strategic planning that helped win it.

To this top-down tale, the next chapter adds a bottom-up perspective to demonstrate how strategy alone is not enough to explain the production of territory in places with longer pasts and uncertain futures. By zooming down to regional and district scales during the Điện Biên Phủ Campaign, it explores how mass participation in logistics work not only transformed political relations and generated new solidarities but also exhausted participants and emptied their cupboards. Binding the Black River region to Vietnam through mass mobilization raised expectations, depleted resources, and generated unintended consequences. Just below the sounds of planning and the fury of combat, a more contingent story of Vietnamese territory was unfolding on the ground.

CHAPTER 5

Struggles at Điện Biên Phủ

THE LIVED EXPERIENCE OF LOGISTICS built tensions into Vietnamese territory. During early stages of the Điện Biên Phủ Campaign in late 1953, a DRV political cadre reported "increasing tensions" and "many anxieties" and "worries about production" among the people from Yên Bái and Sơn La working on Road 13. After the new road's completion, the central government issued another order to "guarantee traffic flows," requiring a "large number" of workers to return to the construction site all over again. Each wave of labor mobilization followed on the one previous, the cadre wrote, such that many dân công had time neither to rest and recover nor to harvest the last rice crop, plant the next one, and pay the agricultural tax. As a result, "all" of the approximately three thousand farmers turned workers were "anxious" (thắc mắc), a term that indicated political relations as much as affect. The political cadre forwarded complaints from two groups. "The Government liberated places where we built roads, but when we went home to increase production," one group said, "we had to depart again immediately, leaving nothing to eat." Another group argued, "The agricultural tax is heavy but, because we're not at home to increase production, there's nothing left to take for contributions."[1]

Months if not years of heavy logistics labor was extracting a human toll and exposing contradictions from militarization of the Black River region's agrarian economy. Even before the latest push, as of October 1953 and from Sơn La alone, some fourteen thousand Tai (Thái), Mường, Hmong (Mèo), Dao, Tày (Thổ), and Kinh (Việt) people had worked 840,000 workdays, or an average of two months per person, to blaze Road 13. Now, moving earth, making gravel, cutting wood, and cooking camp food added to their exhaustion and kept them from tending home and field. Even the specialists and political cadres who watched over them now clamored for "rest" and to see their families again. Even as these cadres carried out the central government's orders, however, they had "not followed correct policy" aiming to ensure "equitable and fair" service. In practice, dân công service spared the rich and fell heavily on poor and vulnerable people. Recruiting "by rooftop," or on a household basis, yielded many children, the elderly and infirm, and women in the second trimester of pregnancy. Some villagers hid from recruiters while others, back on site, tried to escape or wept openly, begging to go home.[2] Not only had transportation trumped provisions, fulfilling one item at the expense of another on the DRV state's logistics agenda, the state itself was showing deep strains at its territorial interface, exposing a gap between central ideals and priorities on the one hand and local realities and consequences on the other.

Conditions on the Road 13 site indicate broader, more intimate tensions caused by the work of constructing Vietnamese territory in the Black River region at a pivotal moment. Whereas the last chapter emphasized institutional development and elite decision making in the Điện Biên Phủ Campaign, this chapter tells the campaign's story from the bottom up. It excavates negotiations over resources and subject positions to examine the many ways in which DRV state power was deployed and contested on the ground and at home. Analyzing a pivot in Vietnam's postcolonial history, the narrative uses contests over food, labor, and citizenship to investigate everyday territorialization processes in a crucible of anti-colonial warfare and mass mobilization. During the military campaign and ensuing siege on French fortifications, the People's Army of Vietnam pursued a policy to "mobilize logistics in place," relying on local farm households for daily rations, porters, and popular support. The strategy linked the national geobody to Black River bodies in everyday ways but to uncertain effect.

Not simply commandeering resources, cadres socialized the Vietnamese geobody through supply duty, encouraging consent backed by military force. As a result, from late 1953 until the battle's end on 7 May 1954, state and military claims on local resources increased in line with vocal concerns about their social costs, indicating how the home front had emerged in war as a contested site within Vietnam's territorial rear. As armed struggle for national liberation (dấu tranh) approached a turning point, local struggles proliferated over the rightful disposition of people and things, bodies and belongings.[3] When the former ended in triumph, the latter continued and questioned its outcome. Agrarian resources were at the center of embattled political relationships during the First Indochina War's peak phase and would remain a focus of contest and negotiation long afterward.

Like chapters 2 and 3, this chapter, "Struggles at Điện Biên Phủ," zooms down from the logistics of territory to examine resource contests on the ground. Whereas chapter 4 discussed the invention and operation of logistics among elite actors, this chapter opens with a cadre's story to humanize the forceful and lasting relations forged through logistics work in the rear and embedded in Vietnamese territory. Unlike the statistical abstractions generated through governing logistics, a supply cadre's memoir foregrounds the cultural encounters, political negotiations, and ambivalent affect that accompanied the everyday grind of logistics work. The next two sections read lived experience on the home front against DRV military-spatial categories in the "free" Northwest Zone, "recently liberated" Lai Châu, and "temporarily occupied" Điện Biên Phủ.[4] The following and final chapter carries the Black River's story beyond combat's conclusion at Điện Biên Phủ to examine the hidden costs and unexpected outcomes of making Vietnamese territory in the Black River borderlands.

A CADRE'S STORY

In October 1953, Hoàng Công Phẩm was appointed a political specialist in Brigade 325 of the People's Army of Vietnam.[5] Born in 1925 in Thừa Thiên Province, near the old imperial capital of Huế, he had to leave his family behind. When his wife gave birth to a girl, Phẩm's commanding officer denied his request for leave, citing a "very urgent situation," and said, "Let us worry about your family." In December, while a brigade cadre evacuated his family to a safe zone, Phẩm reported to the Việt Bắc base area in Tuyên Quang. He received orders directly from the army's high command: march to the Điện Biên Phủ battlefield immediately.

Over the next year and a half, cadre Phẩm's service in the First Indochina War would trace an arc through Vietnam's endgame with France and, decades later, he would record his experiences in a short but moving memoir. First, he supervised logistics work among civilian porters and monitored morale among soldiers through the battle's end. Then, drawing on his knowledge of French, he negotiated prisoner exchanges and secured former colonial territory, including the port of Hải Phòng in spring 1955. Among a copious literature chronicling events at Điện Biên Phủ in 1954, his memoir offers a vivid contrast to French and American authors preoccupied with guns, tanks, and generals, virtually all of which neglect Vietnamese-language sources. Though Vietnamese authors and sources acknowledge the significance of logistics and local participation in the outcome, the cadre's story complicates official valorizations of "voluntary contributions" and reifications of people as statistics.[6] One of many Kinh cadres participating in the Điện Biên Phủ Campaign, he was one of very few to observe ethnographically his everyday encounters with the region's culturally diverse peoples. His reflections stand out for what he witnessed and enacted, how he felt and remembered. His narrative humanizes ambivalent but lasting relations between Vietnamese officials and Black River peoples. It also records a pivotal moment when boundaries were visibly in the making.

Attached to the army's General Supply Department, Phẩm mobilized transportation labor along the Northwest Zone's border with China. As a political cadre, he worked for the Department of Politics and reported to its head, Trần Lương, whom he described as "very upright and kind-hearted."Phẩm and two other cadres oversaw "the Glorious Line," the newest of three routes funneling supplies to the battlefield. On the first line, from Điện Biên's southeast, porters from Thanh Hóa pushed pack bicycles uphill and along the Mã River. From its east, trucks plied Road 13 back and forth to the Việt Bắc base. When these two sources of supply ran low, the Glorious Line opened a third route with China to receive aid from Mengste, Yunnan (see figure 9 in chapter 4).[7] Along this northern route—which passed through the small town of Ba Nậm Cúm, followed treacherous waterways, climbed high passes, and ended in a depot at Mường Tòng (now, Mường Pồn)—rice and labor moved under Phẩm's watchful eye.

As with other routes into the Black River region, opening passage to China required destroying natural barriers but, unlike those routes, the latter required also the recognition and reconstruction of territorial boundaries. The Glorious Line entered Vietnam at Ba Nậm Cúm along a river from China that, according to cadre Phẩm, was called different names on each side of the border. Known "on our side" by its local Tai name, the Nậm Na River, he writes, was full of rapids and waterfalls that blocked transportation. He therefore spent his first week with a battalion of sappers who, drawing on experience taming the Mã River a year ago, detonated mines on each fall, creating explosions so large that each one "blocked the light of day." After rendering the river navigable, "Chinese *dân công*" delivered rice and bamboo to a wharf at Ba Nậm Cúm, where "Vietnamese *dân công*" fashioned rafts from the timber and floated the rice downstream on the Nậm Na. Although the Chinese and Vietnamese were joined in revolutionary solidarity, what distinguished Chinese from Vietnamese territory for Phẩm was a division of labor based on citizenship. Even while destroying physical barriers to movement, he helped construct an international border through which goods flowed freely—but not people. As was true of the late twentieth-century North American Free Trade Agreement, the bordering states regulated labor differently than commodities. Though goods and weapons flowed "freely" across the Sino-Việt border, labor mobility was sharply restricted: only senior Chinese advisors were present at the Điện Biên Phủ front.[8]

Demolishing physical barriers did not eliminate danger but, in fact, exposed Vietnamese subjects to new bodily perils, including forms of social differentiation. "One thing still troubles me from this period," Phẩm wrote, recalling that one day a raft carrying porters from Phú Thọ Province and two cadres drifted into a cave, where they were all lost. Mourning their deaths, he also wondered whether they had yet been recognized as "martyrs," invoking an official category of commemoration reserved for wartime "sacrifice."[9] Whereas these workers had come from downstream Vietnam and their Kinh identity goes without saying, most of the workers Phẩm supervised were local. For example, a photograph held in Vietnam's National Archives (figure 15) shows men and women

FIG. 15. Unloading a sampan at Lai Châu. The woman hefting a sack of rice wears a brocade common among Hmong peoples in the Black River region. (3113a/BNG/NAVC 3.)

in Lai Châu unloading a boat of rice on its way to feed soldiers on the Điện Biên front; the woman hefting a heavy load wears a brocade on her back identifying her as Hmong. Recalling his own experience with similar people doing similar work, cadre Phẩm described them as Tai and Hmong and ascribed each "a way of life." His encounters with local peoples, recognized as Vietnamese citizens but still somehow different from Kinh people, suggest the ways in which powerful ideas of ethnicity emerged out of the myriad everyday struggles accompanying and enabling warfare.

The Glorious Line ascended the Sinh Hồ plateau and threaded through Hmong villages where, Phẩm recalled, their particular way of life disrupted his logistics routine but led him to accept their different customs. In addition to supervising journeys on the Glorious Line, the cadre also organized meals for workers who portaged rafts and rice around waterfalls. "On one occasion," he wrote, "a Hmong woman *dân công* sat down crying and ceased working. I was perplexed because I did not speak their language, did not understand the reason." Phẩm sought advice from another cadre who "specialized in work in ethnic regions." His colleague explained, "Their custom is that men and women must be together in one place and, when night falls, they sing and dance happily." He continued, "If you force them to live separately from one another, like people downstream, they do not work at all." Even though her reason for being upset was unfamiliar to him, Phẩm nonetheless accommodated what he understood to be her different culture of work. He no longer felt a need to "remind" or "pester" the Hmong workers on his crew—he simply let them finish assigned tasks on their own.

In March 1953, when the People's Army commenced attack on French positions at Điện Biên Phủ, cadre Phẩm arrived at a supply depot where he remembered military valor and everyday life but forgot their historic entanglements. While the battle raged at Mường Thanh, Phẩm awaited reassignment at Mường Tòng. Based on the muang, both place-names indicate long Tai settlement and cultural influence. Located just fifteen kilometers from the battlefield, the depot at Tòng sat astride an old route connecting Điện Biên Phủ to Lai Châu. The route was known in French as the "piste Pavie" (Pavie trail), its name honoring colonial cartographer Auguste Pavie who, in the late nineteenth century, had negotiated with local ruler Đèo Văn Trì to explore the region, map and delimit its borders, and claim it for France. More recently, it was along this route that Trì's grandson by marriage had retreated from Lai Châu town to join French forces in their fortified positions, only weeks before his father's final abandonment of the Tai Federation capital and its subsequent capture by the People's Army. Rather than this Tai heritage, colonial history, and associated place-names, however, cadre Phẩm evoked the more recent traces of the region's Vietnamese conquerors.

Proud to be stationed at a hallowed military site, cadre Phẩm remembered how, in early December, a Vietnamese soldier named Bế Văn Đàn achieved recognition as a martyr and hero. During the disastrous final retreat from Lai Châu, in an operation called "Pollux" by the French, several Tai battalions fought desperate rearguard battles against advancing People's Army forces.[10] Among others, Bế Văn Đàn and another gunner blocked the battalions' retreat at Mường Tòng. Because high shrubs and tall grass obscured the gunner's view, Đàn positioned the machine gun over his head, propped the bipod on his shoulders, and faced the oncoming enemy. Holding his head under the barrel and gripping one hand on each leg of the bipod, Đàn instructed the gunner to fire at will. He died in the battle. Yet, wrote Phẩm admiringly, Đàn's "sacrifice" achieved state recognition befitting a "martyr" and in 1955 earned him the military's highest honor, Hero of the Armed Forces. As such, and unlike the river rafters lost forever in a cave, Bế Văn Đàn's memory lives on. In addition to martial tunes, iconic poses, and internet memes, roads and schools throughout Vietnamese sovereign territory now bear his name.

More prosaically, while awaiting reassignment at Mường Tòng, cadre Phẩm grew acquainted with what he called the "Tai way of life" which, based on another encounter with local women, he described as "far different" from that of the Hmong. Having completed supply duty, he awaited his new post with his comrade on the Glorious Line, Bằng Giang, who was born in Cao Bằng, ethnically Tày (Thổ), and evidently familiar with local custom. On his way to becoming a general in the People's Army, Giang was, according to Phẩm, "vivacious" and "very open." Living close to Tai villages and visiting frequently, the two officers sometimes stayed into the wee hours during local dance routines (*xòe*) featuring young women (figure 16). Phẩm was blissfully unaware that

FIG. 16. Vietnamese photograph of Tai xòe dancers, 1954. On hearing the news of victory at Điện Biên Phủ, these dân công celebrated by breaking into dance on the tarmac. Note the discarded shoulder poles in the background. (3309/BNG/NAVC 3.)

FIG. 17. French photograph of Tai xòe dancers at Lai Châu, 1952. Note the dignitaries in attendance. This image of elite audience, official pomp, and careful stagecraft contrasts with the folk tradition, spontaneity, and informality portrayed in figure 16. (© Aubin/ECPAD/Defense.)

DRV administrators had cited these same routines, when performed before French and Tai military audiences, as typifying the colonial exploitation of women (figure 17).[11] "Tai women are sentimental," advised Giang; "make sure you don't get reprimanded for that!" For Phẩm, who had a family he had not seen in months, the Tai women—whom he called "sweet" and "gentle"—were a source of temptation. "Sometimes they would call out to us very endearingly," he recalled. "Oh, Mr. Soldier! Over here, Mr. Soldier!"

At this point in his narrative, before turning to his duties "watching over" soldiers at the front, Phẩm paused to reflect on his experiences during the Điện Biên Phủ Campaign once he had "returned downstream" to regular work as well as home and family. Presaging his own feelings, he records the lyrics of a still popular song, "Remember the Northwest" ("Nhớ Tây Bắc"). It begins: "I remember always the spring afternoon of separation / The clouds dimming, sliding down the hills / In my heart a dream glows, out in the open." Full of vivid imagery and written in rhyme, the song conjures a land of stunning natural beauty, pretty smiling women, and everlasting nostalgia. Each time he hears the song, Phẩm "remembers a struggle that was arduous but dreamy and romantic." In mid-June 1954, on the eve of departure from "beloved Điện Biên," he and his fellow officers enjoyed one last dance with Tai women, leaving the Kinh men "feeling melancholy." In sum, Phẩm remembers a time of trials and loss, novelty and excitement. He evokes the place in terms of rugged landscape, masculine bravery, and feminine beauty.

In contrast to an official notion of struggle and its abstract, nationalist representations, the cadre's story represents wartime logistics through a series of political-economic negotiations, cultural encounters, and affective responses. By participating in grounded resource contests and observing actual human subjects, Phẩm elucidates the many struggles that accompanied the making of Vietnamese territory in the Black River region. Like the people he supervised, he suffered loss and worried for his family's safety. He, too, built enduring relationships, encountered novel customs, and felt meaningful if ambivalent emotions.

His narrative also captures a powerful moment in the longer making of spatial, social, and temporal boundaries conditioning Black River relations with the larger world and with Vietnam in particular. Phẩm helped sever links to France and build new ones with China. Aided by others, he constructed a semi-porous border between China and the Northwest Zone still recognized as the limit of Vietnam's sovereign territory. Far from a nation rising sui generis to beat foreign invaders on its own, as official narratives would have it, Vietnam benefited from timely international aid to achieve independence and remains a national community in the making, sometimes violently. Within DRV sovereign space, Phẩm wielded power not only to mobilize labor and allocate things but also to sort peoples and place them according to a culturalist logic of ethnicity. For Phẩm, whose embodied Kinh-ness was the norm, the social difference he ascribed to Tai-ness held a gendered allure while that he attributed to Hmong-ness was confusing and, ultimately, inscrutable. Caught within Vietnamese space but not culturally Vietnamese, such forms of social difference—recognized and regulated as ethnicity—came with the territory.

When the military campaign ended, Phẩm—like so many other Kinh participants—returned downstream with new ideas of nation, ethnicity, and territory. Phẩm's experience then remained vivid in memory, bounded in time and subject to nostalgia. The people he met upstream, meanwhile, continued everyday struggles, but not as before. Black River peoples inhabited a world they helped transform, in ways not always of their choosing but nonetheless a product of their labors.

THE NORTHWEST ZONE AT WAR

The experiences of cadres and transportation crews on the Glorious Line, like those on Road 13, indicate how Vietnam's Northwest Zone was a work in progress during the Điện Biên Phủ Campaign. After-the-fact representations of the zone at war, especially those recounted in statistics and derived from the geobody, construct its space abstractly as singular, homogenous, and already part of Vietnam. At the time, however, the region was vast, heterogeneous, and only partially accessible to Kinh peoples. Moreover, its space was violently contested not just by soldiers and statesmen but in everyday ways involving its diverse population. The territorial outcome, therefore, like Vietnam's victory in the First Indochina War more broadly, was highly contingent.[12] It was far from certain whether the DRV would actually secure the Black River region, and success depended crucially on local participation in everyday struggles over logistics.

On the ground, the work of territory and logistics unfolded according to the DRV's reappraisal of Northwest Zone space as free, recently liberated, or temporarily occupied. The spatial categories were based on the length of time since the military defeat of colonial forces and formal establishment of DRV territorial administration. Not simply temporal, the tripartite zonation was explicitly spatio-teleological, expressing an anticipated postcolonial sovereignty regarding territory claimed but not (yet) secured. In effect since the late 1952 Northwest Campaign (see figure 5 in chapter 2), the zonation shifted again in late 1953 to reflect the rapidly evolving politico-military situation, especially the threat posed by the bristling French base at Điện Biên Phủ. Accordingly, the Northwest Zone was now largely free while part of Điện Biên was temporarily occupied. After the victorious People's Army assault in December 1953, northern Lai Châu—including the Tai Federation's former capital—was liberated.[13] In each case, the spatial categories organized strategies of logistics mobilization and generated relations of territorial rule—though not always as planned.

Recently liberated one year earlier, most Northwest Zone territory was officially free in late 1953 even as its population was increasingly policed by security forces and burdened with heavy logistics duties. Encompassing the provinces of Sơn La, Yên Bái, Lào Cai, and southern Lai Châu, the free Northwest Zone fell under the bailiwick of the Northwest Zone Administrative Committee. The committee administered territory and governed population by way of local government in district, commune, and village—units nominally the same throughout DRV territory. But here, in a region of historic Tai rule, these local institutions rationalized muang-based relations of domination, especially control of land and labor. Tai power broker Lò Văn Mười, for example, served on the Sơn La Province Administrative Committee for the duration of the long military campaign. In this role, he strengthened DRV local government not just in valley spaces, as in the late 1940s, but also in the neighboring midlands and highlands. Hitching muang to district and commune combined the capacities of like-minded Tai elites with Kinh cadres, extending their reach to elevations historically beyond either's grasp. So, in July 1953, when the zone's administrators complied with centrally issued guidelines emphasizing "battlefield service" and "mass mobilization" over the next year, they ratcheted up resource claims on Tai peoples and extended them to non-Tai peoples, especially Dao and Hmong swidden cultivators. Threatened by French forces and increasingly radical in agenda, the administrators also wielded new coercive tactics to intimidate opponents and appropriate resources on a grand scale.[14]

The Northwest Administrative Committee's October 1954 summary report, cited above and signed "Lê Trung Đình," discussed tactics used to secure the zone and, intriguingly, gestured to the heroic failure of earlier efforts to do so. The named signatory likely did not refer to any member on the zone's committee. Rather, it seems to hark back to a mandarin named Lê Trung Đình who, seventy years before, had died serving Vietnam's deposed king in a failed movement against French conquest known as Cần Vương.[15] Although the committee's full composition remains an open question for scholars, in 1954 it was still led by VWP-insider Nguyễn Kháng (aka Bùi Quang Tạo) from Thái Bình and featured a regional power broker and rising star from Điện Biên Phủ, Lò Văn Hặc. Indicating less an actual continuity than an imagined one, invoking a bygone royalist rebel cloaked the real authors' identity behind a collective nom de guerre and a cheeky allusion. Nonetheless, the report's authorship and the committee's composition indicate a tight loop between Tai regional elites, Kinh cadres, and DRV leaders joined in anticolonial resistance, territorial pursuit, and ruling ambitions.

Solidarity between regional and central elites notwithstanding, the issue of land reform highlights tense processes of mass mobilization in the Northwest Zone and offers an important point of comparison with Vietnam more broadly. Consistent with central policy to withhold land reform from the Northwest Zone in favor of ethnic unity, state-led social transformation was sharply limited both spatially to free zones and programmatically to rent and interest reduction. The pattern departed from other DRV free zones where land reform would move through these early stages, culminate in land redistribution, and terminate in 1957. As of October 1954, only in Lào Cai and Yên Bái did cadres lead poor and middle peasants of "many ethnicities"—Tày (Thổ), Kinh, Mường, Tai, Nùng, Động, and Chinese—to demand lower payments to landlords. Yet mobilizing 62,248 people, one-fifth of the zone's population, generated mixed results, including "errors" typical of agrarian reform elsewhere and, more particularly, "deep ethnic contradictions." Cadres and peasants publicly tried and convicted sixty eight landlords of "tyranny and wickedness," seized 911 tons of rice, and redistributed the rice to "working people." In the process, they constructed local government and institutions, including Farmers Councils, and trained 209 local recruits to staff them. But the radical recruits entered "old organizations," the elite leadership of which constrained their efforts to challenge entrenched political-economic relations. Furthermore, out of forty-three communes mobilized to reduce rent and interest, landlords in twenty-six communes counterorganized a United Anti-Communist Insurgent Army, a Peasants' Party, and a Catholic Youth Union. Allegedly, the landlords aimed to "topple the local government, destroy policy, and welcome the French."[16]

It is unclear whether the countermovement really aimed to overthrow the DRV, reflected the paranoia of Kinh officials working in unfamiliar places, or represented some combination thereof. Nonetheless, the actions of local elites certainly destabilized local government and demonstrated their ongoing power in face of radical social change. As such, the episode offers three insights into local conditions. First, what the report called "ethnic contradictions" was less about class and ethnicity per se, as though these categories were given and somehow independent of state. Rather, the tension grew out of a contradiction within a DRV state that aimed, on one hand, to maintain local power structures while, on the other, to regulate group identities and transform property relations. In the Northwest Zone, the former took precedence, indicating how DRV state formation incorporated rather than dissolved indigenous ruling relations, especially the muang. Second, given that land reform did not proceed as elsewhere in Vietnam, mass enthusiasm for imminent resource redistribution cannot explain mass support for the war effort. As discussed below, why peasants yielded resources in spite of long hardship involved a complex and variable mix of terror and coercion, legitimacy and consent. Third, Yên Bái was a stronghold of the Vietnam Nationalist Party (VNQDĐ) which, in 1929–30, led a brief and bloodily suppressed rebellion against French rule.[17] At the end of World War II, Việt Minh agents had assassinated leading Nationalists and, since then, DRV security forces had arrested many more. By 1953–54, evidently, party-state leaders still interpreted organized opposition in Yên Bái as a grave threat. The resulting crackdown on landlords and rival mass organizations demonstrates how violence figured in political struggles not just on the front but in the rear as well, emplacing tensions deep in emergent DRV territory.

Largely independent of actual land reform, the language of class struggle spread through the Northwest Zone with the Điện Biên Phủ Campaign, inflecting other forms of state violence that built terror into territory. Acting in the name of mass mobilization and battlefield service, regional leaders prioritized campaigns to "crush traitors to the Vietnamese nation," that is, detain people of suspect loyalty or class background, and "eliminate bandits" (*tiễu phỉ*), that is, destroy French-allied militia units. By year's end in 1953, some 1,609 vaguely defined "traitors" were in jail, relatively few of whom had been tried. Security forces added another 406 in the first six months of 1954. As for so-called bandit elimination, in just one late 1953 operation aiming to secure Road 41 through Thuận Châu, security forces "wiped out" 2,300 "bandits," including five Frenchmen, and captured a thousand rifles, neutralizing a French counterinsurgency cell (*maquis*). Next, they targeted pro-French maquis in Than Uyên and Lào Cai before fixing on Tai Federation remnants in recently liberated northern Lai Châu. Throughout the Northwest Zone by June 1954, security forces operating under the banner of bandit elimination killed a total of 7,469 people and collected five thousand firearms. Through it all, the meaning of the word bandit (*phỉ*) was shifting away from banditry proper (that is, outlaw) to denominate a wide range of allegedly counterrevolutionary activity, spanning from French partisans to almost any opposition in highland areas. Until the program's end in 1978, bandit elimination disproportionately affected Hmong people who—whether for reasons of political difference, tax and labor grievances, religious affiliation, or agricultural practice—seemed to oppose the DRV agenda.[18]

Alongside such overt state violence, a more mundane but pervasive and lasting form of policing and surveillance emerged with the campaign, helping to secure agrarian resources and discipline DRV subjects. Beginning in March 1953, on his return home from sojourns in Thailand and the Việt Bắc, Lò Văn Hặc put his local knowledge to work by leading Điện Biên District's police force. A year later, Politburo member and rising star Lê Duẩn enhanced police powers to "watch over" and investigate local political conditions and, in line with VWP policies, to detain suspects, try and imprison them, and eliminate bandits. "In order to protect the rear and serve the front," he integrated police work with mass mobilization and agrarian reform by "trying and punishing spies, commandos, bandits, traitors, reactionaries, and cruel tyrants." A savvy and brutish political operator, Lê Duẩn hailed from southern Vietnam and, by marginalizing rival Politburo members a decade later, including President Hồ and General Giáp, would lead Hanoi's war against the Republic of Vietnam in the Second Indochina War. Acting on his orders in March 1954, Northwest Zone cadres led by Lò Văn Hặc embraced his integrated agenda and months later advanced it into the postcolonial era. In July 1954, noting a time when "peace had returned," regional leaders established a branch office of the Ministry of Internal Affairs to coordinate the work of watching over individuals, supervising local government, surveilling the masses, and pursuing bandits.[19] No longer just an external foreign foe, the enemy was being reconstructed as an internal threat worthy of coercive suppression, even violent attack.

Because of the economy's militarization as well as the accompanying political terror and heightened surveillance, it is not surprising that logistics mobilization proceeded, as the region's summary report observed, "in an orderly routine."[20] Though made in reference to the agricultural tax that provided military provisions, the observation applies equally to the dân công labor service that provided military transport. Indeed, archival documents from late 1953 to mid-1954 do not dwell on gathering provisions and labor from residents of the Northwest's free zones. The archival silence speaks as much to the normalization of citizenship duties since their introduction with the Northwest Campaign as it does to the coercion and suppression of dissent that rose with the Điện Biên Phủ Campaign. The project that Commissar Nguyễn Kháng had outlined in late 1952—to remake the Northwest's population into a military reserve—appeared now, one year later, to bear fruit. Yet, just below the surface and, moreover, following the latter campaign's formal conclusion, both labor service and taxation remained at the heart of tense relations of DRV territorial rule. Any routine or apparent order achieved during the campaign came at the cost of political instability and social disorder rising in its wake.

Although labor service in general had entered a process of normalization, intense labor mobilization accelerated gender and ethnic transformations already under way. A year after the Northwest Campaign had introduced dân công requirements, local peasant subjects were increasingly accustomed to working on behalf of nation and at behest of state. Many had already served in one or more military campaigns. Though legitimation of bodily claims in relation to national citizenship was novel, the jobs they did—including roadwork, office construction, food preparation, and irrigation repair—were not new. In muang communities, Tai nobles had long required commoners to perform such duties, and the French had used the system to provide corvée labor. When the Điện Biên Phủ Campaign began, village-based public assessments (*bình nghị*) apportioned duties and assigned villagers mainly to road and transport crews.[21] Faced with unprecedented demand for transportation labor matched by growing capacities to coerce and cajole compliance, the DRV state recruited ever increasing numbers of women and exposed highland peoples, especially Hmong and Dao, to new claims on their bodies and labor power. A campaign photograph shows men and women dân công fording a swift river and carrying supplies to the Điện Biên front (figure 18). Wading hip-deep, crossing en masse, and wearing disheveled clothes, their appearance contrasts with the neat line of uniformed porters pictured on a bamboo bridge (see figure 13 in chapter 4). The two photographs highlight a gap between state dreams of orderly service and the actual conditions of heavy manual labor.

During the Điện Biên Phủ Campaign, even more women generally and Tai women particularly encountered new risks and rewards by engaging in dân công service outside the household and beyond the village. Official statistics do not break down labor participation by gender. Yet, as recorded during and after the Northwest Campaign, local recruitment favored women because most able-bodied men were soldiering in the colonial Tai battalions. Further, photographic evidence of dân công transport

FIG. 18. Dân công fording a swift river. Looking tired and heavily burdened, the men and women here contrast with the anonymity, order, and practiced ease conveyed in figure 13. (3143/BNG/NAVC 3.)

FIG. 19. Roadwork by Tai "compatriots." Tai women in black haul rocks while Tai men in berets and a helmeted soldier swing sledgehammers, breaking rocks into gravel and leveling the road. (3191/BNG/NAVC 3.)

workers from the Vietnamese archives shows Tai women wielding pickaxes, hauling rocks, and marching in line (figure 19).

Part of an emerging home front, women's participation in the DRV's civilian labor corps challenged patriarchal traditions and delighted egalitarian, productionist cadres. In Tuần Giáo District, for example, women had initially been reluctant to "serve the campaign" after liberation in late 1952. But over the next year, more and more women began to process rice, heft weaponry, and above all work on road crews. In addition to maintaining Road 41 over the epic Pha Đin Pass (1,648 meters), road crews blazed an 80-kilometer spur connecting Tuần Giáo to Điện Biên. The heavy, dangerous, and embattled off-farm work, according to Lò Văn Hặc in 1955, had helped transform Tai society for the better. Now chairman of Lai Châu Province, he praised women's increased participation as a "general advance among the broader population." Not all officials shared his views, however, and Hặc used the report to position himself as a modernizing figure. "Women are certainly not able to do *dân công*," stated a Tai village chief. "Were the Government to capture and kill them, I would pay it no mind."[22] Whereas the chairman praised women for working on behalf of the state, the chief dismissed any who ventured beyond his village as unworthy of his care. For the working women themselves, the DRV's egalitarian gender ideology had ambivalent effects: loosening old ties of patriarchy but engendering new forms of state servitude.

Aside from formal labor service, women's work was and remained part of the longer revolutionary struggle—even when not acknowledged as so. Even as male household members left to go soldiering or attend trainings, home and family stayed central in struggles over power and position. Spared from labor service due to her elite status, Quàng Thị Pánh, for instance, had become enmeshed in deeply familial political contests when she married Lò Văn Hặc. In 1943, the French-appointed official Đèo Văn Long dismissed Hặc from his post as tri châu of Điện Biên in favor of his own son, Đèo Văn Ún. Hặc fled underground, leaving Pánh to hold the family together in the face of violence and sexual coercion. Soon enough, the younger Đèo confiscated their property, torched their homestead, arrested her and her children at gunpoint, and threw them all in jail. Subjected to repeated interrogations regarding her revolutionary activities, Pánh professed ignorance as to her husband's whereabouts. But she gave a response that subtly combined the personal and the political: "My work," she said simply, "is to raise children."[23]

In keeping with a larger pattern, Đèo Văn Ún saw Pánh's children as central to his consolidation of power. After her eldest son, Lò Văn Xương, died suspiciously in detention, his body dumped in a river, Ún forced Xương's widow to marry him. After a hunger strike won her release from jail, Pánh returned home to raise her surviving children, taking in her grandchildren as well. She held fast until 1952 when, with the Northwest Campaign, Hặc finally returned and toppled Ún. Captured in June 1954, one month after the People's Army victory, Ún was tried publicly and executed by firing squad. Pánh's difficult experience helps explain why Hặc brought a personal animus to bear on former colonial officials and members of the Đèo family. In Vietnam as in Laos, for Tai peoples as for Hmong, family disputes became enmeshed in Cold War politics. During the Indochina Wars more broadly, women all over Vietnam's contested territory had to shoulder the increased burden and endure the heightened danger that men's work on the front lines left them at home and in the rear.[24]

As dân công labor service intensified among lowland Tai communities during the Điện Biên Phủ Campaign, it also expanded spatially within the Northwest Zone, climbing the hills to enlist Hmong and Dao peoples. Although the highlanders had begun to serve the DRV after the Northwest Campaign, on Road 13, for example, their mass enlistment represented a significant departure from French colonial precedent exempting them from corvée duties. Furthermore, Hmong peoples had long expressed concern about working at low altitudes, preferring to stay in the cooler heights.[25] Their participation, therefore, visited considerable hardship, as cadre Phẩm recalled about the Hmong woman on his road crew who cried inconsolably. While Phẩm figured out a short-term solution to keep her and other Hmong participants working, senior officials worried about the long-term political consequences of doing so. Of the Northwest Zone more generally, Commissar Kháng observed: "Mobilizing all the Hmong compatriots to descend to the plains without making special considerations for their circumstances—they are accustomed neither to hot weather nor to going far for long—has already affected the compatriots' health; some return home wasting away, sick and dying, such that the political influence is not good."[26] Mustering Hmong people to descend from the heights and perform dân công duties in the valleys, on the road, or by the riverside caused them misery, frequent illness, and sometimes death. It is hard to imagine that any amount of "special considerations," except perhaps continued exemption from labor service, might have prevented these deadly circumstances. Despite his circumspect language, however, Kháng observed astutely how labor service had a political effect that was "not good." In other words, dân công service was seen as illegitimate among many Hmong peoples who, collectively, recognized a contradiction. By returning laborers home in poor health and near death, the DRV failed to adhere to its own rhetoric of caring for and watching over national citizens. More than a short-term failure, increasing claims on Hmong people's bodies (as labor power) and in time their agricultural produce (as tax revenue) bore long-term consequences for the regime's political legitimacy among Hmong communities.

Like participation in the civilian labor corps, taxation was a tense and everyday way of attaching people to national territory and constructing relations of rule. First implemented a year earlier and then intensifying throughout the Điện Biên Phủ Campaign, the agricultural tax remained the principal means through which the DRV state collected rice from farmers in the rear and fed its army on the front. To do so, the Northwest Zone's territorial administration exercised local government and mass organizations, especially Farmers Councils, to levy the tax on cultivators in free and newly liberated zones. After public assessments determined the state share of household harvest, farmers delivered it to storehouses, at which point the military's distribution network, using local labor, ferried the food to the front. Following these procedures, in what its leaders called an "orderly routine," the zone gathered 14,400 tons of rice in the fall 1953 tax and another 2,413 tons in winter/spring 1954, exceeding targets in both cases.[27] During the campaign, therefore, taxation in the Northwest Zone accounted for more than double the amount of rice reported as its "contributions" by the Front Supply Council in its landmark July 1954 report.

Like statistical abstractions and geobody representations wielded by central decision makers, any reported order at a regional scale obfuscated underlying spatial heterogeneity and temporal uncertainty experienced by cadres and peasants on the ground. Spatially, swidden cultivators enjoyed a tax holiday through the campaign and into 1955, exempting most highland communities from an unpopular program. Although labor service had recently expanded to Hmong and Dao peoples, then, suspending their tax payments enabled cadres to maintain relatively harmonious relations during the war and political transition. The agricultural tax, therefore, fell heavily on wet-rice farmers in Tai muang communities. Meanwhile, Tai elites continued to dominate local government agencies and Farmers Councils, enabling them, as before, to evade taxes and foist the burden onto poor peasants.[28] Temporally, prior to November 1953, the zone's leadership had planned to expand the agricultural tax to newly upgraded free zones in southern Lai Châu Province, including Điện Biên District. Yet French reoccupation of Điện Biên threw the plans into disarray and led to many "errors" in tax implementation, such as wielding command tactics instead of educating consent, official confusion about tax liability, and widespread popular anxiety. Furthermore, General Giáp's January 1954 decision to delay the People's Army assault outstripped the ability of taxation to supply the needed extra provisions. As a result, peasants "temporarily loaned" more rice to the government on ad hoc terms negotiated by field cadres. In return, they received assurance that these payments would count toward the next round of DRV taxation in fiscal year 1954.[29] Such assurances, however, depended crucially on a military and territorial outcome that was far from certain.

At the height of the First Indochina War, the logistics demands that the DRV placed on local participants bound them ever tighter to Vietnamese territory. During the Điện Biên Phủ Campaign, diverse peoples of the Black River region yielded still more of their scarce agrarian resources, sometimes against their will, for use by state and military in pursuit of territory. Recounted as contributions to politico-military struggle, their food and labor resources were, in fact, the product of everyday struggles over homes and bodies as well as community and ruling relations. Zooming down still further, it is evident that residents of free zones shared such struggles with those living even closer to the battlefield at Điện Biên Phủ. Far from free, not simply occupied, and only partially liberated, the local peoples who contested powerful resource claims brought negotiations over the terms of DRV territorial rule down to the ground.

THE CRUCIBLE OF ĐIỆN BIÊN PHỦ

The closer one gets to the ground in war, the more uncertain, contested, and entangled the spaces of territory and logistics become. Their histories change too, in this case departing from a tale of singular glorious struggle against foreign oppression to the multiple mundane struggles of local participants. At the regional scale of the Northwest Zone, the social relations constituting territorial domination and logistical mobilization varied by place, built on local histories, and articulated with ethnic and gender differences. Here, by zooming down to a local scale, powerful contests over the rightful placement of people and things come into sharper focus, tracing how Vietnamese territory was formed in the crucible of Điện Biên District.

By the time French paratroopers landed at Điện Biên Phủ on 20 November 1953, the supposedly remote place's landscape and terrain had been contested by global forces for a decade. Opium and rice attracted powerful trade interests. An airfield and mountain passes made it a transport hub. Since World War II, Japan, China, France, and Vietnam had all occupied the strategic site. Now, China and the United States complicated questions of sovereignty by backing proxies in a blazing Cold War conflict. In sum, by late 1953, which state controlled Điện Biên was openly contested and deeply uncertain. So too was the underlying legitimacy of any claim on its territory and population.

What distinguished the DRV claim among others was its commitment to popular legitimacy, its capacity to enlist mass participation, and the forms of power that resulted. All the armies that visited Điện Biên in the 1940s–50s had appropriated local food and labor resources, often with force. Both French Indochina and the DRV incorporated local male elites into administrative posts. But the DRV alone enrolled the masses, educating men and women in radical ideas and mobilizing them in the work of anti-colonial nationalism. Through ground-level processes of state learning, local peoples learned from cadres how to articulate demands for freedom, equality, and prosperity. Like others before them, they embraced the French revolutionary ideals that France had long denied its colonial subjects.[30] As a result, many not only expected a better future but were willing to work—even die—for it. Yet throughout claimed DRV territory by the early 1950s and particularly in Điện Biên, long and escalating warfare deferred such visions, threatening an ideological source of legitimacy and compromising a material source of supply. Cadres and officers, therefore, drew increasingly on coercive tactics, such as surveillance and taxation, to secure necessary logistical resources. Out of these political negotiations and everyday struggles emerged the tense relations constitutive of Vietnamese territory.

Concentrating on Điện Biên District's plain, the French attack split the district and its resident population of 22,640. Five valley communes that the DRV had just upgraded from liberated to free were now occupied by French forces. Tai residents were "confused and worried," according to native son and Tai power broker Lò Văn Hặc. Faced with heavy weapons and crack troops, "most of the upper strata," he continued, "slid towards the enemy and no longer believed in us." The DRV's popular legitimacy was shaken, in other words, and local elites saved their skins. Common folk then had to decide whether to go or stay, a decision faced

FIG. 20. Tai women and children in Muang Thanh, November 1953. (© Daniel Camus/ECPAD/Defense.)

by the Tai women and children in a French photograph taken shortly after the aerial invasion (figure 20). Those who fled for free zones in the hills wound up shuttling supplies to People's Army soldiers. Having abandoned home and farm, they subsisted on forest tubers and lived in constant fear of starvation. Any who remained, however, saw their houses dismantled, rice snatched, gardens burned, and livestock shot and eaten by the Expeditionary Forces. Forced to gather in internment camps (*bản tập trung* in Vietnamese; *gros villages* in French), they faced depredation and corvée labor as well as heightened vulnerability to untimely death, corporeal violence, and sexual assault (figure 21).[31]

Only kilometers away but a world apart from the combat below, five Tai communes in the foothills and five Hmong communes in the moun-

FIG. 21. An internment camp, Muang Thanh, 1954. (© Jean Péraud, Daniel Camus/ECPAD/Defense.)

tains of Điện Biên District remained subject to DRV state power and intensifying claims on its behalf. As in the Northwest's other free zones but even more embattled, Điện Biên's intact DRV institutions were one year young and evolving rapidly through militarized social mobilization. "Through the processes of serving the front," stated an early 1954 Lai Châu Province report, "the infrastructure of local government has been consolidated; armed militia and police forces have also been selected." Serving the front strengthened institutions by vetting personnel. Old and new officials then integrated food and labor collection into established programs called "improving the countryside," such as boosting production, serving soldiers, and taxing grains. Police work also secured manpower and meat. "Watching over" the civilian population prevented people, and their livestock, from fleeing Vietnam for Laos.[32]

For many if not all of the district's population, the wartime atmosphere was terrifying. French aircraft dropped bombs and napalm, killing upstream residents and downstream laborers. Warplanes lit entire villages afire. For much of 1954, DRV state shops—a pillar of the planned economy—ceased to operate, and already scarce supplies of salt, farm tools, and tobacco largely dried up. Water buffalo were butchered or killed by bombs and mines, leaving farmers short of draft labor. People displaced from the plain wandered the hills, begging for food. Beset with "anxiety" and "worry," people "all over" feared starvation, particularly if the People's Army did not fulfill its promised "certain victory." Seven weeks into bitter siege warfare, on 25 April a massive explosion in Noong Nhai Village on the occupied plain killed upward of 444 Tai residents, mostly women and children. The blast fanned persistent fears that the Americans would drop an atomic bomb any day, especially if Vietnam were to win.[33] As for soldiers, so too for civilians: mass death at Điện Biên Phủ was a lived experience.

DRV leaders responded to these deadly conditions—and the existential threat facing their political struggle—by intensifying institutional development and legitimation work at the grassroots. The Military Central Party Committee identified the commune as a foundational institution of DRV government, stressing its role as a mediator between districts, which set targets, and villages, which fulfilled them. To build ground-level support for its logistics agenda, the command ordered cadres to recruit local villagers into commune leadership. Meanwhile, responding to charges of Kinh domination in upstream communes of the Việt Bắc, the Politburo ordered recruitment to reflect a locality's given ethnic composition. Following these instructions "from above," the Điện Biên District Party Leadership Council created special Village Head and Stalwart Committees in each commune to coordinate logistics work in villages. Chosen "stalwarts," according to the District Council, were "good people" from poor families who counterbalanced suspect village leaders from rich families. To avoid the appearance of ethnic domination and because Kinh cadres knew little of local languages and customs, Tai and Hmong stalwarts took the lead as interpreters in village-based meetings. Working in teams, they stressed local participation in military supply and national unity against a singularized enemy.[34]

Led by cadres and guided by stalwarts, the meetings illustrate how logistics mobilization and state formation worked reciprocally and iteratively to secure territory. First, households yielded rice, corn, vegetables, and livestock as payment of the 1953 agricultural tax, sold them outright to procurement officers, or loaned grains against the projected 1954 tax. Laborers ferried supplies from depot to trench, built artillery roads, maintained bridges, and milled rice. Second, assessments provided quantitative, household-level data on production capacity and manpower availability, knowledge used to plan and conduct more taxation and labor recruitment. Third, cadres selected candidates for the bureaucracy. Of the district's forty-nine stalwarts, thirty-nine "vigilant" ones became commune officials and ten were dismissed.[35] Aiming to embed state in society, the militarist measures also collapsed the calculative spaces of logistics and territory.

In addition to gathering resources, gleaning data, and building institutions, the myriad meetings socialized the Vietnamese geobody. Cadres educated largely illiterate village audiences by reading aloud Hồ Chí Minh's "Letter to Compatriots and Cadres of Lai Châu." Stressing loyalty to the DRV, the president called for unity and mutual assistance in the Vietnamese homeland (*tổ quốc*), invoking an idiom that mixed nation, ancestry, and geobody. He promised leniency for anyone who had followed the "wrong path" but now wished to "return to Government and homeland." "For over 80 years now," he wrote of Điện Biên's encompassing province, "the compatriots of Lai Châu have been exploited, oppressed, and tricked by French colonialists and reactionary Vietnamese traitors."[36] This is history in service to the present. He projected Vietnam's geobody back in time to serve an ongoing politico-military struggle. In order for the DRV to liberate Lai Châu and relegate exploitation to the past, in other words, the rising postcolonial state required food, labor, and loyalty—now and in the future.

Differentiating between the two armies' provisioning strategies was itself an important ideological tactic. Cadres pointed to French combatants who "took pigs, chicken, water buffalo . . . but offered no money in return." By contrast, "the Government did not allow the People's Army to take anything from the people." In one lesson, residents were encouraged to think of the army as akin to a water buffalo: "It protects the country, protects the house, so one must care for it so that it has energy." But equating a complex, coercive institution with a tame animal avoided mention of its politically organized violence. It also advanced the territorial agenda by linking civilian safety in the rear to the army's frontal attack. "We in the rear who are able to eat well and sleep peacefully," continued the lesson, "must thank the sibling soldiers out on the front."[37] If a farmer appreciates a draft animal, then so too must "we"—that is, a national we in the making—thank the army. Whether or not local people actually ate well or accepted these terms of citizenship are other questions, discussed below.

The meetings allowed villagers to discuss state claims, offering scholars rare insight into both contests over legitimacy and the genesis of additional, coercive state powers. In sessions called "airing grievances" (*tố khổ*), literally, "eating bitterness," peasants criticized themselves or denounced others as class enemies in line with Maoist models of class struggle and downstream land reform.[38] But in this upstream region where struggle was decoupled from land reform and hitched instead to logistics, the sessions gave peasants a chance to vent feelings about household assessments, even challenge their suitability. Written up in reports and stored in the archives, their reactions also indicate how cadres monitored public morale. Classifying reactions as either "good" or "bad" equipped officials with disciplinary capacities to reward or punish participants as they saw fit.

On the good side, peasants spoke to desired legitimation effects by accepting claims and welcoming service. "Selling pigs and chickens and paying the agricultural tax," stated a Hmong resident, "enables the army to eat and gain energy to fight the enemy and protect the order of our *bản muang*."[39] Referring to mountain villages by the Tai term (*bản*) organized by the Tai governing unit (*muang*), the Hmong respondent harbored no illusions about how the Vietnamese government incorporated preexisting relations of spatial domination. She added, "Caring for the military is like caring for a sibling who leans on me." By associating army with family, she recognized the duties that both bonds imply.

Other reactions demonstrate how Hồ Chí Minh's charisma animated emancipatory ideas, encouraging recognition of DRV authority and stimulating emotive responses. "Before we were as though deaf and mute," stated one poor peasant; "now, enabled by the Government, great-grandfather Hồ sends cadres back here to announce all kinds of differences, as though my deaf ears and blind eyes are clear again." The president's extraordinary qualities both personified complex institutions and extended his legitimacy to the ordinary cadres who worked in his name. Another Hmong villager likened the military to a guest for whom residents played host: "This year while the bandits are in Điện Biên, we all celebrated Tết by going on *dân công* to deliver rice to the army to eat." Appealing to the Lunar New Year ritualized logistics duty and legitimized the force used to secure Vietnam's territorial claim. By contrast, invoking the ancient word bandit (*giặc*) to characterize French forces dehumanized the enemy, delegitimized a rival claim, and accepted their violent treatment.[40]

Exchanging sentiments between prospective leaders and followers figured as opening lines in a longer process of state making. Next, cadres expected citizens to fulfill assessments materially. For example, Lò Văn Ếng embraced the state agenda as his own, helped it succeed on the ground, and earned approval as a peasant champion. Hailing from Nà Tấu Commune, the Tai man had been poor during French rule, leaving his wife and infant child hungry. So, he had "requested" that President Hồ and the government liberate Điện Biên District. He had the good fortune to live next door to Mường Phăng Commune, site of General Giáp's command, where People's Army officers and Chinese advisors purchased scarce meat from local villagers.[41] He seized on the opportunity—and then some. Ếng increased his agricultural output, paid the rice tax (330 kilograms), and served time as a dân công (fifty-seven days). His service included two stints guiding "secret" road construction, presumably for artillery. He also loaned rice to the army (450 kilograms), led a work team that boosted the commune's output, and sold produce to officers, including two water buffalo wounded by warplanes and one ton of green vegetables. Ếng's exemplary service earned the district's recommendation for the zone's highest commendation. He was one of dozens of "outstanding individuals" upon whom the district bestowed a medal, 1 kilogram of salt, and a shovel in elaborate ceremonies.[42] Aside from alleviating real scarcity, the awards indicate official emphasis on agriculture and trade for the shared benefit of state and society. The exchange also underscores a reciprocal relationship between territorial security and rural livelihood that drove the People's War and sealed Vietnam's military victory.

In addition to enshrining the values of the People's War and its exemplary participants, the award ceremonies provided a second stage on which to solicit broader consent to rule. Staged at all levels of government, especially in newly created districts like Điện Biên, the ceremonies featured personnel who represented relations between territorial units and enacted their hierarchical organization. Furthermore, the theatrical performances portrayed a complex array of institutions as a singular entity called "Government," individualized collective duties and collectivized their individual experiences, and finally, praised the citizen subjects who defended the Vietnamese geobody. The ideological performance figured in a longer making of "the state" as a unified body representing, caring for, and watching over national society.

Not everyone consented, indicating how territory—on and off the battlefield—was always negotiated, often partial, and sometimes openly contested. Recorded "bad" reactions feature people of suspect class backgrounds who rejected DRV overtures and challenged egalitarian ideals. "Why all these meetings?" asked a Tai lord. "Just take the rice and meat already." His sharp question recognized legitimation work as such and expressed impatience with its recital. His terse command refused discussion, and he resigned himself to material loss. To relinquish food and *still* earn a bad grade underlines the political significance of imbuing resource flows with meaning. A Tai noble grumbled about the erosion of patriarchy that came through exposing women to work outside the household. He complained: "Requiring women to go work emboldens and ruins them" as future wives. Labor service introduced women to ideas and practices that led them to challenge customary forms of gender subordination.

The noble also questioned prevailing DRV Ethnic Policy. He opined that Kinh people, faced with French military superiority downstream, had decamped to favorable conditions upstream. He declared: "The Kinh come up here and eat the rice of Tai people. So, no way am I doing any *dân công* work at all." Not everyone in Điện Biên's diverse population shared the Ethnic Policy's prescribed unity between peoples conceived first as nationally Vietnamese and second as ethnically Tai, Hmong, or Kinh. On the contrary, the noble asserted that Kinh people were taking advantage of him and other Tai people. Viewing soldiers and cadres not as fellow Vietnamese but as unwelcome visitors, he refused to play host.

Finally, critical responses astutely warned of resource mobilization's escalating social costs. A rich peasant linked consumption by visitors to effects on their host. "The army eats up all the rice and goes back downstream," he reasoned, asking pointedly, "How can we save anything?" Rising state claims on local resources did, in fact, deplete household food and labor stores. Likewise, a Hmong compatriot observed, "This year requires going on *dân công* a lot such that many people fall ill." In addition to the health effects stemming from difficult and dangerous conditions, putting Hmong people to work reversed colonial precedent exempting them from corvée. Classifying this response as "bad" confirmed what Commissar Kháng had called its "not good political influence," that is, damaging DRV legitimacy. In short, military supply was exacting a human toll, even endangering social reproduction. The unintended consequences threatened to unravel carefully constructed ideas of the state as caring for the people.

When peasants aired grievances that questioned ideological and material claims, the stalwarts assumed another role: generating coercive state power inside village communities. Stalwarts "watched over" disgruntled elites to compel compliance with assessed duties. At first, they staged unannounced home visits. Yet early monitoring worsened class-status relations and caused stalwarts "pain." So the district appointed senior cadres to accompany these recruits. Acting as mentors in the arts of surveillance, the cadres taught them how to "observe discreetly."[43]

Just as good reactions and fulfillment of assessed duties merited reward, so too did bad reactions and failure to fulfill them deserve punishment. If peasant champion Lò Văn Ếng demonstrates the former, then Hmong leader Vàng Sông (Chong) exemplifies the latter. Allied with French forces and operating from Laos, Vàng tried to organize resistance to labor service but was foiled by Hmong residents of Độc Lập Commune who reported on the "traitorous commando" and invited district officials to "capture" him. Although he and his men were soon killed by artillery fire, his counter organizing nonetheless struck a chord, one that grew louder after the battle's conclusion. By then, the new branch office of the Ministry of Internal Affairs had taken the lead in "watching over" such suspect individuals.[44] Through it all, the DRV enlisted peasants to police the conduct of neighbors, kin, and clan.

Lodged even in the face of such coercive state power, discontent pointed again to the problem of hunger and its political significance. Since the 1945 famine under Japanese occupation and through the war with France, the DRV had blamed food scarcity on foreign enemies, often with good reason, while advancing rural development to remediate conditions. Development certainly bolstered regime legitimacy among the peasantry. Now, however, it was the DRV that was causing food insecurity in its own Northwest Zone, a region where seasonal hunger was and would remain a hazard of agrarian livelihood. The Northwest and Điện Biên Phủ Campaigns had increased aggregate consumption and decreased production, amplifying local hunger. As of February 1954, Black River peoples were desperately hungry once again, reaching scattered starvation in highland Hmong and Dao communities of Văn Chấn District.[45] Acute as they were, their struggles were muted by the sound and fury of war.

Human bodies were suffering the hard work they did to expand the Vietnamese geobody. Compared with the hunger that followed earlier phases of territorial expansion in 1948 and 1952, the effects of early 1954's hunger on regime legitimacy had shifted. After a year and more of DRV hegemony and intense resource appropriation, it was becoming harder to cast blame for suffering and scarcity on foreign enemies. Further, land reform was not on the region's development agenda, empowering local elites and removing an incentive for poor peasants to endure hardship in favor of an egalitarian future. Warnings of bare cupboards and sick workers, then, raised valid concerns. By spring 1954, signs of growing food shortage were clear even as the consequences for the DRV were still unknown.

In March, after just the latest of many waves of mobilization, Điện Biên District conducted a survey of two "typical" communes to assess manpower availability and food security.[46] In the Hmong commune of Vinh Quang (now Phì Nhừ), a total of 229 residents, or one-quarter of the population, had performed 2,952 labor days, averaging almost two weeks per person. One out of six families had no grain left to eat, only seed stock; just half overall had enough corn and rice to last four months. In the Tai commune of Mường Luân, 776 residents, or 37 percent of the population, had served 10,253 labor days, averaging almost two weeks per person. One-quarter of its families had no rice to eat, just seed stock; a quarter had but a month's supply, and less than 5 percent had enough to last four months.

Though small in scope, the study opens onto larger tensions and foreshadowed struggles still to come. Logisticians calculated population and provisions by territory at a moment in time, but their data overlooked cumulative effects. Gathering quantitative data according to central accounting parameters failed to factor how preceding mobilizations had *already* exhausted food and bodies. Hmong villagers yielded less rice than their Tai neighbors, yet their bushels of corn bought, borrowed, or taxed went uncounted. So too with opium. Similarly, the service durations in previous waves of dân công mobilization were not recorded. Lastly, an entire cornucopia of other food gathered by district, registered in its survey, and distributed to the army—including 101 water buffalo, 567 pigs, 1,173 chickens and ducks; 4,000 pomelos, 4,460 oranges, and 650 sugarcane stalks—did not count beyond the district because the Central Front Supply Council accounted for rice and meat only in metric units.

Discounted by the central government, the agricultural produce certainly mattered to the people who had so little left after years of embattled supply work. Indeed, the author of the March study made an ominous, if understated, observation: "If the rains don't come, [they] will be hungry." In fact, not one family had rice enough to last until October when, if the rains did fall, the next rice harvest would come in. But the battle's most intense combat would come first, destroying great swathes of Điện Biên's productive landscape through April into May. Hunger and starvation, then, loomed over many for whom the Black River region was home.

Never foreordained, the outcome of combat on the Mường Thanh plain rested heavily on the shoulders of local civilians. The dramatic result achieved at Điện Biên Phủ was a contingent product of embattled, interlocking processes that endured long beyond 7 May 1954: securing territory through physical force; mobilizing a differentiated peasantry; legitimating state resource appropriation; acculturating diverse peoples to Kinh social norms, especially the Vietnamese language; and institutionalizing DRV rule in a historically autonomous space. To remember the result only as "national victory" denies the uncertainty of constructing a community isomorphic with territory and overlooks the lingering, cumulative effects of everyday struggles endured by citizens, most of whom were civilians. Constructing territory through logistics work did more than help win the battle that won the war. As the next chapter illustrates, it also built cracks into Vietnam's national territory that would destabilize postcolonial rule for years to come.

CHAPTER 6

Revolutionary Alternatives

IN EARLY 1955 the police arrested a man in Yên Bái for telling fabulous stories. A veteran of the revolutionary war now employed as a DRV cadre, Ngoc Son supervised workers at a rice granary in Lào Cai and inspected upland villages for compliance with mandatory labor service. While on an inspection tour, Son told assembled villagers that a woman had given birth to a winged child who took flight upon delivery. He described how grasshoppers and birds waged war in the skies of Than Uyên, and the grasshoppers killed all their adversaries. To these strange omens, he added apocalyptic predictions of hunger and dislocation: a fisherman had caught an enormous frog that promised, "Butcher me not and I will tell your future," before declaring that the next year would begin peacefully but end in deadly flood.[1]

The villagers who heard Son speak—and helped fill his rice and labor quotas—knew well a tension at the core of Vietnam's rural revolution. Just as promises of freedom, equality, and prosperity inspired peasants to fight French colonial rule, so too did an emerging Vietnamese nation-state appropriate ever-larger shares of their household resources. After independence in 1954, unrest on Vietnam's Sino-Lao frontier grew with taxes on food and bodies, inspiring supernatural visions and millenarian calls for a king to right a world turned upside down. Tapping oral traditions and cultural scripts specific to the upland region, especially among

Hmong peoples, Son's stories amplified tense struggles over labor, food, opium, and an unsettled social order.[2] In so doing, his fabulism revealed an underlying truth: embedded in processes of state making and nation building, resource contests constructed Vietnamese territory in everyday but potent ways.

Through war and into peace, the DRV's heavy claims on the Black River region's agrarian economy bent its political trajectory in unexpected ways. On 7 May 1955, a year to the day after the great victory at Điện Biên Phủ, establishment of the Thái-Mèo [Tai-Hmong] Autonomous Zone celebrated national ethnic unity under revolutionary socialism. Yet local critics decried the zone's resemblance to the colonial Tai Federation, protesting its similar spatial expanse, muang-based administration, and bureaucratic composition dominated by Tai and Kinh cadres. Further, enforcing a DRV opium monopoly in 1956 on the Indochinese model brought simmering discontent among Hmong, Khmu, and Dao swidden cultivators to a boil. Amid this continuity in government, however, the region's diverse peoples had changed as a result of intensive engagement with revolutionary ideals and the work of anti-colonial struggle.[3] In this context, fabulous stories and flood forecasts articulated a potent critique of DRV rule. Rising up in 1957, subaltern groups protested state resource claims and appealed to a supernatural sovereign to deliver justice, topple an ethnicized hierarchy, and unite kin across borders. Crushed by security forces, the movement's activities built on and widened cleavages embedded in postcolonial territory. Its political vision—a highland geobody ruled by a divine king—challenges how scholars conceptualize hegemonic spaces of nation-state rule.

This chapter unearths a buried history of a world-historical place, but it does more. By analyzing the countermovement's formative conditions and alternative visions, it enriches a geographic concept of territory as an uncertain outcome of grounded struggles. To theorize territory as a calculative strategy of rule encompassing land and terrain, as scholars have done, offers important insight into powerful processes governing territorial production and, in the Vietnamese case, helps explain elite actions and policies. By overlooking what happens on the ground, however, a strategic definition of territory sometimes misses contingency and everyday practice. In other words, such a definition does not account for the unplanned consequences of territory's actual construction—in this case, the social tensions and embodied dispositions accumulated through logistics work that destabilized Vietnamese territory in lasting ways. Explaining such unexpected territorial outcomes requires historical and other approaches attentive to setting, agency, and accident, not textual exegesis and conceptual genealogy alone.[4]

Not just a technology of spatial rule and more than a powerful social process, territory is also an indeterminate product specific to context and contingent on its politics. What helped Vietnam win the Black River region in 1954 were the very same territorial strategies, rooted in socializing the geobody through logistics work, that undermined the region's attachment to Vietnam shortly thereafter. The unplanned outcome must be understood in relation to underlying and enduring struggles over resources and sovereignty, space and community. Such popular actions—whether in Vietnam or against it, or in different contexts altogether—influence the state of territory, including how scholars conceptualize it. Understanding the construction of territory and its indeterminate outcome, therefore, only benefits from incorporating histories of place attuned to context, contingency, and conjuncture.

"Revolutionary Alternatives" explores the unexpected and contradictory outcomes of making Vietnamese territory in the Black River region. By picking up narrative threads left dangling in chapters 4 and 5, this sixth and final chapter continues when stories about Điện Biên Phủ conventionally end: after the battle. Their farms, bodies, and households depleted by war, hungry people sought not just food but meaningful political change. Enacting an alternative to state-led revolution, they animated an idea of autonomy that was as rooted in local cultural practice and environmental conditions as it was versed in national policy and transnational organization. The movement's fall marks the end of the long 1950s, ushering in an era when DRV leaders in Hanoi watched over territory and population to their northwest as warily and militaristically as they did to their south.

BEYOND THE BATTLE OF ĐIỆN BIÊN PHỦ

The battle at Điện Biên Phủ ended on 7 May 1954, but the local struggles that had enabled and accompanied it continued long afterward. In fact, according to regional power broker Lò Văn Hặc, now the chairman of Lai Châu Province, the Điện Biên Phủ Campaign lasted locally through

July 1954. Just one of "three large tasks requiring human and material resources" that year, the campaign proper endured into summer when the People's Army moved onto "other battlefields" aiming to "eliminate bandits," thus requiring another round of local logistical support. After the Geneva Agreement ceasefire took effect in late July, roadwork started anew in August. In this third task, local dân công workers repaired Road 41 and paved the Glorious Line, turning the supply line into a sealed road to the Chinese border. As in northern Vietnam more broadly, such infrastructure work—and the labor and food it required—then carried into 1955 and beyond.[5]

Bounding the Điện Biên Phủ Campaign temporally and considering it a discrete event, as with the First Indochina War more broadly, overlooks the ongoing construction and reconstruction of Vietnamese territory. After May 1954, the DRV state continued to appropriate local food through agricultural taxation and labor through dân công service. As before, collecting these resources helped build the material and political infrastructure connecting the upstream Black River region to downstream Vietnam. But even as skirmishing continued, war's end brought two significant changes to spaces no longer contested by France. First, large-scale combat ceased, and people throughout northern Vietnam began a process of economic recovery under conditions of dire scarcity. Second, when the Front Supply Council dissolved in May 1954 and the army's Department of Politics decamped Lai Châu in August, the DRV state's capacity to govern the Northwest Zone diminished sharply. Further, central elites in Hanoi turned their attention elsewhere, not only managing partition between north and south, rebuilding the economy, and pursuing land reform, but also splitting factionally over the pace of socialist transformation and the means of national reunification.[6] As a result, local elites like Lò Văn Hặc managed upstream affairs with more control and less oversight, suggesting a state of de facto regional autonomy one year before its de jure declaration.

Whereas state use of local resources continued much as before, subtle changes in its accounting hint at the larger power shift inside the DRV state tipping the scales to the advantage of local elites. Reporting on 1954 Lai Châu to superiors in the Ministry of Internal Affairs, Chairman Hặc discussed the three tasks outlined above and complied with directives mandating numeric resource counts by standard metric units and labor days. For the first task, he listed the province's six districts and enumerated each one's logistical supply by tons of meat and rice and by number of workers and labor days through June. But then the Central Front Supply Council disbanded, and with it a crucial mechanism of accounting and accountability. Revealingly, under the second task of eliminating bandits in July and August, his report claims, "No district provided specific numbers," adding offhandedly that only in Mường Lay and Quỳnh Nhai was labor usage "heavy." In fact, Mường Lay District had filed several detailed reports registering exact amounts of what its chairman originally called "heavy" labor usage and agricultural taxation, adding that its population was "exhausted" and "anxious" as a result.[7] The third task of road construction from August onward resumes a quantitative narrative, listing by project the thousands of workers and the number of months they worked. So, why obfuscate the second task? Site of the former Tai Federation capital, Mường Lay (Lai) had also been home to its deposed ruler, Đèo Văn Long, and all the other people who had terrorized Hặc's family prior to his return in 1953. The province chairman, in short, may have used an accounting sleight of hand to hide a vendetta from superiors.

The withdrawal of centralized institutions bolstered Tai power and reproduced conditions of partial legibility. As part of broader bureaucratic reform (chỉnh đốn) begun in July 1953, the central government aimed to "destroy feudalism" in the Northwest Zone by purging local government of colonial officials and Tai "lords" (phìa tạo) as well as by increasing the representation of historically disenfranchised groups, especially poor peasants, women, and "small ethnicities" like Khmu (Xá) and Dao (Mán) peoples. Results were decidedly mixed. Redrawing some commune (xã) borders and recruiting eligible candidates did enhance participation. In a new commune in Thuận Châu, for example, a Khmu representative on the district's People's Committee heaped praise on the army and President Hồ for ending long traditions of Tai domination, chauvinism, and exclusion. But he was one of just twelve Khmu representatives in a prominent district; the other hundred seats were held by Tai representatives in the future capital of the Thái-Mèo Zone. Indeed, two-thirds of the zone's communes endured the reforms as before, that is, dominated by local ethnic majorities, mostly Tai. By the end of 1954, commune staff overall was "still not yet clean," or employed old colonial functionaries, wealthy peasants, and nobles. In the region's thirteen districts (huyện), meanwhile, reformists struggled to balance a candidate's background (gender, ethnicity, class) with his or her qualifications (skills, language, attitude), leaving many positions empty and offices understaffed. Deemed a "mess" and "the least stable unit" at reform's conclusion, districts were run by Tai insiders and Kinh cadres who, together, outmaneuvered new officials from historically disenfranchised groups. In spite of calls from "worried" officials to renew the reforms and carry them into 1955, the bureaucratic agenda shifted toward preparing for regional autonomy.[8]

At issue was not a simple personnel matter but instead a complex legacy of multiple sovereignty. In a region long characterized by the hierarchical layering of sovereign claims, the ideas and capacities vested in the Tai muang persisted in new guise and gained new purchase through incorporation as Vietnamese commune and district. Now hegemonic throughout the Northwest Zone, DRV administrative transformation extended the Tai unit's power to encompass non-Tai peoples and upland spaces historically out of reach. Not surprisingly, old practices survived the transition. In general, Tai peoples "disdained" their Khmu and Hmong neighbors, discriminated against them, and still held choice irrigated bottomland while the latter worked sloping, rain-fed swiddens. Change came slowly for the many women, poor peasants, and non-Tai peoples long denied access to formal education and office. In the few cases in which women earned a seat at the table, their male, mostly Tai, upper-crust colleagues greeted them with "surprise and ridicule."[9]

Even a man as committed to socialist ideals as Chairman Hặc remained a product of his own privileged background. Below the itemized resources pursuant to year 1954's three tasks, for example, he stated simply that "routine *dân công* mobilization goes on for the army, building granaries, building roads, welcoming delegations, and for all the other miscellaneous, trifling work that cannot be counted." His blithe statement shows how widespread the official use of labor was and remained in relation not just to centrally approved military and infrastructure work, but also to any of the myriad additional locally mandated tasks that went largely unreported—and unaccounted. Like other male Tai elites recognized as DRV officials and accustomed to muang hierarchy, Hặc drew on bureaucratic and traditional powers to command land and labor.

With the weakening of centralized administrative rule after May 1954, he and his peers also faced fewer checks on their exercise of those powers.

Such resurgent local power—what Hặc himself called "large feudal influence and small cadre presence"—complicates scholarly understandings of Vietnam's highlands and of legibility itself. Historically, it challenges simplistic narratives of steadily increasing Kinh domination of so-called ethnic minorities and indigenous peoples.[10] Although classified as national ethnic minorities, indigenous Tai peoples constituted a demographic majority in the region and drove DRV local government. These empirical facts call for nuanced understandings of state in relation to ethnicity and indigeneity as well as attention to underlying and enduring forms of muang power. Analytically, the idea that labor's use cannot be counted, its literal "incalculability" (*không thống kê được*), speaks to a reconfigured problem of partial legibility, or the state's limited capacity to know and reorder society. Here, illegibility was produced not by society, as scholar James Scott argues, but by changes in the state itself.[11] Never evenly distributed, the balance between official knowledge and ignorance now tilted in favor of local officials.

Their enhanced capacities notwithstanding, local officials faced complex political problems inherited from wartime logistics work and deeply embedded in Vietnamese territory. Labor service was never "trifling" for peasants. Rather, like taxing food, it featured in embodied and still contested relations of spatial rule, particularly among Khmu peoples chafing at Tai domination as well as Dao and Hmong peoples newly subject to claims on their bodies and labor power. Regarding dân công labor in Mường Lay, for example, Chairman Hặc had to admit that supply was insufficient, mobilization violated policy, and many people hid or fled rather than serve. Year 1954's agricultural tax in Sơn La and Lai Châu, too, recapitulated old problems with a vexing twist. Ordered to clear official balance sheets of debt accumulated during the Điện Biên Phủ Campaign, assessors discovered instead a widespread legacy of "grave errors in policy" that had split communities by class and ethnicity, damaged poor people's livelihoods, and gave grist to anti-government propaganda. While such problems dated to the onset of DRV taxation in 1952, they had expanded broadly and rapidly with the great military campaign. Amortizing government debt, therefore, was no simple matter. Because frenzied cadres and supply officers had not left a paper trail in 1953, assessors in 1954 had to negotiate with exhausted, hungry, and sometimes angry peasants.[12] In short, the Northwest Zone assumed responsibility for an accounting mess the central government had created.

Overcoming these bureaucratic problems, the DRV's regional tax haul increased. The zone's gross agricultural tax receipts in 1954 reached 17,005 tons of rice, averaging 366 kilograms per capita, and exceeded the Ministry of Finance's target. These raw numbers only hint at negotiations between assessors and assessed and between zone and center over a range of credits. For example, swidden cultivators in newly liberated areas still enjoyed a tax holiday and people suffering crop damage received exemptions. One-half of previously loaned rice applied to the current tax; the balance was amortized by state payments in salt, cloth, and farm tools.[13] Nonetheless, the 1954 gross was still greater than the 1953 figure and more than twice the region's so-called contribution to the Điện Biên Phủ Campaign.

The tax windfall came in spite of worsening conditions of resource scarcity and food insecurity. Levied year on year and season after season, iterative state appropriation of scarce food resources, like diverting labor from farm to road, was wreaking a grim toll. Contingency also played a role in the region's dwindling food supply. The cadre's prediction, reported in March 1954 after studying mobilization's effects on food stocks in Điện Biên District, rang all too true: monsoon rains did not come that summer and people went hungry, in places even starving. Building on and similar to previous People's Army campaigns, the largest one ever featured a pattern of unintended consequences—combat and hunger, then more hunger—that embedded social tensions still deeper into territory.

Riding in the wake of earlier logistical cycles and compounding prior landscape damage, the 1954 Điện Biên Phủ Campaign exhausted cultivators and depleted cupboards on the largest scale yet. In this context, conditions in 1954–55 were not what Chairman Hặc dismissed casually as "perennial compatriot hunger," as though outside of history. Nor did a monsoon failure simply trigger a hunger event, though weather was a factor. Rather, drought amplified historically produced conditions of food scarcity and household insecurity, resembling what geographer Michael Watts argued was Africa's structural vulnerability in a memorable debate about famine causality with economist Amartya Sen.[14] Precipitated by a contingent weather change, in other words, this latest hunger resulted as much from the DRV's strategic maneuvers to secure the Black River region—namely, intense appropriation of logistical resources and militarization of an agrarian economy—as it did from a legacy of colonial deprivation. Now, however, neither France nor the Tai Federation were there anymore to shoulder the blame, leaving a sovereign Vietnamese nation-state to bear hunger's political consequences.

Hunger radiated outward from battlefields in waves, first during campaigns and then in the lean months that followed. The first wave crested in April/May 1954, coinciding with fierce combat at Điện Biên Phủ and before the corn crop matured. In Sơn La, one-seventh of the province's population was hungry while residents throughout the zone found food "only by going into the forest to dig tubers and collect plants." From June to August, the corn harvest helped tide over fortunate Hmong growers and communities with which they traded. But erratic rainfall meant many more swidden farmers saw their corn crops wither and fail. At hunger's center was Điện Biên Phủ's mined, cratered, and trenched plain: 367 hectares of choice land in what had been a regional rice basket remained unusable for years afterward. When the monsoon rains failed, it was as the official had predicted: drought exacerbated food shortages. Consequently, before the rice crop matured in autumn, a second, more severe wave of hunger rippled through Lai Châu. Residents of Điện Biên District benefited from leftover military stores but neighboring districts scraped by on emergency food aid. By the Lunar New Year (*Tết*) in early 1955, downstream youth brigades working on road crews did not celebrate with glutinous rice cakes but subsisted on rations of gruel instead.[15]

Hunger indicates tenuous economic conditions, and in postwar Vietnam more broadly, it posed a grave political threat to DRV legitimacy. "The food problem during the resistance was extremely difficult. Now that peace has returned," opens a 1955 report, it "has only become more difficult." If officials did not solve the problem, the report predicted that conditions in urban and rural areas "will become unstable," the "elation" people felt with peace will dissipate, "and the prestige of the Party and local government will suffer harm." In stark contrast to rhetoric premised on postcolonial development, destitution did not end with colonial rule. Rising from 800,000 in February to 1.2 million in April 1955, the number of severely undernourished people peaked at about 8 percent of the DRV's total population.[16]

Not distributed evenly, the hungriest people clustered in areas where warfare had been destructive and logistics work intense, seasonal hunger was the norm, and land reform ongoing. Further, a cyclone struck the Red River Delta in late June, flooding hundreds of homes and destroying thousands of hectares of a newly planted rice crop. Conditions were most severe in Interzone 4, in north-central Vietnam, where over six hundred thousand people suffered dire hunger and five thousand died of starvation and related disease. Another thousand people perished nearby.[17] Included in Interzone 4 was Thanh Hóa, the province that had given by far the most food and labor to the Điện Biên Phủ Campaign. Also affected was the western Red River Delta which, together with Interzone 4, had been devastated by the Great Famine of 1945. Just ten years after the historic famine, when the Việt Minh had earned legitimacy by organizing relief efforts under colonial rule, the second famine threatened tired, hungry, and worried people as well as the postcolonial government claiming to represent them.

If the 1955 report described the DRV as a whole, then the political problems associated with hunger and food security went double for its newly liberated northwest corner. In contrast with downstream Vietnam, less reliable figures point back to the problem of partial legibility and diminished central administration. When the Ministry of Agriculture and Forestry reported in mid-1955 that hunger had declined overall to 431,489 people, its report stipulated, "The Northwest Zone does not yet have data." Drawing on an old idiom, the ministry offered an explanation for the paucity of data and for the difficulty of improving conditions among diverse and famished peoples scattered across a rugged landscape. Owing to the region's "vast land [and] sparse people, both differing from place to place," stated another report, "careful research is necessary before leading production." Even amid such agro-ecological and cultural uncertainties, however, hunger persisted in places affected not by drought alone but also by combat and logistics in 1953–54, including the districts of Điện Biên and Mộc Châu, Sinh Hồ and Than Uyên. Though emergency food aid pulled some out of desperate straits, its provision nonetheless ran up against two regionally typical problems.

Literally and figuratively, aid had to flow uphill on infrastructure built to extract, not deliver, agrarian resources, leaving out-of-the-way peoples largely to fend for themselves. Second, many well-off farmers and officials charged with distributing aid instead hoarded and consumed it, or resisted efforts to tap and redistribute their own stores.[18]

If farmers survived 1954's hunger by tightening their belts, then they had diminished reserves—energy, livestock, and food stocks—to survive in 1955. Hunger rose alarmingly in early 1955 as household consumption of seed stock tracked the exhaustion of forest tubers. The "hungriest people," according to a secret July 1955 police report, were subaltern Xá (Khmu) and Puộc (Xinh Mun) peoples as well as highland Mèo (Hmong) and Mán (Dao) peoples. Either their rain-fed swidden rice crops failed for the second year in a row, depleting saved seeds, or they missed the rice-planting season and ate their seed because of mandatory dawn-to-dusk government meetings, as with Khmu farmers in Thuận Châu. Wet-rice farmers suffered too because water buffalo, which supplied meat and draft labor, were another casualty of war. An irrigation assessment described dire conditions in 1956 Điện Biên District: before 1946, one plains commune had 2,500 head; by 1953, when French paratroopers landed, 1,000 remained; a year later, after 350 died from land mines, only 310 head survived—just 12 percent of the initial herd. Other communes "had no animals at all."[19]

Repeatedly gathering provisions and recruiting labor from chronically hungry people reached a logical, sad conclusion. While a mid-1955 report claimed that the total dead from starvation numbered "only" 4 or 5 people, a top-secret police report listed over 50 dead from eating poisonous tubers. A 1956 review found conditions hit a nadir in mid-1955, when 32,503 people were desperately hungry—10 percent of the zone's population—and 41 died of "exhaustion."[20] By way of comparison, more of the region's people went hungry in the year after the Điện Biên Phủ Campaign than the number who had labored in it.

Though fewer people died of starvation in 1954–55 than the hundreds who did in colonial internment camps in 1951–52, the political context had shifted. Franco-Tai rulers had grounded legitimacy in paternalist tradition and racial superiority, not prosperity and full stomachs. Proclaimed by Hồ Chí Minh in his 1945 Declaration of Independence, by contrast, the association of food and happiness with rightful power still echoed through the Northwest Zone in 1955–56. Cadres deemed DRV Ethnic Policy "successful" and recorded a "good influence" when people thanked "great-grandfather Hồ" for providing salt, tools, and seed. Yet cadres seemed unable or unwilling to link sliding DRV legitimacy with deteriorating social conditions, even where the two converged conspicuously. The 1955 police report describing Dao and Hmong peoples as the "hungriest," for instance, went on to describe how they had begun in January to meet in secret, sacrifice animals, and "call for a king" (*xưng vua*) who could drive out Kinh people and deliver a happier life.[21] Just as the police cast blame for hunger solely on colonial rule and capricious nature, so too did they point to French and American machinations as the only cause of political unrest, countermovement, and so-called bandits who, akin to foreign enemies, merited "elimination." Like DRV officials more generally, the police failed to connect the dots between increasing criticism of DRV tax and labor policy and the increasing movement of people to places outside DRV territory—although the report presented abundant evidence of both.

Conditions of hunger indicated and contributed to broader tensions along a still-contested and increasingly restive frontier of Vietnamese territory. In September 1954, Lai Châu Province organized border police units, part of a Northwest Zone program to restrict cross-border movement. Bureaucrats linked border patrols to other "large official business," especially labor service and agricultural taxation. A month later, in October, as the meager rice harvest approached and the tax season loomed, "enemy propaganda" targeted an audience for whom taxes and labor service loomed as grievances. "Over in Laos," went a typical line, "there are no obligations to work as *dân công*, no obligations to pay taxes, and the Việt Minh cannot stop you."[22] Whether or not the Americans or French were really to blame for such (mis)information is an open question. Certainly, counterinsurgency warfare before and after 1954 fostered ideological claims aiming to undermine tax and labor claims and, more broadly, to discredit and destabilize DRV rule (see chapter 3). But identifying sources of ideological production alone cannot explain the reasons for the mass circulation and consumption of ideas, much less why counterpropaganda proved, so often in this instance, more persuasive than DRV propaganda.

If ruling population by way of territory aims to fix people in space, many people slipped the knot by mobilizing themselves, thereby avoiding state claims on food and body, land and labor. In increasing numbers through January 1955, peasants voted with their feet. In an age-old Southeast Asian pattern, some swidden cultivators crossed from district to district—or muang to muang—seeking lighter labor and tax obligations. Many more fled across the DRV's new interstate border, some for China but most for Laos. In one instance, after officials persuaded a group of Hmong families to return, the erstwhile migrants explained, "Only because of fear of going on *dân công* and paying taxes did we flee." From October 1954, "reactionaries in Điện Biên were hectically mobilizing the people to cross to Laos."[23] Over the next year, ever larger numbers heeded the call, not just to escape but also to reunite with kin, ply old trade routes, or simply start over. By December 1955, out-migration had reduced the population of Điện Biên District by 14 percent, or over thirty-two hundred people.[24] Such movements illustrate a broader trend of boundary-crossing behavior happening simultaneously for similar reasons all across the Northwest Zone.

Population flight and persuasive arguments in its favor demonstrate both the contested legitimacy of resource claims and the fragility of state efforts to govern a footloose population territorially. In a region with long, arbitrary, and permeable borders, transnational mobility demonstrated the limits of territorial sovereignty vested in the nation-state. Meanwhile, a millenarian movement was rising that would challenge postcolonial territory in other ways. Hungry for more than food, movement members articulated a vision of self-rule that challenged the Vietnamese geobody, exposing the artifice of a space imagined nationally. Though specific to the mountains of mainland Southeast Asia, Calling for a King presented a radical alternative not just to Vietnam's democratic republic but to the very idea of territory as stable, homogenous, and bounded state space. By way of historical accident and local initiative, not strategic design, postcolonial Vietnamese territory entered a new phase, one highlighting territory's fragility, heterogeneity, and fluidity.

AUTONOMY, REAL AND IMAGINED

Calls for an alternative to state-led revolution emerged during broad discussions about forms of regional autonomy and national unity. Signed into law on 29 March 1955 (229-SL), the Thái-Mèo Autonomous Zone was the de jure form of self-rule granted by the DRV to diverse peoples of its northwest region. Named after the two largest groups among twenty-two recognized ethnicities (dân tộc), the Tai (Thái) at 57 percent and the Hmong (Mèo) at 19 percent, the zone fulfilled a key measure of Ethnic Policy. Articulated as "administrative autonomy" by Party Secretary Trường Chinh in 1951 and explained as "self-management" by President Hồ in 1955, formal autonomy allowed for distinctive local government based on the "county" (châu), officially abolished province and district, and stressed unity with Vietnam's national population and territory.[25]

However small the Thái-Mèo Zone's population of 312,000 was relative to the DRV's 16 million, its share of territory was enormous, estimated at one-third the total (158,000 square kilometers). Significantly, officials also reported its territorial swath as one-sixth of a unified Vietnam. Given Vietnam's ongoing partition into northern and southern republics, this measurement of Thái-Mèo space in relation to one imaginary Vietnam was not just anachronistic. It also signified the geobody's ongoing influence among (northern) ruling elites. The map of the zone (figure 22) is based on a regional geography published by the Northwest Zone's Office of Politics in 1956.[26] While the main map portrays the Thái-Mèo's internal and external borders, its inset plays a neat cartographic trick. By denying any space to the actually existing southern Republic of Vietnam, the inset positions the zone within the DRV's officially recognized Vietnamese geobody, as though always already unified.

Still, the Thái-Mèo Autonomous Zone did not emerge simply from top-down policy. Rather, local actors actively negotiated the terms of self rule, complicating scholarly notions that "autonomy" (tự trị) was merely a means to "subordinate" the region to the ruling Marxist-Leninist party, a fig leaf for Kinh territorial domination, a step to inevitable lowland state expansion, or a coordinated betrayal of "ethnic minorities" by socialist states that "cunningly backtracked in unison" on revolutionary promises.[27] Contemporary documents tell a different, more contingent story. Initiated by the central government in late 1954, regional discussions about Ethnic Policy and a proposed "Thái Autonomous Zone" invited input from 1,041 cadres, 1,333 organization leaders, and 2,334 civilians. A central part of a larger DRV survey, the discussions informed the state's adoption of ethnology as both a field of study and a means to enumerate and classify ethnic groups toward its goal of interethnic equality. Yet equality, like autonomy, was a work in progress. At the time,

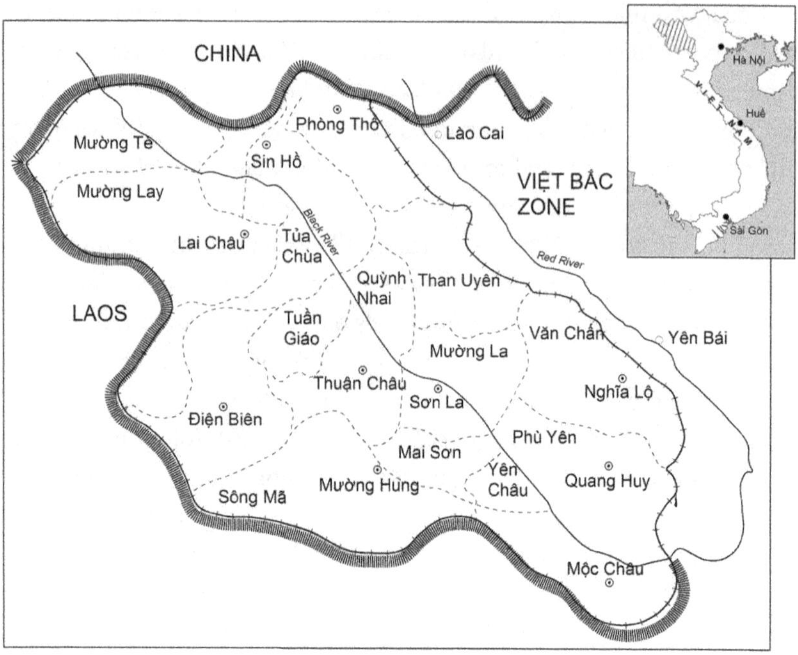

FIG. 22. Map of the Thái-Mèo Autonomous Zone, 1956. The map shows counties (châu) in dashes, international borders in cross-hatches, and the zone's eastern boundary by a crossed line. The inset displays the area's position relative to the Vietnamese geobody. (Map by Hannah Reckhow, based on Ban biên tập Sở Giáo dục Khu, *Địa lý Khu tự trị Thái-Mèo*.)

few if any knew the outcome. Even today, scholars know little about this historic process of negotiation and debate that unfolded on a cutting edge of claimed DRV space. Tracing these processes and following the visions they inspired heeds historian Patricia Pelley's call to study the "historicity of frontiers," or the contingencies, conflicted local agency, and historic dead ends that figured significantly in the longer making of Vietnamese territory.[28]

The forums opened a space for critical engagement. Local participants vented anger at Kinh cadres, particularly for their "disdainful attitude" toward compatriots they called "backwards, lazy, and superstitious." Such ethnic chauvinism was both a persistent problem for the party and one its policies consistently sought to correct.[29] Yet the VWP's egalitarian efforts would be stymied by 1958 not necessarily because of old Kinh cultural arguments. Rather, as this chapter discusses, Kinh chauvinism would articulate with rising Tai chauvinism for an unexpected reason—in response to radical enactments of autonomy led by Khmu, Hmong, and Dao peoples.

What stood out from these 1954–55 discussions was the diversity of opinions regarding Kinh cadres and the unanimity about the Ethnic Policy's fundamentally egalitarian principles. Many Tai cadres, particularly those from elite backgrounds, initially resented working for Kinh superiors. Some of them, in order to avoid a "Kinh Autonomous Region," suggested they pack up and leave. For their part, Mường, Nùng, Tày (Thổ), Dao, and Nhắng cadres "feared lying down without any rights" before the Tai, given the latter's regional demographic majority and historic rule. They also questioned a name—the proposed Thái Autonomous Zone—that privileged Tai peoples over all others. Even further, Hmong, Dao, and Khmu cadres "worried" that were Kinh cadres to return downstream, "no one would resolve ethnic contradictions" or act as a neutral arbiter should interethnic conflict rise again. Above all, virtually everyone agreed to leave divisive French rule behind and instead embraced the policy's principles of unity and rights to equality and democratic participation. As a result, de jure autonomy reflected two significant concessions. First, the "Thái-Mèo" name broke with long precedent by recognizing more than just the one group's regional claim. Second, in addition to the sixteen predominantly Tai counties grounded in valley muang spaces, Hmong peoples earned their own equivalent units in the highlands of Tủa Chùa, Mù Cang Chải, and Hmong Zone 99.[30]

Even as such negotiation characterized the Thái-Mèo Zone in general, the region's historical trajectory advanced autonomy far beyond what the central government ever intended. Three long-standing trends propelled self-rule in an indeterminate direction, initiating a de facto state lasting several years and peaking in a radical countermovement. First, concessions to and opportunities for non-Tai peoples notwithstanding, culturally Tai norms, practices, and spaces were deeply embedded in DRV local government. Despite the name change from "district" (huyện) to "county" (châu), the underlying administrative unit was still the Tai muang. Much as before, the sixteen to nineteen counties oversaw the smaller commune (xã) and village (bản) units where socially diverse residents had long tended to sort themselves according to cultural habit and ethno-linguistic commonality. Therefore, and notwithstanding DRV efforts to preserve ethnic autonomy, the zone's territorial administration "fostered Tai hegemony over other ethnic groups," according to anthropologist Yukti Mukdawijitra. In fact, so powerful were ideas of Tai governance that they decentered, even inverted, conventional representations of ethnicity and power. For example, a commune chairman who toured Hanoi and met President Hồ in 1955 expressed surprise and approval at what he called a "very large, densely populated *bản muang*" belonging to Kinh people.[31] For him, the Red River Delta and its urban center displayed all the features of space organized on the Tai model.

Empowered administratively and drawing on deep local knowledge and traditional mass influence, male Tai elites continued to mediate between center and region, counterbalance any one-way Kinh domination, and negotiate terms of centralized rule. Exemplifying this second trend, regional Tai power brokers Lò Văn Hặc and Xa Văn Minh steered the Zonal Administrative Committee, the region's highest body. In his analysis of this period, Tai-Vietnamese historian Cầm Trọng equated Kinh majority "at the center" with Tai majority "in the Northwest" and endowed both with the normative task of "helping small ethnicities to speed development."[32] His statement speaks as much to the expectation of postcolonial progress as to the reconfiguration of socio-spatial relations empowered to deliver it.

Yet postwar development did not come quickly to the Black River region, especially for the highland swidden cultivators and other non-Tai peoples facing severe economic hardship and turning increasingly to an alternative political order. Discussions of autonomy encouraged "people and cadres to connect concrete, post-liberation conditions with Party and Government capacity to care for and help everyday lives."[33] As such, the lived reality of hunger and scattered starvation undermined the state's popular appeal, a third trend propelling autonomy in uncertain directions. Felt most acutely in out-of-the-way highland places, the stagnating economy and dire material shortages raised questions about a self-professed political revolution that, in actual practice, both preserved hereditary Tai ownership of choice bottomland and privileged Tai-ness and Kinh-ness at the expense of hard-fought rights to interethnic equality.

More and more in years to come, growing awareness of such contradictions led many Dao, Hmong, and Khmu peoples to articulate a sharp critique of DRV territorial rule as configured in their homeland. One

Hmong resident looked out over the frontier in 1958 and gave voice to sentiments animating highland peoples divided by borders, estranged from muang politics, and sidelined by Vietnam's national society: "Over there is Lao land, over here—actually, the Northwest in general—is Tai land, downstream is Kinh land."[34] He was one of many marginalized by de jure autonomy and de facto Tai hegemony who, from 1955 to 1958, searched for, and tried to enact, a form of sovereign rule alternative to DRV territory.

If these social conditions still needed a match to catch fire, then the DRV's ratcheting claims on labor, food, and opium provided the proverbial spark. In a region where land was relatively abundant but people few and far between, conscripting labor remained the principal mechanism to recruit manpower for infrastructure work. In addition to roadwork, the construction of irrigation facilities in landscapes suitable for wet rice, such as the plains of Điện Biên and Nghĩa Lộ, required more workers but benefited mostly Tai growers. In 1956, the zone called for nearly thirty-two thousand conscripts and, because many had already served longer than two months in 1955, required them to work "only 30 days per person." But in practice, service duration and frequency continued to vary by class and status position, falling disproportionately on poor women and men.[35] As a result, any nominal distinction between citizen worker (dân công), colonial corvée (phu), or Tai bonded labor (cuông) was wearing thin, especially for the Hmong and Dao peoples recently called to heel and the Khmu folk serving Tai elites all over again.

Meanwhile, the agricultural tax provided the zone's principal source of revenue during a postwar budget deficit, balanced by central government transfers. In 1955 the Thái-Mèo Zone's People's Assembly set rates at 23 percent of household production for wet rice and 13 percent for swidden rice. Like labor service, actual taxation varied due to rampant "errors," a temporary exemption on swidden, and credits for hazards. Nonetheless, taxation expanded and intensified in 1956 by creeping up from the lowlands, where wet-rice farmers paid one-fifth of their harvest, to include swiddeners on an experimental basis. That same year, the central government sought to reduce subsidies by increasing revenue from the region's most valuable cash crop—derived from poppies grown at elevations above a thousand meters. Though state shops had been buying up opium for years, levying the DRV's first ever tax on it in 1956 both overruled the protests of regional officials and caught cultivators by surprise. Apoplectic poppy farmers accused the DRV of "being no different from the French" while officials representing center, county, and region bickered over responsibility for a witch's brew of popular discontent, "policy errors," and dismal yields. Adding fuel to the fire, the swidden tax holiday expired in 1957. That year, less than half of the zone's counties even filed tax returns as swidden communities left fields fallow, slaughtered livestock, sold their opium on the sly, fled to Laos, hid in the forest, or some combination thereof. A regional tax official blamed low compliance on a "not yet stable political situation" and "heavy propaganda for a king," indicating broad protest against the DRV and support for an alternate sovereign.[36]

CALLING FOR A KING AND OTHER FABULOUS STORIES

In this context of cultural ferment, political instability, and economic hardship, fabulous stories and other strange events make more sense and offer insight into the topsy-turvy state of territory in the postcolonial Black River region. However much Ngoc Son may have perplexed the police in early 1955, his story of a frog that predicted flood actually fit the heavy 1956 monsoon and resulting damage. Then, the cloud of locusts he foresaw in Than Uyên really arrived, alongside swarms of rats and other pests sweeping the region. As for his story of a winged child born in such grim conditions, many people did, in fact, find similarly good reason to leave the familiar behind and take flight for a safer place and a better future, especially by crossing the border to Laos.[37] As for Son himself, it remains unclear whether he was a prophet or a messenger and what role, if any, he played in the larger movement for a just king.

Though questions remain about Son, his biography grounds an understanding of territory in history, geography, and conjuncture, all born as much from agency as accident. Born in the mountains of Yên Bái, he came of age during the wars and long privation that accompanied French, Japanese, Chinese, and multiple Vietnamese claims on its space. After fighting on the Lai Châu front during the revolution, he worked as a government inspector at the central granary in Lào Cai. Based at this warehouse of taxed rice, he visited surrounding villages and communes to conscript dân công labor. These small traces of his past lead to a larger story. Like an earlier generation of proto-nationalist Kinh soldiers and civil servants who worked for and against colonial Indochina, he traveled the circuits of the military and bureaucracy generating collective identities and ideas about their rightful spaces. Having fought against empire, he made nation in the same space, both applying and undermining territory's calculative logic—not as ordered by law but as he saw fit. As a low-level cadre in postcolonial Vietnam, he occupied what scholar Ken MacLean calls a "structural location" and an "ambiguous position" where the party/state and the people visibly meet. Positioned at the blurred boundaries of state and society, where ideas of sovereignty and legitimacy operate in everyday ways, he embodied authority over others, enacted material and ideological claims, and mediated the resulting contests.[38] Finally, his arrest in February 1955 came at a conjuncture in the Black River region's historic trajectory: when popular debates about autonomy and ethnicity tested the DRV's claim to represent the Vietnamese nation. In sum, his actions and stories threatened an emergent national state of territory by questioning the ideas and relations grounding its power in highly contested, socially diverse places.

Even as traces of Son and his stories flash briefly in Vietnam's National Archives, records of other strange events appear from the same spatio-temporal conjuncture—likewise shaped by and shaping the shaky state of Vietnamese territory in the Thái-Mèo Zone. Beginning in September 1956, as the main rice crop matured and the tax season approached, reports of vampires (*ma cà rồng*) spread through Nghĩa Lộ's once fertile plain and surrounding hills, now damaged by war and flood. In one case, a mother and child, suspected of spectral blood drinking, were beaten to death by six conspirators and tossed in a river. In another case, a man named Dựng organized trials in two villages to "denounce" a pregnant woman, who narrowly survived. While she recovered in a clinic, police officers cleared her of suspicion. But they discovered that the man "hated" her because, at a prior revolutionary tribunal, she had "accused" him of being "the enemy's left hand," evidence that had helped punish him with jail and political reeducation. As police officers scrambled to shut down more planned trials around Nghĩa Lộ, popular fears and suspicions spread far west to the zone's capital of Thuận Châu where, in December, a man boasted of "grinding a blade to behead vampires."[39]

Although officials did not always recognize it, ideas of vampirism and accusatory practices sometimes indicated popular attempts to grasp intimate, power-laden social relations transformed through revolution and decolonization. The police chief noted that vampire stories had been circulating for some time, at least since the colonial era, but without anyone acting on them. So, he asked, what had changed? Drawing on his investigation, the chief speculated that Dựng had consorted with a "bandit" in jail and a "reactionary" during reeducation before hatching his plan. After conspiring behind bars, he then took advantage of the people's naiveté and "superstition" to destabilize local government. Though he asked the right question, the chief fingered the usual suspects, that is, enemy provocateurs and local backwardness, and left the woman out of his explanation. In so doing, he also overlooked evidence suggesting more diffuse but systemic causes. Not surprisingly, personal vendettas predating or generated by decolonization carried into the postcolonial era. But old disputes, once reworked by the passion of mass politics and the violence of revolution, assumed new organizational forms. The practices of public accusation (*tố cáo*) and denunciation (*đấu*)—recently introduced by radical cadres to mobilize the masses and to root out class enemies, bandits, and traitors—now served to try other friends, neighbors, and kinfolk for wildly different but locally meaningful reasons.

Vampirism and associated violence emerged in close-knit communities at a time when community social reproduction was increasingly determined by forces beyond local control. As in other agrarian societies where the appearance of witches marked periods of rapid social change, vampires appeared when struggles over hunger and food, life and untimely death—what historian Ralph Austen calls "the forces constituting reproduction in everyday life"—spilled from the domestic into the public sphere.[40] It was no mere coincidence that both alleged vampires were women actively reproducing family and household. Furthermore, the upcoming rice harvest and agricultural tax structured reproductive relations between household, village, and national community. The act of drinking someone's blood resembles that of taxing a household's food, both of which consume one's vital, bodily material to enliven and empower a spectral other. In revolutionary and postcolonial Vietnam, that spectral other was also "the state," an imaginary but powerful entity constructed in everyday ways, like taxing food and conscripting labor.

Even as reports of vampires came and went in a Vietnamizing Black River region, an idea of state—as well as governing institutions, practices, and relations—endured.[41] By ordering his officers to "watch over public opinion" in response to vampirism and calls for a just king, the police chief did more than empower them to monitor morale, check residency permits (*hộ khẩu*), inspect goods, and other "routine work." He also indexed a powerful idea of state rising with the DRV, one that shadowed the care cadres professed for peasants. For subjects watched over in such personal and disembodied ways, this idea of state may have even haunted them.

Of all these unusual stories and events, the mounting cries for deliverance by a divine sovereign most directly contested DRV territorial hegemony in the Black River region. Beginning peacefully in late 1954 and peaking violently in mid-1957, popular cries for a just king sounded from highland Hmong and Dao and midland Khmu peoples. Their appeals resonated among communities disaffected with DRV rule and attracted followers in most if not all the zone's counties.[42] Crossing new interstate borders, similar calls and responses followed old cultural and geographic ties east to Hà Giang and the Việt-Bắc Autonomous Zone (established in July 1956), south and west to Laos, and north to China. Fragmented by topography but continuous at altitude, the social movement challenged DRV rule by redefining the terms of autonomy and enacting a revolutionary alternative.

Not surprisingly, the movement's growth tracked official anxieties about its real and perceived security threat, bequeathing scholars a record steeped in misunderstandings and paranoia but nonetheless indicative of deep territorial anxieties and powerful arguments. Written in Vietnamese, all relevant reports stored in Vietnam's National Archives, like sources found in its National Library, refer to a singular movement as "Calling for a King" (*xưng vua đón vua*). Yet it is not clear whether it was, in fact, just one movement or a whole series of movements named as such. Moreover, Vietnamese-language texts inhibit an emic understanding of activities undoubtedly spoken about in local, mutually unintelligible languages. Reflecting more an epistemic problem than a linguistic one, the documents rehearse what historian Ranajit Guha memorably called "the prose of counterinsurgency" in reference to biased English sources on rebellions in colonial India. But, again, context matters. In the Vietnamese postcolony, official primary and secondary sources do more than deny the movement any internal reason and attribute its causal logic to unreason. The sources also lay blame on external, allegedly neocolonial agents. By linking local activists to a foreign threat, DRV officials resorted to what geobody scholar and historian of Thailand Thongchai Winichakul identified as "one of the most persistent strategies of counterinsurgency" in Southeast Asia's Cold War context. Whether in anti-communist Thailand or communist Vietnam, state efforts to other and isolate internal nationals by association with an external enemy legitimized state violence against the polity's own citizens and subjects.[43]

Thinking politically about the movement's pitch for sovereignty destabilizes powerful conventions underlying the state of territory, especially its assumed spatial, communal, and temporal dimensions. Followers of an imaginary sovereign crossed the external boundaries of Vietnamese territory and took advantage of its internal patchiness and instability, demonstrating the spatial heterogeneity of rule. Participants hailed from diverse ethnic groups, notably Hmong, Dao, and Khmu, each with different histories and sometimes diverging cosmologies. But they advanced a remarkably consistent, pan-ethnic vision of renewal, lending credence to more synthetic treatments of millenarianism and prophecy.[44] Versed in emancipatory ideas and practiced in anti-colonial struggles, they pursued a vision of self-rule untethered from the nation-state. In so doing, they strove to reset the clock on community liberation.

Popular stories of a just king whose imminent arrival would inaugurate a bounteous new age offered a potent counternarrative to state stories about national liberation and the reality of postcolonial deprivation. For Hmong, Dao, and Khmu adherents, the "true" or "just" king would appear in response to expressions of popular devotion such as fasting, animal sacrifice, dance, and prayer. Once the supernatural sovereign appeared on earth, prophecies told how he would vanquish enemies, especially Tai and Kinh peoples; free devotees from their present miseries, particularly taxes and labor service; and deliver them youth and wealth, bounty and happiness. Followers quit work, butchered livestock, abandoned fields, and declared days of sabbath to fast and rest, all of which contested the DRV's developmentalist and productionist agenda. The movement mixed clandestine organizing—by building hideouts deep in the forest, for example—with public protest, including marches on towns and military posts. The latter offered cutting critiques of the postcolonial social order. One slogan echoing across the heights of Điện Biên in 1957 went: "Strike the Kinh, strike the Tai! Seize wet-rice land, seize rifles, seize freedom! Unify Hmong and Khmu peoples!"[45] Participants did more than correctly identify which groups constituted the backbone of regional government, penetrating any mystifying veil of "the state." Just three short years after liberation from colonial rule, these activists appropriated revolutionary principles of freedom (*tự do*) and unity (*đoàn kết*), urged radical land reform, and embraced violent tactics—not in support of DRV rule but in opposition to it.

Not simply state concerns over security, what emerges from the sources is an anxious awareness that national territory was not the only—nor even the most popular—understanding of how power operates in space. The movement seemed to confirm the worst fear of DRV officials, one grounded in the historical experience of colonial divide-and-rule and Cold War anti-communist machinations: namely, foreign-led ethnic division and regional separatism. A police report from October 1956, for example, lists the security threats facing the Thái-Mèo Zone, describing DRV officials as "anxious" and indicating a very real possibility of territorial disintegration should two factions join forces. First, "spies" and "bandits" included agents affiliated with French military and intelligence (2B, GCMA, 6ème Section), Lao Royalists, Vietnamese Nationalists (QDĐ), and Chinese Nationalists (GMD/KMT), many of whom had been expelled from the zone but were now rallying in Laos and moving back across the border. Second, "local reactionaries" included unnamed people or groups who, supposedly, took advantage of superstition, low culture, and popular grievance among "small minorities" to call for a Khmu king in Sông Mã, Điện Biên, and Tuần Giáo; a Dao king in Sin Hồ, Phòng Thổ, and Phù Yen; and a Hmong king in Thuận Châu and Mộc Châu.

Significantly, the same police report credits the local faction with "creating a psychology that does not believe in our regime," a statement that confirms an alternative source of territorial legitimacy and betrays the failure of official nationalism to do so. Nonetheless, the report attributed causes of the internal movement(s) to discontents from the ancien régime and Franco-American imperialists who, allegedly, capitalized on local gullibility. The externalization of causality is common in official histories as well, which only rarely name individuals, such as Dao leader

Tẩn A Lồng in Sìn Hồ and Hmong partisan Vàng Súa Báo (aka Sáy Gâu) in Điện Biên, quickly dismissing them as prestigious but traitorous "bandits" led by foreigners. Although the official explanation was plausible given recent French counterinsurgency maneuvers and ongoing U.S. anti-communist operations, such interpretations occlude the possibility that local people knew what they wanted and that the DRV was not delivering it.[46] In so doing, officials overlooked historical antecedents and abundant evidence of their own government's complicity.

A longer view of the 1955–57 Calling for a King movement suggests comparisons with prophetic rebellions across the global south and fits a millenarian tradition among highland peoples of mainland Southeast Asia. As in the era of European imperial expansion, rapid social transformation unsettled livelihood, custom, and belief, prompting prophetic calls to rejuvenate older religio-cultural-political traditions in pursuit of a new era granting community self-rule. Historically, messianic calls for revitalization, widespread belief in the imminent dawn of a new epoch, and resistance against the prevailing social order all echo the 1918–21 Pa Chay Rebellion when Hmong peoples mounted a massive uprising in the Black River region against French rule in Laos and Tonkin. Though the postcolonial movement never amounted to a full-scale armed rebellion, both social movements appealed to Hmong peoples, featured messianic activities, and aired popular grievances, especially over Tai domination and opium taxation. Politically, Kinh officials, like French administrators before them, were relatively unfamiliar with the region's complex social landscape and worked with hereditary Tai elites to manage local affairs. Culturally, much of the above seems to evince what scholar Nicholas Tapp calls the "main elements" in Hmong messianic activity, including a notion that an army of grasshoppers would drive out Kinh and Tai peoples and the ritual practice of sacrificing white livestock to hasten the king's arrival.[47]

Notwithstanding these similarities with earlier Hmong messianic movements, Calling for a King in the Thái-Mèo Zone displayed important differences and invites further study in relation to lasting political unrest in highland Southeast Asia. First, there is little evidence of discussion in 1955–57 about literacy and writing which, in other movements, gave voice to lamentations about a lost form of power. Second, the movement never crystallized around a singular charismatic leader. That no one had emerged by September 1957 to rally the faithful led knowledgeable members of the Hmong community in Điện Biên to withhold their support and warn of consequences. Compared with the "gifted Pa Chay" forty years ago, argued one elderly shaman (*thầy mo*) and veteran of the 1918 movement, "no one has his talents and capacities to rise as king. I've lived 100 years now and still have yet to see a Hmong or Khmu king." The stakes of false recognition were high, and climbing. His colleague, another prestigious shaman, warned of starvation if sacrificial activities continued: "Last year, I believed in the king but lost all my pigs to ritual." Indeed, ritual activity and work abstention combined with ongoing drought and economic stagnation to depress regional food production, increasing the prevalence of hunger yet again.[48]

Such internal splits point to another feature of the 1955–57 movement. Though identified ethnically in DRV reports, Hmong peoples did not act as one according to some predetermined ethno/communal logic. The shamans from Điện Biên inhabited communities that had split factionally over how to conduct relations with the reigning DRV. Differing sharply over how to treat Kinh cadres dispatched "to raise consciousness," some tolerated their earthly efforts while others "hated them and their Kinh king" in solidarity with a heavenly and vengeful Hmong king. As a result, village spaces fractured: one faction traveled on one road, fetched water from one spring, and denied their rivals access. Pivoting on whose vision of sovereignty was morally correct and how to conduct one's self on earth accordingly, such divisions likely have roots in competing family and clan lineages within Hmong society—an issue analyzed astutely by scholar Mai Na Lee.[49]

In the significant but tragic case of Mộc Châu, such divisions internal to Hmong communities helped hasten the broader movement's end. Located at a strategic crossroads and a gateway to Laos, Mộc Châu County was home to Hmong communities who had hosted a guerilla base in the mountains of Kiến Thiết Commune since early 1952, if not earlier. Right from the start, strong revolutionary support mixed with heavy logistics work to produce ambivalent responses to the DRV. Faced with the agricultural tax, some farmers abandoned cassava fields and fled to Laos rather than pay up. Others protested under slogans like "Liberate yourselves from the agricultural tax" and "Free the *dân công*."[50] Employing clever wordplay, these Vietnamese-language phrases mix the radical ideas and concrete grievances stirred by revolutionary participation. As elsewhere, the political mix was unstable and the territorial outcome uncertain.

Then, during escalating millenarian activities in April 1957, a young Hmong swidden farmer born in Kiến Thiết returned from a visit to Laos and declared a vision of apocalyptic renewal, attracting a militant core but repelling others. So, he and a border-crossing coterie intimidated Hmong nonfollowers, stole their livestock, and forced them to watch as they turned the village commons into a veritable abattoir. They also abducted four opponents, including a member of the county's Administrative Committee, and forced their prisoners into servitude. Admonishing adherents to "ignore the Government" as soldiers and police officers scrambled, they marched reticent villagers to a hideout, ordered them to pray alongside followers, and awaited deliverance. When confronted by DRV armed forces in May, the ringleaders murdered the four prisoners, butchering one person as though an animal. As many as seven died in the resulting shootout and confusion.[51] After that, the DRV no longer countenanced open protests against tax and labor policy nor earthly activities organized around ideas of an alternate if still supernatural sovereign. More than simply jail the movement's leaders, officials even locked up its textual traces deep inside the archives for over sixty years.

Although well documented in Vietnam's National Archives, the 1955–57 movement is virtually unknown to scholars. While Vietnamese secondary sources mention king calling only in passing and just in reference to Hmong cultural practice, an American anthropologist reported ritual activities and messianic ideas already widespread among many Khmu and some Hmong communities around Luang Prabang in 1956. Analyzing the movement in more detail and, if possible, through oral histories with former participants, promises significant historical insight. Notably, Calling for a King predates later, richly studied Hmong movements, such as the "mother of writing" in Laos from 1959–67 and the evangelical Protestant awakening in Vietnam in the 2000s. The former became violently embroiled in the Second Indochina War, especially the so-called Secret War in Laos when CIA-sponsored Hmong militias fought the People's Army of Vietnam, the DRV's Pathet Lao allies, and among themselves. Their defeat in 1975 stimulated an exodus from Laos, resulting in a Hmong diasporic community with large populations in the U.S. and France. The latter movement illustrates how Hmong messianism often overlaps with Christianity and persists in novel yet still contested forms in Vietnam to this day.[52]

In sharp contrast to the Pa Chay movement when Hmong rebels brutalized Khmu, Lao, and Tai peoples, Calling for a King in postcolonial Vietnam assembled a broad coalition of disaffected peoples across significant cultural and agro-ecological cleavages. Sharing everyday hardships as swidden-cultivating "small ethnicities" in the postcolony, Khmu, Dao, Akha (U Ni), and Lao peoples joined forces with their more numerous Hmong neighbors. Influenced by nationalist organizing but embracing their own kind of unity, they articulated a potent critique of the ethnic bias inflecting DRV regional administration, one that hitched downstream Kinh political cadres to upstream Tai power brokers. For the king callers, the Thái-Mèo Zone built on long patterns of Tai domination dating from the precolonial Sip Song Chau Tai through colonial rule under the Đèo clan and into the neocolonial Tai Federation. Seen from this angle, the zone's 1956 decision to tax opium represented only the latest in a series of powerful efforts to wrest from swidden cultivators control over their resources, bodies, and collective destiny. Although their grievances with the DRV began with logistics service during war, the departure of the People's Army in 1954 opened new space for protest just as socio-natural conditions failed to improve with peace. In fact, so persuasive was the swidden cultivators' supernatural vision of a better future that even Tai wet-rice farmers in the valleys began to issue calls for deliverance by a divine sovereign. In 1958, recalling a mythical past when having "Royalty" (*Rồng*) meant adequate rainfall, Tai peoples in Mường Lay and Mường Tè called for a Tai king "to release the *bản muang* from drought."[53]

Movement participants believed in revolutionary social transformation but took it their own way, serving the spirit if not the letter of a people's revolution. By embracing an idea of self-rule and carrying it far beyond regional autonomy, they cast doubt on Vietnam's national unity and revealed splits within the DRV state itself. "Autonomy," snorted one man in Văn Chấn, "only when there are no more Kinh people will there be real autonomy."[54] Neither nation nor the state claiming to represent it were monolithic. Local ideas of autonomy etched these cleavages in space. In its attempt to break with the colonial past, the DRV had introduced historically marginalized peoples to radical ideas of equality and freedom, trained them in guerilla warfare to achieve these aims, offered positions in the regional bureaucracy, and held out the possibility of autonomy. Yet there was no guarantee that anyone's subsequent political activities would proceed as intended.

Like low-level cadres, high-ranking local officials in the Thái-Mèo Zone negotiated terrain unsettled by revolution and war, underlining their complex subject positions and the ambiguous spaces produced through ongoing contests over territorial sovereignty. In August 1956, the police uncovered two plots in which senior Hmong and Khmu cadres had, beginning with discussions of autonomy in winter 1955, used their positions to reach DRV subjects and organize them for the arrival of an alternate sovereign. First, by greeting large audiences under the pretense of tax education, two upper-level Khmu officials—one a representative on the Thái-Mèo Zone's People's Assembly and the other the vice chairman of Mai Sơn County's Administrative Committee—had mobilized dozens of supporters who then sacrificed hundreds of white animals, built a fort in Sông Mã, and stocked it with provisions. Second, and acting in concert with their Khmu colleagues, several Hmong cadres—one of whom was a party member and decorated veteran—leveraged their bureaucratic mobility to build solidarity between far-flung Hmong communities in Điện Biên and Thuận Châu. They supervised ritual activities, mobilized veterans into platoons, and warned that any "western" (*tây*) cadres disloyal to the Hmong king would die on his arrival.[55] Revolutionary shorthand for the French enemy, the reference to "western" opponents bespeaks an anti-colonial spirit lingering in the postcolony.

Analytically, these complex political actions do not fit what influential scholarship glosses as a neat binary of state or anti-state, and their theater of operations blurs state and nonstate spaces. Indeed, the biographies of these DRV leaders and king callers resemble that of the visionary cadre Ngoc Son. Educated in freedom and autonomy by state agents, they acted like loyal cadres but enacted interpretations that strayed from the official script. In so doing, they inverted the process of state learning that had won the First Indochina War but failed to deliver prosperity afterward. Even as the DRV used local officials to increase society's legibility, these local officials used their DRV positions to escape the state's gaze. In short, they embodied a strategic stance that alternately resisted, accommodated, and allied with the state in order to achieve their own ideal form of spatial sovereignty.[56]

Emerging from the ashes of empire, their radical vision of sovereign space transcended nation-state territory fitted out in colonial spaces. Movement participants in Vietnam reached across the French-demarcated border to Laos, invigorated old ties of kin and clan, and united communities across a shared landscape of mountains and forests, villages and swidden fields. Riding with flows of people moving back and forth across the fluid frontier, the Hmong and Khmu leaders coordinated with counterparts in Laos likewise inspired by radical anti-colonial struggle but facing similar hardship under a revolutionary government. In Houa Phan Province, where the Pathet Lao allied with the DRV against the anti-communist Royal Kingdom, Khmu activists prepared to welcome a "Heavenly Lord" (*Châu Phạ*) and rallied supporters with the slogan "Kill the Kinh, marry the Tai, and wipe out the Lao Government," referring to the Pathet Lao. Though nominally different, idiomatic references to "western" and "Kinh" political opponents share origins in Indochinese colonialism: whereas "westerner" indexed French colonials in Vietnam, Kinh officials had occupied over half the posts in the Lao colonial bureaucracy but constituted only 2 percent of the protectorate's population.[57] Further, they all recognized the power of the Tai muang even as they differed over whether to incorporate or drive out its leaders. Taken together, the border-crossing activities suggest how movement participants embraced anti-colonial revolution, mobilized against its intended, statist beneficiaries, and strove to create a space of their own. Informed by radical ideals and steeped in guerilla warfare, they struggled within and across nation-state territory to establish their own vision of autonomy. In so doing, they generated a vision of sovereign space that suited their social terrain.

Calling for a King activities coalesced around a cutting critique of DRV tax and labor policies, one that severed its most devoted followers' everyday ties to the Vietnamese geobody. In early 1957, cadres redoubled their efforts to legitimize resource appropriation by redeploying a nationalist territorial discourse among disaffected Hmong, Khmu, Dao, Xinh Mun, and Akha peoples. Aiming to link policy mandates to duties of citizenship, cadres stressed, "Contributing energy, contributing belongings, and then contributing again builds the country and defends the homeland." Yet at the movement's peak a few months later, an investigation of Hmong communities in Điện Biên found abandoned opium fields, empty corrals, and rice plants gone to seed. Their owners "mocked and complained about labor service and opium policies." Some even "held forth that now [tax collectors] take our opium, tomorrow swidden rice, and perhaps even all pigs and chickens too." Not simply populist sentiment, such popular protest emerged out of longer contests over the rightfulness of sovereign claims levied territorially on things and bodies. In fact, many protesters there and elsewhere did "contribute" their labor and land—just not exactly as cadres instructed.[58] They danced, prayed, fasted, and offered rice, livestock, and coin not to the DRV and Vietnamese geobody, but to an alternate sovereign and spatial imaginary.

As movement activities reached a fever pitch in mid-1957, the DRV countered with a broad crackdown that, with no hint of irony, drew on colonial expertise to jail movement leaders. After an incident in Quan Hóa District, Thanh Hóa Province in April and the deadly confrontation in Mộc Châu County in May, the central government coordinated efforts among police, military, and courts to break up devotional gatherings, reoccupy restive areas, and arrest, try, and imprison prominent participants. When Division 335 of the People's Army deployed to the Mộc Châu plateau, some five hundred people to the west in Sông Mã bolted across the border to Laos, taking steam out of the movement. Although popular calls for a king continued to sound from the zone's heights in years to come, the DRV drew on the expertise of a regional power broker to silence the movement's chief visionaries. Lò Văn Mười—former corrections officer at the notorious Sơn La Penitentiary, partisan in the Vietnamese revolution, and DRV territorial administrator—now served as chief justice of the Thái-Mèo Zone's People's Tribunal.[59] It was an ironic twist in Mười's long revolutionary career: from subverting colonial rule within its prison system, he had come full circle to enforce nation-state rule by jailing postcolonial radicals. Then again, he acted consistently in support of revolutionary state formation and a particular vision of Vietnam's national unity.

Mười's biography and regional ideas informed a verdict on Calling for a King that reoriented the Black River region in relation to Vietnamese territory in powerful and lasting ways. As jailer turned judge, he still operated on home turf: born in Thuận Châu to an elite Tai family, he now presided there over the zone's highest court. Tellingly, the opening lines of his March 1958 verdict on movement participants revived a geographic discourse that traces the region's longer transformation through revolution and DRV rule. He began: "The region's rolling forests and mountains, where land is spacious and people sparse, have a 700-km long border that is difficult to patrol." A decade after Mười coined the phrase, the idea of "vast land sparse people" once again conjured a Vietnamese geobody: framing the mountainous frontier by way of comparison with the Kinh-Việt heartland in the Red River Delta where, the saying goes, there is "little land, many people." In so doing, Mười gestured to an old notion of Tai-Kinh unity, one he now embodied in conjunction with the DRV prosecutor, a Kinh man named Lê Văn Lợi.

Alongside these continuities and connections, however, were important changes regarding the Black River region's place in the Vietnamese geobody as of 1958. A decade earlier, cadre Mười's discourse had smoothed the region's physical and cultural differences in favor of revolutionary solidarity and national, interethnic unity. Now, Justice Mười highlighted these geographic differences as a means to consolidate state territorial power and criminalize what he deemed a "counterrevolutionary" movement. His decision justified state violence against movement leaders, called foreign "spies" and domestic "reactionaries," with police force and prison sentences up to twenty years. It also marginalized movement followers as ethnically other, culturally inferior, and physically remote. He invoked the region's rugged, inaccessible terrain and its allegedly poor, backward, and superstitious peoples—"especially those ethnic minorities in the highlands"—as reason to secure territorial borders against foreign enemies and boost development and education among peoples with a "low cultural level." By explicitly othering peoples based on ethnicity, isolating them by elevation, minimizing them by population count, and dismissing their opinions as uninformed, he ruled against the legitimacy of their aspirations and grievances, crediting both to external sources instead. In so doing, he implicitly posited the cultural superiority of demographic majorities—Kinh in nation, Tai in region—and legitimized their paired role in the DRV state as guardians of territory.

At another moment of broad uncertainty and deep official anxiety about Vietnamese territorial integrity, Mười once again played the key role of regional power broker.[60] His 1958 ruling decided that Calling for a King resulted from local gullibility and enemy subversion, sentenced participants to jail and, most of all, buttressed the DRV's claim to sovereign rule of a contested region. Backed by renewed force, the territorial claim reduced autonomous spaces within the Thái-Mèo Zone just as it reproduced contest along its borders.

Much more than any real or perceived external security threat, however, popular calls for a king destabilized nation-state territory by advancing a sovereign alternative to the DRV and a spatial imaginary alternative to the Vietnamese geobody. Ever since guerilla warfare in the late 1940s, DRV claim-making processes were as material as ideological: striving not simply to appropriate resources but also to bind citizen to nation through ideas of contribution, patriotism, and rightful duty in a shared space of struggle. Such arguments socialized the Vietnamese geobody in everyday ways yet emplaced tensions deep inside DRV territory. In addition to exposing these tensions, Calling for a King generated a regional geobody that departed from one imagined nationally. Movement participants advanced a way of thinking about power in space that mapped old social topographies, crossed new interstate borders, and granted sovereignty over bodies and land.

WATCHING OVER A NEW ERA

Delivered toward the end of the long 1950s, Justice Mười's 1958 verdict on Calling for a King capped a larger transformation of community and space in former Indochina broadly, Vietnam generally, and the Black River region particularly. The period began with a small nationalist revolt in 1945, traced an escalating people's war to victory over French rule in 1954, split into an indeterminate autonomy movement, and ended with coercive national integration around 1960. Along the way, the once obscure border outpost at Điện Biên Phủ became a beacon of anticolonial liberation before quietly but forcefully staking a sovereign claim at territory's edge. Through it all, the realization of DRV territory in line with a Vietnamese geobody—one tracing the colonial space of Tonkin, bounding its rugged northwest quadrant, and stopping short of Laos and China—was always uncertain and anxious, debated and contested. By the late 1950s, however, the signs of growing Vietnamese territorial domination in the Black River region were hard to ignore, inaugurating a new era in the region's longer history.

Even as policies displayed a measure of continuity beyond the late 1950s, Calling for a King fundamentally changed how the DRV approached diverse peoples throughout the highlands of northern Vietnam. Development and Ethnic Policy remained top state priorities, but their justification tilted from arguments favoring material progress and social equality toward rectifying weak security and disloyal politics. In a November 1958 decision advancing economic and cultural development in the uplands, party leaders in Hanoi placed "special emphasis" on links between "politics, economics, and defense" across "vast mountain areas" and, in novel language, "border zones" (*vùng biên giới*). Old policies that sought to strengthen state shops and extend transportation infrastructure assumed new meaning in light of this dawning border awareness and growing concern with domestic political stability. The decision also targeted swidden cultivators for "forest protection" and "fixed cultivation," part of a larger shift away from tolerating the agricultural practice toward regulating it ever more tightly. "Doing so is not just a matter of Ethnic Policy," read the decision, "but also relates to maintaining security and order, to creating a good political influence."[61] The party's increasing preoccupation with security, order, and legitimacy among non-Kinh peoples, especially in the highlands and along borders, would inform DRV policy for decades to come.

Far from marginal, the Thái-Mèo Zone was at the territorial center of the DRV's broader push to securitize external borders and regulate internal forms of socio-environmental difference. When drought and agrarian contests carried into 1958, hunger spread to its highest rate yet among the zone's wet-rice and swidden cultivators, affecting ninety-five thousand people, or almost one-third of the population. As before, official reports mention nothing of hunger's political causes even as welfare agencies seized the opportunity to legitimize state power in line with a broader postcolonial development agenda. But now, in wake of their popular challenge to DRV sovereign authority, Hmong, Khmu, Akha, Dao, and other hungry swidden cultivators earned an extra helping of ideology along with food aid and agricultural assistance. Infusing state-society relations with a dose of paternalism, Vice Chairman Hặc ordered the zone's cadres to stress that "the Government and Party always cares for the ethnic minorities on the homeland's borders." Delivering emergency rice, he explained, "causes a good political influence and makes peoples on the border see clearly the beauty of our regime."[62] Hặc's provision of food aid in January 1958, then, shared the same ethno-spatial security logic underlying Justice Mười's pitch for development and education in March. In turn, party leaders in Hanoi expanded on the regional approach later that November and made it national policy, even rehearsing Hặc's idiom for its desired legitimation effects.

If increasing access to scarce resources was a carrot for wayward subjects of the DRV regime, then the stick came with increasing use of police and military force. The zone's police force watched over Calling for a King obsessively. More than simply inform zone and center about the movement's perceived security threats, the police argued consistently for more funding and manpower to reach places far from their gaze; they found strong support among the zone's party leadership. So, in addition to training local militias, surveilling suspects, inspecting cadres, and securing borders, the police activated a feedback loop with policy makers that strengthened such forms of state security and scrutiny. The bureaucratic mechanism propelled the DRV state back up mountains, through forests, and over hills to "follow closely" (theo dõi) those swidden communities that had long inhabited terrain beyond lowland control. Five years after withdrawing its formidable logistics apparatus, this time the state was here to stay. Soldiers, too, were deployed internally, both to stabilize areas recently shaken by violent protest, like Mộc Châu, Điện Biên, and Sông Mã, and to enforce the DRV monopoly on opium. Meanwhile, as the Lao Civil War escalated and China's Great Leap Forward gained momentum in Yunnan, refugees spilled into the Thái-Mèo Zone, reversing prior flows. In response, the People's Army stepped up patrols along its long external border, sometimes stepping across it in what American diplomats at the United Nations called "incursions" into Lao territory.[63]

In tandem with the use of force, the social process of militarization reintensified with the DRV's embrace of culture as a weapon in a longer war of revolutionary enlightenment. Inspired by Prime Minister Phạm Văn Đồng's militarist declaration that "culture is an ideological weapon," popular education stressed the zone's "strategic location" and aimed to "instill patriotism" through films, picture shows, theater, and handicrafts. Cultural outreach and education expanded throughout the zone but, like food aid and in hand with its provision, focused suspicious attention on highlands and borders. While developing both Tai- and Hmong-language scripts, for example, the government focused surveillance and propaganda on the Hmong and other groups who lived outside the muang but inside DRV borders. Worried that these groups often knew no Vietnamese and worse, could not differentiate colonial from postcolonial regimes, cultural cadres accompanied police and army patrols to collect knowledge and disseminate DRV propaganda. They introduced ideas of material development and linear progress, strove to eliminate "superstitious" and "backward" behaviors, and targeted "mountain society" for long-term "reform" (*cải tạo*), using a term reserved for coercive political reeducation.[64] In short, the coordinated security response to Calling for a King meant that autonomous spaces alternative to the Thái-Mèo Autonomous Zone were closing fast.

At this moment of coercive regional integration, General Giáp stepped into the breach and foretold of a Vietnam that was as fabulous as any realm imagined by recently vanquished Hmong, Dao, or Khmu prophets. Speaking in Thuận Châu in June 1958 before an assembly of the Thái-Mèo Zone's bureaucratic corps, he announced the central government's policy shift from war recovery and economic rebuilding (1954–57) to its second three-year plan emphasizing preparations for socialism (1958–60).[65] Deferring a policy discussion, he devoted his speech instead to elucidating a bold regional imaginary, what he called a "dream for the Northwest." His dream (*mơ màng*) cast the Black River region as an integral part of "our country"—a singular nation temporarily divided into north and south by the Geneva Agreement but one soon to reunite through renewed struggle. By colloquially equating country with water, as in "our water" (*nước ta*), he argued that the northwest helped make Vietnam whole by joining upstream and downstream, mountain to delta, "ethnic minority" with majority Kinh. Ever the people's general, he stressed how integrating national defense with economic transformation would enable the "most backward" region in a backward nation to catch up with advanced socialist societies.

With faith in Marxism-Leninism, he promised not only enough to eat for "isolated ethnic minorities" but also prosperity for all so long as everyone believed in communism and saw his or her duties clearly. He envisioned hydroelectric dams on the Black River, aircraft carrying civilians to Điện Biên Phủ and Nà Sản, farmers working in collectives and harvesting ever more rice, mines plundering Lai Châu's underground riches, and the mountain masses cured of malaria. With a wry sense of humor, he foretold how soldiers on state farms (*nông trường*) would plow Điện Biên's plain and Mộc Châu's plateau using "iron water buffalos," investing tractors with a fabulism not far from talking frogs. He admitted that such a modern vision of the Thái-Mèo Zone sounded fanciful, even unrealistic, and that achieving it would be difficult. But he expressed faith in Lò Văn Hặc and party leaders, praised their commitment to overcoming hardship, chastised downstream cadres for homesickness, and exhorted them all to "embrace the spirit of sacrifice" and "contribute to the zone's construction." Moreover, he encouraged his audience to draw inspiration from how the Soviet Union had developed Uzbekistan and China Xinjiang: both united multiple ethnicities through socialist development, built schools to educate backward peoples, watered cotton in deserts and, in sum, delivered on dreams of prosperity. "If the Soviet Union and China can do it," he concluded to rousing applause, "we can too."

Although a highland kingdom and socialist modernity in Vietnam sounded like equally fanciful geobody visions, what enabled the realization of Giáp's dream was his capacity to wield the powers of state to mobilize population, administer territory, and deploy an army. When he returned to Thuận Châu in May 1959 to celebrate the fifth anniversary of victory at Điện Biên Phủ, he let his charismatic fellow traveler President Hồ Chí Minh offer the rousing vision of party-state leadership, national unity, and socialist prosperity.[66] Sharing the stage was Lò Văn Hặc, now the zone's chairman (figure 23).

Flanked by the regional and national leaders, General Giáp got down to business, discussing tactics necessary to prepare for the DRV's first five-year plan, scheduled to begin in 1961. Citing the massive irrigation works under way to water Điện Biên's plain, he encouraged ongoing cooperative labor performed by upstream and downstream peoples alongside cadres and soldiers, especially those veterans who had "made the Northwest their second home." Here, he pointed to landscape transformation and resettlement programs that were relocating Kinh peoples to the uplands and urging swidden cultivators to adopt sedentary agriculture.[67] Continuing, he acknowledged increases in grain production but

FIG. 23. Hoisting a banner in Thuận Châu, 1959. Celebrating the fifth anniversary of victory at Điện Biên Phủ with General Võ Nguyên Giáp (in cap), zone chairman Lò Văn Hặc and President Hồ Chí Minh display a bilingual banner that reads, "Unity, Emulation, Victory." (© Khu di tích Chủ tịch Hồ Chí Minh tại Phủ Chủ tịch.)

called for still higher targets the next year. He appreciated the smooth ride from Hanoi to Lai Châu but ordered even more road construction and river traffic to increase the flow of goods between upstream and downstream.

He also intensified the DRV's aggressive turn on highland areas generally and in the Black River region particularly as sites of territorial insecurity, popular ignorance, and ethnic difference. Though he did not mention Calling for a King, his speech drew on party-state orders that explain the escalating security measures as its direct result: Directive 128 of 24 February 1959 (128-CT/TW), for example, equates Calling for a King with the threat posed by none other than President Ngô Đình Diệm in the breakaway southern Republic of Vietnam.[68] Whereas confronting the latter precipitated the Second Indochina War, pacifying the Lao-Viet border and highland spaces was a low-intensity conflict that nonetheless fed back into these larger, hotter Cold War struggles. The directive increased monitoring and surveillance (literally, "watching over"), mobilized rapid response forces, and ordered "full implementation" of a program euphemistically called "Democratic Improvement" (*Cải cách dân chủ*).

It was this program that Giáp spent much of his May 1959 speech introducing. He stated that center and region had decided now was the time to solve three old problems: unequal land distribution, "feudal" local government, and popular ideology that failed to identify the proper "enemy." Aiming to solve each of these problems, Democratic Improvement tailored land and labor collectivization to upstream peoples who had thus far escaped land reform and had only begun to pool their labor; concentrated state economic planning at the commune (xã) and purged local government of "reactionaries"; and targeted people in the highlands and along borders for intensive political education and surveillance.[69] In short, he announced a program to centralize control over land, labor, and governance in the Thái-Mèo Zone—with force as necessary.

Though Giáp granted local authorities leeway to adjust collectivization to local conditions, he emphasized the central government's priority: securing territory and mobilizing population. Vested with these powers to watch over space and people, he anticipated new contests to come. The DRV's 1959 Constitution eliminated private property in the north and subsumed all "ethnicities" firmly within Vietnamese nation and territory. Moreover, the Politburo was shifting toward war against President Diệm and the breakaway southern republic, a decision that intensified the Lao Civil War and its border-crossing effects. Lê Duẩn was on the rise, and he was leading the party toward a more aggressive stance on both fronts.[70] Elected VWP secretary in 1960, he sidelined moderates, stressed military solutions, and oversaw two more Indochina wars. Shaping and shaped by all these decisions and policies, the Black River region would remain at war for two more decades.

Another round of territorial construction was about to begin, one that still featured negotiations over regional linkages but now offered much less space for autonomy. As such, Giáp's acknowledgment that "collectivization would entail a process of struggle" only hinted at hardships on the horizon for peoples in the Black River region and in a divided Vietnam more broadly. The legacy of Calling for a King was seen as much in how the DRV treated the northwest as in how the DRV treated any claims of territorial sovereignty that rivaled its own.

Epilogue

RECOUNTING ĐIỆN BIÊN PHỦ

TERRITORY, ĐIỆN BIÊN PHỦ TEACHES US, is contested in the realm of ideas and on the ground. Arguing against territory as a given spatial container, critical geographers have advanced significant insights into how territory is produced. First, powerful processes drive territorial production at multiple scales, from bodies and local social movements to armies, government policies, and transnational economic flows. Even if they appear complete, these processes continue to mold and reflect power relations in space through memory, legitimacy, and representation, including maps. Second, territory is also a strategy of rule, a political technology that operates on society and space through property and economy as well as possession and organized violence. To these important ideas, *Contested Territory* has added a conceptualization of territory as a spatial outcome of contingent contests in specific contexts. If scholars' early theorizations of territory tended to generalize from a Euro-American norm, this book thinks through the context of Southeast Asia and the Himalayan massif.

Centering the many contests around Điện Biên Phủ brings Vietnamese history into dialogue with theories of space and power. In turn, situating these contests in the Black River region highlights the work that went into conceiving Vietnam at a conjunctural moment. Territory in the First Indochina War was contested—but not simply between France and an already extant Vietnam. Rather, Vietnam was and remains a project, much like the Democratic Republic that led its postcolonial construction. Making nation and state was coeval with making an associated territory, including its mutably imagined expanse, or geobody. The project was fraught with multiple contests internal to its space, the final shape of which was never predestined.

Likewise, many of the people now called "Vietnamese" only became so during the period in question. Most people in the Black River borderlands had more in common with their neighbors in Laos and China than downstream Kinh (Việt) peoples. Socially diverse and environmentally adapted, very few spoke the Vietnamese language before 1954. Their fate, like the nation itself, was neither inevitable nor foreordained. Scholars must therefore attend both to the ways in which territory was understood and experienced by the people essential in its making as well as to how territory shaped their understandings of self, other, and community.

Vietnam's anti-colonial victory over France was but one of many struggles that enlisted local peoples as the embattled place of Điện Biên Phủ became a crucible in the longer transformation of the Black River borderlands into Vietnam's northwest frontier. Place, region, and people became Vietnamese through mass mobilization of residents, incorporation of Tai muang political structures, and military conquest of space. The associated contests then carried into the postcolony. Debates over autonomy inspired ideas of self-rule that were as informed by revolutionary equality, national solidarity, and socialist prosperity as they were grounded in traditions of millenarian renewal and prophetic rebellion. Among its Hmong, Dao, and Khmu adherents, Calling for a King advanced a vision of sovereign space and community that mapped onto the region's rugged topography and social diversity. The movement was brutally suppressed, even its history largely erased. Coming to terms with its erasure and what remains in the archives is also part of the process of territorial (re)construction.

Constructed hand in hand with state power, the Vietnamese National Archives chronicle the construction of territory through the eyes of officials and, sometimes, the voices and feelings of the people they watched over. Inadvertently, this surveillance sometimes records the ambiguity that nationalist narratives so often suppress. An idiom of how state power operates in space, "watching over" captures the ambivalence of being protected by a kind policeman but suspiciously surveilled, or of being cared for by a parent but disciplined for bad behavior. Such was the experience of working as a dân công laborer, of being a citizen (công dân) and a resource-bearing subject simultaneously. Operating on bodies but often in a distant way, watching over was also a tactic rising with DRV state capacity to police and protect individuals within its claimed territory. It partially, but not fully, displaced the revolutionary exchange, an earlier mode of state-society relations built on reciprocity in and across the shifting spaces of guerilla warfare. Whereas mixing terms of trade and rule had produced an affect approaching unconditional love in 1950, watching over thereafter generated a distinctly ambiguous sense about state power. Emerging with individualized claims on bodies and food made in the name of nation, the affective oscillation between enthusiasm and anxiety carried into the postcolony.

As state tactic and social effect, watching over grew more pervasive over the long 1950s as DRV state capacity expanded and intensified throughout its claimed territory. The Điện Biên Phủ Campaign of 1953–54 was a crucial moment when agrarian resources in northern Vietnam reached a character of calculability, thus becoming appropriable for the logistics so central to the army's ultimate victory. But counting and accounting practices also discounted social costs, overlooking hunger and spreading discontent. Elites in Hanoi were caught by surprise when the calculative strategies they had pursued in war wound up backfiring years later in peacetime. Nonetheless, the enumerative practices had already begun to assume another role, this time by recounting a particular history of people and things in space. If watching over and its ambivalent effects characterized territorial construction in the moment, then recounting territory has rendered this historical process in starkly nationalist and militarist terms.

Not built in the moment alone, territory is continually constructed through memory and history. The archives are not neutral, nor are the documents they contain. Powerful silences punctuate the record, and very few people have a say. Nonetheless, archives offer primary source material that, if read critically, reveals ambiguity about power relations and uncertainty about the future. By contrast, Vietnamese commemoration in and of Điện Biên Phủ erases such ambiguity and uncertainty. For example, cadre Hoàng Công Phẩm's memoir, discussed in chapter 5, may valorize the Vietnamese-ness of the Black River region, but he observed and experienced varying responses to military intervention all the same. His editors upped the ante by stressing a timeless isomorphism between nation, state, and territory.

Featured in an edited volume celebrating the great victory's fiftieth anniversary, the cadre's memoir was enlisted in a much larger, officially sanctioned commemoration of the battle and its meaning. Authored by the publishing house in Huế, the introduction captures a curious paradox characteristic of this effort. The corporate author writes, "The Điện Biên Phủ Campaign has entered the history of twentieth-century mankind as a noble and eternal history." Even as Phẩm dated his experiences meticulously, the publisher presents them as outside of history. It goes further still: by equating military triumph with "victory for the strength and unity of the Vietnamese people," the introduction extricates a particular idea of nation from the vicissitudes of contingency, contest, and disunity.[1] Published in 2004, the volume does not specify when Phẩm wrote his piece. As such, it represents a historically specific recollection as one that stands both outside time yet always with and for Vietnam.

Part and parcel of territorial construction, commemoration is a powerful process that has shaped not just the memory of Điện Biên Phủ but the place itself. The centralized construction of its official meaning began immediately after combat's conclusion. Two days after People's Army soldiers had planted the DRV's red flag with gold star on General De Castrie's command post, the Executive Committee of the Vietnam Workers' Party celebrated the outcome but overlooked its terrible toll. In a letter to campaign participants dated 9 May 1954, VWP leaders hailed "our full win, the elimination of all enemy forces at Điện Biên Phủ, and the complete liberation of all the Northwest Zone." Its triumphal tone left little room for nuance and less for messy reality. Moreover, even while praising "the great (*vĩ đại*) victory at Điện Biên Phủ" and the campaign's "selfless struggle," the party's leaders warned of more hardship to come. Thus, they urged all cadres, soldiers, and laborers to learn from the experience, strengthen "our forces," and shoulder new duties. Less a place with a long history than an event fixed in time, Điện Biên Phủ now assumed meaning outside this time frame too, as a metaphor.[2] Vietnam's central elites had already begun to pry Điện Biên Phủ loose from the Black River region, reframing it as a mobilization tactic and an exemplary lesson in how Vietnam could win any war against all odds.

The tension between understanding Điện Biên Phủ either as a place with a complex and layered history or as a tactical lesson in state learning grew from there. Two days later, the Politburo instructed all DRV officials to propagate the center's interpretation of Điện Biên Phủ and its geographic representation. Referring repeatedly to the place in terms of "our great victory" there, the instructions of 11 May 1954 stressed what Điện Biên Phủ ought to mean.[3] As the largest victory in the winter/spring offensive, it signaled the strategic defeat of the Navarre Plan and the Franco-American alliance. It was proof that the army could win decisive battles in fixed-position warfare. It was evidence of the extraordinary capacity of people and party to serve military fronts and "organize warfare on a new scale." To disseminate this message throughout DRV territory, the instructions spelled out several slogans, including "Trust thoroughly in the clear-sighted leadership of President Hồ, the Party, and the Government." Written in bold letters and posted on big banners, the slogans were to be displayed where "the masses concentrate," such as traffic intersections.

Alongside the banners, the Politburo ordered the display of one more image: "There should be a map to introduce Điện Biên Phủ." Almost an afterthought, this last item signaled the place's precarious position in relation to the Vietnamese geobody. Even after the all-out, months-long military campaign, many people *still* knew neither the place for which it was named nor where to find it. That Vietnamese people were unlikely to know Điện Biên Phủ and its location only underlines how odd the place's attachment was to their idea of Vietnam at the time. Indeed, what must have stood out in any such map was less the site itself than the borders positioning it just inside the nascent nation's imaginary space. Delineated and claimed by DRV elites, the Vietnamese geobody stretched south to Cambodia, west to Laos, and over the other three regions of Indochina. The DRV's actual hold on the corresponding territory, as this book has demonstrated, was a different matter.

Just because the instructions were created did not mean that everyone followed them. Nonetheless, archival records show how central elites leveraged their position atop DRV territorial administration to correct erroneous interpretations among subordinate officials, officers, and party members. In August 1954, the Northwest Zone's Administrative Committee convened to discuss its past work and plan future endeavors. Its typewritten report was signed by a representative in October, sent to the central government, and is now filed under the Prime Minister's Secretariat (PTTg) record group.[4] One passage edited by hand and in pen—the cuts shown here in strikethrough and the additions in curly brackets—reveals how an anonymous superior had altered the original report's meaning to comply with the instructions described above: "We have already completed two duties: preparing and serving the {great} Dien Bien campaign and mobilizing the masses. In particular, the ~~great~~ service to the {great Dien Bien} campaign surpassed targets and beat deadlines." Writing from a regional perspective, the original author had used the adjective "great" (*vĩ đại*) to modify "service," referring to all the local labor and food logistically necessary to achieve the campaign's outcome. The superior official, however, disagreed with his subordinate's interpretation and corrected it by scratching out "great" in relation to service. Empowered by the party's letter of 9 May that dictated "great" in relation to victory, he moved it to modify the campaign instead. As such, the anonymous editor placed laudatory emphasis on the DRV's leadership of a military tactic rather than on what so many people had done on the ground. In subsequent reports to the center, the zone used "great" in line with the center's corrections.[5]

Far from inconsequential, these orders and edits exemplify state acts of selectively recounting and discounting the past in order to legitimize state political domination over newly won but still contested territory. Embedded in longer state-making processes, recounting Điện Biên Phủ narratively as decisive event and triumphal campaign constructs a lesson to be emulated by people elsewhere and a tactic to be led by an enlightened center. This narrow interpretation requires discounting other stories and experiences, especially those of a place so saturated in meaning and laden with conflict. Such discursive power rests on prior state acts of counting agrarian resources and accounting for their distribution, both of which centralized strategic capacity in service to the territorial project.

Despite the perceived mistake shown above, it is remarkable that the October report affirmed the center's account of Điện Biên Phủ in every other way. Most of all, it cites the same exact statistics on logistical resources amassed by the Central Front Supply Council in its July summary of the Điện Biên Phủ Campaign. Again, by autumn 1954 regional officials knew more than their central superiors about the local resources that had fed and moved the People's Army.[6] Yet, to the single digit, the regional report defers to the council's authoritative counts of labor days, rice tonnage, and so on. In so doing, region fell in line behind center in support of an accounting realm that mapped neatly onto the DRV's national territorial claim.

Precisely because this claim was so contested, however, the 1954 orders and edits were only the opening salvo in an ongoing, commemorative barrage focused on Điện Biên Phủ. The battle's outcome bequeathed an ambiguous and violent legacy both locally, with Calling for a King, and internationally, with the partition of Vietnam. The July 1954 Geneva Agreement ushered in a Cold War territorial compromise akin to Korea and Germany, splitting Vietnam in two at the 17th parallel. Though intended as "provisional," the division between the two "administrative zones" of north and south hardened over two decades into a geopolitical border between states. The southern Republic of Vietnam confounded the DRV's claim to represent all of Vietnam, pitting independence against unification.[7] As much a civil war within and over the south as a war against foreign domination, the ensuing Second Indochina War (1960–75) bequeathed a legacy as ambiguous and violent as its predecessor.

As this next war developed, the DRV advanced military tactics, narrative accounts, and war memorials to affix a singular meaning to Điện Biên Phủ out of a wide range of possibilities. In 1972–73, just shy of the battle's twentieth anniversary, the DRV launched a "Điện Biên Phủ Campaign in the skies" to galvanize air defenses against the U.S. government's ill-conceived Christmas bombing of Hanoi. On the battle's fortieth and fiftieth anniversaries, official historians and military leaders explained how one should interpret Điện Biên Phủ by, for example, invoking the place as a strategic lesson applied successfully in the Second Indochina War. These efforts are ongoing, their legacies written into the landscape. Mường Thanh's valley floor is carpeted with memorials, cemeteries, historical markers, museums, rusty tanks and artillery pieces, preserved battle sites, and the like. Yet recounting this one past still requires active efforts to discount alternative reckonings, even those adhering to a calculative logic but straying from what the government decides should (not) be counted. At a conference held at the Vietnamese Academy of Social Sciences to commemorate the battle's sixtieth anniversary, domestic and international scholars still did not know how many Vietnamese soldiers and civilians had died in combat.[8] A closely guarded state secret, the casualties at Điện Biên Phủ were staggering—so staggering, evidently, that officers and officials still worry about being held accountable for them.

Meanwhile, in the southern Republic of Vietnam in 1967–68, U.S. general William Westmoreland mistakenly anticipated another Điện Biên Phủ at Khe Sanh. As a result, he and President Johnson misread the massive communist buildup for the Tet Offensive targeting urban as well as rural areas. The 1968 offensive would prove to be a turning point in the U.S. government's commitment to the war. This time in its afterlife, Điện Biên Phủ had once again played a crucial, world-historic role.[9]

By excavating Điện Biên Phủ's hidden past, this book has told just some of the many stories that the place can tell and, further, offered a way to think about territory as a contingent outcome of grounded contests. Just as local histories undermine a nationalist telos, so too does the analysis of everyday struggles explain why territorial outcomes stray from strategic design. On 7 May 1964, for instance, the DRV convened mass meetings at Điện Biên Phủ to commemorate the battle's tenth anniversary, celebrate the autonomous zone's ninth birthday (renamed the Northwest Autonomous Zone in 1962), and stage a performance of party-state legitimacy. Yet the grand affair consumed so much food that, even after a bountiful harvest the year before, thousands of residents on the Mường Thanh plain went hungry that summer. Despite months of planning, one official lamented, "the outcome was not as desired."[10] Like the battle itself, its celebration at Điện Biên Phủ a decade later caused hunger, reproducing embodied struggles and tensions emplaced in Vietnamese territory. The unexpected result underlines what scholars can learn about territory by exploring the everyday labors involved in its construction.

ABBREVIATIONS

ANOM:	Archives Nationales d'Outre Mer (National Overseas Territories Archive)
BLĐ:	Bộ Lao động (Ministry of Labor)
BNL:	Bộ Nông lâm (Ministry of Agriculture and Forestry)
BVH:	Bộ Văn hoá (Ministry of Culture)
Conspol:	Conseiller politique (Political Advisor)
CTXH:	Bộ Cứu tế xã hội (Ministry of Social Welfare)
HCI:	Haut Commissariat de France pour l'Indochine (French High Commission in Indochina)
HĐND:	Hội đồng nhân dân (People's Assembly)
KTTTB:	Ủy ban kháng chiến hành chính Khu tự trị Tây Bắc (Northwest Autonomous Zone Resistance and Administrative Committee)
KTTTM:	Khu tự trị Thái-Mèo (Thái-Mèo Autonomous Zone)
NAVC 3:	National Archives of Vietnam Center 3
PTTg:	Phủ Thủ tướng (Prime Minister's Secretariat)
PTTg (1945–54):	Phủ Thủ tướng (1945–54) (Prime Minister's Secretariat [1945–54])

RST:	Résidence Supérieure au Tonkin (Office of the Resident Superior of Tonkin)
SHD:	Service Historique de la Défense (Defense Historical Service)
Sơn-Lai:	Ủy ban hành chính liên tỉnh Sơn La-Lai Châu (Sơn La–Lai Châu Interprovince Administrative Committee)
TAHC:	Trị an hành chính (Security Administration)
UBHC:	Ủy ban hành chính (Administrative Committee)
UBHCKC:	Ủy ban hành chính kháng chiến (Administrative and Resistance Committee)
UTC:	Ủy ban thống nhất của Chính phủ (Government Reunification Committee)
VB:	Ủy ban hành chính Khu tự trị Việt Bắc (Việt-Bắc Autonomous Zone Administrative Committee)

NOTES

INTRODUCTION

1. Logevall, *Embers of War,* 498–501. Of the vast literature on the battle itself, the standard-bearer remains Fall, *Hell in a Very Small Place.*
2. Fanon, *The Wretched of the Earth;* Oey Hong Lee, *Asia Menang di Dien Bien Phu.*
3. On geographic notions of place, see Massey, *Space, Place, and Gender;* Tuan, *Space and Place.*
4. Fall, *Hell in a Very Small Place,* 23; Le Failler, *La rivière Noire,* 424–29.
5. Thongchai, *Siam Mapped;* on multiple Vietnams, see Goscha, *Vietnam: A New History,* 3.
6. Agnew, "The Territorial Trap"; Windrow, *The Last Valley;* Simpson, *Dien Bien Phu;* Đặng Nghiêm Vạn and Đinh Xuân Lâm, *Điện Biên trong lịch sử.*
7. Vandergeest and Peluso, "Territorialization and State Power in Thailand"; Yeh, *Taming Tibet;* Moore, *Suffering for Territory;* Eilenberg, *At the Edges of States;* Rajaram and Grundy-Warr, *Borderscapes;* Sahlins, *Boundaries.*
8. Elden, *The Birth of Territory;* Elden, "Land, Terrain, Territory"; Kratoska, Raben, and Nordholdt, *Locating Southeast Asia;* Lacoste, "An Illustration of Geographical Warfare."
9. Tagliacozzo, "Jagged Landscapes"; Bryan, "Rethinking Territory."
10. Thongchai, *Siam Mapped;* Anderson, *Imagined Communities;* Krishna, "Cartographic Anxiety."
11. Taylor, "Surface Orientations"; Anderson, *The Rebel Den of Nùng Trí Cao;* Baldanza, *Ming China and Vietnam;* Taylor, *A History of the Vietnamese,* 398; Woodside, *Vietnam and the Chinese Model;* Dutton, *The Tây Sơn Uprising;* Davis, *Imperial Bandits.* For comprehensive treatments of Vietnam's borders

and their representation, see Lafont, *Les frontières du Vietnam;* Whitmore, "Cartography in Vietnam." Disputes over the South China Sea—what Vietnamese call the Eastern Sea—testify to the ongoing production of territory and associated imaginaries. Hayton, *The South China Sea.* For more on the Second Indochina War, aka what Americans often call the Vietnam War, see Goscha, *Vietnam: A New History,* ch. 11; Kiernan, *Việt Nam,* ch. 10.

12. Tai, "Introduction to 'Mapping Vietnameseness'"; Scott, *Weapons of the Weak;* Hahn, *A Nation under Our Feet;* Kligman and Verdery, *Peasants under Siege;* Kerkvliet, *The Power of Everyday Politics;* Wolford, *This Land Is Ours Now;* Wolf, "Peasants and Political Mobilization"; Lentz, "Mobilization and State Formation on a Frontier of Vietnam."
13. Smith, Swenson, and Gokariksel, "Territory, Bodies, and Borders"; Vandergeest and Peluso, "Territorialization and State Power in Thailand"; Lockhart, "In Lieu of the *Levée en masse*"; Scott, *Moral Economy of the Peasant;* Ngô Vĩnh Long, *Before the Revolution.*
14. Geyer, "The Militarization of Europe"; McEnaney, *Civil Defense Begins at Home;* Bonker, *Militarism in a Global Age;* Farish, *The Contours of America's Cold War;* Võ Nguyên Giáp, *People's War, People's Army;* Trường Chinh and Võ Nguyên Giáp, *Vấn đề dân cày.*
15. Cowen, *The Deadly Life of Logistics.*
16. On regional millenarian traditions, see Lee, *Dreams of the Hmong Kingdom;* Tapp, "Of Grasshoppers, Caterpillars, and Beans"; Culas, *Le messianisme hmong;* Tai, *Millenarianism and Peasant Politics in Vietnam.*
17. Le Failler, *La rivière Noire;* Sterling, Hurley, and Le Duc Minh, *Vietnam: A Natural History;* Vu Tu Lap, *Vietnam: Geographical Data.*
18. Scott, *The Art of Not Being Governed;* Michaud, *Historical Dictionary;* Van Schendel, "Geographies of Knowing, Geographies of Ignorance"; Di Cosmo and Wyatt, *Political Frontiers, Ethnic Boundaries, and Human Geographies;* Jonsson, *Slow Anthropology;* Lieberman, "A Zone of Refuge in Southeast Asia?"; Anderson and Whitmore, introduction to *China's Encounters,* 15n37.
19. On an analytics of conjuncture, see Li, *Land's End,* 16–20. Anderson and Whitmore, "The Dong World"; Lee, *Dreams of the Hmong Kingdom;* Giersch, *Asian Borderlands;* Tagliacozzo, "Tropical Spaces, Frozen Frontiers"; Davis, *Imperial Bandits,* ch. 4; Walker, *The Legend of the Golden Boat.*
20. Jerusalemy, "Monographie sur le Pays Thaï"; Phan-My, "Bao Cao So Luoc vê tinh hinh cong viec chinh quyên trong hai thang 10 va 11 nam 1952 tai vung moi duoc giai phong o Tây-Bac," 22 December 1952, 1306/PTTg (1945–54)/NAVC 3; "Tinh hinh khai quat vê Khu tu tri dan toc Thai Meo o Tay-Bac," 1955, 22/KTTTB/NAVC 3; "La declaration de M. Rene Pleven sur l'Indochine," 24 October 1952, 23–95/HCI/ANOM.
21. Salemink, *The Ethnography of Vietnam's Central Highlanders,* 130–31; population estimate for unified north and south Vietnam as of 1955, "Data Query," United Nations Population Division, accessed 5 July 2017, https://esa.un.org/unpd/wpp/DataQuery/; Hardy, *Red Hills;* Scott, *The Art of Not Being Governed,* ch. 6.

22. Mullaney, *Coming to Terms with the Nation,* 3–5; Lentz, "Making the Northwest Vietnamese"; Masaka, *Politics of Ethnic Classification in Vietnam;* Leach, *Political Systems of Highland Burma;* Barth, introduction to *Ethnic Groups and Boundaries,* 13; Herman, *Amidst the Clouds and Mist,* 14; Anderson and Whitmore, introduction to *China's Encounters,* 11; Taylor, "Minorities at Large."
23. Izikowitz, "Neighbors in Laos," 138; Izikowitz, *The Lamet.*
24. Izikowitz, *The Lamet;* Evans, "Laos: Minorities"; Halpern, *Economy and Society of Laos;* Scott, *The Art of Not Being Governed,* ch. 6; Condominas, *From Lawa to Mon,* 60–65; Lee, *Dreams of the Hmong Kingdom,* 64–69; Tapp, "Ritual Relations and Identity."
25. Cầm Trọng, *Người Thái ở Tây Bắc,* 312–27; Gourou, *L'utilisation du sol en Indochine,* 349–50; Jerusalemy, "Monographie sur le Pays Thaï," 24–30.
26. Le Failler, *La rivière Noire,* 26. Then located at a rapids, the market is now flooded by the Hòa Bình Dam, as analyzed by Dao, "Damming Rivers in Vietnam." Jerusalemy, "Monographie sur le Pays Thaï," 35–36; Forbes, "The 'Cin-Ho' (Yunnanese Chinese) Caravan Trade"; Shrader, *A War of Logistics,* 348.
27. Condominas, *From Lawa to Mon,* 35–36; Condominas, "Essai sur l'évolution des systèmes politiques thaïs," 11; Scott, *The Art of Not Being Governed,* 65; Turton, introduction to *Civility and Savagery,* 27.
28. Thongchai, *Siam Mapped,* 49; Condominas, *From Lawa to Mon,* 32; Mukdawijitra, "Ethnicity and Multilingualism"; Ha Viet Quan, "Brokering Power in Vietnam's Northwest."
29. Davis, *Imperial Bandits,* 5; Anderson, *Rebel Den of Nùng Trí Cao,* ch. 4; Hickey, "Social Systems of Northern Vietnam"; Marr, *Vietnam: State, War, and Revolution,* 470–71; Halpern, *Economy and Society of Laos,* 10; Evans, "Introduction: What Is Lao Culture?," 14–16; Tappe, "Variants of Frontier Mimesis"; Le Failler, "The Đèo Family of Lai Châu"; Condominas, *From Lawa to Mon,* 71–75; Thongchai, *Siam Mapped,* 99–100.
30. Condominas, *From Lawa to Mon,* 55–64, 74; Evans, "Tai-ization," 279; Turton, introduction to *Civility and Savagery,* 21–22; Tapp, "Ritual Relations and Identity"; Badenoch and Shinsuke, "Mountain People in the *Muang.*"
31. Davis, *Imperial Bandits,* 132–37; Le Failler, *La rivière Noire,* 181–84; Fourniau, "La frontière Sino Vietnamienne"; Goscha, *Vietnam: A New History,* 238, 428–29; Salemink, *The Ethnography of Vietnam's Central Highlanders,* 28; McAlister, "Mountain Minorities and the Viet Minh," 786.
32. Lentz, "Cultivating Subjects"; McCoy, *The Politics of Heroin.*
33. Abrams, "Notes on the Difficulty of Studying the State"; Gupta, "Blurred Boundaries"; Das and Poole, *Anthropology in the Margins of the State;* Mitchell, "Society, Economy, and the State Effect"; Migdal, *State in Society;* Sivaramakrishnan, *Modern Forests;* Vu, "Studying the State through State Formation"; Jones, "State Encounters."
34. Lund, "Rupture and Rule"; Pelley, *Postcolonial Vietnam.*
35. Mayaram, *Against History, Against State;* Trouillot, *Silencing the Past;* Amin, *Event, Metaphor, Memory;* Fuentes, *Dispossessed Lives;* Stoler, *Along the Archival Grain,* 4.

36. For more on holdings, see Phạm Thị Bích Hải et al., *Sách chỉ dẫn các phòng lưu trữ*.
37. MacLean, *The Government of Mistrust*.
38. Scott, *The Art of Not Being Governed*, 34; MacLean, *The Government of Mistrust*, 8; Porter, *Vietnam: The Politics of Bureaucratic Socialism*, ch. 1; Mitchell, *Rule of Experts*, ch. 3; Marx, *Grundrisse*.
39. Ngô Thiếu Hiệu, ed., *Sách chỉ dẫn các phông lưu trữ thời kỳ thuộc địa;* Cons, *Sensitive Space*.
40. Salemink, *The Ethnography of Vietnam's Central Highlanders*, 9–27; Goscha, *Un état né de la guerre*, 13–18. During the American intervention in Vietnam, for example, historian John T. McAlister wrote a brilliant piece on the Black River region ("Mountain Minorities and the Viet Minh") by gaining access to French military records in exchange for protecting their secrecy: as a result, it does not list a single document consulted. Further, his piece adheres to a French military practice of lumping together the DRV, People's Army, mass organizations, and other anti-colonial forces as "the Viet Minh." Not limited to Cold War scholarship, the simplifying but inaccurate label of "the Viet Minh" still permeates many French and American studies of the First Indochina War. Amin, *Event, Metaphor, Memory*, 1.
41. Lentz, "The King Yields to the Village?"
42. Lentz, "Encountering Everyday Perspectives."

CHAPTER ONE: "VAST AREA, SPARSE PEOPLE"

1. Kiernan, *Việt Nam*, 379; Brocheux and Hémery, *Indochina*, 348–49; Bảo tàng Sơn La, *Di tích lịch sử*, 39–40; Cầm Trọng, *Người Thái ở Tây Bắc*, 493, 515.
2. Marr, *Vietnam 1945*, 421; Le Failler, *La rivière Noire*, 418–32.
3. Phạm Quang Trung, "Nhà thơ dân tộc Thái Lò Văn Mười"; Bảo tàng Sơn La, *Di tích lịch sử*, 31; Salemink, "Mois and Maquis," 247; Zinoman, *The Colonial Bastille*, 83.
4. Phạm Quang Trung, "Nhà thơ dân tộc Thái Lò Văn Mười." In a ritual context, *Lak muang* means "spirit of the earth" or "pillar of soil" and ideologically connects Tai elites to their earthly domain. Adapting this icon as their newspaper's name, members of the Tai Youth League (Mu Nom Choet Muang / Hội Thanh niên cứu quốc) invoked a modern interpretation of these old practices. Condominas, *From Lawa to Mon*, 58–59; Mukdawijitra, "Ethnicity and Multilingualism"; Cầm Trọng, *Người Thái ở Tây Bắc*, 505.
5. Lentz, "Making the Northwest Vietnamese"; Zinoman, *Colonial Bastille*, 214. Hỏa Lò would become known as the "Hanoi Hilton" during the Second Indochina War when it housed captured U.S. pilots. Hoàng Điệp and Mai Hoa, "Vua Thái ở Chiềng Mai"; Mukdawijitra, "Ethnicity and Multilingualism," 219. I am grateful to Ha Viet Quan for investigating Mười's (lack of) family connection with Hặc. Lentz, "Making the Northwest Vietnamese," 83; Le Failler, *La rivière Noire*, 494; Fall, *Hell in a Very Small Place*, 24.

6. Goscha, *Vietnam: A New History*, 428–29; Haut Commisariat de France pour l'Indochine, "Note sur les limites du Pays Tai et de la délimation entre les trois provinces de Lai-Chau, Phong-Tho, et Thuan Chau (Son-La)," November 1946, 214/Conspol/HCI/ANOM; Le Failler, "The Đèo Family of Lai Châu"; Nguyên-Dê, preface; McAlister, "Mountain Minorities and the Viet Minh," 786.
7. Ban Chấp hành Đảng bộ huyện Điện Biên, *Lịch sử Đảng bộ*, 52; Đặng Nghiêm Vạn and Đinh Xuân Lâm, *Điện Biên trong lịch sử*, 144; Võ Nguyên Giáp, *Đường tới Điện Biên Phủ*, 355; Furuta, "The Indochina Communist Party's Division into Three Parties," 147; Bộ Chỉ huy quân sự tỉnh Sơn La, *Sơn La: Lịch sử kháng chiến*, 65, 103.
8. Lò Văn Mười, "Bao-Cao 3 tháng 4, 5, 6 năm 1949 của Liên Tinh Sơn La Lai Châu," 18 July 1949, 187/PTTg (1945–54)/NAVC 3. The following discussion draws on this document, unless noted otherwise.
9. Born Phạm Văn Côn in Hà Nam Province, Trần Quyết (1922–90) would go on to command Vietnam's police force and serve in the National Assembly and on the party's Executive Committee.
10. Jerusalemy, "Monographie sur le Pays Thaï," 23.
11. With particular reference to the province of Thái Bình, the matching idiomatic expression is "Thái Bình đất chật người đông." Tạ Long and Ngô Thị Chính, *Sự biến đổi nền nông nghiệp*, 40; Bronson, "Exchange at the Upstream and Downstream Ends."
12. Davis, "States of Banditry," ch. 5.
13. Lò Văn Mười, "Bao-Cao 4, 5, 6 năm 1949"; Đảng Lao động Việt Nam, *Văn kiện của Đảng về Chính sách dân tộc*, 29–31.
14. Brocheux and Hémery, *Indochina*, 62–63.
15. Lò Văn Mười, "Bao-Cao 4, 5, 6 năm 1949."
16. "Báo cáo UBHCKC LT Sơn-Lai 3 tháng 7, 8, 9 năm 1949," 21 October 1949, 187/PTTg (1945–54)/NAVC 3; Lee, *Dreams of the Hmong Kingdom*.
17. Goscha, *Going Indochinese*. Conveying a sense of geographic determinism, for example, Cầm Trọng writes, "This region of high mountains, full of obstacles and difficult of access, where land is vast and people sparse, made for a very complex people, a society that developed very slowly." *Người Thái ở Tây Bắc*, 517. For more contemporary invocations, see Lentz, "Mobilizing a Frontier," 5, 23.
18. Ginsburgs, "Local Government and Administration in North Vietnam," 203; Fall, "Local Administration under the Việt Minh," 56.
19. Lockhart, *Nation in Arms*, 195–96; Pelley, *Postcolonial Vietnam*, 111; Scott, *The Art of Not Being Governed*, 54.
20. Sa Văn Minh, "Bao cao nam 1948 cua UBHCKC Sơn-Lai," 15 January 1949, 78/PTTg (1945–54)/NAVC 3. 254/SL-CTN (19/11/48) "Sắc lệnh tổ chức lại chính quyền nhân dân trong thời kỳ kháng chiến" and 255/SL-CTN (19/11/48) "Sắc lệnh ấn định cách tổ chức và cách làm việc của HĐND và UBHCKC

trong vùng tạm thời bị địch kiểm soát hoặc uy hiếp," Government of Vietnam Portal, accessed 27 March 2015, http://www.chinhphu.vn.

21. Woodside, *Vietnam and the Chinese Model,* 141–52; Lof-Vawn-Muowif, "Bao-cao 3 thang 1, 2, 3 năm 1949 của UBHCKC Liên tỉnh Sơn-La Lai-Châu," 5 April 1949, 187/PTTg (1945–54)/NAVC 3; Lò Văn Mười, "Bao-Cao 3 tháng 4, 5, 6 năm 1949."
22. Unless noted otherwise, the following discussion draws on Lò Văn Mười, "Bao-Cao 3 tháng 4, 5, 6 năm 1949."
23. Cầm Trọng, *Người Thái ở Tây Bắc,* 327.
24. Condominas, *From Lawa to Mon,* 36; Brocheux and Hémery, *Indochina,* 86–87; Thongchai, *Siam Mapped,* 120, 134; LeFailler, *La rivière Noire,* 432–39.
25. Ch. Deligne, "Conseiller politique pour les regions thais à msr. L'amiral, haut commissaire de France pour l'Indochine," 30 October 1946, 214/Conspol/HCI/ANOM.
26. In Vietnamese, *bộ máy hành chính* and *chính quyên.*
27. Duong Manh Hung, "Ty Nông chính Sơn-Lai kinh gửi Ông tổng Giám đốc Nhà nông chính VN," 15 May 1950, 3058/BNL/NAVC 3; Lò Văn Mười, "Bao-Cao 3 tháng 4, 5, 6 năm 1949"; Turton, introduction to *Civility and Savagery.*
28. Duncan, *Civilizing the Margins;* Dove, "Writing for, versus about, the Ethographic Other"; Sa Văn Minh, "Bao cao nam 1948"; Lò Văn Mười, "Bao-Cao 3 tháng 4, 5, 6 năm 1949."
29. Mau, "The Training of Cadres in the Lao Dong Party"; Evans, "Vietnamese Communist Anthropology," 140; Lò Văn Mười, "Bao-Cao 3 tháng 4, 5, 6 năm 1949."
30. Poisson, "Unhealthy Air of the Mountains."
31. Marr, *Vietnam 1945,* 105; Gunn, *Rice Wars in Colonial Vietnam,* ch. 8; Huỳnh Kim Khánh, *Vietnamese Communism,* 312–15; Hy V. Luong, *Revolution in the Village,* 137–39; Hồ Chí Minh, "Tuyên Ngôn Độc Lập," in *Hồ Chí Minh toàn tập.*
32. Yeh, *Taming Tibet,* 14–17; Bourdieu, *Outline of a Theory of Practice;* Mauss, *The Gift.*
33. Scott, *The Moral Economy of the Peasant;* Tran Quyet, "Bao cao thang 6 nam 1948," 20 July 1948, 78/PTTg (1945–54)/NAVC 3.
34. Brocheux and Hémery, *Indochina,* 91–100; Sa Văn Minh, "Bao-Cao ba thang (thang 7, 8, 9 nam 1948)," 1948, 78/PTTg (1945–54)/NAVC 3; Sa Văn Minh, "Bao cao nam 1948."
35. Tran Quyet, "Bao cao thang 6 nam 1948," 20 July 1948, 78/PTTg (1945–54)/NAVC 3.
36. Marr, *Vietnam 1945,* 246. In 1951, for example, a French officer argued that increasing the supply of salt to highland Laos would work in favor of "our psychological actions in that state." Le Colonel de Brebisson, "Fiche pour le Directeur du Cabinet Civil," 24 January 1951, 274/783/Conspol/HCI/ANOM.
37. Lò Văn Mười, "Bao-Cao 3 tháng 4, 5, 6 năm 1949"; Jerusalemy, "Monographie sur le Pays Thaï," 33–34; J. Briand, "Le conseiller provincial à msr. Le

directeur des douanes et régies à Saigon," 19 January 1948, and R. Lebca, "Le directeur fédérale des douanes et régies de l'Indochine à msr. le conseiller provinciale," 31 January 1948, 83/Conspol/HCI/ANOM; Lof-Vawn-Muowif, "Báo cáo 3 tháng 1, 2, 3 năm 1949."

38. Day, *Fluid Iron*. Arendt writes dismissively of "exploitation," and Marxist thought by extension, as a mode of revolutionary logic. She considers the "social question," or mass poverty, to be a revolutionary dead end, one that mistakenly substitutes economic "abundance" for political "freedom." *On Revolution*, 50–55. However, her logic, as spelled out in *The Human Condition*, rests on a normative binary between "private" and "public" spheres (the Greek *oikos* and *polis*) as realms for economic and political action, respectively.
39. Bronson, "Exchange at the Upstream and Downstream Ends," 50; Sa Văn Minh, "Bao cao nam 1948."
40. Sa Văn Minh, "Bao cao nam 1948"; Lof-Vawn-Muowif, "Báo cáo 3 tháng 1, 2, 3 năm 1949."
41. Lof-Vawn-Muowif, "Báo cáo 3 tháng 1, 2, 3 năm 1949."
42. Malarney, "'The Fatherland Remembers Your Sacrifice'"; Lof-Vawn-Muowif, "Báo cáo 3 tháng 1, 2, 3 năm 1949."
43. Balibar, "The Nation Form," 347; Nancy, *The Inoperative Community*, 15.
44. Italics added. Lof-Vawn-Muowif, "Báo cáo 3 tháng 1, 2, 3 năm 1949"; Sa Văn Minh, "Bao cao nam 1948."
45. Lof-Vawn-Muowif, "Báo cáo 3 tháng 1, 2, 3 năm 1949."
46. Lof-Vawn-Muowif, "Báo cáo 3 tháng 1, 2, 3 năm 1949"; Sa Văn Minh, "Bao cao nam 1948."
47. Lò Văn Mười, "Bao-Cao 3 tháng 4, 5, 6 năm 1949."
48. Lò Văn Mười, "Bao-Cao 3 tháng 4, 5, 6 năm 1949."
49. Sa Văn Minh, "Bao cao nam 1948."
50. Lò Văn Mười, "Bao-Cao 3 tháng 4, 5, 6 năm 1949."
51. Lò Văn Mười, "Bao-Cao 3 tháng 4, 5, 6 năm 1949."
52. Dutton, *The Tây Sơn Uprising*, ch. 3.
53. Tran Quyet, "Bao cao thang 6 nam 1948," 20 July 1948, and Sa Văn Minh, "Bao cao nam 1948," 78/PTTg (1945–54)/NAVC 3; Lò Văn Mười, "Bao-Cao 3 tháng 4, 5, 6 năm 1949."
54. Sa Văn Minh, "Bao cao nam 1948."
55. Woodside, "The Triumphs and Failures of Mass Education in Vietnam"; Ninh, *A World Transformed;* Sa Văn Minh, "Bao cao nam 1948"; Lof-Vawn-Muowif, "Báo cáo 3 tháng 1, 2, 3 năm 1949."
56. Enfield, "Areal Linguistics and Mainland Southeast Asia"; Mukdawijitra, "Ethnicity and Multilingualism," 222–23; Phan-My, "Bao Cao So Luoc vê tinh hinh công viêc chinh quyên trong hai thang 10 và 11–1952 tai vùng moi duoc giai phong o Tây-Bac," 22 December 1952, 456/PTTg (1945–54)/NAVC 3; McAlister, "Mountain Minorities and the Viet Minh," 789.
57. Mukdawijitra, "Contesting Imagined Communities"; Lò Văn Mười, "Bao-Cao 3 tháng 4, 5, 6 năm 1949."

58. Anderson, *Imagined Communities,* 42–46.
59. Sa Văn Minh, "Bao-Cao ba thang (thang 7, 8, 9 nam 1948)," 1948, 78/PTTg (1945–54)/NAVC 3; Lò Văn Mười, "Bao-Cao 3 tháng 4, 5, 6 năm 1949."
60. Passage from Sa Văn Minh, "Bao-Cao ba thang (thang 7, 8, 9 nam 1948)."
61. Cầm Trọng, *Người Thái ở Tây Bắc,* 500–503.
62. Abrams, "Notes on the Difficulty of Studying the State."
63. Italics added. Lò Văn Mười, "Bao-Cao 3 tháng 4, 5, 6 năm 1949"; Bộ Chỉ huy quân sự tỉnh Sơn La, *Sơn La: Lịch sử kháng chiến,* 99.
64. Lof-Vawn-Muowif, "Báo cáo 3 tháng 1, 2, 3 năm 1949."
65. Lò Văn Mười, "Bao-Cao 3 tháng 4, 5, 6 năm 1949."
66. McHale, "Freedom, Violence, and the Struggle over the Public Arena"; Ch. Deligne, "Conseiller politique pour les regions thais à msr. L'amiral, haut commissaire de France pour l'Indochine"; Sa Văn Minh, "Bao-Cao ba thang (thang 7, 8, 9 nam 1948)" and Sa Văn Minh, "Bao cao nam 1948."
67. Lof-Vawn-Muowif, "Báo cáo 3 tháng 1, 2, 3 năm 1949" and Lò Văn Mười, "Bao-Cao 3 tháng 4, 5, 6 năm 1949."
68. Lò Văn Mười, "Bao-Cao 3 tháng 4, 5, 6 năm 1949."
69. Lò Văn Mười, "Bao-Cao 3 tháng 4, 5, 6 năm 1949."
70. Here I refer to an exchange between Duara's *Rescuing History from the Nation* and Taylor's "Surface Orientations in Vietnam." Their debate hinges on a critique of History and its guiding telos as stated in Hegel, *The Philosophy of History.*
71. A few documents subsequent to this date and credited to the Sơn-Lai Committee are held in the Việt Bắc record group, but they discuss plans for return, not direct in situ observations.
72. McAlister, "Mountain Minorities and the Viet Minh," 772–73; Duiker, "Ho Chi Minh and the Strategy of People's War"; Goscha, *Vietnam: A New History,* 255; Mao Tse Tung, "On Protracted War," in *Selected Works,* 186.
73. "Báo cáo kiểm điểm công tác năm 1950 của Liên Khu Việt Bắc," 1951, 3/VB/NAVC 3; Jerusalemy, "Monographie sur le Pays Thaï," 55–58; Colonel de Castries, "Objet: Bande de surveillance," 18 June 1951, and subsequent correspondence through December 1952, 2377/10H/SHD; Logevall, *Embers of War,* 266–73.
74. Bộ Chỉ huy quân sự tỉnh Sơn La, *Sơn La: Lịch sử kháng chiến,* 124–33; Ban Chấp hành Đảng bộ huyện Điện Biên, *Lịch sử Đảng bộ,* 75–94; Đảng Cộng sản Việt Nam, *Ba mươi năm phấn đấu,* 30–42.
75. Italics added (*không biết thế nào mà tình được nữa*). Nguyễn Ba Kinh, "Báo cáo 6 tháng đầu năm 1950," 15 June 1950, 309/PTTg (1945–54)/NAVC 3.
76. Nonini, *Getting By,* 34–38; Goscha, *Vietnam: A New History,* 246.
77. Nguyễn Ba Kinh, "Báo cáo 3 tháng thứ III (7,8,9–1950)," 20 November 1950, 309/PTTg (1945–54)/NAVC 3.
78. Cam Van Bieu, "Quyêt Nghi An gâp rut xây dung bô dôi dia phương va fat triên dân quân du kich xa, ban 6 tháng cuối năm 1951," 3 August 1951, 1188/VB/NAVC 3.

CHAPTER TWO: VIETNAM ON THE MARCH

1. Võ Nguyên Giáp, *Đường tới Điện Biên Phủ*, 361–62.
2. Trường Chinh, "Chỉ thị của ban thường vụ trung ương về mở chiến dịch Tây Bắc và chuẩn bị chiến trường Đông Bắc," 6 January 1950, in Đảng Cộng sản Việt Nam, *Văn kiện Đảng*, 7–9; "Chỉ thị của Ban Chấp hành Trung ương về mở chiến dịch Quang Trung," 28 September 1952, in Đảng Cộng sản Việt Nam, *Văn kiện Đảng*, 304–6; McAlister, "Mountain Minorities and the Viet Minh," 772–73; "Nghị quyết của ban bí thư thành lập Khu Tây Bắc," 17 July 1952, in Đảng Cộng sản Việt Nam, *Văn kiện Đảng*, 210–13.
3. Le Failler, *La rivière Noire;* Condominas, *From Lawa to Mon*, 70.
4. Winichakul, *Siam Mapped*, 17.
5. Lawrence and Logevall, *The First Vietnam War;* Goscha and Ostermann, *Connecting Histories.*
6. Hồ Chí Minh (or "Hồ the enlightened") was known then by his alias Nguyễn Ái Quốc ("Nguyễn the patriot"); Kiernan, *Việt Nam*, 364–65; Huỳnh Kim Khánh, *Vietnamese Commumism*, 126–29; Goscha, *Going Indochinese*, 83; Furuta, "The Indochina Communist Party's Division into Three Parties."
7. The question of Vietnam or Indochina has also intrigued scholars of Southeast Asian nationalisms. See Goscha, *Going Indochinese* and *Vietnam or Indochina?;* Henley, "Ethnographic Integration and Exclusion in Anticolonial Nationalism"; Anderson, *Imagined Communities;* Kiernan, *How Pol Pot Came to Power*, 51–52; Huỳnh Kim Khánh, *Vietnamese Communism*, 332–33.
8. Originally titled "Luận cương cách mạng Việt Nam" (Thesis on the Vietnamese Revolution), reprinted as "Hoàn thành giải phóng dân tộc, phát triển dân chủ nhân dân, tiến tới chủ nghĩa xã hội" (Completely Liberate the Nation, Develop the People's Democracy, Advance to Socialism), in Đảng Cộng sản Việt Nam, *Văn kiện Đảng*, 40–175; for a cursory English translation, see Truong Chinh, "On the Vietnamese Revolution," in *Truong-Chinh: Selected Writings*, 279–426; Lentz, "Making the Northwest Vietnamese," 75.
9. "Bản đồ chiến dịch Tây Bắc," 1952, 1306/PTTg (1945–54)/NAVC 3; discussed in more detail below.
10. "Hoàn thành giải phóng dân tộc," in Đảng Cộng sản Việt Nam, *Văn kiện Đảng*, 40–41, 82; Goscha, *Thailand and the Southeast Asian Networks*, 345–47; Kiernan, *How Pol Pot Came to Power*, chs. 2–4.
11. Elden, "Land, Terrain, Territory," 804; Furuta, "The Indochina Communist Party's Division into Three Parties," 161; Goscha, *Thailand and the Southeast Asian Networks*, 348. Trường Chinh stated, "cứ làm mà không nói." "Chỉ thị của Ban Bí thư về việc tuyên truyền Chiến dịch Thượng Lào," 4 May 1953, in Đảng Cộng sản Việt Nam, *Văn kiện Đảng*, 199–200.
12. Lentz, "Cultivating Subjects," 901; Viện Lịch sử Quân sự Việt Nam, *Lịch sử cuộc kháng chiến*, 234–48; Brown and Zasloff, *Apprentice Revolutionaries*, 47–53; Hồ Chí Minh, "Thư gửi đơn vị bộ đội ta có nhiệm vụ tác chiến ở Thượng Lào," 3 April 1953, in *Hồ Chí Minh toàn tập*, 64.
13. Thongchai, *Siam Mapped*, 165–67.

14. Thongchai, *Siam Mapped*, 165; Ninh, *A World Transformed*, 26–31, 90–91; Pelley, *Postcolonial Vietnam*, 81–91; Phan Văn Các, *Từ điển Hán Việt*, 116–17, 417; Đặng Chấn Liêu, Lê Khả Kế, and Phạm Duy Trọng, *Từ điển Việt-Anh*, 195; Verdery, "Ethnicity, Nationalism, and State-Making," 50.
15. My discussion of ethnic classification in Vietnam fits between that of Charles Keyes (who traces a longer genealogy to Soviet, Chinese, and French influences) and Ito Masako (who begins a sustained analysis in 1959) in order to focus on how the geobody structured ethnicity as a secondary identification; Keyes, "Presidential Address: 'The Peoples of Asia'"; Masako, *Politics of Ethnic Classification in Vietnam;* Mullaney, *Coming to Terms with the Nation.*
16. Quotes from Trường Chinh here and below in "Hoàn thành giải phóng dân tộc," in Đảng Cộng sản Việt Nam, *Văn kiện Đảng*, 139–40.
17. On the Montagnard Countries, see Salemink, *The Ethnography of Vietnam's Central Highlanders*, ch. 5. For relevant policies of autonomy, see "Trích Nghị quyết Hội nghị Trung ương lần thứ VIII của Đảng Cộng sản Dông-dương," 10–19 May 1941 and "Trích Nghị quyết Hội nghị cán bộ Trung ương," 3–6 April 1947, in Đảng Lao động Việt Nam, *Văn kiện của Đảng về Chính sách dân tộc*, 21–27. Excised by the editors of *Văn kiện Đảng*, this section of Trường Chinh's speech is in Đảng Lao động Việt Nam, *Văn kiện của Đảng về Chính sách dân tộc*, 36.
18. Anderson, *The Spectre of Comparisons*, 318; Gladney, *Making Majorities;* Burguière and Grew, *The Construction of Minorities.*
19. "Hoàn thành giải phóng dân tộc," in Đảng Cộng sản Việt Nam, *Văn kiện Đảng*, 140.
20. Lieberman, *Strange Parallels*, ch. 4.
21. For example, "Desiring to implement this ethnic policy above," he stated, "we must implement the following points."
22. "Chính sách dân tộc thiểu số của Đảng hiện nay (Nghị quyết Bộ Chính trị)," August 1952, in Đảng Cộng sản Việt Nam, *Văn kiện Đảng*, 259–82; "Chỉ thị của Ban Bí thư thi hành chính sách dân tộc thiểu số ở Khu QT," 16 August 1952, in Đảng Cộng sản Việt Nam, *Văn kiện Đảng*, 241–58. Note that "QT" in the title refers to "Quang Trung" (aka Khu XX), military code for the Northwest Zone.
23. Hồ Chí Minh, "Báo cáo trước Hội nghị lần thứ tư an chấp hành Trung ương Đảng," 25 January 1953, in *Hồ Chí Minh toàn tập*, 18.
24. "Báo cáo tại Hội nghị Ban chấp hành Trung ương lần thứ tư về công tác mặt trận," 1953, in Đảng Cộng sản Việt Nam, *Văn kiện Đảng*, 117.
25. Pham-văn-Đông, "Ban 'Chinh sach dân tôc' sô 281-TTg: Chinh sach dan toc hien nay cua Chinh phu nuoc Viet Nam Dan Chu Cong hoa," 22 June 1953, 1332/PTTg (1945–54)/NAVC 3.
26. Thongchai, *Siam Mapped*, 123; Muelle, *Combats en Pays Thaï;* McAlister, "Mountain Minorities and the Viet Minh," 803–4.
27. "Nghị quyết của ban bí thư thành lập Khu Tây Bắc," 17 July 1952, in Đảng Cộng sản Việt Nam, *Văn kiện Đảng*, 211; McAlister, "Mountain Minorities and

the Viet Minh," 773; Duiker, "Ho Chi Minh and the Strategy of People's War," 170–71; "Chỉ thị của Ban Bí thư," 16 August 1952, in Đảng Cộng sản Việt Nam, *Văn kiện Đảng*, 245.

28. Cao Văn Lượng, Nguyễn Văn Nhật, and Võ Kim Cương, *Lịch sử kháng chiến*, 339–40; Võ Nguyên Giáp, *Đường tới Điện Biên Phủ*, 411; Marr, *Vietnam: State, War, and Revolution*, 26, 387; "Di tích lịch sử—cách mạng Khu ủy Tây Bắc," Government of Yên Bái Province, accessed 27 February 2015, http://yenbai.gov.vn/vi/Pages/chitietkhuuytaybac.aspx; Ho-Chi-Minh, 134-SL, 28 January 1953, 1268/PTTg (1945–54)/NAVC 3.
29. ". . . đất rộng, người thưa" in "Nghị quyết của Ban Bí thư thành lập Khu Tây Bắc," 17 July 1952, in Đảng Cộng sản Việt Nam, *Văn kiện Đảng*, 210.
30. "Chỉ thị của Ban Bí thư," 16 August 1952, in Đảng Cộng sản Việt Nam, *Văn kiện Đảng*, 243, 245, 248; "Dự thảo đề án phát triển chiến tranh du kích và củng cố cơ sở chính trị năm 1952," 1951, 1125/PTTg (1945–54)/NAVC 3; "Chính sách dân tộc thiểu số của Đảng hiện nay," August 1952, in Đảng Cộng sản Việt Nam, *Văn kiện Đảng*, 270; Vu, "Triumphs or Tragedies."
31. Anderson and Whitmore, introduction to *China's Encounters*, 3, 21–30.
32. "Chỉ thị của Ban Bí thư," 16 August 1952, in Đảng Cộng sản Việt Nam, *Văn kiện Đảng*, 248.
33. Lo Van Muoi, "Trich yeu: Hoan thanh giam to thuc hien giam tuc," 12 December 1950, 3093/BNL/NAVC 3; "Chỉ thị của Ban Bí thư," 16 August 1952, in Đảng Cộng sản Việt Nam, *Văn kiện Đảng*, 249.
34. "Chỉ thị của Ban Chấp hành Trung ương về mở chiến dịch Quang Trung," 28 September 1952, in Đảng Cộng sản Việt Nam, *Văn kiện Đảng*, 304–6; Krishna, "Cartographic Anxiety," 508.
35. "Carte du Pays Tai," 1946, 214/Conspol/HCI/ANOM; "Bản đồ chiến dịch Tây Bắc," 1952, 1306/PTTg (1945–54)/NAVC 3.
36. Sa-văn-Minh, "Thông Cáo về việc hủy bỏ các thể lệ cấm đoán tàn ác của giặc Tây," 16 October 1952, 1306/PTTg (1946–54)/NAVC 3.
37. For more on the knots and entanglements of postcolonial territory, see Moore, *Suffering for Territory*, 3–5; Vandergeest and Peluso, "Territorialization and State Power in Thailand," 389.
38. Mỹ would become a minister without portfolio. Marr, *Vietnam: State, War, and Revolution*, 211, 661n177.
39. Scott, *Seeing Like a State*. Unless otherwise noted, the following discussion draws from Phan-My, "Bao Cao So Luoc vê tinh hinh công viêc chinh quyên trong hai thang 10 và 11–1952 tai vùng moi duoc giai phong o Tây-Bac," 22 December 1952, 456/PTTg (1945–54)/NAVC 3; and Nguyen Khang, "Bao Cao Cong tac vung moi giai phong trong 2 thang 10, 11/1952," 29 December 1952, 1306/PTTg (1945–54)/NAVC 3. "La Declaration de M René Pleven sur l'Indochine," 24 October 1952, 23/95/HCI/ANOM.
40. Elden, "Land, Terrain, Territory."
41. Phan-My, "Bao Cao So Luoc."
42. Woodside, *Vietnam and the Chinese Model*.

43. Cầm Trọng, *Người Thái ở Tây Bắc,* 312–27; Scott, *The Art of Not Being Governed,* 36–37; Le Failler, *La rivière Noire,* 386–95; McAlister, "Mountain Minorities and the Viet Minh," 813.
44. Phan-My, "Bao Cao So Luoc."
45. Condominas, *From Lawa to Mon,* 80.
46. Thongchai, *Siam Mapped,* 120.
47. Nguyen Khang, "Bao Cao Cong tac vung moi giai phong." Because the report lacks diacritical marks, the exact titles are ambiguous. Nonetheless, possible renderings such as "thống quân," or military general, date to the Northern Wei (Bắc Ngụy) and Tang (Đường) periods. Đỗ Văn Ninh, *Từ điển chức quan Việt Nam.*
48. ĐLĐVN, "Bao Cao Tinh Hinh Tay Bac Va Nhiem Vu Nam 1953," March 1953, 471/PTTg (1945–54)/NAVC 3; "Tinh hinh khai quat Khu tu tri dan toc Thai Meo o Tay-Bac," May 1955, 22/KTTTB/NAVC 3.
49. Phan-My, "Bao Cao So Luoc."
50. Weber, "The Types of Legitimate Domination," in *Economy and Society,* 212–31; Corrigan and Sayer, *The Great Arch.*
51. Nguyen Khang, "Bao Cao Cong tac vung moi giai phong."
52. Nguyên Khangs, "Bao-Cao 3 thang dâu nam 1953," 15 April 1953, 471/PTTg (1945–54)/NAVC 3; Sa Văn Minh, "Bao Cao Tinh hinh cong tac Noi chinh," 9 July 1953, 772/KTTTB/NAVC3.
53. Phan-My, "Bao Cao So Luoc"; Nguyen Khang, "Bao Cao Cong tac vung moi giai phong"; Nguyên Khangs, "Bao-Cao 3 thang dâu nam 1953."
54. Ethnic background of the remaining seventy cadres is unclear, and figures do not necessarily count officials in local government. The districts were Mường La, Phù Yên, Mộc Châu, Mai Sơn, Yên Châu, and Điện Biên. ĐLĐVN, "Bao Cao Tinh Hinh."
55. Nguyên Khangs, "Bao-Cao 3 tháng đầu năm 1953."
56. ĐLĐVN, "Bao Cao Tinh Hinh."
57. Pham-van-Dông, "Thong Tu [Sô 265-TTg] ve viec chinh don chinh quyen cap xa qua phat dong quan chung," 16 May 1953, 1376/PTTg (1945–54)/NAVC 3.
58. Pham van Dông, "Thông tu bô khuyêt Thông tu sô 265-TTg ngay 16-5-1953 cua Thu tuong Phu vê viêc chinh dôn chinh quyên câp xa qua phat dông quân chung," 4 October 1953, 1376/PTTg (1945–54)/NAVC 3.
59. Dang Phong and Beresford, *Authority Relations,* 17; Anderson, "Old State, New Society."

CHAPTER THREE: ANXIOUS ECONOMIES

1. Ministère des Relations avec les États-Associés, "Note Hebdomadaire de Renseignement," 15–21 December 1952, 23/95/HCI/ANOM; Le Colonel Sizaire, "Bulletin Hebdomadaire de Renseignments," 15 January 1953, 5636/10H/SHD; État Major, 3ème Bureau, "Ordre Particulier pour les Sous Groupement Opérationnel Nord," 21 October 1953, 2699/10H/SHD.

2. On affect and anxiety in social analysis, see Middleton, *The Demands of Recognition;* Lindquist, *The Anxieties of Mobility;* Krishna, "Cartographic Anxiety."
3. On similarly transformative processes and the evocation of a similar "structure of feeling" but in a capitalist context, see Williams, *The Country and the City.*
4. Nguyen Khang, "Bao Cao Cong tac vung moi giai phong trong 2 thang 10, 11/1952," 29 December 1952, 1306/PTTg (1945–54)/NAVC 3.
5. Nguyen Khang, "Bao Cao Cong tac vung moi giai phong"; Phan-My, "Bao Cao So Luoc vê tinh hinh công viêc chinh quyên trong hai thang 10 và 11–1952 tai vùng moi duoc giai phong o Tây-Bac," 22 December 1952, 456/PTTg (1945–54)/NAVC 3.
6. MacLean, *The Government of Mistrust,* 51; Ninh, *A World Transformed,* 122–23.
7. Nguyên Ba Kình, "Báo cáo v/v tạm cấp ruộng đất," 18 May 1950, 3093/BNL/NAVC 3; Lo Van Muoi, "Trich yeu: hoan thanh giam to thuc hien giam tuc," 12 December 1950, 3093/BNL/NAVC 3. Nguyen Khang, "Bao Cao Cong tac vung moi giai phong"; the Cầm case is discussed in more detail below; Phan-My, "Bao Cao So Luoc."
8. Lentz, "The King Yields to the Village?," 3; Condominas, *From Lawa to Mon,* 47, 56; Cầm Trọng and Hữu Ưng, "Chế độ ruộng công"; Adas, "From Foot-dragging to Flight"; Li, "What Is land?"; Elden, "Land, Terrain, Territory."
9. Le Failler, "The Đèo Family of Lai Châu," 59; Chánh văn phòng Thủ tướng Phủ, "Báo cáo tình hình sản xuất huyện Yên Châu," 5 December 1952, 3501/BNL/NAVC 3; "Bao cao so kêt tinh hinh ruong dat o huyen Moc tinh Son La," n.d. [1952], 3225/BNL/NAVC 3.
10. Moise, *Land Reform;* Kerkvliet, *The Power of Everyday Politics;* Vo, "Nguyễn Thị Năm and the Land Reform"; Holcombe, "Socialist Transformation"; Trần Phương, *Cách mạng ruộng dất,* 218; McAlister, "Mountain Minorities and the Viet Minh," 812; Sikor and Dao Minh Truong, "Agricultural Policy and Land Use"; Mellac, "Land Reform and Changing Identities." For an early statement on land reform's revolutionary significance, see Trường Chinh and Võ Nguyên Giáp, *Vấn đề dân cày,* translated by Christine White as *The Peasant Question.*
11. Hồ Chí Minh, "Báo cáo tại Hội nghị lần thứ tư Ban Chấp hành Trung ương Đảng," 25 January 1953, in Đảng Cộng sản Việt Nam, *Văn kiện Đảng,* 14–29; Trường Chinh, "Báo cáo của Tổng Bí thư tại Hội nghị lần thứ tư Ban Chấp hành Trung ương Đảng (khoá II)," in Đảng Cộng sản Việt Nam, *Văn kiện Đảng,* 30–83.
12. Moise, *Land Reform,* 170–73; Kiernan, *Việt Nam,* 422–25; MacLean, *The Government of Mistrust,* 43–48; Kerkvliet, *The Power of Everyday Politics,* ch. 3.
13. "Bao-Cao tinh hinh Tay bac va nhiem vu nam 1953 Trong Hoi nghi Can Bo Tay Bac (tu 22 den 27/2/53)," March 1953, 471/PTTg (1945–54)/NAVC 3; "Bao-Cao kiem diem chuong trinh cong tac thang 12/52 va 1/1953 vung moi giai phong," February 1953, 471/PTTg (1945–54)/NAVC 3.

14. White, "Agrarian Reform," 158–64. On the difficulties of translating class terminology in the Vietnamese context, see MacLean, *The Government of Mistrust,* 41–43; Pham Van Dông, "Thông tu bô khuyêt Thông tu sô 265-TTg ngay 16-5-1953 cua Thu tuong Phu vê viêc chinh dôn chinh quyên câp xa qua phat dông quân chung," 4 October 1953, 1376/PTTg (1945–54)/NAVC 3.
15. "Số 149-SL của Chủ tịch nước," 12 April 1953, Ministry of Justice, accessed 2 December 2015, http://moj.gov.vn/; Holcombe, "Socialist Transformation," 102–3; "Chỉ thị của Ban Chấp hành Trung ương về phát động quần chúng trong năm 1953," 24 April 1953, in Đảng Cộng sản Việt Nam, *Văn kiện Đảng,* 182.
16. "Cung co kinh te tai chinh vung tu do xay dung kinh te tai chinh vung moi giai phong," 12 March 1953, 472/PTTg (1945–54)/NAVC 3. Even in official correspondence, this terminological distinction between "assign" (*giao*) and "redistribute" (*chia lại*) was not always clear, resulting in errors and impromptu edits. The following report discussing land allocation shows the typed word "grant" (*cấp*) scratched out in favor of a handwritten "assignment" (*giao*): Bui Quang Taoj, "Bao-Cao So luoc tinh hinh phuc hoi san xuat o vung moi giai phong Tay bac," 8 July 1953, 3501/BNL/NAVC 3; Nguyên-Khangs, "Bao-Cao 3 thang dâu nam 1953," 15 April [May?] 1953, 471/PTTg (1945–54)/NAVC 3.
17. "Bao-Cao tinh hinh Tay bac"; Nguyên-Khangs, "Bao-Cao 3 thang dâu nam 1953"; Bui Quang Taoj, "Bao-Cao So luoc tinh hinh."
18. "De Nghi vê viêc vân dông quần chung o vùng dân tôc thiêu sô moi giai phong thuôc Tây-bac," September 1953, 1258/PTTg (1945–54)/NAVC 3.
19. "De Nghi vê viêc vân dông quần chung."
20. Nguyen Khang, "Bao Cao Cong tac vung moi giai phong"; Tong cuc Cung Cap, "Bao Cao So Ket Cong tac dan cong cong trong chien dich Q.T.," 1952, 624/BLĐ/NAVC 3.
21. "Bao cao tinh hinh cong tac cua phai doan o Tây bac," 11 November 1953, 1357/PTTg (1945–54)/NAVC 3; Lê Văn Kim, "Báo cáo tình hình cán bộ và dân công (công tác chính trị tháng 12–53)," 15 January 1954, 647/BLĐ/NAVC 3.
22. Thongchai, *Siam Mapped,* 17; Pham-van-Dong, "Dieu Le tam thoi so 183-TTg ngay 14-7-1952 ve huy dong su dung dan cong," 14 July 1952, 1296/PTTg (1945–54)/NAVC 3; *Những điều cần biết về huy động và sử dụng dân công;* Nguyen Khang, "Bao Cao Cong tac vung moi giai phong." For more on emulation (*thi đua*) and mirroring (*gương mẫu*), see Woodside, *Community and Revolution,* 70–71; MacLean, *The Government of Mistrust,* 14.
23. Đặng Chấn Liêu, Lê Khả Kế, and Phạm Duy Trọng, *Từ điển Việt-Anh,* 194; 2ème Bureau, Forces Terrestres du Nord Vietnam (FTNV), "L'Economie Viet-Minh: Indochine du Nord," May 1953, 2370/10H/SHD; "Dự thảo nội quy dân công đi phục vụ," n.d., 635/BLĐ/NAVC 3; and Văn Hào, *Nghĩa vụ đi dân công;* Pham-van-Dong, "Dieu Le tam thoi so 183-TTg."
24. Elden, "How Should We Do the History of Territory?"; Nguyen Khang, "Bao Cao Cong tac vung moi giai phong."
25. Phan-My, "Bao Cao So Luoc." On unceremonious death (*chết đường*), see Kwon, *Ghosts of War.*

26. Nguyen Van Tao, "Thong Tu vê viêc thuc hiên chinh sach huy dông và su dung dân công," 26 April 1951, 612/BLĐ/NAVC 3; Pham-van-Dông, "Nghi Dinh sô 308-TTg ngay 10 thang 9 nam 1953 vê huy dông va su dung dân công," 10 September 1953, 1296/PTTg (1945–54)/NAVC 3. Regarding French intelligence, see records of prisoner interrogations conducted in January 1954 by 2ème Bureau, FTNV, 2699/10H/SHD.
27. Pham-van-Dong, "Dieu Le tam thoi so 183-TTg"; Nguyen Chi Nhi, "Báo cáo về sản xuất nông nghiệp trong 3 tháng thứ 3," 5 October 1953, 196/BNL/NAVC 3.
28. Le Trung Dinh, "Bao Cao kiem diem cong tac xay dung khu Tay Bac tu khi thanh lap den nay (7-1952 đen 7-1954)," 16 October 1954, 520/PTTg (1945–54)/NAVC 3; Cong Truong Son La, "Tong ket kinh nghiem lanh dao dan cong mien nui t[ai] Son La," 21 October 1953, 647/BLĐ/NAVC 3; Scott, *The Art of Not Being Governed*, 40–50; Tsing, *Friction*, 5–6.
29. "Bao-Cao tinh hinh Tay bac"; Nguyên-Khangs, "Bao-Cao 3 thang dâu nam 1953."
30. Nguyên-Khangs, "Bao-Cao 3 thang dâu nam 1953."
31. "Bao-Cao tinh hinh Tay bac"; Lentz, "Mobilization and State Formation," 560; Cong an Tay Bac, "Kiêm soat trên sông dê fong Biêt-Kich," 1 July 1953, 2350/KTTTB/NAVC 3.
32. Cong Truong Son La, "Tong ket kinh nghiem lanh dao."
33. Cong Truong Son La, "Tong ket kinh nghiem lanh dao."
34. Lò Văn Mười, "Bao-Cao 3 tháng 4, 5, 6 nam 1949 của Liên Tinh Sơn La Lai Châu," 18 July 1949, 187/PTTg (1945–54)/NAVC 3; Le Failler, *La rivière Noire*, 405.
35. Or, "làm yên lòng dân . . . ," in Nguyen Khang, "Bao Cao Cong tac vung moi giai phong."
36. Nguyen Khang, "Bao Cao Cong tac vung moi giai phong"; Nguyen Chi Nhi, "Báo cáo về sản xuất nông nghiệp."
37. "Sắc lệnh của Chủ tịch nước Việt Nam Dân chủ Cộng hoá số 13-SL, 1/5/1951," Ministry of Justice, accessed 20 February 2016, http://moj.gov.vn/; Lockhart, *Nation in Arms*, 248–50. On taxes in French Indochina, see Brocheux and Hémery, *Indochina*, 91–97; on early DRV tax policy, see Marr, *Vietnam: State, War, and Revolution*, 344–46.
38. Nguyen Khang, "Bao Cao Cong tac vung moi giai phong."
39. Scott, *Seeing Like a State;* Nguyên-Khangs, "Bao-Cao 3 thang dâu nam 1953."
40. Elden, *The Birth of Territory*, 8.
41. General de Linares, Commandant de FTNV à Msr Colonel, Commandant la Zone de Haiphong, 4 July 1952, 2370/10H/SHD; Deuxième Bureau, FTNV, "L'Economie Viet-Minh: Indochine du Nord," May 1953, 2370/10H/SHD; Ministère des Relations avec les États Associés, "Notes Hebdomadaires de Renseignments," 15–21 December 1952, 23–95/HCI/ANOM.
42. Phòng T-T Thị xã Kiến An, "Đồng bào trong vùng tạm chiếm thi đua yêu nước như thế nào?" 1948–49, 2369/10H/SHD.
43. "Tài liệu của địch tuyên truyền về công tác cuộc cải cách điền địa do Thủ tướng bù nhìn Nguyễn Văn Tâm chủ trương và xuyên tạc chính sách phát động quần chúng của ta năm 1953," 1953, 1394/PTTg (1945–54)/NAVC 3.

44. "*Bao-Cao* tinh hinh Tay bac"; "Tổng kết thuế nông nghiệp vùng mới giải phóng Tây Bắc," 1953, 5810/KTTTB/NAVC 3.
45. "Cung co kinh te tai chinh vung tu do"; Nguyên-Khangs, "Bao-Cao 3 thang dâu nam 1953"; "Tổng kết thuế nông nghiệp."
46. Nguyen Chi Nhi, "Báo cáo về sản xuất Nông nghiệp."
47. "Giai gong thue nong nghiep" and "Giai fong dan cong." In "Tổng kết thuế nông nghiệp."
48. "Tổng kết thuế nông nghiệp"; Lentz, "Cultivating Subjects"; Nguyễn Văn Dự, "Về tình trạng nghiện hút."
49. Thao Fim Som Fu, "Ủy ban Quân Dân Chính L/T Sam Nưa-Phong Saly kính gửi UBHCKC tỉnh Sơn La," 27 February 1953, 8930/KTTTB/NAVC 3.
50. Nguyên-Khangs, "Bao-Cao 3 thang dâu nam 1953"; Le Trung Dinh, "Bao Cao kiem diem cong tac"; Triệu, Công an Khu Tây Bắc, "Báo cáo 3 tháng 6, 7, 8-1953," 12 September 1953, 2349/KTTTB/NAVC 3; Nguyen Chi Nhi, "Báo cáo về sản xuất nông nghiệp."
51. Particularly when reporting sensitive issues, reports often obscure agency by using intransitive verbs, as in "Presently, hunger has appeared (*xuất hiện*)," Nguyên-Khangs, "Bao-Cao 3 thang dâu nam 1953"; another report reads, "After liberation, hunger happened (*xảy ra*)," Le Trung Dinh, "Bao Cao kiem diem cong tac."
52. On the Laos Campaign and People's Army movements in spring 1953, see Võ Nguyên Giáp with Hữu Mai, *The Road to Điện Biên Phủ*, 440–61; Viện Lịch sử Quân sự Việt Nam, *Tóm tắt các chiến dịch trong khang chiến*, 411–23; Nguyen Chi Nhi, "Bao cao tinh hinh san xuât nông nghiêp thang 7/1953," 24 August 1953, 3478/BNL/NAVC 3.
53. Gourou, *L'utilisation du sol en Indochine*, 347–51; Savina, *Histoire des Miao*, 213–22; Lentz, "Cultivating Subjects," 901–3; "Bao-Cao tinh hinh Tay bac."
54. Bố Canh nông, "Đề án kế hoạch phòng chống đói," 1953, 3601/BNL/NAVC 3; Devereux, "Why Does Famine Persist in Africa?"
55. Italics in original. Bố Canh nông, "Đề án kế hoạch phòng chống đói," 1953, 3601/BNL/NAVC 3; "Bao-Cao tinh hinh Tay bac"; Nguyên-Khangs, "Bao-Cao 3 thang dâu nam 1953." "Drought and flood are one part caused by climate," stated the central party order, "while another part is caused by forest destruction from opening swiddens carelessly." "Chỉ thị của Ban Bí thư về phòng đói và cứu đói," 12 May 1953, in Đảng Cộng sản Việt Nam, *Văn kiện Đảng*, 207–8. Here, party leaders blamed the victims.
56. Nghiêm Xuan Yem, "Sô 99 NN/GG v/v Phuc hôi san xuât cac vung moi giai phong," 28 November 1952, 3501/BNL/NAVC 3; italics in original, "Chỉ thị của Ban Bí thư," in Đảng Cộng sản Việt Nam, *Văn kiện* Đảng, 212.
57. "Chỉ thị của Ban Bí thư," in Đảng Cộng sản Việt Nam, *Văn kiện Đảng*, 211; Le Trung Dinh, "Bao Cao kiem diem cong tac"; Nguyen Chi Nhi, "Báo cáo về sản xuất Nông nghiệp."
58. Duong-Hông-Quang, "Viêc chiêm huu ruông dât và thê luc phong kiên tai vùng dân tôc Thai o Tây-bac," 22 November 1953, 1370/PTTg (1945–54)/NAVC 3. Unless noted otherwise, the following discussion draws on this document.

59. The original statement reads, "Tich cuc tiên hành viêc 'thanh tru cac phan tu không trong sach thuôc tâng lop trên.'" Note that the author quoted the phrase beginning with *thanh trừ*, a verb carrying violent potential.
60. Evans, "Tai-ization," 274; Condominas, *From Lawa to Mon*, 59.
61. I translated this aphorism from Vietnamese into English, added more formal and consistent breaks, imputed diacritical marks, inserted quote marks, and cleaned up the punctuation. The original reads "'Hoa sen trong ao, mây nam không no, nam nay da nơ', ho Câm [?]èn noi: 'vi nhà ho Câm tan cu nên hoa không no, nay nhà ho Câm da vê nên hoa lai no,['] viec nay rât nhiêu nguoi tin là thuc." Duong-Hông-Quang, "Viec chiêm huu ruông dât."

CHAPTER FOUR: DIỆN BIÊN PHỦ AND THE LOGISTICS OF TERRITORY

1. Võ Nguyên Giáp, *Đường tới Điện Biên Phủ*, 356, 403.
2. Van Creveld, *Supplying War*, 1; Cowen, *The Deadly Life of Logistics*, 5, 26; Elden, "How Should We Do the History of Territory?"
3. Geyer, "The Militarization of Europe," 76.
4. Scott, *Seeing Like a State;* Foucault, *Space, Knowledge, and Power*, 182.
5. Jessop, "From Micro-powers to Governmentality"; MacLean, *The Government of Mistrust*, 11; Lentz, "The King Yields to the Village?"; Italics in original, Weber, "Bureaucracy," in *Economy and Society*, 975; Cowen, *The Deadly Life of Logistics*, 4; Mills, *The Power Elite*, 185.
6. Mitchell, *Rule of Experts*, ch. 3; Võ Nguyên Giáp, *Đường tới Điện Biên*, 365–66; Võ Nguyên Giáp, *Điện Biên Phủ: Điểm hẹn*, 346.
7. Scott, *The Art of Not Being Governed*, 18.
8. Phan Văn Các, *Từ điển từ Hán Việt*, 262; Nguyen Chi Nhi, "Bao cao tinh hinh san xuât nông nghiêp thang 7/1953," 24 August 1953, 3478/BNL/NAVC 3; Nguyen Ba Kinh, "B/C vê thi hanh chinh sach ruông dât," 17 July 1951, 3225/BNL/NAVC 3.
9. Salemink, *The Ethnography of Vietnam's Central Highlanders*, 129–30; McAlister, "Mountain Minorities and the Viet Minh," 788–89, 837; Jerusalemy, "Monographie surs le Pays Thaï," 58; Lentz, "Frontier Making and Erasing."
10. Le Failler, *La rivière Noire*, 29–30; Phan-My, "Bao Cao So Luoc vê tinh hinh công viêc chinh quyên trong hai thang 10 và 11 1952 tai vùng moi duoc giai phong o Tây-Bac," 22 December 1952, 456/PTTg (1945–54)/NAVC 3.
11. Viện Lịch sử Quân sự Việt Nam, *Tóm tắt các chiến dịch*, 390; Viện Lịch sử Quân sự Việt Nam, *Lịch sử cuộc kháng chiến*, 207; "Chính sách dân tộc thiểu số của Đảng hiện nay (Nghị quyết Bộ Chính trị)," August 1952, in Đảng Cộng sản Việt Nam, *Văn kiện Đảng*, 277.
12. Viện Lịch sử Quân sự Việt Nam, *Lịch sử cuộc kháng chiến*, 206–7; Viện Lịch sử Quân sự Việt Nam, *Tóm tắt các chiến dịch*, 393; Bo Lao dong, "Bao cao cong tac dan cong nam 1952," 1953, 623/BLĐ/NAVC 3; Bộ Lao động, "Báo cáo sơ kết Chiến dịch Quang Trung," 1 January 1953, 624/BLĐ/NAVC 3; Phan-My, "Bao Cao So Luoc"; Nguyen Khang, "Bao Cao Cong tac vung moi giai phong trong 2 thang 10, 11/1952," 29 December 1952, 1306/PTTg (1945–54)/NAVC 3;

"Bao-Cao tinh hinh Tay bac va nhiem vu nam 1953 trong Hoi nghi Can Bo Tay Bac (tu 22 den 27/2/53)," March 1953, 471/PTTg (1945–54)/NAVC 3; Le Trung Dinh, "Bao Cao kiem diem cong tac xay dung khu Tay Bac tu khi thanh lap den nay (7-1952 đen 7-1954)," 16 October 1954, 520/PTTg (1945–54)/NAVC 3.

13. Dove, "The Epistemology of Southeast Asia's Anthropogenic Grasslands"; Thompson and Warburton, "Uncertainty on a Himalayan Scale."
14. Mitchell, *Rule of Experts*, 111.
15. Võ Nguyên Giáp, *Đường tới Điện Biên*, 402; Gourou, *Les paysans du Delta tonkinois;* Van Creveld, *Supplying War*, ch. 2; Kleinen, "Tropicality and Topicality"; Joseph Gregory, "Gen. Vo Nguyen Giáp, Who Ousted US from Vietnam, Is Dead," *New York Times*, 4 October 2013.
16. Lockhart, *Nation in Arms*, 246–47; Bộ Lao động, "Báo cáo sơ kết Chiến dịch Quang Trung," 1 January 1953, 624/BLĐ/NAVC 3; Fall, *The Viet-Minh Regime*, 77; Võ Nguyên Giáp, *Đường tới Điện Biên*, 402; Nguyễn An, "Công tác vận tải trong chiến dịch," 176.
17. "Nghị quyết của Hội nghị lần thứ tư Ban Chấp hành Trung ương Đảng Lao động Việt Nam," 25–30 January 1953, in Đảng Cộng sản Việt Nam, *Văn kiện Đảng*, 131; Hoàng Văn Thái, *Cuộc tiến công chiến lược*, 34; Nguyễn An, "Công tác vận tải trong chiến dịch," 174–75; "Chỉ thị của Ban Bí thư về công tác kinh tế tài chính và sản xuất tiết kiệm," 30 July 1953, in Đảng Cộng sản Việt Nam, *Văn kiện Đảng*, 274.
18. Võ Nguyên Giáp, *Đường tới Điện Biên*, 403; Goscha, *Un état né de la guerre*, 268; Lockhart, *Nation in Arms*, 121, 236; Viện Lịch sử Quân sự Việt Nam, *Tóm tắt các chiến dịch*, 414.
19. Tilly, *Coercion, Capital, and European States;* italics in original, "Chỉ thị của Ban Bí thư về công tác kinh tế," 30 July 1953, in Đảng Cộng sản Việt Nam, *Văn kiện Đảng*, 267.
20. "Thông tri của Ban Bí thư về nhiệm vụ cung cấp cho mặt trận," 9 November 1953, in Đảng Cộng sản Việt Nam, *Văn kiện Đảng*, 346.
21. Đỗ Hữu Lễ, "Quân và dân Tây Bắc," 229–30.
22. Tran Dang Khoa, "Tinh hinh vân tai trên Sông Da," 9 March 1953, 2492/PTTg (1945–54)/NAVC 3; "Chỉ thị của Ban Bí thư," 15 June 1953, in Đảng Cộng sản Việt Nam, *Văn kiện Đảng*, 244; Scott, *The Art of Not Being Governed*, 166; Harvey, *The Condition of Postmodernity*, 240.
23. Võ Nguyên Giáp, *Đường tới Điện Biên*, 407–8; Võ Nguyên Giáp, *Điện Biên Phủ: Điểm hẹn*, 189–90.
24. Hoàng Văn Thái, *Cuộc tiến công chiến lược*, 34; Viện Lịch sử Quân sự Việt Nam, *Lịch sử cuộc kháng chiến*, 263–64; Đỗ Hữu Lễ, "Quân và dân Tây Bắc," 229–30; Võ Nguyên Giáp, *Điện Biên Phủ: Điểm hẹn*, 188; Võ Nguyên Giáp, *Đường tới Điện Biên*, 408.
25. Logevall, *Embers of War*, 388, 427–29; Lockhart, *Nation in Arms*, 230–35, 243, 261.
26. Nguyễn Văn Thuận, "Một số vấn đề về công tác chính trị," 113.

27. Bộ Lao Động, "Thông tư số 12 LĐ / TTg ngày 12-10-1953 v/v thi hành Nghị định số 308-TTg ngày 10-9-1953 sửa đổi điều lệ tạm thời số 183-TTg ngày 14-7-1952 về huy động sử dụng dân công," 12 October 1953, 1296/PTTg (1945–54)/NAVC 3; Pham-van-Dông, "Nghi Dinh sô 308-TTg ngay 10 thang 9 nam 1953 vê huy dông va su dung dân công," 10 September 1953, 1296/PTTg (1945–54)/NAVC 3.
28. Geyer, "The Militarization of Europe," 76; Phan Văn Các, *Từ điển Hán Việt,* 98–103. I am grateful to Hue-Tam Ho Tai for her insight into this meaning of "công."
29. "Thư gửi cán bộ và đồng bào dân công cầu đường," 16 September 1953, in *Hồ Chí Minh toàn tập,* 140; Đặng Chấn Liêu, Lê Khả Kế, and Phạm Duy Trọng, *Từ điển Việt-Anh,* 690.
30. "Chỉ thị của Ban bí thư," 15 June 1953, in Đảng Cộng sản Việt Nam, *Văn kiện Đảng,* 244.
31. Cowen, *Deadly Life of Logistics,* 4, 8; Elden, *The Birth of Territory,* 322–23; on militarization and the compression of social formations, see Geyer, "The Militarization of Europe," 79.
32. Foucault, *Society Must Be Defended,* 48; Febvre, *A New Kind of History,* 208–18; Phan Văn Các, *Từ Điển Hán Việt,* 184; Nguyễn Như Ý, *Đại từ điển tiếng Việt,* 687–88, 1015. Mao Tse Tung, "Problems of Strategy in China's Revolutionary War," December 1936, cited in Roberts, *A Concise History of China,* 235; Heuser, *The Evolution of Strategy,* 402–3.
33. Ferguson, *The Anti-politics Machine;* Feldman, "Social Regulation in a Time of War"; "Cung co kinh te tai chinh vung tu do xay dung kin te tai chinh vung moi giai phong," 12 March 1953, 472/PTTg (1945–54)/NAVC 3.
34. "Cung co kinh te tai chinh vung tu do."
35. McMichael, *Contesting Development.*
36. Vandergeest and Peluso, "Territorialization and State Power in Thailand"; "Cung co kinh te tai chinh vung tu do."
37. Italics in original, Bo Canh nong, "Dự án ve van de thong ke san xuat non-lam-nghiep," 7 July 1953, 176/BNL/NAVC 3. Scott, Tehranian, and Mathias, "The Production of Legal Identities Proper to States," 7; Lentz, "Mobilization and State Formation," 576.
38. Bo Canh nong, "Dự án ve van de thong ke."
39. "Cung co kinh te tai chinh vung tu do"; "Bao-Cao Tinh hinh san xuat nong nghiep thang 12–53," 5 January 1954, 3478/BNL/NAVC 3.
40. Bui Quang Tao, "Bao cao san xuât Nông-nghiêp Khu Tây Bac thang 4 va 5, 1953," 1953, 3478/BNL/NAVC 3; "Cung co kinh te tai chinh vung tu do"; Nguyen Chi Nhi, "Bao cao tinh hinh san xuât nông nghiêp thang 8/1953 (da duoc UBHCKC K. thong qua)," 15 September 1953, 3478/BNL/NAVC 3.
41. Lockhart, *Nation in Arms,* 254; Prados, "Assessing Dien Bien Phu."
42. Võ Nguyên Giáp, *Điện Biên Phủ: Điểm hẹn,* 19–20; Zhai, *China and the Vietnam Wars,* 45; Viện Lịch sử Quân sự Việt Nam, *Lịch sử cuộc khang chiến,* 285–88; "De Nghi vê viêc vân dông quần chung o vùng dân tôc thiêu sô

moi giai phong thuôc Tây-bac," September 1953, 1258/PTTg (1945–54)/ NAVC 3.

43. Cao Văn Lượng, Nguyễn Văn Nhật, and Võ Kim Cương, *Lịch sử kháng chiến,* 437; "Thông tri của Ban Bí thư về nhiệm vụ cung cấp cho mặt trận," 9 November 1953, in Đảng Cộng sản Việt Nam, *Văn kiện Đảng,* 344.
44. "Thông tri của Ban Bí thư," in Đảng Cộng sản Việt Nam, *Văn kiện Đảng,* 345; "Chỉ thị của Ban Bí thư về công tác kinh tế tài chính và sản xuất tiết kiệm," 30 July 1953, in Đảng Cộng sản Việt Nam, *Văn kiện Đảng,* 269–70; Viện Lịch sử Quân sự Việt Nam, *Lịch sử cuộc kháng chiến,* 291; Hoàng Văn Thái, *Cuộc tiến công chiến lược,* 47.
45. "Thông tri của Ban Bí thư về nhiệm vụ cung cấp cho mặt trận," 9 November 1953, in Đảng Cộng sản Việt Nam, *Văn kiện Đảng,* 345–46. See also Nguyễn Đình Hưng, "Sức mạnh dân công trong chiến dịch Điện Biên Phủ," in Lê Dần, *Điện Biên Phủ,* 84–85.
46. Viện Lịch sử Quân sự Việt Nam, *Lịch sử cuộc kháng chiến,* 326; Nguyễn Văn Thuận, "Một số vấn đề về công tác chính trị," 113.
47. Fall, *Hell in a Very Small Place,* 19–20, 63.
48. Fall, *Hell in a Very Small Place,* 30–35, 50; Võ Nguyên Giáp, *Điện Biên Phủ,* ch. 2.
49. McAlister, "Mountain Minorities and the Việt Minh," 826–27.
50. Cao Văn Lượng, Nguyễn Văn Nhật, and Võ Kim Cương, *Lịch sử kháng chiến,* 432; Hồ Chí Minh, *Hồ Chí Minh toàn tập,* 597.
51. "Gen Giáp's Strategic Rethink a Decisive Factor," *Việt Nam News,* 4 May 2014, 8–9; Phan Huy Lê, "Một Quyết đoán táo bạo, kịp thời."
52. Võ Nguyên Giáp, *Điện Biên Phủ: Điểm hẹn,* 107, 112; Hoàng Văn Thái, *Cuộc tiến công chiến lược,* 48–53; Zhai, *China and the Vietnam Wars,* 46–47.
53. Võ Nguyên Giáp, *Điện Biên Phủ: Điểm hẹn,* 137.
54. Logevall, *Embers of War,* 414–17; Viện Lịch sử Quân sự Việt Nam, *Lịch sử cuộc kháng chiến,* 378–79; Fall reports a total of forty-eight 105-millimeter howitzers in *Hell in a Very Small Place,* 127; Võ Nguyên Giáp, *Điện Biên Phủ: Điểm hẹn,* 187–88.
55. "Chỉ thị của Bộ Chính trị: Động viên quân đội và nhân dân tiếp tục đánh giặc và phục vụ tiền tuyến," 8 February 1954, in Đảng Cộng sản Việt Nam, *Văn kiện Đảng,* 15; Cao Văn Lượng, "Đường lối giương cao ngọn," 43; Võ Nguyên Giáp, *Điện Biên Phủ: Điểm hẹn,* 187.
56. Baubeau, "Aspects logistiques de la bataille de Dien Bien Phu," 6 July 1954, 1176/10H/SHD; Fall, *Hell in a Very Small Place,* 479–82; Cao Văn Lượng, Nguyễn Văn Nhật, and Võ Kim Cương, *Lịch sử kháng chiến,* 436.
57. Quoted in Hoi dong Cung cap Mat tran, "Bao Cao Cong tac phuc vu chien dich Dien Bien Phu," 10 July 1954, 1692/PTTg (1945–54)/NAVC 3; italics in original, Baubeau, "Aspects logistiques de la bataille"; Shrader, *A War of Logistics,* xv.
58. Unless otherwise noted, all references are to Hoi dong Cung cap Mat tran, "Bao Cao Cong tac phuc vu chien dich Dien Bien Phu," 10 July 1954, 1692/PTTg (1945–54)/NAVC 3; A summary of this "secret" document (with slightly

different statistics) is available at "Công tác phục vụ chiến dịch Điện Biên Phủ qua một tài liệu lưu trữ," State Records Management and Archives Department of Vietnam, accessed 4 February 2018, http://www.archives.gov.vn.

59. See "Góp công sức cho Điện Biên đánh thắng," in Vũ Hải Đăng, *Điện Biên Phủ*, 317–18; Đặng Đức Quy, "Vai trò của đồng bào Tây Bắc với thế trận lòng dân trong chiến dịch Điện Biên Phủ," in Nguyễn Bá Dương, *Thế trận lòng dân*, 213–25.
60. Thongchai, *Siam Mapped*, 164–70.
61. Hồ Chí Minh, "Thư gửi cán bộ và đồng bào dân công cầu đường," 16 September 1953, in *Hồ Chí Minh toàn tập*, 140.
62. Estimates from Nguyễn Hào Hùng, "Chiến thắng Điện Biên Phủ—Bản anh hùng ca của liên minh đoàn kết chiến đấu Việt Nam-Lào-Campuchia," in Viện Sử học, *Mấy vấn đề về chiến thắng*, 161–62; Nguyễn An, "Công tác vận tải trong chiến dịch," 176; Vũ Văn Thông, "Công tác vận tải," 165; Võ Nguyên Giáp, *Điện Biên Phủ: Điểm hẹn*, 190; Viện Lịch sử Quân sự Việt Nam, *Lịch sử cuộc kháng chiến*, 388.
63. For example, the military's Central Party Command roundly criticized the civilian supply agency's "simplistic organization" before the Politburo in Tổng Quân ủy, "Kế hoạch quân sự năm 1954," 20 December 1953, in Trần Trọng Trung, *Một số văn kiện chỉ đạo*, 235.
64. Nguyễn An, "Công tác vận tải trong chiến dịch," 177.
65. Nguyễn Kháng, "Báo cáo kiểm điểm công tác 6 tháng đầu năm 1954," 24 June 1954, 519/PTTg (1945–54), NAVC 3; Le Trung Dinh, "Bao Cao kiem diem cong tac"; Bùi San, "Bao-Cao ve thuc-hien chinh-sach dan-toc trong nam 1954," 29 December 1954, 1465/PTTg (1945–54)/NAVC 3. Uncounted data in "Tập báo cáo thành tích 8 năm khang chiến 1946–1954 của các tỉnh thuộc Khu Tây Bắc," 1955, 577/PTTg (1945–54)/NAVC 3; Ban Chấp hành Khu Tây bắc, "Báo cáo tổng quát công tác phục vụ chiến dịch Điện Biên Phủ," 14 June 1954, 665/BLĐ/NAVC 3.
66. The Central Highlands Campaign required upward of 200,000 laborers and 6 million labor days, according to Viện Lịch sử Quân sự Việt Nam, *Lịch sử cuộc kháng chiến*, 385; Nguyễn Kháng, "Công tác tiễu phỉ tru biệt kích," 17 March 1954, 519/PTTg (1945–54)/NAVC 3
67. Cao Văn Lượng, Nguyễn Văn Nhật, and Võ Kim Cương, *Lịch sử kháng chiến*, 442; Bộ Chỉ huy Quân sự tỉnh Sơn La, *Sơn La*, 171; Đỗ Hữu Lễ, "Quân và dân Tây Bắc với công tác bảo đảm hậu cần," 231.
68. Pelley, *Postcolonial Vietnam*, 3–4.
69. Like Indonesian and other Southeast Asian languages, the Vietnamese language distinguishes between a first-person plural inclusive (*chúng ta*) and exclusive (*chúng tôi*).
70. Official population figures from Phan-My, "Bao Cao So Luoc" and "Tinh hinh khai quat vê Khu tu tri dan toc Thai Meo o Tay-Bac," May 1955, 22/KTTTB/NAVC 3. My estimate is based on 261,000 dân công and approximately 53,000 People's Army logisticians, soldiers, and officers. The latter figure, to

this day, remains obscure: Vũ Văn Thông lists 53,800 soldiers in "Công tác vận tải," 157; Simpson estimates 47,500 in *Dien Bien Phu,* 35. The calculated figure of 314,000 does not include another estimated 500,000 women working to support the soldiers from home, the 2,800 Youth Volunteers (*Thanh niên xung phong*), nor myriad others serving elsewhere, as discussed in Nguyễn Hữu Hợp and Nguyễn Hữu Đạo, "Chiến thắng Điện Biên Phủ," 98–100.

CHAPTER FIVE: STRUGGLES AT ĐIỆN BIÊN PHỦ

1. Lê Văn Kim, "Báo cáo tình hình cán bộ và dân công (công tác chính trị tháng 12–53)," 15 January 1954, 647/BLĐ/NAVC 3.
2. "Tổng kết kinh nghiệm lãnh đạo dân công miền núi t[ại] Sơn La," 21 October 1953, 647/BLĐ/NAVC 3; Lê Văn Kim, "Báo cáo tình hình."
3. For a comparative perspective on the "front lawn as the front line" influencing 1950s domestic life in the United States, see McEnaney, *Civil Defense Begins at Home.* Võ Nguyên Giáp, *People's War, People's Army.*
4. Or, *vùng tự do, vùng mới giải phóng, vùng tạm bị chiếm.* To reduce clutter, the text eschews quotation marks for these terms.
5. Unless otherwise noted, discussion below draws on Hoàng Công Phẩm, "Chúng tôi đi chiến dịch Điện Biên Phủ" and on "Hồ sơ về Hoàng Công Phẩm," 53076/UTC/NAVC 3.
6. See Simpson, *Dien Bien Phu;* Windrow, *The Last Valley;* Roy, *La bataille de Dienbienphu;* Ban Chấp hành Đảng bộ tỉnh Lai Châu, "Vai trò của Đảng bộ."
7. Both Hoàng Công Phẩm and Trần Lương (aka Trần Nam Trung) continued military service in the Second Indochina War, the latter as the DRV's secretary of defense for southern Vietnam; Chen, *Vietnam and China,* 275.
8. Andreas, *Border Games,* 103–6; Zhai, *China and the Vietnam Wars,* 46–49.
9. On "martyrs" (*liệt sỹ*), "sacrifice" (*hy sinh*), and commemoration in Vietnam, see Tai, *The Country of Memory.*
10. Muelle, *Combats en Pays Thaï,* ch 3.
11. Bằng Giang (aka Nguyễn Cao Cơ), like Phẩm, would later serve with distinction in the Second Indochina War; Phan-My, "Bao Cao So Luoc vê tinh hinh công viêc chinh quyên trong hai thang 10 và 11–1952 tai vùng moi duoc giai phong o Tây-Bac," 22 December 1952, 456/PTTg (1945–54)/NAVC 3.
12. Bradley, *Vietnam at War,* 73.
13. For more on the town of Lai Châu during this tumultuous period, see Lentz, "Making the Northwest Vietnamese."
14. UBHCKC Tinh Son La, "Bao-cao công tac xay-dung và cung-cô Chinh-quyen tu thang 1/1954 den thang 7/1954," 1954, 826/KTTTB/NAVC 3; Le Trung Dinh, "Bao Cao kiem diem cong tac xay dung khu Tay Bac tu khi thanh lap den nay (7-1952 đen 7-1954)," 16 October 1954, 520/PTTg (1945–54)/NAVC 3.
15. Brocheux and Hémery, *Indochina,* 51–64; Le Failler, *La rivière Noire,* ch 3.

16. Kerkvliet, "Agricultural Land in Vietnam"; White, "Peasant Mobilization and Anti-colonial Struggle." The organizations are listed as Liên hiệp Nghĩa bình chống Cộng, Nông dân Đảng, Liên đoàn Thanh niên Công giáo; Le Trung Dinh, "Bao Cao kiem diem cong tac."
17. On unstable social categories, see MacLean, *The Government of Mistrust*, ch. 1; Lentz, "Making the Northwest Vietnamese," 73–82. On explanations for mass participation, see Lockhart, *Nation in Arms*, 256–58; White, "Agrarian Reform and National Liberation," 241. On the Yên Bái Uprising, see Brocheux and Hémery, *Indochina*, 315–16; Zinoman, *The Colonial Bastille*, 203–4.
18. Elden, *Terror and Territory;* Le Trung Dinh, "Bao Cao kiem diem cong tac"; Roger Trinquier, Groupement de Commandos Mixtes Aeroportes, "Études general d'un programme d'action," 8 August 1952, 2375/10H/SHD; Viện Khoa học Công an, "Công tác bảo vệ trong cuộc tiến công chiến lược Đông Xuân 1953–1954 và trong chiến dịch Điện Biên Phủ," in Viện Sử học, *Mấy vấn đề về chiến thắng*, 135–37; Davis, *Imperial Bandits*, 9–12; Ngô, *The New Way*, 28.
19. Công an tỉnh Lai Châu, *Lịch sử Công an*, 24; Lê Duẩn, "Chỉ thị của ban bí thư về việc tăn cường lãnh đạo công tác công an," 20 February 1954, in Đảng Cộng sản Việt Nam, *Văn kiện Đảng*, 25; Nguyen, *Hanoi's War*, ch. 1; Quang Van Dai, "Báo cáo cong tac noi chinh nam 1954," 3 May 1955, 1401/PTTg (1945–54)/NAVC 3.
20. Le Trung Dinh, "Bao Cao kiem diem cong tac."
21. Ban Chấp hành Đảng bộ tỉnh Lai Châu, "Vai trò của Đảng bộ," 112.
22. Lò Văn Hạc, "Bao-cao tong ket cong tac nam 1954," 5 March 1955, 542/PTTg (1945–54)/NAVC 3.
23. Nguyễn Thị Lâm Hảo, *Điện Biên—Đất và Người*, 164–69.
24. Công an tỉnh Lai Châu, *Lịch sử Công an*, 35; Lee, *Dreams of the Hmong Kingdom*, ch. 8; Werner and Bélanger, "Gender and Vietnam Studies," in Werner and Bélanger, *Gender, Household, State*.
25. Catholic priest François Savina recorded many reasons why Hmong people preferred the highlands, including, "We prefer the mountains to the plains because the former is less hot, less humid, and less unhealthy." Savina, *Histoire des Miao*, 174–75.
26. Nguyễn Kháng, "Báo cáo kiểm điểm cộng tác 6 tháng đầu năm 1954," 24 June 1954, 519/PTTg (1945–54)/NAVC 3.
27. Ban Chấp hành Đảng bộ tỉnh Lai Châu, "Vai trò của Đảng bộ," 112; Le Trung Dinh, "Bao Cao kiem diem cong tac."
28. "Bao cao cong tac thue nong nghiep 1954 Khu Tây Bắc (Tai Hôi nghi tông kêt cua Bô 27/4/55)," 27 April 1955, 2621/PTTg (1945–54)/NAVC 3; letter from Buy Quang Tao, Chủ tịch UBHCKC Khu Tây Bắc to UBHCKC các tỉnh trong Khu v/v thuế nông nghiệp, 23 September 1954, 2621/PTTg (1945–54)/NAVC 3; Nguyen huy Thanh, "Bao Cao (So ket dot 1 cong tac thue nong nghiep vu dong 54 o hai tinh Son la va Lai chau)," 13 November 1954, 2621/PTTg (1945–54)/NAVC 3.

29. Lee San, "Bao-Cao tông kêt thuên N.N. 1954," 31 December 1954, 102/Sơn-Lai/NAVC 3; "Bao cao cong tac thue nong nghiep 1954 Khu Tây Bắc," 27 April 1955, 2621/PTTg (1945–54)/NAVC 3.
30. Vietnam's anti-colonial nationalism contrasts with the European, American, and Israeli contexts discussed in Weiner, *Landscaping the Human Garden;* James, *The Black Jacobins.*
31. Ty Cong an Lai Chau, "Bao cao cong tac nam 1954 cua Ty CA LC," 25 December 1954, 90/Sơn-Lai/NAVC 3. The five occupied communes are listed as Xa Thanh-yen, Thanh-tieng, Thanh-luong, Sam-mun, and Nong-het. Tinh Lai Chau, "Ke hoach cong tac Huyen Dien Bien," 1954, 10/KTTTB/NAVC 3; Lò Văn Hạc, "Bao-cao tong ket cong tac nam 1954." In this report, Lò Văn Hặc cited "specific" damages in Điện Biên as "328 dead, 283 wounded, 157 women raped, 1255 houses destroyed, 671 water buffalo [dead] . . ." (ellipses in original). It is unclear whether his figures account for residents killed in Noong Nhai, discussed below. Duc Binh, "Bao Cao Thang 2 Nam 1954," 28 February 1954, 2194/KTTTB/NAVC 3.
32. The five "Ethnic Tai communes" are listed as Na-Taus, Muong-luan, Muong-nha, Muong-muon, and Muong-fang; the "Ethnic Hmong communes" as Vinh Quang, Đoc-lap, Hanh phuc, Na-u, Quang-trung, and Tan-lap. Tinh Lai Chau; "Ke hoach cong tac Huyen Dien Bien"; Duc Binh, "Bao Cao Thang 2 Nam 1954."
33. Lò Văn Hạc, "Bao-cao tong ket cong tac nam 1954"; Duc Binh, "Bao Cao Thang 2 Nam 1954"; Tinh Lai Chau, "Ke hoach cong tac Huyen Dien Bien." The explosion killed 444 people, "almost all of whom were women and children." Cited from a memorial in Thanh Xương Commune photographed by the author in January 2007. For more on Noong Nhai, see Công an tỉnh Lai Châu, *Lịch sử Công an,* 30–31; Ty Cong-An Lai-Chau, "Bao-Cao 'Tinh hinh giai fong Dien-Bien fu' Ngay 15-5-1954," 15 May 1954, 2376/KTTTB/NAVC 3. On high-level diplomatic discussions regarding the use of American nuclear weapons, see Logevall, *Embers of War,* 498–501.
34. "Lời hiệu triệu của Tổng quân ủy gửi toàn thể các đồng chí đảng viên trong chiến dịch XX," in Trần Trọng Trung, *Một số văn kiện Chỉ đạo,* 294–96; Trường Chinh, "Về mấy vấn đề cần chú ý trong việc phát động quần chúng giảm tô vùng dân tộc thiểu số ở lẫn với người Kinh," 5 December 1953, in Đảng Cộng sản Việt Nam, *Văn kiện Đảng,* 532. For more on recruitment, known as "striking the root to string the beads" (*bắt rễ xâu chuỗi*), see MacLean, *The Government of Mistrust,* 45. On the local Ban Cán sự huyện Điện Biên and Uy bản xã Trưởng bản Trung kiên, see Hoàng Trang, "Bao Cao Tông kêt huy dông nhân vât luc fuc vu chiên truong," 29 March 1954, 2194/KTTTB/NAVC 3.
35. Tinh Lai Châu, "Ke hoach cong tac Huyen Dien Bien"; Hoàng Trang, "Bao Cao Tông kêt huy dông nhân vât luc."
36. Duc Binh, "Bao Cao Thang 2 Nam 1954"; Tinh Lai Chau, "Ke hoach cong tac Huyen Dien Bien"; Tréglodé, *Heroes and Revolution,* 214; Hồ Chí Minh, "Thư

gửi đồng bào và cán bộ Lai Châu," 12 December 1953, in *Hồ Chí Minh toàn tập*, 190.

37. Duc Binh, "Bao Cao Thang 2 Nam 1954."
38. MacLean, *The Government of Mistrust*, 43.
39. Unless otherwise noted, all quoted responses are from Hoàng Trang, "Bao Cao Tông kêt huy dông nhân vât luc."
40. Weber, *Economy and Society*, 241–45; Goscha, *Vietnam: A New History*, 229.
41. Duc Binh, "Bao Cao Thang 2 Nam 1954."
42. Hoàng Trang, "Bao Cao Tông kêt huy dông nhân vât luc."
43. Hoàng Trang, "Bao Cao Tông kêt huy dông nhân vât luc."
44. Hoàng Trang, "Bao Cao Tông kêt huy dông nhân vât luc." On Vàng Chong and French sponsorship of Hmong militias, see Lee, *Dreams of the Hmong Kingdom*, 288–94; Quang Van Dai, "Báo cáo cong tac noi chinh nam 1954," 3 May 1955, 1401/PTTg (1945–54)/NAVC 3.
45. Trần Quyết, "Bao-Cao San xuat nong nghiep tu ngay giai phong den thang 2 nam 1954," 14 May 1954, 3624/BNL/NAVC 3.
46. Unless otherwise noted, data are from Hoàng Trang, "Bao Cao Tông kêt huy dông nhân vât luc."

CHAPTER SIX: REVOLUTIONARY ALTERNATIVES

1. Written "Ngocj Sown," his name is most likely rendered with diacritics as Ngọc Sơn. Khu Công an Tây Bắc, "Bao-Cao Ve nhung tin tuc hoang duong va de cao My tung ra o Luc-Yen," 21 February 1955, 2350/KTTTB/NAVC 3.
2. Lee, *Dreams of the Hmong Kingdom;* Tapp, "Of Grasshoppers, Caterpillars, and Beans."
3. Khu ủy Tây Bắc, "Bao Cao thang 10, 1954," 1 November 1954, 519/PTTg (1945–54)/NAVC 3; Lentz, "Cultivating Subjects," 879–918; McCoy, *The Politics of Heroin*. An advocate of the continuity thesis goes so far as to argue for over a century of stasis in highland-lowland relations, summarizing that, as of 1989, "in the mountains, very little indeed had changed since the time of Imperial Vietnam." Michaud, "The Montagnards and the State," 360.
4. Elden, "Land, Terrain, Territory." For similar findings in China if for different reasons, see Yeh, *Taming Tibet*, 5–10; Elden, "How Should We Do the History of Territory?"
5. Lò Văn Hạc, "Bao-cao tong ket cong tac nam 1954," 5 March 1955, 542/PTTg (1945–54)/NAVC 3; MacLean, "Bodies in Perpetual Motion."
6. Kirsch and Flint, *Reconstructing Conflict;* Goscha, *Un état né de la guerre*, 13; Logevall, *Embers of War*, 619–20; Lam Sung, "Bao-Cao tong ket cong tac trong 1954," 12 December 1954, 90/Sơn-Lai/NAVC 3; Asselin, *Hanoi's Road to the Vietnam War*, 17–33; Szalontai, "Political and Economic Crisis in North Vietnam."
7. Unless otherwise noted, the discussion draws on Lò Văn Hạc, "Bao-cao tong ket cong tac nam 1954"; UBHC Huyen Muong Lay, "Bao-Cao Tong ket Thue

Nong Nghiep," 25 November 1954, 102/Sơn-Lai/NAVC 3; Lam Sung, "Bao-Cao tong ket cong tac trong 1954."

8. "Nghi Quyet: Cong tac chinh quyen Khu Tay Bac nam 1953," 1953, 836/KTTTB/NAVC 3; UBHC Khu Tay Bac, "Bao cao 'Cong tac chinh quyen 6 thang dau nam 1954,'" 6 July 1954, 836/KTTTB/ NAVC 3; UBHCKC Tinh Son La, "Bao-cao công tac xay-dung và cung-cô Chinh-quyen tu thang 1/1954 den thang 7/1954," 1954, 826/KTTTB/NAVC 3; "Đề án công tác chính quyền 6 tháng cuối năm 1954," 1954 and "Đề án công tác chính quyền khu Tây Bắc năm 1954," n.d., 836/KTTTB/NAVC 3.
9. Thongchai, *Siam Mapped*, 88; UBHC Khu Tay Bac, "Bao cao 'Cong tac chinh quyen.'"
10. Michaud, "Handling Mountain Minorities"; McLeod, "Indigenous Peoples and the Vietnamese Revolution"; Turner, "Making a Living the Hmong Way."
11. Mukdawijitra, "Ethnicity and Multilingualism"; Cầm Trọng, *Người Thái ở Tây Bắc;* MacLean, *The Government of Mistrust*, 11–16; Scott, *Seeing Like a State*, 76–80.
12. Buy Quang Tao, Chủ tịch UBHC Khu Tây Bắc gửi thư đến các tỉnh trong Khu v/v thuế nông nghiệp, 23 September 1954, 2621/PTTg (1945–54)/NAVC 3; Nguyen huy Thanh, "Bao Cao (So ket dot 1 cong tac thue nong nghiep vu dong 54 o hai tinh Son la va Lai chau)," 13 November 1954, 2621/PTTg (1945–54)/NAVC 3.
13. "Bao cao cong tac thue nong nghiep 1954," 27 April 1955, 2621/PTTg (1945–54)/NAVC 3.
14. Watts, "Entitlements or Empowerment?"; Watts and Bohle, "Hunger, Famine, and the Space of Vulnerability"; Sen, *Poverty and Famines*.
15. Lê-Van-Khiêu, "Bao-Cao Tinh hinh san xuat nong lam nghiep (6 thang dau nam 54)," 10 July 1954, 272/BNL/NAVC 3; Ty Cong an Lai Chau, "Bao cao cong tac nam 1954 cua Ty CA LC," 25 December 1954, 90/Sơn-Lai/NAVC 3; "Bao cao cong tac thue nong nghiep 1954 Khu Tây Bắc," 27 April 1955, 2621/PTTg (1945–54)/NAVC 3; Tran-quoc-Manh, "Bao-Cao tom tat tinh hinh cong tac thang 1 nam 1955," 31 January 1955, 90/Sơn-Lai/NAVC 3.
16. "Bao cao ve van de luong thuc," 1955, 2632/PTTg (1945–54)/NAVC 3; Ủy ban Cứu tế xã hội, "Báo cáo trước Hội nghị Ủy ban Cứu tế xã hội TW," 13 February 1955, 4071/BNL/NAVC 3; "Tổng kết công tác lãnh đạo sản xuất chống đói năm 1955," 1955, 4072/BNL/NAVC 3.
17. MacLean, *Government of Mistrust*, 62; "Tổng kết công tác lãnh đạo sản xuất chống đói năm 1955"; UBHC Liên Khu IV, "Bao cao tinh hinh doi va benh tat o lien Khu IV," 19 April 1955, 2/CTXH/NAVC 3; "Tinh hinh đoi, benh, san xuat: b/c của anh Nhắng ở Hội ban Bí thư, ở Hội đồng Chính phủ," 18 July 1955, 4072/BNL/NAVC 3.
18. "Tinh hinh đoi rach va benh tat o cac lien khu," 1955, 4072/BNL/NAVC 3; "Kế hoạch sản xuất nông lâm nghiệp," 1955, 305/BNL/NAVC 3; Ha Xuan Tu, "So bo bao cao cong tac va tinh hinh san xuat nong lam nghiep nam 1955 cua so Nong lam Khu Tu tri Thai Meo," 7 December 1955, 3167/KTTTB/NAVC 3; Le

Trung Dinh, "Bao-cao tong ket cuu doi và san xuat Khu Tay Bac," 6 June 1956, 305/CTXH/NAVC 3; Trần Quyết, "Bao-cao san xuat nong nghiep tu ngay giai phong den thang 2 nam 1954," 15 May 1954, 3624/BNL/NAVC 3.

19. Phòng TAHC, "Báo cáo tình hình 6 tháng đầu năm 1955," 1 July 1955, 2379/KTTTB/NAVC 3; Fong Thuy loi Kien truc, "Bao-Cao cong tac dieu tra tinh hinh ruong dat hoang chau Dien Bien," 15 May 1956, 3177/KTTTB/NAVC 3.
20. Sở Nông lâm, "Bao Cao tinh hinh san xuat 6 thang dau nam 1955 trong Khu Tu tri Thai-Meo," 28 July 1955, 305/BNL/NAVC 3; Sở Công an, "Báo cáo tổng kết công tác năm 1955," 13 October 1955, 2379/KTTTB/NAVC 3; Quầng Văn Đức, "Kiểm điểm thực hiện chính sách dân tộc thiểu số qua công tác chống đói," July 1956, 2756/KTTTB/NAVC 3.
21. Quầng Văn Đức, "Kiểm điểm thực hiện chính sách"; Phòng TAHC, "Báo cáo tình hình 6 tháng đầu năm 1955."
22. Ty Cong an Lai Chau, "Bao cao cong tac nam 1954"; Nguyen Khangs, "Bao cao thang I/1955," 1 February 1955, 6/PTTg/NAVC 3; Lò Văn Hạc, "Bao-cao tong ket cong tac nam 1954."
23. Tappe, "A Frontier in the Frontier"; Tran-quoc-Manh, "Bao-Cao tom tat tinh hinh cong tac thang 1 nam 1955," 31 January 1955, 90/Sơn-Lai/NAVC 3; Lò Văn Hạc, "Bao-cao tong ket cong tac nam 1954"; Ty Cong an Lai Chau, "Bao cao cong tac nam 1954"; Nguyen Khangs, "Bao cao thang I/1955."
24. District populations of 22,600 (late 1954), 19,372 (late 1955), and 19,875 (mid-1956) in Ty Cong an Lai Chau, "Bao cao cong tac nam 1954"; UBHC Chau Dien Bien, "Bao-Cao tong ket cong tac 1 nam 1955," 5 January 1956, 26/KTTTB/NAVC 3; Fong Thuy loi Kien truc, "Bao-Cao cong tac dieu tra tinh hinh ruong dat hoang."
25. Hồ Chí Minh, "Thư gửi đồng bào Khu tự trị Thái-Mèo," 7 May 1955, in *Hồ Chí Minh toàn tập*, 543; *Những Tài liệu về Tổ chức Chính quyền Khu tự trị Thái-Mèo;* "Tinh hinh khai quat vê Khu tu tri dan toc Thai Meo o Tay-Bac," May 1955, 22/KTTTB/NAVC 3.
26. "Tinh hinh khai quat vê Khu tu tri"; Ban biên tập Sở Giáo Dục, *Địa lý Khu tự trị Thái-Mèo.*
27. Connor, *The National Question*, 115; Pholsena, *Post-war Laos*, 158; Michaud, "The Montagnards and the State," 356; Scott, *The Art of Not Being Governed*, 10–11; Michaud and Forsyth, "Rethinking the Relationships between Livelihoods and Ethnicity in Highland China, Vietnam, and Laos," in Michaud and Forsyth, *Moving Mountains*, 5.
28. Nguyen Khangs, "Bao cao thang I/1955"; Masako, *Politics of Ethnic Classification in Vietnam*, 17–20; Bui San, "Bao-Cao ve thuc-hien chinh-sach dan-toc trong nam 1954," 29 December 1954, 1465/PTTg (1945–54)/NAVC 3; Taylor, "Surface Orientations in Vietnam"; Pelley, *Postcolonial Vietnam*, 70.
29. Nguyen Khangs, "Bao cao thang I/1955"; Đảng Lao động Việt Nam, *Văn kiện của Đảng về Chính sách dân tộc.*

30. Khu uy TB, "Báo cáo tháng 10, 1954," 1 November 1954 and Nguyễn Kháng, "Báo cáo tháng 11, 1954," 2 December 1954, 519/PTTg (1945–54)/NAVC 3; "Chinh sach dan toc thieu so ——," 1954, 2745/KTTTB/NAVC 3; Bui San, "Bao-Cao ve thuc-hien chinh-sach dan-toc trong nam 1954," 29 December 1954, 1465/PTTg (1945–54)/NAVC 3; "Tinh hinh khai quat vê Khu tu tri."
31. Mukdawijitra, "Ethnicity and Multilingualism," 244; Le Trung Dinh, "Bao-Cao ve viec dua cac dai bieu ve Ha noi du le don mung Ho chu tich, Dang, và Chinh phu ve thu do," 7 January 1955, 6/PTTg/NAVC 3.
32. "Hội đồng Nhân dân Khu tự trị Thái-Mèo đã bầu Ủy ban Hành chính Khu," *Nhân dân*, 13 May 1955; Cầm Trọng, *Người Thái ở Tây Bắc*, 566.
33. Nguyen Khangs, "Bao cao thang I/1955."
34. "Báo cáo tổng kết của khối miền núi," 1958, 927/BVH/NAVC 3.
35. Nguyên-Viết-Thành, "Làm hồ chứa nước trên cánh đồng Điện-Biên," *Nhân dân*, 5 April 1959; Lentz, "Mobilization and State Formation," 575; Lo-Van-Hac, "Bao-Cao tinh hinh chung 6 thang đauf nam 1957," 6 September 1957, 52/PTTg/NAVC 3; "Báo cáo cong tac cai thien doi song vat chat va tinh than cho nhan dan cac D.T.," 10 January 1957, 2765/KTTTB/NAVC 3.
36. Uy ban Ke hoach, "Bao-Cao tong ket tinh hinh thuc hien ke hoach nha nuoc nam—1956," 1957, 38/KTTTB/NAVC 3; Lò Văn Minh, "Quyết nghị số 227/Qn của UBHC Khu TTTM về điều lệ tạm thời thuế nông nghiệp," 18 October 1955; 5823/KTTTB/NAVC 3; Lò Văn Hặc, "Báo-Cáo 3 thang 7, 8, 9–1956," 5 October 1956, 17/PTTg/NAVC 3; Lentz, "Cultivating Subjects," 906–8; "Báo cáo tổng kết công tác thuế thuốc phiện năm 1956," 14 January 1957, 5869/KTTTB/NAVC 3; Lâm Liên, "Báo cáo v/v thu thuế sản phẩm miền núi 1957," 23 May 1957, 5953/KTTTB/NAVC 3.
37. Lò Văn Hặc, "Báo-Cáo 3 thang 7, 8, 9-1956," 5 October 1956, 17/PTTg/NAVC 3; Châu Điện Biên, "Báo cáo gia đình chạy sang Lào từ tháng 11 đến hết tháng 12 năm 1954," 1955, 8930/KTTTB/NAVC 3.
38. Khu Công an Tây Bắc, "Bao-Cao Ve nhung tin tuc hoang duong"; Goscha, *Going Indochinese*, 31; Zinoman, *The Colonial Bastille*, 4–5; Anderson, *Imagined Communities;* Elden, *The Birth of Territory*, ch. 7; MacLean, *The Government of Mistrust*, 16–17; Migdal, "Mental Maps and Virtual Checkpoints," in Migdal, *Boundaries and Belonging.*
39. Unless otherwise noted, references to vampires and vampirism come from Sở Công an Khu, "Bao-Cao Thang 10 nam 1956 cua Phong 2," 25 October 1956 and Sở Công an Khu, "Báo cáo từ 25/11 đến 25/12 năm 1956," 26 December 1956, 2389/KTTTB/NAVC 3.
40. Austen, "The Moral Economy of Witchcraft," 91.
41. Abrams, "Notes on the Difficulty of Studying the State."
42. "Bao cao bo sung tinh hinh va cong tac tri an," 1957, 2389/KTTTD/NAVC 3.
43. Mayaram, *Against History, Against State;* Guha, "The Prose of Counterinsurgency"; Ban Chấp hành Đảng bộ huyện Điện Biên, *Lịch sử Đảng bộ huyện;* Thongchai, *Siam Mapped*, 169–70. On Cold War political violence in Thailand, see Haberkorn, *Revolution Interrupted.*

44. Proschan, "Peoples of the Gourd"; Évrard, "Oral Histories and Migration under Socialism"; Litzinger, *Other Chinas;* Scott, *The Art of Not Being Governed,* ch. 8.
45. Nguyễn Thuân, "Báo cáo tổng kết công tác tuyên truyền chống âm mưu xưng vua của địch ở xã Độc Lập," 12 September 1957, 2413/KTTTB/NAVC 3.
46. Sở Công an Khu, "Báo cáo tổng kết kiểm điểm tình hình và công tác từ 1/56 đến 10/56," 18 October 1956, 2389/KTTTB/NAVC 3; Bộ Nội vụ, *Công an nhân dân Lai Châu,* 54–59; Công an tỉnh Lai Châu, *Lịch sử Công an,* 41–48; Lentz, "Cultivating Subjects," 891; McCoy, *The Politics of Heroin;* Trinquier, *Modern Warfare.*
47. Adas, *Prophets of Rebellion;* Baird, "Millenarian Movements"; Leach, *Political Systems,* 10–14; Kirsch, *Feasting and Social Oscillation,* 12; Culas, *Le messianisme hmong;* Lee, *Dreams of the Hmong Kingdom,* 103–20; Le Failler, *La rivière Noire,* ch. 8; Gunn, "Shamans and Rebels"; Tapp, "Of Grasshoppers, Caterpillars, and Beans"; Đinh Sơn, "Báo-Cáo cong tac cai thien doi song vat chat va tinh than cho nhan dan cac dan toc," January 1957, 3215/KTTTB/NAVC 3.
48. Scott, *The Art of Not Being Governed,* ch. 6 1/2; Nguyễn Thuân, "Báo cáo tổng kết công tác tuyên truyền chống âm mưu xưng vua"; UBHC KTTTM, "Báo-Cáo cong tac quy III," 19 October 1957, 52/PTTg/NAVC 3.
49. Nguyễn Thuân, "Báo cáo tổng kết công tác tuyên truyền chống âm mưu xưng vua"; Lee, *Dreams of the Hmong Kingdom,* 40–42.
50. "Tổng kết thuế nông nghiệp vùng mới giải phóng Tây Bắc," 1953, 5810/KTTTB/NAVC 3.
51. Giám đốc Sở Công an Khu gửi Ông Bộ trưởng bộ Công an, 29 July 1957, and Trần Quyết, "Tình hình xưng đón vua ở xã Kiến Thiết Chiềng Tương thuộc Mộc Châu," 15 November 1957, 2414/KTTTB/NAVC 3.
52. Vương Duy Quang, "Hiện tượng 'Xưng vua' ở Người Hmông"; Cao Văn Lượng, *Lịch sử Việt Nam,* 67; Halpern, *Economy and Society of Laos,* 121–22; Smalley, Chia Koua Vang, and Gnia Yee Yang, *Mother of Writing;* Ngô, *The New Way;* Tapp, Michaud, Culas, and Lee *Hmong/Miao in Asia;* Jonsson, "War's Ontogeny"; McCoy, "America's Secret War in Laos"; Ngô, "Protestant Conversion and Social Conflict."
53. Chef de Bataillon Lacordaire, "Rapport d'inspection du 11 au 22 Oct 1924 4eme TM circonscription de Lai Châu," 30 October 1924, 1397/RST/ANOM; "Dien Bien Phu," 1933(?), 1178/10H/SHD; Đinh Sơn, "Báo-Cáo cong tac cai thien doi song vat chat"; Lò Vặn Hạc, "Báo-Cáo tinh hinh chung trong thang 7/1958," 2 August 1958, 134/KTTTB/NAVC 3.
54. Phòng TAHC, "Báo cáo tình hình 6 tháng năm 1955."
55. Sở Công an KTTTM, "Báo cáo về tình hình 'Vua Xá và Vua Mèo' trong Khu," 16 February 1957, 2414/KTTTB/NAVC 3.
56. Scott, *The Art of Not Being Governed;* Lee, *Dreams of the Hmong Kingdom,* 49.
57. Sở Công an KTTTM, "Báo cáo về tình hình 'Vua Xá và Vua Mèo'"; Goscha, *Going Indochinese,* 28.

58. “Báo cáo cong tac cai thien doi song vat chat va tinh than cho nhan dan cac D.T.”; Nguyễn Thuân, “Báo cáo tổng kết công tác tuyên truyền chống âm mưu xưng vua”; Sở Công an KTTTM, “Báo cáo về tình hình ‘Vua Xá và Vua Mèo.’”
59. Nguyên Trac, “Số 2103 VHH/CT nhắc để phòng âm mưu xưng vua,” 31 May 1957, 2414/KTTTB/NAVC 3; Nguyen Dui Trinh, “Chỉ thị số 36 CT/TW v/v giải quyết vấn đề ‘xưng vua đón vua’ và các vấn đề tương tư ở miền núi,” 10 July 1957, 2413/KTTTB/NAVC 3; “Báo cáo bổ sung tình hình và công tác trị an,” 1957, 2389/KTTTB/NAVC 3; Trần Quyết, “Tình hình xưng đón vua ở xã Kiên Thiêt Chiềng Tương thuộc Mọc Châu,” 15 November 1957, 2414/KTTTB/NAVC 3. Unless otherwise noted, discussion of Mười’s service on the People’s Tribunal draws on Lò Văn Mười (Chánh an TAND phúc thẩm KTTTM) and Lê Văn Lợi (Công tố ủy viên), “Đường lợi truy tố xét xử bọn phản động—phá hoại,” 13 March 1958, 2440/KTTTB/NAVC 3.
60. Davis, “Black Flag Rumors”; Ha Viet Quan, “Brokering Power in Vietnam’s Northwest.”
61. “Trích nghị quyết hội nghị Trung ương lần thứ 14,” November 1958, in Đảng Lao động Việt Nam, *Văn kiện của Đảng về Chính sách dân tộc,* 85; McElwee, *Forests Are Gold,* 82–83.
62. Harms, “The Critical Difference”; UBHC KTTTM, “Báo-Cáo tinh hinh cong tac cuu te xa hoi 3 thang quy 3 nam 1958,” 30 October 1958, 56/CTXH/NAVC 3; Yeh, *Taming Tibet,* 163; Gupta, *Postcolonial Developments;* Đinh Sơn, “Chỉ thị số 278 v/v tổng kết công tác phòng chống và cứu đói 1958 chuẩn bị kế hoạch phòng chống cứu đói năm 1959,” 16 October 1958, and Lò Văn Hặc, “Chỉ thị số 32 v/v tập trung cán bộ làm công tác cứu đói,” 21 January 1958, 353/CTXH/NAVC 3.
63. Ban Chấp hành Khu Tây Bắc, “Nghị quyết số 2/NG/TB ‘Công tác vùng cao của Khu năm 1957,’” 24 March 1957, and Trần Quốc Mạnh, “Báo cáo ‘Kết quả thi hành Nghị Quyết vùng cao,’” 22 November 1957, 2777/KTTTB/NAVC 3; Cao Văn Lượng, *Lịch sử Việt Nam,* 122; Lentz, “Cultivating Subjects,” 910–13; Jonsson, “War’s Ontogeny,” 132; Ma, *The Lahu Minority,* 30–32; Litzinger, *Other Chinas,* 87; Collins, “Situation in Laos,” in Cavell, Stevenson, and Spooner, *Documents relatifs aux relations extérieures du Canada,* 857–58.
64. Sở Văn Hoá, “Tong ket cong tac van hoa trong ba nam 1956–58 o Khu tu tri Thai Meo,” 29 November 195[8?], 46/BVH/NAVC 3. On local scripts, see Mukdawijitra, “Ethnicity and Multilingualism,” ch. 6; Nguyen Manh Chat, “Ke hoach cong tac o Khu tu tri Thai Meo,” 4 September 1957, 898/BVH/NAVC 3; Lê-Liêm, “Đe cương cong tac van hoa phuc vu ke hoach phat trien san xuat nong nghiep dai han o mien nui,” 14 July 1958, 927/BVH/NAVC 3.
65. Unless noted otherwise, the following discussion draws on “Bai noi chuyen cua Pho Thu tuong Vo Nguyen Giap truoc can bo trung cap va nghien cuu Tay Bac,” 1 June 1958, 144/KTTTB/NAVC 3.
66. Hồ Chí Minh, “Đồng báo Khu tự trị Thái-Mèo cần ra sức thi đua sản xuất và tiết kiệm để tiến dân lên chủ nghĩa xã hội,” *Nhân dân,* 9 May 1959. Unless

noted otherwise, the following discussion draws on "Tom tat bai noi chuyen cua đ/c Vo-Nguyen-Giap ngay 8/5/59," 8 May 1959, 182/KTTTB/NAVC 3.

67. Hardy, *Red Hills*, chs. 8–9; McElwee, *Forests Are Gold*, ch. 2; De Koninck and Déry, "Agricultural Expansion as a Tool of Population Redistribution."
68. Nguyễn Duy Trinh, "Chỉ thị số 128-CT/TƯ v/v đẩy mạnh hơn nữa việc thi hành chủ trương tăng cường công tác vùng cao," 24 February 1959, in Đảng Lao động Việt Nam, *Văn kiện Đảng về Chính sách dân tộc*, 86–97.
69. Lentz, "Mobilization and State Formation," 574–81.
70. Pelley, *Postcolonial Vietnam*, 102; MacLean, *The Government of Mistrust*, 83; Nguyen, *Hanoi's War*, 45; Asselin, *Hanoi's Road to the Vietnam War*, 45; Goscha, *Vietnam: A New History*, 307.

EPILOGUE

1. Nhà xuất bản Thuận Hoá, "Thay lợi giới thiệu," 7–8.
2. "Thư của Ban chấp hành Trung ương Đảng Lao động Việt Nam," 9 May 1954, in Đảng Cộng sản Việt Nam, *Văn kiện Đảng*, 94–95; Amin, *Event, Metaphor, Memory*, 3.
3. "Chỉ thị của Ban Bí thư về việc tổ chức cuộc tuyên truyền động viên mở rộng thắng lợi của Chiến dịch Điện Biên Phủ," 11 May 1954, in Đảng Cộng sản Việt Nam, *Văn kiện Đảng*, 99–105.
4. Le Trung Dinh, "Bao Cao kiem diem cong tac xay dung khu Tay Bac tu khi thanh lap den nay (7-1952 đen 7-1954)," 16 October 1954, 520/PTTg (1945–54)/NAVC 3.
5. Nguyen huy Thanh, "Bao Cao (So ket dot 1 cong tac thue nong nghiep vu dong 54 o hai tinh Son la va Lai chau)," 13 November 1954, 2621/PTTg (1945–54)/NAVC 3.
6. Hoi dong Cung cap Mat tran, "Bao Cao Cong tac phuc vu chien dich Dien Bien Phu," 10 July 1954, 1692/PTTg (1945–54)/NAVC 3; Ban Chấp hành khu Tây bắc, "Báo cáo tổng quát công tác phục vụ chiến dịch Điện Biên Phủ," 14 June 1954, 665/BLĐ/NAVC 3; "Tập báo cáo thành tích 8 năm kháng chiến 1946–1954 của các tỉnh thuộc khu Tây Bắc," 1955, 577/PTTg (1945–54)/NAVC 3.
7. "Agreement on the Cessation of Hostilities in Viet-Nam," 20 July 1954, *Geneva Agreements*, accessed 28 October 2017, http://peacemaker.un.org/node/1477; Pelley, *Postcolonial Vietnam*, 4–5; Thayer, *War by Other Means*, 1–7.
8. *Hà Nội—Điện Biên Phủ;* Viện Lịch sử Quân sự Việt Nam, *Lịch sử cuộc kháng chiến*, preface and ch. 26 ("Some Lessons of the Anti-French Resistance War as the Foundation for Developing the Path and Means of the Anti-American Resistance War"); Võ Nguyên Giáp, *Điện Biên Phủ*, 314–19, appendix ("Appraising the Meaning of the Điện Biên Phủ Campaign [*a guide for reporters*]"); Chu Ngọc Sơn, Đỗ Thuận Lan, Nguyễn Tuấn Anh, *Ấn tượng Điện Biên*. For more on this 2014 conference, see Viện Hàn lâm Khoa học xã hội Việt Nam, *Hội thảo khoa học quốc tế*.
9. I am grateful to Ben Kiernan for this insight. For more on this moment, see Kiernan, *Việt Nam*, 443.

10. Lo Van Hac, "Chi thi Ve viec to chuc ky niem ngay 7-5 Chien thang Dien bien Phu va thanh lap [Khu] tu tri," 22 April 1964, 384/KTTTB/NAVC 3; Trần Quốc Mạnh, "Báo cáo của Thường vụ Tỉnh ủy về vụ đói ở đồng bằng Điện Biên," 22 October 1964, 9816/KTTTB/NAVC 3.

BIBLIOGRAPHY

ARCHIVAL SOURCES

Vietnam

Bảo tàng Lịch sử Quốc gia (Vietnam National Museum of History), Hanoi

Khu di tích Chủ tịch Hồ Chí Minh tại Phủ Chủ tịch (President Hồ Chí Minh Heritage Site at the Presidential Palace), Hanoi

Thư viện Quốc gia (National Library of Vietnam), Hanoi

Thư viện tỉnh Điện Biên (Điện Biên Province Library), Điện Biên Phủ

Trung tâm Lưu trữ Quốc gia Việt Nam I (National Archives of Vietnam Center 1), Hanoi

Gouvernement Général de l'Indochine

Résidence Supérieure au Tonkin

Service Géographique de l'Indochine

Trung tâm Lưu trữ Quốc gia Việt Nam III (National Archives of Vietnam Center 3), Hanoi

Bộ Cứu tế Xã hội (Ministry of Social Welfare)

Bộ Lao động (Ministry of Labor)

Bộ Ngoại Giao (Ministry of Foreign Affairs)

Bộ Nông lâm (Ministry of Agriculture and Forestry)

Bộ Văn hoá (Ministry of Culture)

Phủ Thủ tướng (Prime Minister's Secretariat)

Phủ Thủ tướng (1945–54) (Prime Minister's Secretariat [1945–54])

Ủy ban Hành chính Khu tự trị Việt Bắc (Việt-Bắc Autonomous Zone Administrative Committee)

Ủy ban Hành chính liên tỉnh Sơn La-Lai Châu (Sơn La–Lai Châu Interprovince Administrative Committee)

Ủy ban Kháng chiến Hành chính Khu tự trị Tây Bắc (Northwest Autonomous Zone Resistance and Administrative Committee)

Ủy ban Thống nhất của Chính phủ (Government Reunification Committee)

France

Archives Nationales d'Outre Mer (National Overseas Territories Archives), Aix en Provence

Cartes et Plans

Gouvernment Géneral de l'Indochine

Haut Commissariat de France pour l'Indochine

Résidence Supérieure au Tonkin

Établissement et Centre d'Archives Production Audiovisuelle de la Défense (Defense Communication and Audiovisual Establishment), Fort d'Ivry, Paris

Dien Bien Phu

Lai Chau

Lao divers

Tonkin (batailles, vie quotidienne)

Service Historique de la Défense (Defense Historical Service), Château de Vincennes, Paris

Archives de l'Indochine (10H)

ORAL HISTORIES

City of Hanoi and provinces of Điện Biên, Sơn La, Lào Cai, and Lai Châu (2006, 2007, 2012, 2014); Madison, WI (2013)

NEWSPAPERS

Le Monde

New York Times

Nhân dân

Quân đội nhân dân

Tuổi trẻ

Việt Nam News

PUBLISHED SOURCES

Abrams, Philip. "Notes on the Difficulty of Studying the State (1977)." *Journal of Historical Sociology* 1, no. 1 (1988): 58–89.

Adas, Michael. "From Footdragging to Flight: The Evasive History of Peasant Avoidance Protest in South and South-east Asia." *Journal of Peasant Studies* 13, no. 2 (1986): 64–86.

———. *Prophets of Rebellion: Millenarian Protest Movements against the European Social Order.* Chapel Hill: University of North Carolina Press, 1979.

Agnew, John. "The Territorial Trap: The Geographical Assumptions of International Relations Theory." *Review of International Political Economy* 1, no. 1 (Spring 1994): 53–80.

Amin, Shahid. *Event, Metaphor, Memory: Chauri Chaura, 1922–1992*. Berkeley: University of California Press, 1995.

Anderson, Benedict. *Imagined Communities: Reflections on the Origins and Spread of Nationalism*. New York: Verso, 1991.

———. "Old State, New Society: Indonesia's New Order in Comparative Historical Perspective." *Journal of Asian Studies* 42, no. 3 (1983): 477–96.

———. *The Spectre of Comparisons: Nationalism, Southeast Asia and the World*. New York: Verso, 1998.

Anderson, James. *The Rebel Den of Nùng Trí Cao: Loyalty and Identity along the Sino-Vietnamese Frontier*. Seattle: University of Washington Press, 2007.

Anderson, James, and John Whitmore, eds. *China's Encounters on the South and Southwest: Reforging the Fiery Frontier over Two Millennia*. Boston: Brill, 2015.

———. "The Dong World: A Proposal for Analyzing the Highlands between the Yangzi Valley and the Southeast Asian Lowlands." *Asian Highland Perspectives* 44 (2017): 8–71.

Andreas, Peter. *Border Games: Policing the US-Mexico Divide*. Ithaca: Cornell University Press, 2000.

Arendt, Hannah. *The Human Condition*. Chicago: University of Chicago Press, 1989.

———. *On Revolution*. New York: Penguin Classics, 2006.

Asselin, Pierre. *Hanoi's Road to the Vietnam War*. Berkeley: University of California Press, 2013.

Austen, Ralph. "The Moral Economy of Witchcraft: An Essay in Comparative History." In *Modernity and Its Malcontents: Ritual and Power in Postcolonial Africa*, edited by Jean Comaroff and John Comaroff, 89–110. Chicago: University of Chicago Press, 1993.

Badenoch, Nathan, and Tomita Shinsuke. "Mountain People in the *Muang*: Creation and Governance of a Tai Polity in Northern Laos." *Southeast Asian Studies* 2, no. 1 (April 2013): 29–67.

Baird, Ian. "Millenarian Movements in Southern Laos and North Eastern Siam (Thailand) at the Turn of the Twentieth Century: Reconsidering the Involvement of the Champassak Royal House." *South East Asia Research* 21, no. 2 (June 2013): 257–79.

Baldanza, Kathlene. *Ming China and Vietnam: Negotiating Borders in Early Modern Asia*. Cambridge: Cambridge University Press, 2016.

Balibar, Etienne. "The Nation Form: History and Ideology." *Review* 13, no. 3 (1990): 329–61.

———. "What Makes a People a People? Rousseau and Kant." In *Masses, Classes, and the Public Sphere*, edited by Mike Hill and Warren Montag, 105–31. New York: Verso, 2000.

Ban Biên tập Sở Giáo dục. *Địa lý Khu tự trị Thái-Mèo*. Thuận Châu: Phòng Chính trị Khu Tây Bắc, 1956.

Ban Chấp hành Đảng bộ huyện Điện Biên. *Lịch sử Đảng bộ huyện Điện Biên*. Hanoi: NXB Chính trị quốc gia, 2005.

Ban Chấp hành Đảng bộ tỉnh Lai Châu. "Vai trò của Đảng bộ và nhân dân tỉnh Lai Châu trong cuộc tiến công chiến lược đông-xuân 1953–1954 và chiến dịch Điện Biên Phủ." In *Mấy Vấn đề về chiến thắng lịch sử Điện Biên Phủ*, edited by Viện sử học, 107–18. Hanoi: NXB Khoa học xã hội, 1985.

Bảo tàng Sơn La. *Di tích lịch sử cách mạng nhà tù Sơn La*. Sơn La: NXB Văn hóa dân tộc, 2009.

Barth, Fredrik, ed. *Ethnic Groups and Boundaries: The Social Organization of Culture Difference*. Boston: Little, Brown, 1969.

Bộ Chỉ huy quân sự tỉnh Sơn La. *Sơn La: Lịch sử kháng chiến chống thực dân Pháp (1945–1954)*. Hanoi: NXB Quân đội nhân dân, 1995.

Bonker, Dirk. *Militarism in a Global Age: Naval Ambitions in Germany and the United States*. Ithaca: Cornell University Press, 2012.

Bộ Nội vụ. *Công an nhân dân Lai Châu: Lịch sử biên niên (1945–1975)*. Hanoi: NXB Công an nhân dân, 1995.

Bourdieu, Pierre. *Outline of a Theory of Practice*. Translated by Richard Nice. Cambridge: Cambridge University Press, 1998.

Bradley, Mark. 2009. *Vietnam at War*. New York: Oxford University Press.

Brocheux, Pierre, and Daniel Hémery. *Indochina: An Ambiguous Colonization, 1858–1954*. Translated by Ly Lan Dill-Klein with Eric Jennings, Nora Taylor, and Noémi Tousignant. Berkeley: University of California Press, 2009.

Bronson, Bennett. "Exchange at the Upstream and Downstream Ends: Notes towards a Functional Model of the Coastal State in Southeast Asia." In *Economic Exchange and Social Interaction in Southeast Asia: Perspectives from Prehistory, History, and Ethnography*, edited by Karl Hutterer, 39–52. Ann Arbor: Michigan Papers on South and Southeast Asia, 1978.

Brown, MacAlister, and Joseph Zasloff. *Apprentice Revolutionaries: The Communist Movement in Laos, 1930–1985*. Stanford: Hoover Institution Press, 1986.

Bryan, Joe. "Rethinking Territory: Social Justice and Neoliberalism in Latin America's Territorial Turn." *Geography Compass* 6, no. 4 (2012): 215–26.

Burguière, André, and Raymond Grew, eds. *The Construction of Minorities: Cases for Comparison across Time and around the World*. Ann Arbor: University of Michigan Press, 2001.

Cầm Trọng. *Người Thái ở Tây Bắc Việt Nam*. Hanoi: NXB Khoa học xã hội, 1978.

Cầm Trọng and Hữu Ứng. "Chế độ ruộng công và hình thái xã hội của người Thái Tây-Bắc trước đây." *Nghiên cứu lịch sử* 151 (July–August 1973): 50–57.

Cao Văn Lượng. "Đường lối giương cao ngọn cờ độc lập dân tộc và chủ nghĩa xã hội với chiến thắng Điện Biên Phủ." In *Mấy vấn đề về chiến thắng lịch sử Điện Biên Phủ*, edited by Viện sử học, 31–48. Hanoi: NXB Khoa học xã hội, 1985.

———, ed. *Lịch sử Việt Nam, 1954–1965*. Hanoi: NXB Khoa học xã hội, 1996.

Cao Văn Lượng, Nguyễn Văn Nhật, and Võ Kim Cương. *Lịch sử kháng chiến chống thực dân Pháp của quân và dân khu Tây Bắc (1945–1954)*. Hanoi: NXB Khoa học xã hội, 2003.

Cavell, Janice, Michael Stevenson, and Kevin Spooner, eds. *Documents relatifs aux relations extérieures du Canada: Documents on Canadian External Relations.*

Vol. 26. Ottawa: Department of Foreign Affairs and International Trade, 2006.

Chabant, Edmond. "Notes sur l'histoire des haut-pays du Nord-Ouest Vietnam." Lai Châu: Typescript, 1951.

Chen, King C. *Vietnam and China, 1938–1954*. Princeton: Princeton University Press, 1969.

Chu Ngọc Sơn, Đỗ Thuận Lan, and Nguyễn Tuấn Anh, eds. *Ấn tượng Điện Biên: Dien Bien Impression*. Hanoi: NXB Văn hoá thông tin, 2004.

Condominas, Georges. "Aspects of a Minority Problem in Indochina." *Pacific Affairs* 24, no. 1 (1951): 77–82.

———. "Essai sur l'évolution des systèmes politiques thaïs." *Ethnos* 41, nos. 1–4 (1976): 7–67.

———. *From Lawa to Mon, from Saa' to Thai: Historical and Anthropological Aspects of Southeast Asian Social Spaces*. Edited by Gehan Wijeyewardene with the assistance of Judith Wilson and Paula Harris. Translated by Stephanie Anderson, Maria Margannon, and Gehan Wijeyewarndene. Canberra: Department of Anthropology, Research School of Pacific Studies, the Australian National University, 1990.

Công an tỉnh Lai Châu. *Lịch sử Công an nhân dân huyện Điện Biên (1952–1975)*. Hanoi: NXB Công an nhân dân, 1994.

Conklin, Harold. *Hanunóo Agriculture: A Report on an Integral System of Shifting Cultivation in the Philippines*. Rome: FAO, 1957.

Connor, Walker. *The National Question in Marxist-Leninist Theory and Strategy*. Princeton: Princeton University Press, 1984.

Cons, Jason. *Sensitive Space: Fragmented Territory at the India-Bangladesh Border*. Seattle: University of Washington Press, 2016.

Cons, Jason, and Michael Eilenberg, eds. *Frontier Assemblages: The Emergent Politics of Resource Frontiers in Asia*. Antipode Book Series. Malden, MA: Wiley, forthcoming.

Corrigan, Philip, and Derek Sayer. *The Great Arch: English State Formation as Cultural Revolution*. Oxford: Basil Blackwell, 1985.

Cowen, Deborah. *The Deadly Life of Logistics: Mapping Violence in Global Trade*. Minneapolis: University of Minnesota, 2014

Culas, Christian. *Le messianisme hmong aux XIXe et XXe siècles: La dynamique religieuse comme instrument politique*. Paris: CNRS, 2005.

Đặng Chấn Liêu, Lê Khả Kế, and Phạm Duy Trọng. *Từ điện Việt-Anh*. TP HCM: NXB Thành phố Hồ Chí Minh, 2001.

Đảng Cộng sản Việt Nam. *Ba mươi năm phấn đầu và xây dựng của Đảng bộ Lai Châu, 1949-1979*. Lai Châu: Ban nghiên cứu lịch sử Đảng Lai-Châu, 1980.

———. *Văn kiện Đảng toàn tập*. Multiple vols. Hanoi: NXB Chính trị quốc gia, 2001.

Đảng Lao động Việt Nam. *Văn kiện của Đảng về Chính sách dân tộc (Lưu hành nội bộ)*. Hanoi: NXB Sự thật, 1965.

Đặng Nghiêm Vạn and Đinh Xuân Lâm. *Điện Biên trong lịch sử*. Hanoi: NXB Khoa học xã hội, 1979.

———. "Truyền thống chống xâm lăng của Điện Biên trong lịch sử." *Nghiên cứu lịch sử* 102 (September 1967): 47–53, 60.

Dang Phong, and Melanie Beresford. *Authority Relations and Economic Decision-Making in Vietnam: An Historical Perspective.* Copenhagen: NIAS, 1998.

Đảng ủy Quân sự Trung ương. *Một số văn kiện chỉ đạo chiến cuộc đông xuân 1953–1954 và chiến dịch Điện Biên Phủ.* Hanoi: NXB Quân đội nhân dân, 2004.

Dao, Nga. "Damming Rivers in Vietnam: A Lesson Learned in the Tây Bắc Region." *Journal of Vietnamese Studies* 6, no. 2 (Summer 2011): 106–40.

Das, Veena, and Deborah Poole, eds. *Anthropology in the Margins of the State.* Santa Fe: School of American Research Press, 2004.

Davis, Bradley. "Black Flag Rumors and the Black River Basin: Powerbrokers and the State in the Tonkin-China Borderlands." *Journal of Vietnamese Studies* 6, no. 2 (Summer 2011): 16–41.

———. *Imperial Bandits: Outlaws and Rebels in the China-Vietnam Borderlands.* Seattle: University of Washington, 2017.

———. "States of Banditry: The Nguyen Government, Bandit Rule, and the Culture of Power in the Post-Taiping China-Vietnam Borderlands." PhD diss., University of Washington, 2008.

Day, Tony. *Fluid Iron: State Formation in Southeast Asia.* Honolulu: University of Hawaii Press, 2002.

De Koninck, Rodolphe, and Steve Déry. "Agricultural Expansion as a Tool of Population Redistribution in Southeast Asia." *Journal of Southeast Asian Studies* 28, no. 1 (1997): 1–26.

Devereux, Stephen. "Why Does Famine Persist in Africa?" *Food Security* 1 (February 2009): 25–35.

Di Cosmo, Nicola, and Don Wyatt, eds. *Political Frontiers, Ethnic Boundaries, and Human Geographies in Chinese History.* New York: Routledge, 2003.

Đỗ Hữu Lễ. "Quân và dân Tây Bắc với công tác bảo đảm hậu cần cho chiến dịch Điện Biên Phủ." In *Công tác bảo đảm hậu cần trong chiến dịch Điện Biên Phủ: Bài học, kinh nghiệm, và thực tiễn,* edited by Tổng cục Hậu cần, 226–45. Hanoi: NXB Quân đội nhân dân, 2004.

Đỗ Văn Ninh. *Từ điển chức quan Việt Nam.* Hanoi: NXB Thanh niên, 2006.

Dove, Michael. "The Epistemology of Southeast Asia's Anthropogenic Grasslands: Issues of Myth, Science, and Development." *Southeast Asian Studies* 35, no. 2 (September 1997): 223–39.

———. "Writing for, versus about, the Ethographic Other: Issues of Engagement and Reflexivity in Working with a Tribal NGO in Indonesia." *Identities* 6, nos. 2–3 (1999): 225–53.

Duara, Prasenjit. *Rescuing History from the Nation.* Chicago: University of Chicago Press, 1995.

Duiker, William. *The Communist Road to Power in Vietnam.* Boulder, CO: Westview, 1996.

———. "Ho Chi Minh and the Strategy of People's War." In *The First Vietnam War: Colonial Conflict and Cold War Crisis,* edited by Mark Lawrence and Fredrik Logevall, 152–74. Cambridge, MA: Harvard University Press, 2007.

Duncan, Christopher, ed. *Civilizing the Margins: Southeast Asian Government Policies for the Development of Minorities.* Ithaca: Cornell University Press, 2004.

Dutton, George. *The Tây Sơn Uprising: Society and Rebellion in Eighteenth Century Vietnam.* Honolulu: University of Hawaii Press, 2006.

Eilenberg, Michael. *At the Edges of States: Dynamics of State Formation in the Indonesian Borderlands.* Leiden: KITLV, 2012.

Elden, Stuart. *The Birth of Territory.* Chicago: University of Chicago Press, 2013.

———. "How Should We Do the History of Territory?" *Territory, Politics, Governance* 1, no. 1 (2013): 5–20.

———. "Land, Terrain, Territory." *Progress in Human Geography* 34, no. 6 (2010): 799–817.

———. *Terror and Territory: The Spatial Extent of Sovereignty.* Minneapolis: University of Minnesota Press, 2009.

Enfield, N. J. "Areal Linguistics and Mainland Southeast Asia." *Annual Review of Anthropology* 34 (2005): 181–206.

Evans, Grant. "Introduction: What Is Lao Culture and Society?" In *Laos: Culture and Society,* edited by Grant Evans, 1–34. Singapore: Institute of Southeast Asian Studies, 2000.

———. "Laos: Minorities." In *Ethnicity in Asia,* edited by Colin MacKerras, 210–24. New York: Routledge-Curzon, 2003.

———. "Tai-ization: Ethnic Change in Northern Indochina." In *Civility and Savagery: Social Identity in Tai States,* edited by Andrew Turton, 263–89. Richmond, UK: Curzon, 2000.

———. "Vietnamese Communist Anthropology." *Canberra Anthropology* 8, nos. 1–2 (1985): 116–47.

Évrard, Olivier. "Oral Histories and Migration under Socialism and Post-Socialism among the Khmu of Northern Laos." In *Moving Mountains: Ethnicity and Livelihoods in Highland China, Vietnam, and Laos,* edited by Jean Michaud and Tim Forsyth, 76–99. Vancouver: University of British Columbia Press, 2011.

Fall, Bernard B. *Hell in a Very Small Place: The Siege of Dien Bien Phu.* Philadelphia: Lippincott, 1967.

———. "Local Administration under the Viet Minh." *Pacific Affairs* 27, no. 1 (1954): 50–57.

———. *The Viet Minh Regime: Government and Administration in the Democratic Republic of Vietnam.* Ithaca: Southeast Asia Program, Department of Far Eastern Studies; issued jointly with the Institute of Pacific Relations, 1954.

Fanon, Frantz. *The Wretched of the Earth.* Translated by Constance Farrington. New York: Grove, 1963.

Farish, Matthew. *The Contours of America's Cold War.* Minneapolis: University of Minnesota Press, 2010.

Febvre, Lucien. *A New Kind of History: From the Writings of Febvre.* Edited by Peter Burke. Translated by K. Folca. London: Routledge and Kegan Paul, 1973.

Feldman, Shelley. "Social Regulation in a Time of War." *Globalizations* 4, no. 4 (2007): 445–59.

Ferguson, James. *The Anti-politics Machine: Development, Depoliticization, and Political Power in Lesotho*. Minneapolis: University of Minnesota Press, 1994.

Forbes, Andrew D. "The 'Cin-Ho' (Yunnanese Chinese) Caravan Trade with North Thailand during the Late Nineteenth and Early Twentieth Centuries." *Journal of Asian History* 21, no. 1 (1987): 1–47.

Foucault, Michel. *Society Must Be Defended*. Translated by David Macey. New York: Picador, 2003.

———. *Space, Knowledge, and Power: Foucault and Geography*. Edited by Jeremy Campton and Stuart Elden. Burlington: Ashgate, 2007.

Fourniau, Charles. "La frontière Sino-Vietnamienne et le face à face Franco-Chinois à l'epoque de la conquête du Tonkin." In *Les frontières du Vietnam: Histoire des frontières de la péninsule indochinoise*, edited by P. B. Lafont, 85–103. Paris: Éditions l'Harmattan, 1989.

Fuentes, Marisa. *Dispossessed Lives: Enslaved Women, Violence, and the Archives*. Philadelphia: University of Pennsylvania Press, 2016.

Furuta, Motoo. "The Indochina Communist Party's Division into Three Parties: Vietnamese Communist Policy towards Cambodia and Laos, 1948–1951." In *Indochina in the 1940s and 1950s*, edited by Takashi Shiraishi and Motoo Furuta, 143–63. Ithaca: Southeast Asia Program, Cornell University, 1992.

Geyer, Michael. "The Militarization of Europe, 1914–1945." In *The Militarization of the Western World*, edited by John R. Gillis, 65–102. New Brunswick: Rutgers University Press, 1989.

Giersch, Patterson. *Asian Borderlands: The Transformation of Qing China's Yunnan Frontier*. Cambridge, MA: Harvard University Press, 2006.

Ginsburgs, George. "Local Government and Administration in North Vietnam, 1945–1954." *China Quarterly* 10 (April–June 1962): 174–204.

Gladney, Dru, ed. *Making Majorities: Constituting the Nation in Japan, Korea, Malaysia, Fiji, Turkey, and the United States*. Stanford: Stanford University Press, 1998.

Goscha, Christopher. *Un état né de la guerre, 1945–1954*. Paris: Armand Colin, 2011.

———. *Going Indochinese: Contesting Concepts of Space and Place in French Indochina*. Copenhagen: NIAS, 2012.

———. *Thailand and the Southeast Asian Networks of the Vietnamese Revolution (1885–1954)*. Richmond, UK: Curzon, 1999.

———. *Vietnam: A New History*. New York: Basic Books, 2016.

———. *Vietnam or Indochina? Contesting Concepts of Space in Vietnamese Nationalism (1887–1954)*. Copenhagen: Nordic Institute of Asian Studies, 1995.

Goscha, Christopher E., and Benoît de Tréglodé, eds. *Naissance d'état-parti: Le Viêt Nam depuis 1945 / The Birth of a Party-State: Vietnam since 1945*. Paris: Les Indes Savantes, 2004.

Goscha, Christopher, and Christian Ostermann. *Connecting Histories: Decolonization and the Cold War in Southeast Asia, 1945–1962*. Stanford: Stanford University Press, 2009.

Gourou, Pierre. *Indochine française: Le Tonkin*. Paris: Mâcon, 1931.

———. "Land Utilization in Upland Areas of Indochina." In *The Development of Upland Areas in the Far East*. New York: Institute of Pacific Relations, 1951.

———. *Les paysans du delta tonkinois: Étude de géographie humaine*. Paris: Les Éditions d'Art et d'Histoire, 1936.

———. *L'utilisation du sol en Indochine française*. Paris: Hartmann, 1940.

Guha, Ranajit. "The Prose of Counterinsurgency." In *Culture/Power/History*, edited by Nicholas Dirks, Geoff Eley, and Sherry Ortner, 336–71. Princeton: Princeton University Press, 1999.

Gunn, Geoffrey. *Rice Wars in Colonial Vietnam: The Great Famine and the Viet Minh Road to Power*. Lanham, MD: Rowman and Littlefield, 2014.

———. "Shamans and Rebels: The Batchai (Meo) Rebellion of Northern Laos and North-west Vietnam (1918–21)." *Journal of the Siam Society* 74 (1986): 107–21.

Gupta, Akhil. "Blurred Boundaries: The Discourse of Corruption, the Culture of Politics, and the Imagined State." *American Ethnologist* 22, no. 2 (1995): 375–402.

———. *Postcolonial Developments: Agriculture in the Making of Modern India*. Durham: Duke University Press, 1998.

Haberkorn, Tyrell. *Revolution Interrupted: Farmers, Students, Law, and Violence in Northern Thailand*. Madison: University of Wisconsin Press, 2011.

Hahn, Steven. *A Nation under Our Feet: Black Political Struggles in the Rural South from Slavery to Emancipation*. Cambridge, MA: Harvard University Press, 2004.

Halpern, Joel. *Economy and Society of Laos: A Brief Survey*. New Haven: Southeast Asia Studies, Yale University, 1964.

Hà Nội—Điện Biên Phủ. Hanoi: Sở Văn hoá thông tin Hà Nội, 1973.

Hardy, Andrew. *Red Hills: Migrants and the State in the Highlands of Vietnam*. Honolulu: University of Hawaii Press, 2002.

Harms, Erik. "The Critical Difference: Making Peripheral Vision Central in Vietnamese Studies." *Journal of Vietnamese Studies* 6, no. 2 (Summer 2011): 1–15.

Harvey, David. *The Condition of Postmodernity: An Enquiry into the Origins of Social Change*. Cambridge: Blackwell, 1989.

Ha Viet Quan. "Brokering Power in Vietnam's Northwest: The Case of Ethnic Tai Cadres." PhD diss., Australian National University, 2016.

Hayton, Bill. *The South China Sea: The Struggle for Power in Asia*. New Haven: Yale University Press, 2014.

Hegel, Georg. *The Philosophy of History*. Translated by J. Sibree. New York: Dover, 1956.

Henley, David. "Ethnographic Integration and Exclusion in Anticolonial Nationalism: Indonesia and Indochina." *Comparative Studies in Society and History* 37, no. 2 (1995): 286–324.

Herman, John. *Amidst the Clouds and Mist: China's Colonization of Guizhou*. Cambridge, MA: Harvard University Press, 2007.

Heuser, Beatrice. *The Evolution of Strategy: Thinking War from Antiquity to Present*. New York: Cambridge University Press, 2010.

Hickey, Gerald. "Social Systems of Northern Vietnam." PhD diss., University of Chicago, 1958.

Hoàng Công Phẩm. "Chúng tôi đi chiến dịch Điện Biên Phủ." In *Điện Biên Phủ: ký ức và nhân chứng*, edited by Lê Dần, 63–78. Huế: NXB Thuận Hoá, 2004.

Hoàng Điệp and Mai Hoa. "Vua Thái ở Chiềng Mai." *Tuổi trẻ online* kỳ 1–4 (1 March, 1 April, 1 May, 1 June, 2016). Accessed 22 October 2017, http://tuoitre.vn/vua-thai-o-chieng-mai.html.

Hoàng Văn Thái. *Cuộc tiến công chiến lược Đông Xuân 1953–1954*. Hanoi: NXB Quân đội nhân dân, 1984.

Hồ Chí Minh. *Bác Hồ với đồng bào các dân tộc*. Hanoi: NXB Thông tấn, 2006.

———. *Ho Chi Minh on Revolution: Selected Writings, 1920–66*. Edited by Bernard Fall. New York: Signet, 1968.

———. *Hồ Chí Minh toàn tập*. Multiple vols. Hanoi: NXB Chính trị quốc gia, 1995.

Holcombe, Alec. "Socialist Transformation in the Democratic Republic of Vietnam." PhD diss., University of California, Berkeley, 2014.

Hữu Mai. *Điện Biên Phủ: thời gian và không gian*. Hanoi: Thanh niên, 1979.

Huỳnh Kim Khánh. *Vietnamese Communism, 1925–1945*. Ithaca: Cornell University Press, 1982.

Hy V. Luong. *Revolution in the Village: Tradition and Transformation in North Vietnam, 1925–1988*. Honolulu: University of Hawaii Press, 1992.

Izikowitz, Karl. *The Lamet: Hill Peasants in French Indochina*. Göteborg: Elanders Boktr., 1951.

———. "Neighbors in Laos." In *Ethnic Groups and Boundaries: The Social Organization of Culture Difference*, edited by Fredrik Barth, 135–48. Boston: Little, Brown, 1969.

James, C. L. R. *The Black Jacobins: Toussaint L'Ouverture and the San Domingo Revolution*. New York: Vintage, 1963.

Jerusalemy, Jean. "Monographie sur le Pays Thaï." Typescript, 1952.

Jessop, Bob. "From Micro-powers to Governmentality: Foucault's Work on Statehood, State Formation, Statecraft, and State Power." *Political Geography* 26, no. 1 (2007): 34–40.

Jones, Rhys. "State Encounters." *Environment and Planning D: Society and Space* 30 (2012): 805–21.

Jonsson, Hjorleifur. *Slow Anthropology: Negotiating Difference with the Iu Mien*. Ithaca: Southeast Asia Program Publications, Cornell University, 2014.

———. "War's Ontogeny: Militias and Ethnic Boundaries in Laos and Exile." *Southeast Asian Studies* 47, no. 2 (September 2009): 125–49.

Joseph, Gilbert, and Daniel Nugent, eds. *Everyday Forms of State Formation: Revolution and the Negotiation of Rule in Modern Mexico*. Durham: Duke University Press, 1994.

Kerkvliet, Benedict. "Agricultural Land in Vietnam: Markets Tempered by Family, Community, and Socialist Practices." *Journal of Agrarian Change* 6, no. 3 (July 2006): 285–305.

———. *The Power of Everyday Politics: How Vietnamese Peasants Transformed National Policy.* Ithaca: Cornell University Press, 2005.

Keyes, Charles. "Presidential Address: 'The Peoples of Asia'—Science and Politics in the Classification of Ethnic Groups in Thailand, China, and Vietnam." *Journal of Asian Studies* 61, no. 4 (November 2002): 1163–1203.

Kiernan, Ben. *How Pol Pot Came to Power: Colonialism, Nationalism, and Communism in Cambodia, 1930–1975.* New Haven: Yale University Press, 2004 [1985].

———. *Việt Nam: A History from Earliest Times to the Present.* New York: Oxford University Press, 2017.

Kirsch, Scott, and Colin Flint, eds. *Reconstructing Conflict: Integrating War and Post-war Geographies.* Burlington: Ashgate, 2011.

Kirsch, Thomas. *Feasting and Social Oscillation: Religion and Society in Upland Southeast Asia.* Ithaca: Southeast Asia Program, Department of Asian Studies, Cornell University, 1973.

Kleinen, John. "Tropicality and Topicality: Pierre Gourou and the Genealogy of French Colonial Scholarship on Rural Vietnam." *Singapore Journal of Tropical Geography* 26, no. 3 (2005): 339–58.

Kligman, Gail, and Katherine Verdery. *Peasants under Siege: The Collectivization of Romanian Agriculture.* Princeton: Princeton University Press, 2009.

Kratoska, Paul, Remco Raben, and Henk Nordholt, eds. *Locating Southeast Asia: Geographies of Knowledge and Politics of Space.* Singapore: National University of Singapore Press, 2005.

Krishna, Sankaran. "Cartographic Anxiety: Mapping the Body Politic in India." *Alternatives* 19 (1994): 507–21.

Kwon, Heonik. *Ghosts of War in Vietnam.* New York: Cambridge University Press, 2008.

Lacoste, Yves. "An Illustration of Geographical Warfare: Bombing of the Dikes on the Red River, North Vietnam." *Antipode* 5, no. 2 (1972): 1–13.

Lafont, P. B., ed. *Les frontières du Vietnam: Histoires des frontières de la péninsule indochinoise.* Paris: Éditions L'Harmattan, 1989.

Langer, Paul, and Joseph Zasloff. *North Vietnam and the Pathet Lao: Partners in the Struggle for Laos.* Cambridge, MA: Harvard University Press, 1970.

Lawrence, Mark Atwood, and Fredrik Logevall, eds. *The First Vietnam War: Colonial Conflict and Cold War Crisis.* Cambridge, MA: Harvard University Press, 2007.

Leach, E. R. *Political Systems of Highland Burma.* Boston: Beacon, 1965.

Lê Dần, ed. *Điện Biên Phủ: ký ức và nhân chứng.* Huế: NXB Thuận Hoá, 2004.

Lee, Mai Na. *Dreams of the Hmong Kingdom: The Quest for Legitimation in French Indochina, 1850–1960.* Madison: University of Wisconsin Press, 2015.

Le Failler, Philippe. "The Đèo Family of Lai Châu: Traditional Power and Unconventional Practices." *Journal of Vietnamese Studies* 6, no. 2 (Summer 2011): 42–67.

———. *Le pilori des chimères: Monopole et prohibition de l'opium en Indochine.* Paris: l'Harmattan, 2001.

———. *La rivière Noire: L'intégration d'une marche frontière au Vietnam.* Paris: CNRS, 2014.

Lefebvre, Henri. *The Production of Space.* Translated by Donald Nicholson-Smith. Malden, MA: Blackwell, 1991.

Lentz, Christian C. "Cultivating Subjects: Opium and Rule in Post-colonial Vietnam." *Modern Asian Studies* 51, no. 4 (2017): 879–918.

———. "Encountering Everyday Perspectives on the American War." *Geopolitics* 20, no. 4 (2015): 753–56.

———. "Frontier Making and Erasing: Histories of Infrastructure Development in Vietnam." In *Frontier Assemblages: The Emergent Politics of Resource Frontiers in Asia,* edited by Jason Cons and Michael Eilenberg. Antipode Book Series. Malden, MA: Wiley, forthcoming.

———. "The King Yields to the Village? A Micropolitics of Statemaking in Northwest Vietnam." *Political Geography* 39 (2014): 1–10.

———. "Making the Northwest Vietnamese." *Journal of Vietnamese Studies* 6, no. 2 (2011): 68–105.

———. "Mobilization and State Formation on a Frontier of Vietnam." *Journal of Peasant Studies* 38, no. 3 (July 2011): 559–86.

———. "Mobilizing a Frontier: Điện Biên Phủ and the Making of Vietnam, 1945–1955." PhD Thesis, Cornell University, 2011.

Li, Tania. *Land's End: Capitalist Relations on an Indigenous Frontier.* Durham: Duke University Press, 2014.

———. "What Is Land? Assembling a Resource for Global Investment." *Transactions of the Institute of British Geographers* 39 (2014): 589–602.

Lieberman, Victor. *Strange Parallels: Southeast Asia in Global Context, c. 800–1830.* Volume 1: *Integration on the Mainland.* New York: Cambridge University Press, 2003.

———. "A Zone of Refuge in Southeast Asia? Reconceptualizing Interior Spaces." *Journal of Global History* 5, no. 2 (July 2010): 333–46.

Lindquist, Johan. *The Anxieties of Mobility: Migration and Tourism in the Indonesian Borderlands.* Honolulu: University of Hawaii Press, 2005.

Litzinger, Ralph. *Other Chinas: The Yao and the Politics of National Belonging.* Durham: Duke University Press, 2000.

Lockhart, Greg. "In Lieu of the *Levée en masse*: Mass Mobilization in Modern Vietnam." In *The People in Arms: Military Myth and National Mobilization since the French Revolution,* edited by Daniel Moran and Arthur Waldron, 208–33. New York: Cambridge University Press, 2003.

———. *Nation in Arms: The Origins of the People's Army of Vietnam.* Boston: Allen and Unwin, 1989.

Logevall, Fredrik. *Embers of War: The Fall of an Empire and the Making of America's Vietnam.* New York: Random House, 2012.

Lund, Christian. "Rupture and Rule: State Formation through the Production of Property and Citizenship." *Development and Change* 47, no. 6 (2016): 1199–1228.

Ma, Jianziong. *The Lahu Minority in Southwest China: A Response to Ethnic Marginalization on the Frontier.* New York: Routledge, 2013.

MacLean, Ken. "Bodies in Perpetual Motion: Struggles over the Meaning, Value, and Purpose of Fuzzy Labor on the Eve of Collectivization." In *State, Society and the Market in Contemporary Vietnam,* edited by Hue-Tam Ho Tai and Mark Sidel, 33–54. New York: Routledge, 2013.

———. *The Government of Mistrust: Illegibility and Bureaucratic Power in Socialist Vietnam.* Madison: University of Wisconsin Press, 2013.

Malarney, Shaun. "'The Fatherland Remembers Your Sacrifice': Commemorating War Dead in North Vietnam." In *The Country of Memory: Remaking the Past in Late Socialist Vietnam,* edited by Hue-Tam Ho Tai, 46–76. Berkeley: University of California Press, 2001.

Mao Tse-Tung. *Selected Military Writings.* Peking: Foreign Languages Press, 1963.

———. *Selected Works of Mao Tse-Tung.* Vol. 2. London: Lawrence and Wishart, 1954.

Marr, David. *Vietnam 1945: The Quest for Power.* Berkeley: University of California Press, 1995.

———. *Vietnam: State, War, and Revolution.* Berkeley: University of California Press, 2013.

Marx, Karl. *Grundrisse.* Translated by Martin Nicolaus. New York: Penguin, 1973 [1858].

Masako, Ito. *Politics of Ethnic Classification in Vietnam.* Translated by Minako Sato. Kyoto: Kyoto University Press, 2013.

Massey, Doreen. *Space, Place, and Gender.* Minneapolis: University of Minnesota Press, 1994.

Mau, Michael. "The Training of Cadres in the Lao Dong Party of North Vietnam, 1960–1967," *Asian Survey* 9, no. 4 (1969): 281–96.

Mauss, Marcel. *The Gift: The Form and Reason for Exchange in Archaic Societies.* Translated by W. D. Halls. New York: Norton, 1990.

Mayaram, Shail. *Against History, Against State: Counterperspectives from the Margins.* New York: Columbia University Press, 2003.

McAlister, John T. "Mountain Minorities and the Viet Minh: A Key to the Indochina War." In *Southeast Asian Tribes, Minorities, Nations,* edited by Peter Kunstadter, 771–844. Princeton: Princeton University Press, 1967.

McCoy, Alfred. "America's Secret War in Laos, 1955–75." In *A Companion to the Vietnam War,* edited by Marilyn Young and Robert Buzzanco, 283–313. Malden, MA: Blackwell, 2002.

———. *The Politics of Heroin: CIA Complicity in the Global Drug Trade.* New York: Lawrence Hill Books, 1991.

McElwee, Pamela. *Forests Are Gold: Trees, People, and Environmental Rule in Vietnam.* Seattle: University of Washington Press, 2016.

McEnaney, Laura. *Civil Defense Begins at Home: Militarization Meets Everyday Life in the Fifties.* Princeton: Princeton University Press, 2000.

McHale, Shawn. "Freedom, Violence, and the Struggle over the Public Arena in the Democratic Republic of Vietnam." In *Naissance d'état-parti: Le Viêt Nam depuis 1945 / The Birth of a Party-State: Vietnam since 1945*, edited by Christopher Goscha and Benoît de Tréglodé, 81–99. Paris: Les Indes Savantes, 2004.

McLeod, Mark. "Indigenous Peoples and the Vietnamese Revolution, 1930–1975." *Journal of World History* 10, no. 2 (Fall 1999): 353–89.

McMichael, Philip, ed. *Contesting Development: Critical Struggles for Social Change.* New York: Routledge, 2010.

Mellac, Marie. "Land Reform and Changing Identities in Two Tai-Speaking Districts in Northern Vietnam." In *Moving Mountains: Ethnicity and Livelihoods in Highland China, Vietnam, and Laos*, edited by Jean Michaud and Tim Forsyth, 146–72. Vancouver: University of British Columbia Press, 2011.

Michaud, Jean. "Handling Mountain Minorities in China, Vietnam, and Laos: From History to Current Concerns." *Asian Ethnicity* 10, no. 1 (2009): 25–49.

———. *Historical Dictionary of the Peoples of the Southeast Asian Massif.* Lanham, MD: Scarecrow, 2006.

———. "The Montagnards and the State in Northern Vietnam from 1802 to 1975: A Historical Overview." *Ethnohistory* 47, no. 2 (2000): 333–68.

Michaud, Jean, and Tim Forsyth, eds. *Moving Mountains: Ethnicity and Livelihoods in Highland China, Vietnam, and Laos.* Vancouver: University of British Columbia Press, 2011.

Middleton, Townsend. *The Demands of Recognition: State Anthropology and Ethnopolitics in Darjeeling.* Stanford: Stanford University Press, 2016.

Migdal, Joel, ed. *Boundaries and Belonging: States and Societies in the Struggle to Shape Identities and Local Practices.* Cambridge: Cambridge University Press, 2004.

———. *State in Society: Studying How States and Societies Transform and Constitute One Another.* Cambridge: Cambridge University Press, 1999.

Mills, C. Wright. *The Power Elite.* New York: Oxford University Press, 1956.

Mitchell, Timothy. *Rule of Experts: Egypt, Techno-Politics, Modernity.* Berkeley: University of California Press, 2002.

———. "Society, Economy, and the State Effect." In *State/Culture: State Formation After the Cultural Turn*, edited by George Steinmetz, 76–97. Ithaca: Cornell University Press, 1999.

Moise, Edwin. *Land Reform in China and North Vietnam: Consolidating the Revolution at the Village Level.* Chapel Hill: University of North Carolina Press, 1983.

Moore, Donald S. *Suffering for Territory: Race, Place, and Power in Zimbabwe.* Durham: Duke University Press, 2005.

Muelle, Raymond. *Combats en Pays Thaï de Lai Chau à Diên Biên Phu, 1953–1954.* Paris: Presses de la Cité, 1999.

Mukdawijitra, Yukti. "Contesting Imagined Communities: Politics of Script and Tai Cosmopolitanism in Upland Vietnam." *Cultural Dynamics* 24, nos. 2–3 (2012): 207–25.

———. "Ethnicity and Multilingualism: The Case of the Ethnic Tai in the Vietnamese State." PhD diss., University of Wisconsin, 2007.

Mullaney, Thomas. *Coming to Terms with the Nation: Ethnic Classification in Modern China.* Berkeley: University of California Press, 2011.

Nancy, Jean-Luc. *The Inoperative Community.* Edited by Peter Connor. Translated by Peter Connor, Lisa Garbus, Michael Holland, and Simona Sawhney. Minneapolis: University of Minnesota Press, 1991.

Ngô, Tâm T. T. *The New Way: Protestantism and the Hmong in Vietnam.* Seattle: University of Washington Press, 2016.

———. "Protestant Conversion and Social Conflict: The Case of the Hmong in Contemporary Vietnam." *Journal of Southeast Asian Studies* 46, no. 2 (June 2015): 274–92.

Ngô Thiếu Hiệu, ed. *Sách chỉ dẫn các phông lưu trữ thời kỳ thuộc địa / Guide des fonds d'archives d'époque coloniale.* Hanoi: NXB Thông tin, 2001.

Ngô Vĩnh Long. *Before the Revolution: The Vietnamese Peasants under the French.* New York: Columbia University Press, 1991.

Nguyen, Lien-Hang. *Hanoi's War: An International History of the War for Peace in Vietnam.* Chapel Hill: University of North Carolina Press, 2012.

Nguyễn An. "Công tác vận tải trong chiến dịch Điện Biên Phủ." In *Mấy vấn đề về chiến thắng lịch sử Điện Biên Phủ,* edited by Viện sử học, 173–83. Hanoi: NXB Khoa học xã hội, 1985.

Nguyễn Bá Dương, ed. *Thế trận lòng dân trong chiến dịch Điện Biên Phủ.* Hanoi: NXB Chính trị quốc gia, 2014.

Nguyên-Dê. Preface to "Quelques minorités ethniques du Nord-Indochine." Special issue, *France-Asie* 10, nos. 92–93 (January–February 1954): 141–43.

Nguyễn Hữu Hợp and Nguyễn Hữu Đạo. "Chiến thắng Điện Biên Phủ, sức mạnh tổng hợp của cả nước." In *Mấy vấn đề về chiến thắng lịch sử Điện Biên Phủ,* edited by Viện sử học, 89–106. Hanoi: NXB Khoa học xã hội, 1985.

Nguyễn Như Ý, ed. *Đại từ điển tiếng Việt.* TP Hồ Chí Minh: NXB Đại học quốc gia, 2011.

Nguyễn Thị Lâm Hảo. *Điện Biên—đất và người.* Hanoi: NXB Văn hóa—Thông tin, 2008.

Nguyễn Văn Dự. "Về tình trạng nghiện hút thuốc phiện ở vùng đồng bào các dân tộc tỉnh Lai Châu." *Dân tộc học* 77 (1993): 55–58.

Nguyễn Văn Thuận. "Một số vấn đề về công tác chính trị ngành cung cấp trong chiến dịch Điện Biên Phủ." In *Công tác bảo đảm hậu cần trong chiến dịch Điện Biên Phủ: Bài học, kinh nghiệm, và thực hiện,* edited by Tổng cục Hậu cần, 97–119. Hanoi: NXB Quân đội nhân dân, 2004.

Nhà xuất bản Thuận Hoá. "Thay lời giới thiệu." In *Điện Biên Phủ: Ký ức và nhân chứng,* edited by Lê Dần. Huế: NXB Thuận Hoá, 2004.

Những điều cần biết về huy động và sử dụng dân công. Bộ Lao động, 1951.

Những tài liệu về tổ chức Chính quyền Khu tự trị Thái-Mèo. Hanoi: Ban dân tộc (Thủ tướng phủ), 1955.

Nhung Tuyet Tran and Anthony Reid, eds. *Việt Nam: Borderless Histories.* Madison: University of Wisconsin Press, 2006.

Ninh, Kim. *A World Transformed: The Politics of Culture in Revolutionary Vietnam.* Ann Arbor: University of Michigan Press, 2002.

Nonini, Don. *Getting By: Class and State Formation among Chinese in Malaya.* Ithaca: Cornell University Press, 2015.

Oey Hong Lee. *Asia Menang di Dien Bien Phu.* Jakarta: "A.-A.," 1961.

Pelley, Patricia. *Postcolonial Vietnam: New Histories of the National Past.* Durham: Duke University Press, 2002.

Phạm Quang Trung. "Nhà thơ dân tộc Thái Lò Văn Mười." Accessed 2 February 2018, https://sites.google.com/site/pqtrungdlu/chan-dung-van-nghe-sy/nh-th-dn-tc-thi-l-vn-mi.

Phạm Thị Bích Hải, Vũ Thị Minh Hương, Trần Thị Hương, Philippe Le Failler, and Nguyễn Minh Sơn, eds. *Sách chỉ dẫn các phông lưu trữ bảo quản tại Trung tâm lưu trữ quốc gia III / Guide to the Collections of National Archives Centre III.* Hanoi: NXB Văn hoá thông tin, 2006.

Phan Huy Lê. "Một Quyết đoán táo bạo, kịp thời biểu thị tài năng, bản lĩnh của Đại tướng Võ Nguyên Giáp." In *Hội thảo khoa học quốc tế chiến thắng Điện Biên Phủ: Sức mạnh Việt Nam và tầm vóc thời đại / International Conference on the Điện Biên Phủ Victory: Vietnamese Strength and Lasting Significance,* edited by Viện Hàn lâm khoa học xã hội Việt Nam, 83–92. Hanoi: NXB Khoa học xã hội, 2014.

Phan Văn Các. *Từ điển từ Hán Việt.* TP HCM: NXB Thành phố Hồ Chí Minh, 2003.

Pholsena, Vatthana. *Post-war Laos: The Politics of Culture, History, and Identity.* Ithaca: Cornell University Press, 2006.

Poisson, Emmanuel. "Unhealthy Air of the Mountains: Kinh and Ethnic Minority Rule on the Sino-Vietnamese Frontier from the Fifteenth to the Twentieth Century." In *On the Borders of State Power: Frontiers in the Greater Mekong Sub-Region,* edited by Martin Gainsborough, 12–24. New York: Routledge, 2009.

Porter, Gareth. *Vietnam: The Politics of Bureaucratic Socialism.* Ithaca: Cornell University Press, 1993.

Prados, John. "Assessing Dien Bien Phu." In *The First Vietnam War: Colonial Conflict and Cold War Crisis,* edited by Mark Atwood Lawrence and Fredrik Logevall, 215–39. Cambridge, MA: Harvard University Press, 2004.

Proschan, Frank. "Peoples of the Gourd: Imagined Ethnicities in Highland Southeast Asia." *Journal of Asian Studies* 60, no. 4 (2001): 999–1032.

Rajaram, Prem Kumar, and Carl Grundy-Warr. *Borderscapes: Hidden Geographies and Politics at Territory's Edge.* Minneapolis: University of Minnesota Press, 2007.

Roberts, J. A. G. *A Concise History of China.* Cambridge, MA: Harvard University Press, 1999.

Roy, Jules. *La bataille de Dienbienphu.* Paris: Julliard, 1963.

Sahlins, Peter. *Boundaries: The Making of France and Spain in the Pyrenees.* Berkeley: University of California Press, 1991.

Salemink, Oscar. *The Ethnography of Vietnam's Central Highlanders: A Historical Contextualization, 1850–1990.* Honolulu: University of Hawaii Press, 2003.

———. "Mois and Maquis: The Invention and Appropriation of Vietnam's Montagnards from Sabatier to the CIA." In *Colonial Situations: Essays on the Contextualization of Ethnographic Knowledge*, edited by George Stocking Jr., 243–60. Madison: University of Wisconsin Press, 1991.

Savina, F. M. *Histoire des Miao*. Hong Kong: Imprimerie de la Société des Missions-Étrangères, 1924.

Scott, James C. *The Art of Not Being Governed: An Anarchist History of Southeast Asia*. New Haven: Yale University Press, 2009.

———. *The Moral Economy of the Peasant: Rebellion and Subsistence in Southeast Asia*. New Haven: Yale University Press, 1976.

———. *Seeing Like a State: How Certain Schemes to Improve the Human Condition Have Failed*. New Haven: Yale University Press, 1998.

———. *Weapons of the Weak: Everyday Forms of Peasant Resistance*. New Haven: Yale University Press, 1987.

Scott, James C., John Tehranian, and Jeremy Mathias. "The Production of Legal Identities Proper to States: The Case of the Permanent Family Surname." *Comparative Studies in Society and History* 44, no. 1 (2002): 4–44.

Sen, Amartya. *Poverty and Famines: An Essay on Entitlement and Deprivation*. Oxford: Clarendon, 1981.

Service Géographique de l'Indochine. *Atlas de l'Indochine*. Hanoi: Service Géographique de l'Indochine, 1928.

Shrader, Charles R. *A War of Logistics: Parachutes and Porters in Indochina, 1945–1954*. Lexington: University Press of Kentucky, 2015.

Sikor, Thomas, and Dao Minh Truong. "Agricultural Policy and Land Use Changes in a Black Tai Commune of Northern Vietnam, 1952–1997." *Mountain Research and Development* 22, no. 3 (August 2002): 248–55.

Simpson, Howard. *Dien Bien Phu: The Epic Battle America Forgot*. Washington, DC: Brassey's, 1994.

Sivaramakrishnan, K. *Modern Forests: Statemaking and Environmental Change in Colonial Eastern India*. Stanford: Stanford University Press, 1999.

Smalley, William, Chia Koua Vang, and Gnia Yee Yang. *Mother of Writing: The Origin and Development of a Hmong Messianic Script*. Chicago: University of Chicago Press, 1990.

Smith, Sara, Nathan Swenson, and Banu Gokariksel. "Territory, Bodies, and Borders." *Area* 48, no. 3 (December 2015): 258–61.

Sterling, Eleanor, Martha Hurley, and Le Duc Minh. *Vietnam: A Natural History*. New Haven: Yale University Press, 2006.

Stoler, Ann Laura. *Along the Archival Grain: Epistemic Anxieties and Colonial Common Sense*. Princeton: Princeton University Press, 2009.

Szalontai, Balazs. "Political and Economic Crisis in North Vietnam, 1955–56." *Cold War History* 5, no. 4 (November 2005): 395–426.

Tagliacozzo, Eric. "Jagged Landscapes: Conceptualizing Borders and Boundaries in the History of Human Societies." *Journal of Borderlands Studies* 31, no. 1 (2016): 1–21.

———. "Tropical Spaces, Frozen Frontiers: The Evolution of Border-Enforcement in Nineteenth-century Insular Southeast Asia." In *Locating Southeast Asia: Geographies of Knowledge and Politics of Space*, edited by Paul Kratoska, Remco Ruben, and Henk Nordholt, 149–74. Singapore: National University of Singapore Press, 2005.

Tai, Hue-Tam Ho, ed. *The Country of Memory: Remaking the Past in Late Socialist Vietnam.* Berkeley: University of California Press, 2001.

———. "Introduction to 'Mapping Vietnameseness.'" *Cross-currents* 20 (September 2016): 1–6.

———. *Millenarianism and Peasant Politics in Vietnam.* Cambridge, MA: Harvard University Press, 1983.

Tai, Hue-Tam Ho, and Mark Sidel, eds. *State, Society and the Market in Contemporary Vietnam.* New York: Routledge, 2013.

Tạ Long and Ngô Thị Chính. *Sự biến đổi nền nông nghiệp Châu Thổ-Thái Bình ở vùng núi Điện Biên, Lai Châu.* Hanoi: NXB Nông nghiệp, 2000.

Tapp, Nicholas. "Of Grasshoppers, Caterpillars, and Beans: A Historical Perspective on Hmong Messianism." *TRaNS* 3, no. 2 (July 2015): 289–318.

———. "Ritual Relations and Identity: Hmong and Others." In *Civility and Savagery: Social Identity in Tai States*, edited by Andrew Turton, 84–103. Richmond, UK: Curzon, 2000.

Tapp, Nicholas, Jean Michaud, Christian Culas, and Gary Yia Lee, eds. *Hmong/Miao in Asia.* Chiang Mai: Silkworm Books, 2004.

Tappe, Oliver. "A Frontier in the Frontier: Sociopolitical Dynamics and Colonial Administration in the Lao-Vietnamese Borderlands." *Asia Pacific Journal of Anthropology* 16, no. 4 (2015): 368–87.

———. "Variants of Frontier Mimesis: Colonial Encounter and Intercultural Interaction in the Lao-Vietnamese Uplands." *Social Analysis* 62, no. 2 (2018): 51–75.

Taylor, Keith. *A History of the Vietnamese.* New York: Cambridge University Press, 2013.

———. "Surface Orientations in Vietnam: Beyond Histories of Nation and Region." *Journal of Asian Studies* 57, no. 4 (1998): 949–78.

Taylor, Philip. "Minorities at Large: New Approaches to Minority Ethnicity in Vietnam." *Journal of Vietnamese Studies* 3, no. 3 (2008): 3–43.

Thayer, Carlyle. *War by Other Means: National Liberation and Revolution in Viet-Nam, 1954–60.* Boston: Allen and Unwin, 1989.

Thompson, Michael, and Michael Warburton. "Uncertainty on a Himalayan Scale." *Mountain Research and Development* 5, no. 2 (May 1985): 115–35.

Thongchai Winichakul. *Siam Mapped: A History of the Geobody of a Nation.* Honolulu: University of Hawaii Press, 1994.

Tilly, Charles. *Coercion, Capital, and European States, AD 990–1992.* Oxford: Blackwell, 1992.

Tổng cục Hậu cần, ed. *Công tác bảo đảm hậu cần trong chiến dịch Điện Biên Phủ: Bài học kinh nghiệm và thực tiễn.* Hanoi: NXB Quân đội nhân dân, 2004.

Trần Phương, ed. *Cách mạng ruộng đất ở Việt-Nam*. Hà Nội: NXB Khoa học xã hội, 1968.

Trần Trọng Trung, ed. *Một số văn kiện chỉ đạo chiến cuộc Đông Xuân 1953–1954 và chiến dịch Điện Biên Phủ*. Hanoi: NXB Quân đội nhân dân, 2004.

Tréglodé, Benoît de. *Heroes and Revolution in Vietnam*. Translated by Claire Duiker. Singapore: NUS Press, 2012.

Trinquier, Robert. *Modern Warfare: A French View of Counterinsurgency*. Translated by Daniel Lee. Pall Mall: London, 1964.

Trouillot, Michel-Rolph. *Silencing the Past: Power and the Production of History*. Boston: Beacon, 1995.

Truong Chinh. *Truong-Chinh: Selected Writings*. Hanoi: Thế giới, 1994.

Trường Chinh and Võ Nguyên Giáp. *The Peasant Question, 1937–1938*. Translated by Christine P. White. Ithaca: Southeast Asia Program, Department of Asian Studies, Cornell University, 1974.

———. *Vấn đề dân cày*. Hanoi: NXB Sự thật, 1959 [1937].

Tsing, Anna. *Friction: An Ethnography of Global Connection*. Princeton: Princeton University Press, 2005.

Tuan, Yi-Fu. *Space and Place: The Perspective of Experience*. Minneapolis: University of Minnesota Press, 1977.

Turner, Sarah. "Making a Living the Hmong Way: An Actor-Oriented Livelihoods Approach to Everyday Politics and Resistance in Upland Vietnam." *Annals of the Association of American Geographers* 102, no. 2 (2012): 403–22.

Turton, Andrew, ed. *Civility and Savagery: Social Identity in Tai States*. Richmond, UK: Curzon, 2000.

Van Creveld, Martin. *Supplying War: Logistics from Wallenstein to Patton*. New York: Cambridge University Press, 2004 [1977].

Vandergeest, Peter, and Nancy Lee Peluso. "Territorialization and State Power in Thailand." *Theory and Society* 24, no. 3 (1995): 385–426.

Văn Hào. *Nghĩa vụ đi dân công*. Cao Bằng: Nhà in Việt Lập, 1950.

Van Schendel, Willem. "Geographies of Knowing, Geographies of Ignorance: Jumping Scale in Southeast Asia." *Environment and Planning D: Society and Space* 20 (2002): 647–68.

Verdery, Katherine. "Ethnicity, Nationalism, and State-Making: Ethnic Groups and Boundaries, Past and Future." In *The Anthropology of Ethnicity: Beyond "Ethnic Groups and Boundaries,"* edited by Hans Vermeulen and Cora Govers, 33–58. Amsterdam: Het Spinhuis, 1994.

Viện Hàn lâm Khoa học xã hội Việt Nam, ed. *Hội thảo khoa học quốc tế chiến thắng Điện Biên Phủ: Sức mạnh Việt Nam và tầm vóc thời đại / International Conference on the Điện Biên Phủ Victory: Vietnamese Strength and Lasting Significance*. Hanoi: NXB Khoa học Xã hội, 2014.

Viện Lịch sử Quân sự Việt Nam. *Lịch sử cuộc kháng chiến chống thực dân Pháp, 1945–54*. 2 vols. Hanoi: NXB Quân đội Nhân dân, 1995.

———. *Tóm tắt các chiến dịch trong kháng chiến chống thực dân Pháp (1945–1954)*. Hanoi: NXB Quân đội Nhân dân, 2000.

Viện Sử học. *Mấy vấn đề về chiến thắng lịch sử Điện Biên Phủ*. Hanoi: NXB Khoa học xã hội, 1985.

Vo, Alex-Thai D. "Nguyễn Thị Năm and the Land Reform in North Vietnam, 1953." *Journal of Vietnamese Studies* 10, no. 1 (Winter 2015): 1–62.

Võ Nguyên Giáp. *Điện Biên Phủ*. Hanoi: NXB Chính trị quốc gia, 1994.

———. *Điện Biên Phủ: Điểm hẹn lịch sử*. Hanoi: NXB Quân đội nhân dân, 1999.

———. *Đường tới Điện Biên Phủ*. Hanoi: NXB Quân đội nhân dân, 1999.

———. *People's War, People's Army: The Viet Cong Insurrection Manual for Underdeveloped Countries*. New York: Bantam Books, 1968 [1962].

Võ Nguyên Giáp with assistance from Hữu Mai. *Điện Biên Phủ: Rendezvous with History*. Annotated translation by Lady Borton. Hanoi: Thế Giới, 2004.

———. *The Road to Điện Biên Phủ*. Translated by Tuấn Lan. Hanoi: Thế Giới, 2004.

Vu, Tuong. "Studying the State through State Formation." *World Politics* 62, no. 1 (January 2010): 148–75.

———. "Triumphs or Tragedies: A New Perspective on the Vietnamese Revolution." *Journal of Southeast Asian Studies* 45, no. 2 (June 2014): 236–57.

Vũ Hải Đăng, ed. *Điện Biên Phủ: Nhân chứng sự kiện*. Hanoi: NXB Quân đội, 2004.

Vương Duy Quang. "Hiện tượng 'Xưng vua' ở người Hmông." *Dân tộc học* 122, no. 3 (2003): 28–37.

Vu Tu Lap. *Vietnam: Geographical Data*. Hanoi: Foreign Languages Publishing House, 1979.

Vũ Văn Thông. "Công tác vận tải và những kinh nghiệm vận dụng các phương thức vận tải trong chiến dịch Điện Biên Phủ." In *Công tác bảo đảm hậu cần trong chiến dịch Điện Biên Phủ: Bài học kinh nghiệm và thực tiễn*, edited by Tổng cục Hậu cần. Hanoi: NXB Quân đội nhân dân, 2004.

Walker, Andrew. *The Legend of the Golden Boat: Regulation, Trade and Traders in the Borderlands of Laos, Thailand, Burma, and China*. Honolulu: University of Hawaii Press, 1999.

Watts, Michael. "Entitlements or Empowerment? Famine and Starvation in Africa." *Review of African Political Economy* 51 (July 1991): 9–26.

Watts, Michael, and Hans Bohle. "Hunger, Famine, and the Space of Vulnerability." *Geojournal* 30, no. 2 (June 1993): 117–25.

Weber, Max. *Economy and Society*. Edited by Guenther Roth and Claus Wittich. 2 vols. Berkeley: University of California Press, 1978.

Weiner, Amir, ed. *Landscaping the Human Garden: Twentieth-Century Population Management in a Comparative Framework*. Stanford: Stanford University Press, 2003.

Werner, Jayne, and Danièle Bélanger, eds. *Gender, Household, State: Đổi Mới in Việt Nam*. Ithaca: Southeast Asia Program, Cornell University, 2002.

White, Christine. "Agrarian Reform and National Liberation in the Vietnamese Revolution, 1920–1957." PhD diss., Cornell University, 1981.

———. "Peasant Mobilization and Anti-colonial Struggle in Vietnam: The Rent Reduction Campaign of 1953." *Journal of Peasant Studies* 10, no. 4 (1983): 187–213.

Whitmore, John. "Cartography in Vietnam." In *The History of Cartography*, vol. 2, book 2, edited by J. B. Harley and David Woodward, 478–508. Chicago: University of Chicago Press, 1994.

Williams, Raymond. *The Country and the City*. New York: Oxford University Press, 1973.

Windrow, Martin. *The Last Valley: Dien Bien Phu and the French Defeat in Vietnam*. Cambridge, MA: Da Capo, 2004.

Wolf, Eric. "Peasants and Political Mobilization: Introduction." *Comparative Studies in Society and History* 17, no. 4 (1975): 385–88.

Wolford, Wendy. *This Land Is Ours Now: Social Mobilization and the Meanings of Land in Brazil*. Durham: Duke University Press, 2010.

Woodside, Alexander B. *Community and Revolution in Modern Vietnam*. Boston: Houghton Mifflin, 1976.

———. "The Triumphs and Failures of Mass Education in Vietnam." *Pacific Affairs* 56, no. 3 (1983): 401–27.

———. *Vietnam and the Chinese Model: A Comparative Study of Vietnamese and Chinese Government in the First Half of the Nineteenth Century*. Cambridge, MA: Harvard University Press, 1988.

Yeh, Emily. *Taming Tibet: Landscape Transformation and the Gift of Chinese Development*. Ithaca: Cornell University Press, 2013.

Young, Marilyn, and Robert Buzzanco, eds. *A Companion to the Vietnam War*. Malden, MA: Blackwell, 2002.

Zhai, Qiang. *China and the Vietnam Wars, 1950–1975*. Chapel Hill: University of North Carolina Press, 2000.

Zinoman, Peter. *The Colonial Bastille: A History of Imprisonment in Vietnam, 1862–1940*. Berkeley: University of California Press, 2001.

INDEX